Dictionary of Arabic Loanwords in the Languages of Central and East Africa

Handbook of Oriental Studies

Handbuch der Orientalistik

SECTION ONE

The Near and Middle East

Edited by

Maribel Fierro (*Madrid*)
M. Şükrü Hanioğlu (*Princeton*)
Renata Holod (*University of Pennsylvania*)
Florian Schwarz (*Vienna*)

VOLUME 145

The titles published in this series are listed at *brill.com/ho1*

Dictionary of Arabic Loanwords in the Languages of Central and East Africa

By

Sergio Baldi

TUTA SUB AEGIDE PALLAS · 1683 ·

BRILL

LEIDEN | BOSTON

Cover illustration: Zanzibar, 2016. Photo by author.

Library of Congress Cataloging-in-Publication Data

Names: Baldi, Sergio, author.
Title: Dictionary of Arabic loanwords in the languages of Central and East Africa / Sergio Baldi.
Description: Leiden ; Boston : Brill, 2021. | Series: Handbook of Oriental studies. Section 1, the Near and Middle East, 01699423 ; volume 145 | Includes bibliographical references and index.
Identifiers: LCCN 2020042391 (print) | LCCN 2020042392 (ebook) | ISBN 9789004438477 (hardback) | ISBN 9789004438484 (ebook)
Subjects: LCSH: African languages—Foreign elements—Arabic—Dictionaries. | African languages—Foreign words and phrases—Arabic—Dictionaries. | African languages—Dictionaries—Arabic. | Arabic language—Influence on African languages—Dictionaries. | Africa, Central—Languages—Foreign words and phrases—Dictionaries. | Africa, East—Languages—Foreign words and phrases—Dictionaries.
Classification: LCC PL8009 .B35 2020 (print) | LCC PL8009 (ebook) | DDC 496—dc23
LC record available at https://lccn.loc.gov/2020042391
LC ebook record available at https://lccn.loc.gov/2020042392

Typeface for the Latin, Greek, and Cyrillic scripts: "Brill". See and download: brill.com/brill-typeface.

ISSN 0169-9423
ISBN 978-90-04-43847-7 (hardback)
ISBN 978-90-04-43848-4 (e-book)

This book is printed on acid-free paper and produced in a sustainable manner.

To Angela
and my children
Diego and Roberta

Contents

Preface IX
Abbreviations X

Introduction 1

Dictionary
Alif 9
Bāʾ 21
Tāʾ 46
Ṯāʾ 50
Jīm 53
Ḥāʾ 68
Ḫāʾ 85
Dāl 98
Ḏāl 110
Rāʾ 113
Zāʾ 129
Sīn 135
Šīn 158
Ṣād 174
Ḍād 185
Ṭāʾ 188
Ẓāʾ 196
ʿAin 198
Ġain 220
Faʾ 225
Qāf 240
Kāf 255
Lām 268
Mīm 274
Nūn 285
Hāʾ 296
Wāw 300
Yāʾ 312

Preface

In June 1975, while traveling to the United States to study, I met Professor Pierre Alexandre. He then directed the Cahiers d'Etudes Africaines at the Department of Human Sciences, Boulevard Raspail, and taught Swahili at the Institute of Modern Oriental Languages (now known as INALCO). He suggested that I return to Paris, after my Fulbright scholarship, to do a doctoral dissertation on Arabic loanwords in Swahili. This chance meeting changed almost all of my academic career. A few years later, I began to study in France, where I enrolled in Professor Claude Gouffé's Hausa class. The latter, who was kind enough to take an interest in the work I was doing, suggested that I include Hausa in my research.

The preparation and discussion of my thesis showed that there was a lot of work to be done on Arabic loanwords, especially with regard to Hausa. Many loanwords could not be explained without considering their meaning in relation to neighboring languages.

In 1978, I was appointed to head the Sudanic language courses at the Istituto Universitario Orientale (Naples) and I began to teach Hausa. The academic interest that I hitherto devoted to Swahili was reoriented toward West Africa and I began to produce articles on Arabic loanwords in languages close to Hausa, such as Kanuri, Fulfulde, etc., languages that could explain the route the Arabic loanwords had taken to reach Hausa, in cases in which the loanwords did not come directly from Arabic.

During these years, I greatly benefited from the help and suggestions, first and foremost, of the late Professor Pierre Alexandre and the late Professor Claude Gouffé, whom I can never thank enough. A number of friends and colleagues supported me in one area or another: Norbert Cyffer (Universität Wien), Herrmann Jungraithmayr (Goethe Universität, Frankfurt), and Rudolf Leger (Goethe Universität, Frankfurt) engaged me in very useful discussions during our meetings for Erasmus courses, and Henry Tourneux (CNRS / IRD, Paris) in particular, presented questions on phonetic fonts, and offered academic assistance, suggestions, and encouragement, including with regard to the final format of the publication.

Abbreviations

Dictionaries and Other Works

Daf	*Dictionnaire arabe-français (dialecte du Tchad)*
Dfa	*Dictionnaire français-arabe (dialecte du Tchad)*
EI[2]	*Encyclopaedia of Islam*
Vai	*Vocabolario arabo-italiano*

Grammatical Abbreviations

adj.	adjective
adv.	adverb
arch.	archaic
bib.	Bible; biblical
bot.	botanical
cf.	refer to
coll.	collective
colloq.	colloquial
conj.	conjunction
eg.	Egyptian
excl.	exclamation
expr.	expression
geom.	geometric
gram.	grammar
interj.	interjection
invar.	invariable
jur.	jurisprudence
lit.	literally
n.	noun
n.v.	verbal name
neg.	negation
num.	numeral
part.	particle
pl.	plural
prep.	preposition
refl.	reflexive
s.	singular

s.o.	someone
sp.	species
s.th.	something
syr.	Syrian
t.	transitive
tun.	Tunisian
v.	verb
vulg.	vulgar
v.i.	intransitive verb
voc.	vocative
zoo.	zoological
/	indicates a variant[1]

Authors' Names

Abe	Abe
Ade	Adelaar
B	Baldi
Bal	Balinandi
Ben	Benson
Bla	Blackings
Bo	Bosha
Bot	Botne
Bou	Bouquiaux
Bry	Bryant
B-Z	Bertoncini-Zúbková
Cal	Calloc'h
CAT	Cox, Adamson & Teusink
Cra	Crazzolara
Dal	Dale
Dav	Davis
Dozy	Dozy 1881
Dz	Dzokanga
Ev	van Everbroeck
F	Freytag
FA	Faure

1 In his Arabic dictionary, P. Jullien de Pommerol indicates whether or not a verbal form is incomplete after the verbal form and notes the plural after nouns.

Fel	Felberg
Fis	Fischer
FKM	Ferrari, Kalunga et Mulumbwa
Gh	Ghaleb
Gor	Gorman
Gue	Gueunier
Häf	Häflinger
Han	Hannan
Höf	Höftmann
Hul	Hulstaert
Id	Idris
JdP	Jullien de Pommerol
K&B	Kiraithe & Baden
K&O	Kagaya & Olomi
Ka	Kaji
Kab	Kabuta
Kag	Kagaya
Kaye	Kaye
Kazim	Kazimirski 1860
Kit	Kitching
Koh	Kohnen
Kra	Krapf
Krö	Krönlein
Lam	Laman
Leg	Legère
M&L	Maho & Lodhi
M.A.M.	Mohamed A. Mohamed
Mbi	Mbiti
Mer	Mertens
MMR	Muniko, Muita & Ruel
MN&Z	Mwalonya, Nicolle, Nicolle & Zimbu
Mo	Mosha
Mu	Muratori
Odo	Odonga
P	Prost
P&G	Pillinger and Galboran
Po	Pozzati
PP	Pires Prata
R	Rechenbach

Rd	Rood
Reh	Reh
Ri	Richardson
RL	Roth-Laly
S&A	Smith & Ama
Sacl	Sacleux
Schr	Schrock
Smi	Smith
Sno	Snoxall
Swa	Swartenbroeckk
Tir	Tirronen
Vet	Vettor
Wehr	Wehr
WF	White Fathers
Whi	Whiteley
Wü	Würtz
Yo	Yoneda
Z&T	Zeltner & Tourneux

Introduction

It has now been more than a dozen years since the publication of my work on Arabic borrowing in West African languages[1] and I am just now able to finish my project of mapping Arabic loanwords in East African languages, largely carried through Swahili. My work aims to provide a tool for researchers of African languages, to offer them a lexicon of these languages if they want to indicate Arabic loanwords in their work. During the time I have devoted to the study of these loanwords, I consulted thousands of dictionaries of African languages and other works on the subject, and noticed that words are often presented as Arabic loanwords while they are not, while other words that are taken from Arabic are not declared as such. The mistake, I believe, is due to the acceptance of suggestions made by various informants, the vast majority of whom were Muslims, who were led to see Arabic everywhere and not where it really was! I remember the exclamation of a colleague from Chad, and not the only one in my academic career, to my assertion that the term Hausa *littafi* "book" was a borrowing from Arabic *kitāb*!

This dictionary is structured in the same form as my previous dictionary, with the same numbering, in order to allow a comparison between Arabic loanwords common to the two volumes. The Arabic terms that are not present in these languages have been omitted.

In this work I have organized the Arabic etymons that have been borrowed into East African languages according to the order of the Arabic roots; then, under each entry, the borrowed words are listed according to the alphabetical order of the African languages. In the event an Arabic word has been borrowed in several ways, with different meanings, it is marked twice (*cf.* **ʿāda** 'habit, custom' **1964** and **al-ʿāda** 'commission' **1965**). In these cases, the borrowings are reported twice, though in the source dictionary they appear under a single entry (see Swahili *ada* 'custom, manner, habit' and *ada* 'commission or fee on certain occasion').

In the organization of the data, I adhered to the following methodology: the name of each language is followed by the name of the author (in the form of an acronym) from which the meaning is taken, with the exception Arabic, where I give the author and the page cited, to help non-specialists find the data

1 Sergio Baldi, *Dictionnaire des emprunts arabes dans les langues de l'Afrique de l'Ouest et en Swahili* (*Dictionnaires et Langues*) (Paris: Karthala, 2008).

 | DOI:10.1163/9789004438484_002

in these dictionaries. For languages with dialectical variations (i.e. Malgache), I quoted variants of the individual dialects (i.e., le kiantal,[2] under 507).

I have examined and consulted the following list of languages and texts:

Acooli	Cra (Crazzolara), Mu (Muratori)
Alur	Kna (Knappert[3] 1972–1973)
Ankole	Kna (Knappert 1972–1973)
Ateso	Kit (Kitching)
Anywa	Reh (Reh)
Arabic	Beaussier = Beau;
	Dictionnaire arabe-français (*dialecte du Tchad*) = Daf;
	Dictionnaire français-arabe (*dialecte du Tchad*) = Dfa;
	Dozy 1881 = Dozy;
	Encyclopaedia of Islam[4] = EI^2;
	Faure = FA;
	Freytag = F;
	Ghaleb = Gh;
	Jullien de Pommerol = JdP;
	Kaye 1986 = Kaye;
	Kazimirski 1860 = Kazim;
	Qur'an;
	Roth-Laly = RL;
	Smith & Ama = S&A;
	Taine-Cheikh 1988 = TC1;
	Taine-Cheikh 1990 = TC2;
	Vocabolario arabo-italiano = Vai;
	Wehr;
	Zeltner et Tourneux = Z&T;
	Verbs are indicated in roman characters if they are derived forms.
Bari	Mu (Muratori)
Batéké	Cal (Calloc'h)
Bemba	WF (White Fathers)
Bende	Abe
Ciluba	Kab (Kabuta)
Dholuo	Gor (Gorman);
	Odo (Odonga)

2 One of the sub-dialects of Malagasy from Mayotte (Gueunier 1986: iv).

3 For the data taken from Knappert's articles, in the corpus, I also give the page number.

4 *Encyclopaedia of Islam*, second edition, ed. P.J. Bearman, Th. Bianquis, C.E. Bosworth, E. van Donzel, and W.P. Heinrichs (Leiden: Brill, 1960–2004).

Dinka	Id (Idris)
Gbéa	Cal (Calloc'h)
Gikuyu	Ben (Benson);
	Gor (Gorman)
Gmbwaga	Cal (Calloc'h)
Gwere	Kag (Kagaya)
Haya	Ka (Kaji);
	M&L (Maho & Lodhi)
Ik	Schr (Schrock)
Ila	Smi (Smith)
Jita	Kag (Kagaya)
Kamba	Mbi (Mbiti);
	Whi (Whiteley)
Khoi-Khoin	Krö (Krönlein)
Kikongo	Bent (Bentley);
	Lam (Laman);
	Swa (Swartenbroeckk)
Kiluba	Kna (Knappert 1999)
Kinyarwanda	CAT (Cox, Adamson & Teusink);
	Kna (Knappert 1972–1973)
Kiw'oso	K&O (Kagaya & Olomi)
Kuria	MMR (Muniko, Muita & Ruel)
Lega	Bot (Botne)
Lhukonzo	Balinandi
Lingala	Dz (Dzokanga);
	Ev (van Everbroeck)
Lomongo	Hul (Hulstaert)
Lotuxo	Mu (Muratori)
Luena	Vet (Vettor)
Lunyankole	Dav (Davis)
Lunyoro	Dav (Davis)
Luganda	Mo (Mosha);
	Sno (Snoxall)
Macua	PP (Pires Prata)
Madi	Bla (Blackings)
Malagasy	Ade (Adelaar);
	Gue (Gueunier)
Matengo	Häf (Häflinger);
	Yo (Yoneda)
Ndogo	Po (Pozzati)

Ndonga	Tir (Tirronen)
Ngh'wele	Leg (Legère)
Ngombe	Rd (Rood)
Nyakyusa[5]	Fel (Felberg)
Pokomo	Kra (Krapf);
	Wü (Würtz)
Pokot	Cra (Crazzolara)
Rendille	P&G (Pillinger and Galboran)
Runyankore	Ka (Kaji)
Sango[6]	Bou (Bouquiaux);
	Cal (Calloc'h);
	P (*Prost*);
	Kna (Knappert 1972–1973)
Shilluk	Koh (Kohnen)
Shona	Dal (Dale);
	Han (Hannan)
Sukuma	Ri (Richardson)
Swahili	Bo (Bosha);
	B-Z (Bertoncini-Zúbková);
	FKM (Ferrari, Kalunga et Mulumbwa);
	Gue (Gueunier);
	J (Johnson);
	K&B (Kiraithe & Baden);
	M.A.M. (Mohamed A. Mohamed);
	Mer (Mertens);
	R (Rechenbach);
	Sacl (Sacleux)
Xhosa	Fis (Fischer)
Zande	Kna (Knappert 1972–1973)
Zulu	Bry (Bryant)

Most loanwords are nouns, therefore, I only identified cases in which borrowed words are not nouns; in these cases, I give an abbreviation of their grammatical form as indicated in the source, where possible.

5 Called Ngonde in Malawi.

6 For Sango, the subject of my previous dictionary (Baldi 2018), I have only included the Arabic terms borrowed into East African languages.

My objective was to collect all loanwords, such that this work is as complete as possible, though some words may not be commonly used by speakers of a given language that seem to be pure Arabic xenisms (see Swahili *hamsa* 'five' < **ḫamsa 841**). For the languages which I have personally worked on (see bibliography) with regard to Arabic etymology, I indicate with a degree of certainty; for others, I based myself more on experience than on the indications of the authors of the dictionaries analyzed. The reliability of the works I consulted varies: the Swahili dictionary of Johnson is less reliable than that of father Sacleux with regard to quoting loanwords in general and Arabic in particular.

I tried to reproduce the words as they are given by the authors, but their translations into French were homogenized, so, for example, under **imām 96**, I did not include *imàm, imâm, Imam, iman*, but simply *imam*.

At the end of the book I have included the following:

- an **addenda section** listing words that are not of Arabic origin, although they are recorded by some dictionaries as from an Arabic dialect;
- an **index** of Arabic words in alphabetical order adapted from Latin to facilitate the search of readers unfamiliar with the Arabic alphabetical order. The bilingual dictionaries consulted often follow different forms in the transcription of Arabic that could confuse the reader and for this reason I have collected the most remarkable differences in this table.

Arabic letter	Transliteration [by]	Description or example (from text)
ء	ʔ	initial glottal stop
ع	ɛ [Roth-Laly]	1106, 1459, 1460, 1847, 1923, and 1925
ق	g [Pommerol]	2341a
ج	ǧ [Roth-Laly]	492a
غ	ḡ [Wehr]	297
ج	j [Daf, Dfa, Pommerol, Wehr]	535
ج	ǰ [Kaye]	1192
خ	k [Wehr]	821
ب	p [Pommerol]	357a
خ	x [Pommerol, Roth-Laly, Zeltner and Tourneux]	821
ظ	ẓ [Roth-Laly]	1760

- an **index** of English keywords of the Arabic borrowings in African languages;
- an **index** of French keywords of the Arabic borrowings in African languages; and
- an index of the scientific names of plants and animals in Latin.

Note

In some cases, the numbering of the Arabic etymons is discontinuous (number skipped or accompanied by a letter, see 465a). These features have no special relevance; they are simply due to practical reasons, such as the difficulty of updating the whole.

Dictionary

Alif

abadan always, forever; ever, (with neg.) never (Wehr 1b) 3

Dinka (Id)	abadan	at all
Malagasy (Gue)	abadàny	it is necessary, it is certain
Swahili (J)	abadan (*adv.*)	never (with neg.)

abadī eternal (Wehr 1b) 4

Swahili (J)	abadi (*adv.*)	ever, always

ibra needle; shot, injection (Wehr 1b; Daf 63) 5

Acooli (Cra)	libìrà	needle
Bari (Mu)	libira	needle
Dholuo (Odo)	libira	needle
Dinka (Id)	ebera	needle
Lotuxo (Mu)	alibira	needle
Madi (Bla)	líbīrà	needle; syringe, injection
Ndogo (Po)	libra	needle

ibrīq pitcher, jug (Wehr 2a); ʾ**ibri:g** trough (Z&T 129) 6

Acooli (Cra)	biìnikà	teapot (via Swahili)
Ateso (Kit)	ebinika	kettle
Dholuo (Gor)	birika	kettle
(Odo)	binika	teapot, kettle (via Swahili)
Digo (MN&Z)	birika	container, water tank (via Swahili)
Haya (Ka)	ebinîka	kettle (via Swahili)
Madi (Bla)	bìníkà	kettle
Nyakyusa (Fel)	ilíbílíka	kettle, teapot, jug, reservoir, cistern, tank (via Swahili)
Runyankore (Ka)	ebi-nika	kettle (via Swahili)
Swahili (J)	birika	kettle

 | DOI:10.1163/9789004438484_003

iblīs devil, Satan (Wehr 2a); the Arabic word is a borrowing from Greek διάβολος slanderer, *cf.* Latin *diabolus* devil; **iblīs** devil, Satan (RL 15b) 9

Swahili (J)	ibilisi	Devil, Satan

ab father (Wehr 2b); **abūnā** reverend father, form of address and title of a priest (Chr.) (Wehr 2b); **abba** dad, father (Daf 4) 10

Madi (Bla)	àbʊ́nà	priest

aṯar mark (Wehr 4a) 12

Swahili (J)	athari	mark, spot

ajara (*v.*) to reward, remunerate (Wehr 5b) 15

Swahili (J)	ajara	wages

ujra hire, rent (Wehr 5b) 17

Madi (Bla)	ɨ̄jʊ̄rà (*v.*)	hire
Swahili (J)	ajara, ijara (but more usu. ujira)	hire, wages

ajīr workman, day laborer (Wehr 5b) 18

Malagasy (Gue)	koaĵìry	rent, take on lease or lease
Swahili (J)	-ajiri (*v.*)	hire

ijāra rent; letting (Wehr 5b) 19

Swahili (J)	ijara	hire, wages

li-ajli because of (Wehr 6a) 20

Swahili (J)	ajili	cause, reason

ajal deadline (Wehr 6a) 21

Digo (MN&Z)	ajali	accident (via Swahili)
Malagasy (Gue)	aĵàly, oaĵàly	danger of death, misfortune, mishap
Swahili (J)	ajali	fate, death

[yawm] al-aḥad Sunday (Wehr 6b) 24

Malagasy (Ade)	alahàdy	Sunday
Rendille (P&G)	Ahá'd	Sunday

'ḪR (*v.*) (II) to delay, put off (Wehr 8a); **axxar / yi'axxir** (*v.*) (II) to delay, be late, retard (JdP 212b) 25

Swahili (J)	-ahiri (*v.*)	stand over, be put off

āḫir last, ultimate, extreme (Wehr 8a) 27

Macua (PP)	ahera	future life; paradise; sky
Madi (Bla)	ákīrì	the end
Swahili (J)	aheri	the end, the last stage

al-āḫira the hereafter (Wehr 8a) 29

Swahili (J)	ahera	the next world

ta'ḫīr delay (Wehr 8b) 31

Swahili (J)	taahira	delay

aḫ brother; friend (Wehr 9a); **axu** brother (JdP 212a) 32

Swahili (J)	ahi	brother (sometimes used for friend)
	yahe	ordinary people; brother, friend

adab good manners (Wehr 9b) 35

Digo (MN&Z)	adabu	good manners (via Swahili)
Swahili (J)	adabu	good manners

adīb cultured; well-mannered, civil, urbane (Wehr 10a) 37

Swahili (J)	adibu (*adj.*)	decorous, good mannered, civil, polite

ādam Adam (Wehr 10b) 40

Malagasy (Gue)	Adàmo	Adam, the first man
Swahili (J)	Adamu	Adam

iḏn permission (Wehr 11b) 43

Swahili (J)	idhini	sanction, permission, authorization

aḏān call to prayer (Wehr 11b); **weððân** [one] who often calls for prayer, who often makes the call to prayer (TC1 16) 44

Swahili (J)	adhana	the call of the muezzin

mu'aḏḏin muezzin (Wehr 11b) 45

Digo (MN&Z)	-adhini (*v.*)	call to prayer (via Swahili)
Malagasy (Gue)	koadìny, mikoadìny	sing the call to prayer
Swahili (J)	-adhini (*v.*)	call to public prayers
	mwadhini	muezzin

aḏiya (*v.*) to suffer damage (V) to be hurt (Wehr 12a) 46

Swahili (J)	tadi (+ *v.*), utadi	offense, rudeness, aggression

aḏan, aḏāh trouble, annoyance (Wehr 12a) 47

Swahili (J)	adha	trouble, discomfort

ma'rab purpose, aim (Wehr 12a) 49

Swahili (J)	maarubu	reason, purpose

ta'rīḫ history (Wehr 12b) 50

Digo (MN&Z)	tarehe	date (via Swahili)
Kiw'oso (K&O)	tareê	date
Kuria (MMR)	etarehe	a date, day; (of a woman) menstrual date, periods (via Swahili)
	etariki	date (of the month)
Swahili (J)	tarehe	date, history

arz cedar (Wehr 13a) 53

Swahili (J)	mwerezi	cedar tree (Pygeum africanum)

arḍ earth (Wehr 13a) 55

Digo (MN&Z)	aridhi	earth, land (via Swahili)
Swahili (J)	ardhi	soil, ground, earth

azal eternity (Wehr 14b) 60

Swahili (J)	azali	eternal, without beginning

usquf bishop (Wehr 17a) 68

Nyakyusa (Fel)	askofú	bishop (via Swahili)
Swahili (J)	askofu	bishop

ašir lively, exuberant; insolent (Wehr 18b) 70

Swahili (J)	shere, sheri (?)	fun, [object of] ridicule, joke, derision

mi'šār saw (Wehr 18b); **museer** saw (S&A 61a) 70a

Dholuo (Odo)	mucumeni	saw
Madi (Bla)	mɔ̀sɔ̀mɛ́nì	saw, to cut

aṣl origin; the original (e.g., of a book) (Wehr 19a) **71**

Digo (MN&Z)	asili	origin, inner nature (via Swahili)
Malagasy (Gue)	asoìly, asìly	breed, species, origin
Swahili (J)	asili	origin, source

aṭlas satin (Wehr 20a) **74**

Swahili (J)	atlasi in nguo ya atlasi	satin

ufura crowd, crush; confusion (Kazim: I, 40a); **ufura** confusion, mixture, adversity (F: I, 43a) 75

Swahili (J)	ufuraha (?)	a small box made of tin or silver, in which limes are kept (i.e., limes used in the chewing mixture *uraibu*)

afaf displeasure; grumbling (Wehr 20a) 76

Swahili (J)	ufefe (?)	weakness, uselessness

afandī gentleman (Wehr 20b) **76a**

Swahili (Bo)	afande	sir, master (used only by soldiers and police)

afyūn opium (Wehr 21a) 77

Swahili (J)	afyuni, afiuni	opium

ma'kal food, edibles (Wehr 22a); **ma'akâl** dot, money for a wedding (JdP 780b) 78

Swahili (J)	maakuli	victuals, food

illā unless; except; (after negation) only, but (Wehr 22b); **ellā / llā** (*adv.*) only, no more, nothing; only ... except, apart from; constantly (TC1 24); **'ille** except, apart from (Z&T 129) 79

Swahili (J)	ila *part.*	except, unless, but

alf thousand (Wehr 23a) 81

Acooli (Mu)	alıp	thousand
Bari (Mu)	alıp, alıpan	thousand
Dholuo (Odo)	alip	thousand (via Swahili)
Digo (MN&Z)	elufu	thousand (via Swahili)
Dinka (Id)	alip	thousand
Gikuyu (Ben)	warubu	thousand (via Swahili)
Ik (Schr)	álìf (álìfù-)	thousand
Lotuxo (Mu)	alıf	thousand
Luena (Vet)	élefu	thousand (via Swahili)
Macua (PP)	alfu	thousand
Madi (Bla)	álīfò	thousand
Rendille (P&G)	álif / élif (?)	thousand (via Swahili)
Swahili (J)	elfu	thousand

alif name of the letter ا (Wehr 23a) 82

Macua (PP)	alifu	first letter of the Arabic alphabet
Swahili (Sacl)	alifu, alif	first letter of the Swahili-Arabic alphabet

almās diamond (Wehr 24a) 86

Digo (MN&Z)	alimasi	diamond (via Swahili)
Malagasy (Gue)	almàsy	diamond
Nyakyusa (Fel)	alumasí	diamond (via Swahili)
Swahili (J)	almasi	diamond; a common personal male name

allāh Allah (Wehr 24b) 88

Macua (PP)	Allah / Allahu	God; name used by Muslims
Swahili (J)	Allah	God. Seldom used except in Arabic expressions and formulas. The word is used by Muslims for 'God,' there is a word of Bantu origin, Mungu, used exclusively by Christians.

alā (*v.*) to neglect or fail to do, not to do (Wehr 24b) 90

Swahili (J)	ala! interj.	expression of annoyance, impatience

umma nation, people (Wehr 25b) 94

Swahili (J)	umati	a crowd

amāma (*prep.*) in front of; in the presence of (Wehr 25b) 95

Swahili (J)	omo (?)	forepart of ship, prow
	yahom (?)	a nautical term for straight ahead

imām imam (Wehr 26a) 96

Digo (MN&Z)	imamu	imam (via Swahili)
Malagasy (Gue)	imàmo	imam
Swahili (J)	imamu	imam, leader

a-mā or? (Wehr 26a) 97

Malagasy (Gue)	amà (*conj.*)	and, and then
Swahili (J)	ama (*conj.*)	either ... or

amad end, terminus; period; distance (Wehr 26a) 100

Swahili (J)	mede	goal, winning post

amara, *imperf.* **ya'muru** to order, command (Wehr 26a) 101

Malagasy (Gue)	koamorìŝa	to order
Swahili (Bo)	-amrisha (*v.*)	order, command, prescribe, decide

amr order, command (Wehr 26b) 102

Malagasy (Gue)	amòry	authority, authorization, order
Swahili (J)	amri	command, order

amr order, command (Wehr 26b) and **dunyā** world (Wehr 295a) 102a

Malagasy (Gue)	amorodonìa	expression introducing a declaration that we want to solemnize: I let you know

amr matter, affair, concern, business (Wehr 26b) 104

Swahili (J)	amara	urgent affairs

amīr emir (Wehr 27a) 107

Digo (MN&Z)	amiri	commander (via Swahili)
Swahili (J)	amiri	commander, leader, officer
	-amuru (*v.*)	command, order, direct

ma'mūr commissioner (Wehr 27b) 107a

Dinka (Id)	maamuur	paramount chief

ta'ammul consideration; contemplation (Wehr 28a) 110

Swahili (J)	taamuli	thought, thoughtfulness, meditation

amān security (Wehr 28b) 112

Digo (MN&Z)	amani	peace (via Swahili)
Malagasy (Gue)	amàny	sorry! thanks! (to ask forgiveness from parents, or a teacher)
Swahili (J)	amani	peace, security, safety, confidence

amīn trustworthy (Wehr 28b) 113

Digo (MN&Z)	-amini	to believe
	-aminifu	trustworthy, faithful (via Swahili)
Malagasy (Gue)	koamìny	to believe
Pokomo(Kra)	amánia	believer
Swahili (J)	amini (*n.* + *v.* + *adj.*)	fidelity, faithfulness, honesty
	-aminifu a.	faithful, honest, trustworthy

āmīn amen (Wehr 29a) 114

Digo (MN&Z)	amina	amen (via Swahili)
Swahili (J)	amin	amen, so be it

amāna trust (Wehr 29a); **amân** trust, security, loyalty (JdP 113b) 115

Malagasy (Gue)	amàna	object entrusted to s.o. for a third party, deposit, commission to do, to wear
Swahili (J)	amana	trust, security

īmān faith, belief (Wehr 29a) 116

Digo (MN&Z)	imani	faith (via Swahili)
Malagasy (Gue)	imàny	piety
Swahili (J)	imani	faith, confidence

ma'mūn reliable (Wehr 29a) 117

Swahili (J)	maamuma, mahamuna	an utter fool, simpleton, ignoramus

mu'min believing, faithful; believer (Wehr 29a) 118

Swahili (J)	muminina	a true believer (i.e., a Muslim)

amīrāl admiral (Wehr 29a) 119a

Swahili (Bo)	admeri	admiral

inna verily (Wehr 29b) 120

Swahili (J)	ina (*adj.*)	certainly, truly

anānās pineapple (Wehr 29b) 121a

Kinyarwanda (CAT)	ina-nasi	pineapple (via Swahili)
Kuria (MMR)	enaanaasi	a pineapple
Madi (Bla)	ànànásɨ̀	pineapple
Runyankore (Ka)	enanâ:si	pineapple (via Swahili)
Swahili (J)	nanasi	pineapple

onbaši (Tk. onbaşı) corporal (Wehr 30a) 121b

Acooli (Cra)	òbacà	corporal
Dholuo (Odo)	obaca	corporal (archaic) now *kopolo*
Madi (Bla)	ɔ̀mbásà	corporal

injīl gospel (Wehr 30a) 124

Ateso (Kit)	egiri	gospel
Gikuyu (Ben)	injiri	gospel (via Swahili)
Luganda (Sno)	'Njirì	gospel (via Swahili)
Swahili (J)	injili, anjili	the New Testament

anisa, anusa (*v.*) to be companionable, sociable, friendly (IV) to entertain, delight, amuse (Wehr 30b); **anasa** conversation, chat, talk, rap (JdP 149b); **ânisîn** chatting, friendly conversation, talking nicely (JdP 166b); **anisa, wanasa** (*v.*) to get used to, become familiar with (II) to accustom; to make familiar (Kazim: I, 60b; Kazim: II, 1611b); **wannas / yiwannis** (*v.*) (II) to converse, chat, discuss (JdP 1252b); **wannâs / wannâsîn** (*adj.*) talkative (JdP 1252b); **wannisîn** chat, discussion, conversation (JdP 1252b); **wennes** (*v.*) (II) to court, to tell a story (TC1 36) 125

Swahili (J)	anasa (*n.* + *v.*)	pleasure, enjoyment, luxury
	-anisi (*v.*)	please, cheer
	-anisi (*adj.*)	pleasing, luxurious
	-taanasa (*v.*)	seek pleasure, live luxuriously
	-taanisi (*v.* + *n.*)	please, cheer

nās people (Wehr 30b) 126

Swahili (J)	wadinasi	a man of good birth

ahl relatives, family (Wehr 33a); **ahlī** domestic, family (*adj.*) (Wehr 33a) 129

Malagasy (Gue)	ahàly	parents, relatives, family
Swahili (J)	ahali	wife; family, relations

au or; (with foll. subj.) unless, except, that (Wehr 33b) 130

Digo (MN&Z)	au	or (via Swahili)
Malagasy (Gue)	ào	or
Swahili (J)	au (*conj.*)	or

āfa harm, damage (Wehr 34b) 131

Swahili (J)	afa, mwafa	disaster, damage, calamity, ill luck

ūqīya ounce, a weight of varying magnitude (Wehr 34b) 132

Swahili (J)	wakia	an ounce (weight)

āla, pl. **ālāt** instrument; utensil (Wehr 34b) 133

Swahili (J)	ala	any sort of instrument, apparatus, tool, machine

awwal first, most important (Wehr 35a); **awwalī** prime, fundamental (Wehr 35b) 134

Swahili (J)	awali (*n.* + *adj.* + *adv.*)	beginning, start, first place

ayyil stag (Wehr 35b) 135

Swahili (J)	ayala	a hart

awwah *interj.* oh! (Wehr 36a) 135a

Madi (Bla)	áwà *interj.*	beware! take care!

āya sign, mark; miracle; Qur'anic verse (Wehr 36b) 136

Swahili (J)	aya	a short section or division of a book, esp. of the Qur'an, a paragraph

ayy any, every (Wehr 36b); **ayyi** any (Kaye 15a) 138a

Madi (Bla)	áyɨ́ (*adj.*)	any

aiḍan also; in addition (Wehr 37b) 139

Swahili (J)	aidha (*conj.*)	further, moreover, next, then

Bā'

bi (*prep.*) in; with; by (Wehr 38a) 143

Swahili (J)	bi (*prep.*)	by, with, in (used in a few phrases)

bi-lā without (Wehr 38a) 144

Malagasy (Gue)	bilà	without
Swahili (J)	bila (*prep.*)	without

bābūr locomotive (Wehr 38b) 147

Madi (Bla)	bàbúrú	ship; a small pressure stove which uses paraffin

bāḏinjān, baiḏinjān aubergine (Wehr 38b) 149

Gikuyu (Ben)	mbiringanya	eggplant, aubergine, brinjal (via Swahili mbilinganya)
Nyakyusa (Fel)	ibílíngania	eggplant, aubergine (via Swahili)
Swahili (J)	bilingani	aubergine

biʾr well, spring (Wehr 39a); **bîr / biyâr** well (JdP 274a) **149a**

Madi (Bla)	bírì	(water) well

bārūd saltpeter; gunpowder (Wehr 39a); **bārūd** gunpowder (Daf 15) (probably of Turkish origin into Swahili) **150**

Bende (Abe)	bhalúti	gunpowder
Gikuyu (Ben)	mbaruti	gunpowder
	rabuta	gunpowder, high explosive blasting powder (via Swahili)
Kiw'oso (K&O)	bar'udî	gunpowder
Lingala (Ev)	balúti	explosive black powder, shotgun
Nyakyusa (Fel)	ibalutí	gunpowder (via Swahili)
Pokomo (Wü)	barudi	gunpowder
Shilluk (Koh)	marud	gunpowder
Swahili (J)	baruti	gunpowder

burunji bugle, for the military (JdP 285a); **burūği** bugle, trumpet (RL 46a) **151**

Acooli (Cra)	bùrucì	horn (of band)
(Mu)	buruji	trumpet
Bari (Mu)	buruji	trumpet
Lotuxo (Mu)	aburuji	trumpet

bāmiya gumbo (Wehr 40a) **156**

Dinka (Id)	bamia	gumbo
Nyakyusa (Fel)	ibamía	okra, lady's finger (via Swahili)
Swahili (J)	bamia	okra (Hibiscus esculentus)

batūl virgin (Wehr 41a) **156a**

Swahili (M.A.M.)	batuli	virgin (with special reference to the virgin Mary and Fatima, daughter of the Prophet Muhammad)

bajal syphilis (Wehr 41b); **bağal** gonorrhea (RL 42a) **161**

Bari (Mu)	bejel	[imported] syphilis

baḥr, pl. **biḥār, abḥār** sea; large river (Wehr 42b); **bahar** river, big lake, sea (JdP 233a); **baḥr** river, lake, lagoon (RL 42b) **163**

Digo (MN&Z)	bahari	ocean (via Swahili)
Malagasy (Gue)	ḇahàry, bahàry	sea
Matengo (Yo)	bahâli	sea
Shona (Dal)	bahari	sea (via Swahili)
Swahili (J)	bahari	sea, ocean
	baharia	sailor

baẖt luck; a kind of lottery (Wehr 43a); **baxat** luck (JdP 260b) **163a**

Madi (Bla)	báátɨ̀	luck
Malagasy (Gue)	ḇahàty	luck
Swahili (J)	bahati	luck (good or bad) fortune

buẖār vapor (Wehr 43b) **164**

Acooli (Cra)	màbúùr	steamer
(Mu)	babur	
Bari (Mu)	babur	steamer
Dholuo (Odo)	mabur	steamer, ship, boat
Dinka (Id)	mabu(u)r	steamer
Lotuxo (Mu)	ababur, ababuri	steamer
Ndogo (Po)	babur	boat; ship

baẖūr incense (Wehr 43b) **165**

Malagasy (Gue)	kobohòry	that we incense, that we pass in the smoke (ritual gesture)
Swahili (J)	buhuri	a vapor bath for illness, fumigation

baẖs too little, too low; very low (price) (Wehr 43b) **166**

Swahili (J)	bahasa (*adj.*)	cheap

baḫšīš tip, gratuity (Wehr 43b) **166a**

Acooli (Cra)	bàkàcíìc	payment
Dholuo (Odo)	bakacic	a payment or reward for good work done
Gikuyu (Ben)	mabacici	largess, free gift, s.th. added over and above a transaction (via Swahili)
Madi (Bla)	bàkàsísì	tip; reward (via Swahili)
Swahili (J)	bakshishi	gratuity, gift, dole, tip

baḫīl avaricious (Wehr 44a) **167**

Malagasy (Gue)	b̠ahìly	miser
Swahili (J)	bahili (*n.* + *adj.*)	a miser, parsimonious person

budd way out, escape (Wehr 44a) **168**

Swahili (J)	budi	escape, way out

lā budda certainly (Wehr 44a) **169**

Acooli (Cra)	búlê (*adv.*)	perhaps, possibly; nearly (via Swahili)
Digo (MN&Z)	labuda	maybe, perhaps (via Swahili)
Swahili (J)	labda (*adv.*)	perhaps, it seems so, no doubt, probably, possibly

badr full moon (Wehr 45b) **171**

Malagasy (Gue)	badìry, badrỳ	incantation against an enemy
Swahili (J)	badiri	word used for various celestial phenomena and omens

bidʿ innovator (Wehr 46a) **173**

Swahili (J)	bidii	effort, energy

bidʿa, pl. **bidaʿ** innovation (Wehr 46a) 173a

Swahili (M.A.M.)	bidaa	[in Islam] innovation

badal replacement; price, rate (Wehr 46b); **badal** change [money] (Kaye 16a) 176

Kiw'oso (K&O)	baadala	instead of (via Swahili)
Matengo (Yo)	balálajà	instead of ~
Swahili (J)	badala	a substitute, thing given in exchange

badīl substitute, alternate (Wehr 46b) 177

Gikuyu (Ben)	bandũrithia (*v.*)	change, alter, get s.th. changed, altered (via Swahili badilisha)
Malagasy (Gue)	b̲adìly	change, change money for a ticket
Swahili (J)	badili	change, exchange, alteration
	-badilisha (*v.*)	cause to change or be changed

badan body, trunk, torso (Wehr 47a) 178

Swahili (J)	badani	the front or back piece of a kanzu

badāwa, bidāwa desert life, Bedouin life; nomadism (Wehr 47b) 181

Swahili (J)	bedui	a Bedouin, wanderer, nomad, outcast

baḏara (*v.*) to sow, disseminate (also fig., to spread) (Wehr 48a) 184

Swahili (J)	-badiri (*v.* + *adj.* + *n.*)	squander money, waste money or goods
	budhara	wastefulness in using money

mubaḏḏir spendthrift (Wehr 48b) **186**

Swahili (J)	mbadhiri	an extravagant person, waster of money or property

barra (*v.*) to be reverent (II) to exculpate (Wehr 49a) **187**

Malagasy (Gue)	ḇôra, bôra, ḇôroa, boarà, boôrà	better, [one] who is better
Swahili (J)	bora (*adj.*)	of special quality

barr land (as opposed to sea) (Wehr 49a) **189**

Haya (M&L)	embalabala, embarabara	highway, main road (via Swahili)
Lingala (Ev)	balabála (?)	street, highway, avenue, boulevard
Matengo (Yo)	balabâla-balabâla	car road
Swahili (J)	bara barabara (?)	land (in general, as opp. to sea) a highway

burra cat (RT 45b); **bura** cat (S&A 96a) **190a**

Acooli (Mu)	bura	cat
Bari (Mu)	'burön, 'burönyön	cat
Lotuxo (Mu)	agurre (?)	cat
Ndogo (Po)	bura	cat (domestic)

barī', pl. **burā'** free; innocent; guileless (Wehr 49b) **192**

Swahili (J)	buraa	forgiveness of obligation, debt, offense

burtuqāl orange (Wehr 50b); **burtuxâl** name of a tree, orange, Citrus sp. (J) dP 284b) **194**

Bari (Mu)	burdugan	orange
Dinka (Id)	burtukan, bertukan	orange
Lotuxo (Mu)	aburdukan	orange

burj tower; castle; sign of the zodiac (Wehr 50b) 195

Swahili (J)	buruji	battlement, indented parapet of a house, fort; (Sacl) Zodiac sign

burūda coldness, chilliness (Wehr 51b) 197

Swahili (J)	buruda	prayers for the sick and dying
	-burudi (*v.*)	[to] be cool, be cold

tabrīd cooling; cold storage, refrigeration (Wehr 51b) 199

Swahili (J)	-tabaradi (*v.*)	cool, refresh

bārid cold; cool (Wehr 51b) 200

Gikuyu (Ben)	*mũ*bariti (?)	large tree (Grevillea robusta, gives deep shade) (*cf.* via Swahili)
Swahili (J)	baridi	cold, chill; wind; coolness

mibrad file, rasp (Wehr 51b) 200a

Dinka (Id)	mabrad	lime

barāza field, vast plain without trees (Kazim: I, 110a); **berze** flat sandy space; in arenaceous terrain, small buttonhole beaches devoid of any vegetation and clean of any debris or dung (hence: place, public place) (TC1 77) 202

Ateso (Kit)	ebarasa	veranda
Ciluba (Kab)	dìbàlaasà	veranda (via Swahili)
Gikuyu (Ben)	*ĩ*baratha (*v.*) refl.	make oneself at home, make oneself (lavishly) comfortable
	mbaratha	audience (held by a government official) (via Swahili)
Lingala (Dz)	baraza, barza	veranda (via Swahili)
Runyankore (Ka)	i:baráza	veranda (via Swahili)

Malagasy (Gue)	b̲aràza, baràza	veranda, bench running along the wall of the house outside, where men sit, where one can exhibit goods for sale
Swahili (J)	baraza	place of public audience or reception

barzaḫ interval (Wehr 52b) 204

Swahili (J)	barazahi	paradise

burš mat (Wehr 52b); **biric / burûc** mat (JdP 275a); **burš** doormat made of palm leaves (Kazim: I, 111a) 205

Acooli (Mu)	biris	mat (not of papyrus)
Bari (Mu)	birit	mat (not of papyrus)
Dinka (Id)	biric	mat (of palm leaves)
Lotuxo (Mu)	abiris	mat

baraṣ leprosy (Wehr 53a) 206

Swahili (J)	barasi	black or light-colored patches on the hands or feet, said to be caused by leprosy or yaws

burquʿ, pl. **barāqiʿ** veil (worn by women; long, leaving the eyes exposed) (Wehr 54a) 206a

Swahili (M.A.M.)	barakoa	kind of veil worn by women to cover the face to the mouth, except the eyes

baraka benediction (Wehr 54b) 211

Malagasy (Gue)	b̲aràka	luck, fortune that is due to the blessing of God
Pokomo (Wü)	baraka	benediction
Swahili (J)	baraka	a blessing; prosperity

barlamān parliament (Wehr 54b) 213a

Madi (Bla)	bálīmɛ̄nì, pálīmɛ̄nì	parliament

burma earthenware pot (Wehr 55a) 217

Swahili (J)	buruma	a hookah, a water pipe

burunji bugle, for the military (JdP 285a); **brenği** bugle (RL 49a) 218

Acooli (Cra)	bùrucì	horn (of band)
(Mu)	buruji	trumpet
Bari (Mu)	buruji	trumpet
Lotuxo (Mu)	aburuji	trumpet

barmīl barrel; keg, cask (Wehr 55b; RL 49a); **birmil** barrel (Kaye 19a) 221

Acooli (Mu)	barmil	barrel
Bari (Mu)	börömit	barrel
Dinka (Id)	bermil	barrel
Lotuxo (Mu)	aboromil	barrel
Ndogo (Po)	bormil	barrel

bariha to heal, [recover from] an illness (Kazim: I, 118b) 222

Swahili (J)	buraha	rest, ease, comfort

burhān proof (Wehr 56a) 223

Swahili (J)	buruhani	power of God, i.e., used of holy people

barwa waste, scrap (Wehr 56a) 224

Ateso (Kit)	ebaluwa	letter
Bende (Abe)	bhaalúbha	letter; folder
Dholuo (Gor)	baruwa, barupe	letter
Gikuyu (Ben)	*i*rũa	piece of paper, sheet of writing paper; note, chit, letter
(Gor)	marua	letter (via Swahili)

Haya (Ka)	ebarúwa	letter (via Swahili)
Kinyarwanda (CAT)	i-baruwa	letter (via Swahili)
Kiw'oso (K&O)	baruwô	letter (mail)
Luganda (Sno)	`bbàluwà	letter; note (via Swahili)
Madi (Bla)	bàrúà	letter (via Swahili)
Matengo (Yo)	balûa	letter, folder
Runyankore (Ka)	ebarúha / amabarúha	letter (via Swahili)
Swahili (J)	barua	letter

burzul ignorant man (Freytag: I, 107b); fat, corpulent (Kazim: I, 110b) 225

Swahili (J)	baradhuli	a simpleton, dupe, dull-witted person

bazzāz draper, cloth merchant (Wehr 57a) 226

Swahili (J)	bazazi	trader

bizr spice (Wehr 57a) 228

Gikuyu (Ben)	bitharĩ, bitharĩ	curry powder (via Swahili)
Swahili (J)	bizari	small seed such as pepper, turmeric

ibzīm buckle, clasp (Wehr 57a) 230

Ndogo (Po)	abazin	clip, clasp; loop
Swahili (J)	bizimu	a buckle, brooch, clasp, or fastener

bas (Oriental and Bedouin dialect) only, do not ... that, enough! (JdP 254b); **bas** (*vulg.*) enough (Kazim: I, 124a); **bas** only; it's enough (RL 50b) 231

Madi (Bla)	básɨ̀ (*adv.*)	okay; fine; that's enough (via Swahili)

Malagasy (Gue)	b̲àsy, bàsy	enough, that's enough, stop, thank you (to ask that one stops serving a dish or drink)
Swahili (J)	basi	only; it's enough

basbās mace (*bot.*); (*maġr.*) fennel (Wehr 57b) 233

Swahili (J)	basbasi	mace, inner husk of the nutmeg

busta post (JdP 285b); **busta** post office (RL 50b) 234

Acooli (Mu)	bosta	mail; post office
Bari (Mu)	bosta	mail; post office
Dinka (Id)	posta	post
Lotuxo (Mu)	abosta	mail; post office
Madi (Bla)	bósɨ̄tà / pósɨ̄tà / bósɔ̄tà	post; post office
Swahili (J)	busta	post, mail; mailbag

bustān garden (Wehr 57b) 235

Bende (Abe)	bhusitaáni	garden (near a house)
Digo (MN&Z)	busitani	garden (via Swahili)
Haya (M&L)	obustani, omubustani	garden (via Swahili)
Kiw'oso (K&O)	búsutáni	vegetable garden (near a house) (via Swahili)
Swahili (J)	bustani	a garden

bāsūr, pl. **bawāsīr** hemorrhoids (Wehr 57b) 236

Swahili (J)	bawasiri	piles, hemorrhoids

bušrā glad tidings (Wehr 59b) 236a

Swahili (M.A.M.)	bushura	happiness, joy, gladness

bišāra good news (Wehr 59b) **236b**

Swahili (M.A.M.)	bishara	good news

bašīr bringer of glad tidings (Wehr 59b) **239**

Swahili (J)	-bashiri (*v.*)	foretell

baškīr towel (Wehr 60a); **baškir** towel (RL 51b) **240a**

Madi (Bla)	bìsìkírì	towel

baṣura (*v.*) to look, see; to realize (Wehr 60b) **241**

Swahili (J)	-busuri (*v.*)	observe, be careful, take care

baṣīr, pl. **buṣarā'** endowed with eyesight; acutely aware (Wehr 61a) **243**

Swahili (J)	busara	good sense, practical wisdom, prudence, sagacity

tabaṣṣur reflection, consideration; perspicacity (Wehr 61b) **245**

Swahili (J)	tabasuri	same meaning as busara (rarely heard); *cf.* no. **243**

abṣa', fem. **baṣ'ā'** stupid, fool (Kazim: I, 132b) **246**

Swahili (J)	basua	confusion of mind, weakness of intellect

baṣal onion(s) (Wehr 61b); **besel / baṣal** onion (RL 51a–52a) **247**

Acooli (Mu)	basala	onion
Bari (Mu)	basalatat, basala	onion
Dinka (Id)	bathala	onion
Lotuxo (Mu)	abasyala, abasyalaa'	onion
Madi (Bla)	básālà	onion
Ndogo (Po)	basala	onion

baṣal onion(s) (Wehr 61b) and **ṯūm** garlic (Wehr 109b) 247a

Madi (Bla)	básàlà túmù	garlic

biḍāʿa, pl. **baḍāʾiʿ** merchandise (Wehr 62a) 248

Swahili (J)	bidhaa	merchandise

baṭṭārīya battery (Wehr 62b); **battariye / batâtîr** flashlight, torch (JdP 258a) 249a

Acooli (Mu)	batariya	battery; electric torch
Bari (Mu)	batariya	battery; electric torch
Lotuxo (Mu)	afattariya	battery; electric torch
Madi (Bla)	bàtàríà	torch

biṭṭīḫ, **baṭṭīḫ** melon, watermelon (Wehr 63a) 250

Dinka (Id)	bateka	watermelon

baṭar arrogance, pride, vanity (Wehr 63a) 250a

Swahili (J)	batara	arrogance, vanity, pride

baṭāṭsa potato (RL 53b) 250b

Madi (Bla)	bàtátāsɨ̀	Irish potatoes

bāṭil vain; null (Wehr 63b) 256

Swahili (J)	-batili (*v.*)	annul

baṭana (*v.*) to be hidden (Wehr 64a); **baṭana** (*v.*) to double (a garment) (Kazim: I, 137b); **baṭn** belly, stomach; interior, inside (Wehr 64a) 257

Swahili (J)	batini	the belly (rarely used, fig., of the innermost thoughts or intentions)

baṭāyin small ship (F: I, 133a) 259

Swahili (J)	bedeni	a kind of Arabian sailing vessel

biṭāna lining (of a garment) (Wehr 64b) 260

Swahili (J)	bitana	any thin material used for lining a garment

baṭṭānīya blanket (Wehr 64b); **battâniye** / **batâtîn** blanket (JdP 258a) 260a

Acooli (Cra)	bàṭàniià	blanket (to cover)
(Mu)	bataniya	blanket
Bari (Mu)	bataniya	blanket
Dinka (Id)	batania	blanket
Dholuo (Odo)	bataniya	blanket
Lotuxo (Mu)	abattaniya	blanket
Madi (Bla)	bàtàníà	blanket

bu'bu' bugaboo, bogey (Wehr 65a) 261

Swahili (J)	barubaru (?)	a strong vigorous youth

ba'ṯ sending out; resurrection (Wehr 65a); **yaum al-ba'ṯ** Day of Resurrection (from the dead) 262

Swahili (J)	-baathi, -buathi (*v.*)	[to] raise up (seldom heard, only in the phrase *siku ya kubaathiwa*, or, 'the day of the general resurrection')

ba'du then; still, yet (Wehr 66a) 265

Dinka (Id)	baden	then, later
Swahili (J)	bado (*adv.*)	not yet; still

baʿda after (Wehr 66a); **baʿd** (*adv.*) (particle of insistence, strengthening, more or less so ...) anyway, so, as for (TC1 112) 266

Bende (Abe)	bhaáda	after
	bhaadáye (*interj.*)	then
Digo (MN&Z)	bada ya	after (via Swahili)
Malagasy (Gue)	ḇaàda, ḇaʿàda, ḇaànda, ḇànda	after
Swahili (J)	baada (*adv.*)	after, afterwards

baʿīḍ far, far away; remote (Wehr 66a) 267

Swahili (J)	-baidi (*v.*)	[to] be apart, be separate

baʿḍ portion (Wehr 67a) 268

Swahili (J)	baadhi	some, a portion

baʿā to reach and harm him by his evil eye (Kazim: I, 144b) 269

Swahili (J)	baa	evil, disaster, calamity; anything which brings bad luck or disaster

buġḍ hatred (Wehr 67b) 270

Swahili (J)	bughudha	abhorrence, hatred, ill feeling, slander

baġl mule (Wehr 67b); **baxal** mule (JdP 260b) 271

Acooli (Cra)	bakàlà, bagàlà	mule
Bari (Mu)	bakala, bakalajin	horse or mule
Dholuo (Odo)	bakala	mule
Swahili (J)	baghala	mule

B Ġ M (*v.*) to express oneself confusedly in front of s.th. or in obscure terms, to the point of letting oneself know exactly what one wants (Kazim: I, 146b) 272

Swahili (J)	baghami	a fool

bafta calico, Indian cotton cloth (Wehr 68a) 274

Luganda (Sno)	bafùta	calico
(Mo)	\`bbaf\`uta	bleached calico (via Swahili)
Malagasy (Gue)	ḇafòta	shroud, white cloth for shroud
Swahili (J)	bafta	a kind of thin bleached calico, used for lining garments

baqar bovines, cattle (Wehr 68b); **bagar** bovine (Daf 13) 275

Sango (Bou)	bágàrà	ox; beef; buffalo
Swahili (M.A.M.)	bakari	cow

baqqāriy massive and solid (stick), like that of the drover (F: I, 142a) 277

Digo (MN&Z)	bakora	walking stick, staff (via Swahili)
Gikuyu (Ben)	mbokora	walking stick (via Swahili)
Swahili (J)	bakora (?)	a walking stick, formerly one with a crooked handle; a stroke [given by s.o.] with a stick; a gift given by a father to a master when placing his son with him to learn a trade

B Q ʿ (*v.*) to spot, stain (Wehr 68b) 278

Swahili (J)	baka	mark on the body, birthmark, scar, ringworm; also used of marks on animals

bāqūl porous earthenware jug for water (Dozy: I, 104b) 280

Digo (MN&Z)	bakuli	bowl (via Swahili)
Kamba (Mbi)	mbakũli	bowl (via Swahili)
Luganda (Sno)	\`bbàkulì	basin (via Swahili)

Madi (Bla)	bàkúlì	bowl (via Swahili)
Malagasy (Gue)	ḇakòly	bowl
Matengo (Yo)	bakûli-bakûli	bowl (new style)
Nyakyusa (Fel)	ibakúli	bowl (via Swahili)
Pokot (Cra)	bàkúli	bowl, mug (via Swahili)
Swahili (J)	bakuli	basin, any large deep dish

baqiya (*v.*) to remain, stay; to be left behind (Wehr 69a) 281

Swahili (J)	baki	that which remains over, remainder, residue; in arithmetic, that which remains after subtraction, difference, balance in accounting

bikr firstborn; virgin (Wehr 70a) 283

Acooli (Mu)	bikira	virgin (via Swahili)
Luganda (Sno)	mùbiikìra	virgin, nun
	mùnuubiikìra	nun (via Swahili)
Swahili (J)	bikira	virgin

bal nay, rather ...; (and) even; but, however (Wehr 71a) 284

Malagasy (Gue)	ḇàḏy, ḇàdy, ḇaḏỳ	but, since, on the contrary, and then
Swahili (J)	bali (*conj.*)	but, on the contrary

balla (*v.*) to moisten, wet, make wet (Wehr 71a) 285

Swahili (J)	bilula (?)	a tap, turncock

bulbul nightingale (Wehr 71b) 287

Swahili (J)	bulibuli (*adj.*) in *kofia ya bulibuli*	a white embroidered skull-cap

balaḥ dates (Wehr 72a) 287a

Madi (Bla)	bálà	dates (i.e., fruit)

balad, pl. **bilād** town (Wehr 72a) **287b**

Swahili (M.A.M.)	biladi	town

buldān countries (Wehr 72a) **289**

Swahili (J)	buldani	district

baladī native, indigenous (Wehr 72a) **290**

Swahili (J)	biladia	anything belonging to or appertaining to a town

ballāṣ (*eg.*) earthenware jar (Wehr 72b) **293**

Swahili (J)	balasi	a large jar with a narrow neck

balaġa (*v.*) to attain puberty (Wehr 73a) **297**

Malagasy (Gue)	kob̲alìhy, kobalìghy	to reach puberty, be pubescent; to be old enough to be attracted to girls
Swahili (J)	-balehe (*v.*)	to come to (sexual) maturity

balġam phlegm; expectoration, sputum (Wehr 74a) **302**

Swahili (J)	belghamu	phlegm

ablaq, fem. **balqā'** variegated, two-color, white and black (Kazim: I, 163b) **304**

Swahili (J)	mbalanga, balanga	a skin disease, esp. of the hands which become covered with light- or dark-colored patches

balīya misfortune, calamity (Wehr 75b) **304a**

Swahili (M.A.M.)	balia	calamity, misfortune

balāʾ trial, tribulation, distress, misfortune; plague (Wehr 75b) 308

Swahili (J)	balaa	trouble, difficulty, damage, calamity, pest

ballūr, billaur crystal; crystal glass, glass (Wehr 75b) 310

Bende (Abe)	bhilaúli	glass
Gikuyu (Ben)	*mũ*raũni, *mũ*raũri	metal tumbler for drinking purposes (via Swahili)
Haya (Ka)	ekilaúli	tumbler; goblet (via Swahili)
Luganda (Sno)	kìrawulì	lamp glass; tumbler (via
(Mo)	\`ek\`irawur\`i	Swahili)
Malagasy (Gue)	bilaòry	glass
Runyankore (Ka)	ekirahúri / ebirahúri	glass (via Swahili)
Swahili (J)	bilauri	glass, crystal; a tumbler, wineglass

ibn son (Wehr 76a); **ādam** Adam (Wehr 10b) 312

Digo (MN&Z)	binadamu	human being (via Swahili)
Malagasy (Gue)	binadàmo, b̲inadàmo	man, being human
Swahili (J)	bin	son (of)
	binadamu	member of the human
	binamu	race, human being, man
		a cousin, i.e., son of paternal uncle

ibna, bint daughter; **banat** girl (Wehr 76b) 313

Swahili (J)	binti	a daughter, young lady
(M.A.M.)	banati	girl, damsel

bunn coffee beans, coffee (Wehr 76b) 315

Acooli (Mu)	bun	coffee (tree)
Bari (Mu)	bun	coffee (tree)
Lotuxo (Mu)	abun	coffee (tree)
Swahili (J)	buni	coffee berry, fruit of the mbuni

bunduqīya rifle, gun (Wehr 77a); **bundūg** gun (RL 61a); **bundug** gun (Z&T 121) 317

Knappert (1972–73: 293, note 18) states: "The Hausa *bindiga* form comes from a term of the *Lingua franca* designating the *venediga* rifle; this word, in Portuguese or Spanish, is the adjectival form of Venice, the former port of transfer of firearms."

The word in Luganda is a loan to Swahili *bunduki*, "itself a loan from Turkish via Arabic. The origin of this word is the Greek *pontikòn* (hazelnut), referring to the shape of a musket bullet. The Ganda form of the word can be explained by the 'law of Meinhof,' which states that the first of two consecutive voiced pre-nasalized plosive consonants must become a nasal. The loss of the last syllable is already found in Luo *bunde*; the Nilotic languages prefer words of one or two syllables" (Knappert 1970: 82).

Acooli (Cra)	mùdùku	gun, rifle
(Mu)	mudukú	
Dholuo (Gor)	bunde	rifle
(Odo)	muduku	gun, rifle; also called *luduku*, with *luduku* preferred
Gikuyu (Ben)	bundũki, bindũki	rifle, gun (via Swahili)
Kikongo (Swa)	bindúki[1]	guns, firearms or shooting, bows
Kiw'oso (K&O)	-búnduki	gun (via Swahili)
Kuria (MMR)	imbunduki / ibunduki	gun
Lingala (Kna 1970)	bondúki	gun (via Swahili)
Luganda (Sno)	'mmûndu	gun, rifle (via Swahili)
Luo (Kna 1970)	mbúnduk	gun (via Swahili)
Madi (Bla)	mùndùkú / bùndúkì	gun
Malagasy (Gue)	bondòky	gun
Pokomo(Wü)	bundutyi	gun
Runyankore (Ka)	embû:ndu	gun (via Swahili)
Swahili (J)	bunduki	gun, rifle, musket

1 Swartenbroeckk gives: "Pl – incorrect de *bundúki* fusil, parfois arc."

(Sp. bandera) **bandēra** pennon, flag, banner (Wehr 77a) 318

Acooli (Cra)	bɛɛ́rɛ̂	flag
(Mu)	bɛrɔ, bɛrɛ	banner, flag
Ateso (Kit)	emendera	flag
Bari (Mu)	bɛrɛt, bɛrɛsi	banner, flag
Digo (MN&Z)	bendera	flag, banner (via Swahili)
Lotuxo (Mu)	abɛrɛt	banner, flag
Ndogo (Po)	bere	flag
Runyankore (Ka)	ebe.ndéra	flag (via Swahili)
Swahili (J)	bendera	flag

bannūr glass (Wehr 77a); **ballūr**, **bannūr** crystal (RL 58b) 318a

Madi (Bla)	bònúrù	long glass of water

banzīn, **benzīn** gasoline, benzine (Wehr 77a) 318b

Ndogo (Po)	benjin	gasoline

banā (*v.*) to build, construct (Wehr 77b); agent name **banā** builder 321

Swahili (J)	-buni (*v.*)	construct, contrive, compose, invent; fabricate

banṭalūn (from It. pantaloni) trousers, pants (Wehr 77b); **pantalon** / **panâtilîn** trousers (JdP 1023a), Fr. loanword 321a

Bari (Mu)	pantalon	trousers
Dinka (Id)	mathelon	trousers
Lotuxo (Mu)	amotolon	trousers
Madi (Bla)	bòtòlónì / mòtòlónì	trousers
Ndogo (Po)	mandaloni	trousers

bango hashish, hemp, cannabis, Cannabis sativa indica (JdP 244a) 321b

Madi (Bla)	bánggì	hashish, opium

bank bank, banking house (Wehr 77b) 321c

Madi (Bla)	bɛ́nggɨ̀ / bɛ́ngkɨ̀	bank

binya, bunya structure (Wehr 78a); **bunya / bunyât** punch (JdP 283b) 321d

Madi (Bla)	búnīà	boxing; boxing match

bahta perplexity, stupefaction (Wehr 78b) 323

Swahili (J)	butaa	astonishment

mubhij pleasant, charming, delightful (Wehr 78b) 324

Swahili (J)	mmbuji	an elegant, well-dressed person

bahīma beast, animal, quadruped (Wehr 79b) 324a

Swahili (M.A.M.)	bahaimu	an animal with four legs

bahā (*v.*) to be beautiful (Wehr 80a); **buhya** painting (JdP 282a) 328

Bari (Mu)	buya'	paint
Dinka (Id)	buia	paint
Lotuxo (Mu)	abuya	paint
Madi (Bla)	bóyɛ̀	color; paint

bahw hall; parlor, drawing room, reception hall (Wehr 80a) 329

Swahili (J)	behewa	inner court surrounded by buildings and open to the air; a compartment (or carriage) of a train; an underground storage area

BWB (*v.*) (II) to divide into chapters or sections (Wehr 80b) 329a

Swahili (M.A.M.)	bawibu (*v.*)	divide s.th. into sections or chapters

bāba kind, sort, class, category (Wehr 81a) 331

Swahili (J)	babu, bab	kind, sort, class, used in commerce

bawwāb doorman, gatekeeper (Wehr 81a) 332

Swahili (J)	bawabu	doorkeeper, house porter

bawwāba (large) gate, portal (Wehr 81a) 333

Swahili (J)	bawaba	a hinge

bāḥa (*v.*) to become known; **abāḥa** (IV) to permit, allow; to justify (Wehr 81a) 334

Swahili (J)	-bihi (*v.*)	to repudiate, forego, forgive (i.e., of a debt, obligation)

būr uncultivated, fallow (Wehr 82a) 335

Swahili (J)	pori	steppe, wilderness, uninhabited wilds, grassy [area] without trees

būrī (Tk. *boru*) trumpet, bugle (Wehr 82a); **bûri** horn, buzzer (JdP 284a), Turkish loanword; **būrī** bugle (RT 63a) 335a

Dholuo (Odo)	burugi	a bugle
Madi (Bla)	búrè	vehicle horn; horn sound
Swahili (J)	buri	a small elephant tusk (just beginning to grow)

būza / **būẓa** a beerlike beverage (Wehr 82b) 337

Swahili (J)	boji	a kind of intoxicating liquor
	buza	intoxicating liquor prepared with honey

bāla (*v.*) and (V) to make water, urinate (Wehr 83a) 339

Swahili (J)	-tabawali (*v.*)	urinate

būlīs (Fr. police) police (Wehr 83b); **bôlîs / bawâlîs** police officer, police (JdP 279b), Fr. loanword; **bōlīs** police, police officer (RL 58b) **341a**

Acooli (Mu)	bolis	policeman
Bari (Mu)	bolis	policeman
Dinka (Id)	booliis	police
Lotuxo (Mu)	wahil pl.	policeman

bait verse (Wehr 84b) **344**

Swahili (J)	ubeti	verse, stanza, strophe

bait al-māl treasure house (Wehr 84b) **345**

Acooli (Mu)	mäli	property

baiṭārī veterinary (Wehr 86b); **bēṭarī** veterinary (RT 66b) **347a**

Madi (Bla)	bétērì	veterinarian

bai' sale (Wehr 86b) **348a**

Bende (Abe)	bheéi, bheéji	price
Dholuo (Odo)	bei, beyi	price
Lega (Bot)	i.béi	price (via Swahili)
Matengo (Yo)	bêi	price
Runyankore (Ka)	ebê:yi	price (via Swahili)
Swahili (J)	bei	value, price, cost

bai' sale (Wehr 86b); **šarā** (*v.*) to sell; to buy (Wehr 470a) **349**

Digo (MN&Z)	bishara	business (via Swahili)
Kuria (MMR)	ibiasara	trade, business
Malagasy (Gue)	biaŝàra	merchandise
Swahili (J)	biashara	trade, commerce, buying and selling

baiʿa agreement, arrangement; business deal, transaction; sale (Wehr 86b) 351

Swahili (J)	bia	co-operation, partnership, association in business, pleasure

bīkār compass (Wehr 87a) 353

Swahili (J)	bikari	compass for drawing

baina (*prep.*) between; among, amidst (Wehr 87b) 355

Malagasy (Gue)	ḇaìna, baìna	between, among, from, to (approximately)
Swahili (J)	baina ya (*prep.*)	between, among

bayyin clear, plain, evident (Wehr 88a); **bāin** / **bāyin** visible; clear; apparent; obvious (RL 67a) 356

Swahili (J)	ubaini, ubainifu, ubayana	clearness, demonstrability, evidence

bayān explanation (Wehr 88a) 357

Swahili (J)	bayana, baina	clearness, explanation

pêrik wig, lock of hair (JdP 1024b) 357a

Madi (Bla)	bàrúkà	wig

Tā'

tibġ tobacco (Wehr 91a); **tâba** tobacco (JdP 1155b); **tâba** (borrowed from Spanish tabaco), known in Sudan (Qāsim) tobacco (JdP 1155b); **tumbâk** Arabic word of Iranian, Persian, Turkish loanword (Qāsim; *al-Munjid*, 1975) tobacco, snuff (JdP 1222b) **363a**

Acooli (Cra)	táà, tóbâ, tábâ	tobacco
Bari (Mu)	taba	tobacco
Lotuxo (Mu)	attaba, attabat	tobacco
Ndogo (Po)	taba	tobacco
Pokot (Cra)	tápà	tobacco (via Swahili)
Swahili (J)	tumbako[2]	tobacco
(M.A.M.)	mtumbako	tobacco (plant)
	tumbaku	tobacco

tabalo tank for water (RL 69a); **tabliiya** stall, kiosk (S&A 150b) **363b**

Madi (Bla)	tò'bòlíà	a kiosk

tijāra commerce (Wehr 91b) **365**

Swahili (J)	-tajiri (*v.*), and sometimes tijara (*v.*)	get money by trading, get rich

tājir, pl. **tujjār** merchant (Wehr 91b); **tâjir / tujjâr** (*adj.* + *n.*) shopkeeper, merchant (JdP 1168a) **366**

Digo (MN&Z)	tajiri	master, rich person (via Swahili)
Dinka (Id)	taajir	trader
Madi (Bla)	tōjārɨ̀	trade, trading, business
Swahili (J)	tajiri	a merchant, wholesale trader

2 Johnson (1939: 478a) considers this a loanword from Hindi (under *tumbako*), or Persian (under *mtumbako* at 312a), while Kiraithe and Baden (1976: 24) claim it has a Portuguese origin; Mohammed A. Mohammed (2011: 763a) gives it an English origin.

tarabēza (*eg.*) table (Wehr 93a); **tarbêza / tarâbîz** table, table- 369a
bench, display, counter, stall (JdP 1186b), < Greek τραπεζα

Dinka (Id)	tarabeth, tarabeza	table
Lotuxo (Mu)	attaramɛja	table
Ndogo (Po)	tarabeza	table

turjumān interpreter (Wehr 93a) 371

Acooli (Cra)	tùrjùmáàm	interpreter (now obsolete)

tarzī (*eg.*) tailor (Wehr 93a); **tarzī** tailor (RT 71a); **terezi** tailor 371a
(S&A 153a)

Madi (Bla)	térēzì	tailor

tarifa (*v.*) to live in opulence, in luxury (Wehr 93b) 372

Swahili (J)	-turufu (*v.*)	scorn, slight, treat with contempt

taraka (*v.*) to let be, renounce, to give up; to abstain; to neglect 373
(Wehr 93b)

Malagasy (Gue)	mikotoròko	to lose hope

trimbîl / trimbîlât automobile (JdP 1220a); **trombīl** automobile 374a
(RT 72b et 1220a)

Acooli (Mu)	trumbili	automobile
Bari (Mu)	trumbili, trumbilyet	automobile
Lotuxo (Mu)	attoromile	automobile
Madi (Bla)	tùrùmbílì	automobile
Ndogo (Po)	trombil	automobile

tisʿa nine (Wehr 94b) 375

Digo (MN&Z)	tisiya	nine (via Swahili)
Madi (Bla)	tísà	nine, used in time telling
Swahili (J)	tisa	nine

tusʿ one-ninth, the ninth part (Wehr 94b) **376**

Swahili (J)	-a tisa	ninth

tisʿūn ninety (Wehr 94b), (*acc.*) **tisʿīn** **377**

Digo (MN&Z)	tisini	ninety (via Swahili)
Kiw'oso (K&O)	-tisíni	ninety
Swahili (J)	tisini	ninety

taṭā to be unjust and tyrannical, exert vexations, persecutions (Kazim: I, 199a) **379**

Swahili (J)	-tatai (*adj.*)	cunning, deceitful

taʿab trouble; difficulty; fatigue (Wehr 94b); **taʿab** fatigue, pain, trouble (JdP 1152a) **380**

Madi (Bla)	tá'bò	suffering
Malagasy (Gue)	taʿàbo, taàbo	pain, fatigue, trouble, difficulties
Swahili (J)	taabu	trouble, distress, ado, fatigue, toil, travail

tuffāḥ apple(s) (Wehr 95a) **384**

Swahili (J)	tofaa	fruit of the tree mtofaa (rose-apple, Eugenia jambosa)

taksi / takâsi taxi (JdP 1170b); **taksi** taxi (S&A 151b) **385a**

Madi (Bla)	tékēsì	taxi; a large metal washing basin

tukul kitchen (JdP 1222a); **tukl / tukul** grass kitchen (RL 75b) **385b**

Madi (Bla)	tókōlò	a hut

talifa (*v.*) to be destroyed; to be or become damaged or spoiled (Wehr 96a) **386**

Swahili (J)	-tilifu (*v.*)	destroy, waste

tilifūn telephone (Wehr 96b) 387a

Dinka (Id)	telepuun, telepun	telephone
Madi (Bla)	tèlèfúnì / téléfōnì	telephone

talā (*v.*) to read; to recite (Wehr 97a) 388

Swahili (J)	-taali (*v.*)	study, learn, be a student

tamma (*v.*) to be or become finished (Wehr 97b); **tamma** / **yitimm** (*v.*) to finish, complete, suffice (JdP 1179b); **temm** / **temma** to be finished, be completed, be ended (RL 77a) 391

Malagasy (Gue)	kotsìmo	to be pubescent, to be nubile
Swahili (J)	tamati	used in the sense of "Finis," the end, esp. at the end of poems, stories

tamr, pl. **tamarāt**, **tumūr** dates, esp. dried ones (Wehr 98a) 394

Madi (Bla)	tómōrò	dates, the fruit
Ndogo (Po)	tomoro	dates

tamarǧī nurse, attendant in hospital (RL 78a); **tamaaragi** nurse (S&A 152a) 394a

Dinka (Id)	temerj	nurse
Madi (Bla)	tòmórōgì	nurse

tāba (*v.*) to repent (Wehr 98b); **tauba** repentance (Wehr 98b) 396

Swahili (J)	toba	repentance
	-tubu (*v.*)	repent

tannūr a kind of baking oven, a pit, usually clay-lined, for baking bread (Wehr 98b) 397

Swahili (J)	tanuu, tano, tanu,	native lime-kiln, i.e.
(M.A.M.)	tanuru	limestone piled in a circular
	tanuri	heap of logs and burnt
		kiln, furnace

tanaka tin container, can, pot (Wehr 98b) **397a**

Ndogo (Po)	tanga	barrel

tūtiyā zinc (Wehr 99a); **tûta** zinc (Daf 132); **tûta** name of mineral (JdP 1226a) **399**

Acooli (Cra)	tuutù	sulphate of copper

tāj crown (Wehr 99a) **400**

Gikuyu (Ben)	tanji	crown (via Swahili)
Swahili (J)	taji	a crown, coronet

taurāh Torah, Pentateuch; Old Testament (Wehr 99a) **401**

Swahili (J)	torati, taurati	the law of Moses, the Pentateuch

tīn fig (Wehr 100b) **403**

Swahili (J)	tini	a fig, fruit of the mtini (Ficus carica)

Ṯā'

ṯubūt constancy, immutability; certainty (Wehr 101b) **407**

Gikuyu (Ben)	thubuticia (*v.t.*)	(of Anglican Church rite) confirm, hold confirmation service (via Swahili)
Swahili (J)	-thubutu (*v.*)	have courage to
	-thubutisha (*v.*)	cause courage

ṯābit firm, fixed; permanent (Wehr 102a) **408**

Swahili (J)	thabiti (*adj.*)	firm; brave

ṯurayyā Pleiades (Wehr 103a) 409

Swahili (J)	Thurea	a chandelier; the Pleiades

ṯafar crupper (of the saddle) (Wehr 103b) 410

Swahili (J)	mtafura	crupper – the strap fastened to the saddle passing under the tail of horse, donkey, etc.

ṯulṯ one-third (Wehr 105b) 413

Swahili (J)	theluthi (*adj.*)	one-third (fraction)

ṯalāṯa three (Wehr 105b) 413a

Madi (Bla)	tàlátà	three, used in time telling

ṯalaṯīn thirty (Wehr 105b) 414

Digo (MN&Z)	salasini / thelathini	thirty (via Swahili)
Swahili (J)	thelathini	thirty

ṯalāṯā' Tuesday (Wehr 105b) 415

Malagasy (Gue)	talàta	Tuesday
Rendille (P&G)	Talaa'dá	Tuesday

ṯalj, pl. **ṯulūj** snow, ice (Wehr 106a); **talij** ice (JdP 1175a); **telej** ice (S&A 153a) 416

Dholuo (Gor)	theluji	snow
Digo (MN&Z)	theluji	snow (via Swahili)
Dinka (Id)	talj	ice
Gikuyu (Ben)	therunji, tharunji	snow (via Swahili)
Luganda (Sno)	\`sserùji	snow (via Swahili)
(Mo)	\`sser\`ugi	
Swahili (J)	theluji	snow

ṯallāja refrigerator (Wehr 106a) **416a**

Madi (Bla)	tɛ̀lɛ́jà	refrigerator

ṯamara to bear fruit (Wehr 106b); **ṯamara** fruit (Wehr 106b); **ṯamra** tree (Kazim: I, 236a) **417**

Swahili (J)	thamra	name given to cloves when just beginning to form

ṯaman price (Wehr 107a) **418**

Digo (MN&Z)	samani	value (via Swahili)
Swahili (J)	thamani	price, value

ṯamāniya eight (Wehr 107a) **419**

Madi (Bla)	tàmánīà	eight, used in time telling
Swahili (J)	themani, themanya	eight

ṯamāniyata ʿašara eighteen (Wehr 107a) **420**

Swahili (J)	themntashara	eighteen

ṯumn one-eighth (Wehr 107a) **421**

Swahili (J)	themuni, thumni, sumni	one-eighth (fraction)

ṯamānīn eighty (Wehr 107a) **422**

Digo (MN&Z)	samanini / themanini	eighty (via Swahili)
Kiw'oso (K&O)	-sémaninî	eighty (via Swahili)
Swahili (J)	themanini	eighty

ṯanāʾ commendation, praise, eulogy; appreciation (Wehr 108a) **424**

Swahili (J)	sana (*adv.*)	very much, in a high degree

iṯnāni two (Wehr 108a) 424a

Madi (Bla)	ìtìnínì (*num.*)	two, used in time-telling

iṯnā ʿašara twelve (Wehr 108a) 424b

Gikuyu (Ben)	thinacara	6 AM or 6 PM (via Swahili)
Madi (Bla)	ìtìnásārà	twelve, used in time-telling
Swahili (J)	thenashara (*n.* + *adj.*)	twelve, for *kumi na mbili*

al-iṯnain Monday (Wehr 108a) 425

Malagasy (Ade)	alatsinàiny	Monday
Rendille (P&G)	Alaasmín	Monday

ṯawāb recompense; (*Isl. law*) merit, credit (bestowed by God for good deeds) (Wehr 108b) 427

Digo (MN&Z)	thawabu	reward, particularly from God (via Swahili)
Swahili (J)	thawabu	a reward, gift – but esp. from God

ṯum garlic (Wehr 109b) 429

Swahili (J)	thumu, tumu, saumu	garlic

Jīm

ġāz gas (Wehr 110a); **jâs** oil, kerosene (JdP 652b) 429a

Acooli (Mu)	jas	paraffin
Bari (Mu)	jas	paraffin
Dinka (Id)	jas lamba	paraffin
Lotuxo (Mu)	ajas	paraffin
Madi (Bla)	jásɨ̀	paraffin; fuel in general

ja'š emotional; heart, soul (Wehr 110a) **430**

Swahili (J)	jasho	sweat, perspiration; high temperature

jāh rank, honor, glory (Wehr 110a) **431**

Swahili (J)	jaha	honor, glory, prosperity

jubba a long outer garment, open in front, with wide sleeves (Wehr 110b); **ǧibba** long sleeved cloak (RL 85a) **432**

Malagasy (Gue)	ĵòba	large ceremonial dress in the Muslim costume
Swahili (J)	juba	a kind of coat, open in front, with collar and wide sleeves of cloth

jabara (**jabr**, **jubūr**) (*v.*) to set; to restore; to force; to console (Wehr 110b) **433**

Swahili (J)	-juburu (*v.*)	compel, force, sometimes used in the sense of encourage

'ilm al-jabr algebra (Wehr 111a) **434**

Swahili (Bo)	aljebra	branch of mathematics in which signs and letters are used to represent quantities

jabbār giant; omnipotent (God) (Wehr 111a); **jabbâr** proud, giant (Daf 65) **435**

Swahili (J)	jabari	Supreme Ruler, Islamic name of God; a brave, fearless, proud person; a violent person

jabal mountain (Wehr 111b) 438

Digo (MN&Z)	jabali	rock (via Swahili)
Haya (M&L)	eibale	rock (via Swahili)
Malagasy (Gue)	ĵabàly	mountain
Swahili (J)	jabali	a rock, rocky hill or mountain or cliff

jubn, jubna cheese (Wehr 111b) 439

Madi (Bla)	jɨ́bīnà	cheese
Ndogo (Po)	jibna	cheese
Swahili (J)	jibini	cheese

jaḥama (*v.*) to light (the fire); to open, wide eyes, fix them on a point; (II) to fix s.o., to fix one's gaze at/gaze intently at (Kazim: I, 257a) 441

Swahili (J)	-jugumu (*v.*)	speak scornfully, disparagingly

jaḥīm fire, hellfire, hell (Wehr 113a; Qur'an 79:36) 442

Swahili (J)	jahim	Hell

jaẖẖa (*v.*) (*eg.*) to lord it, give o.s. airs; to boast, brag; (*syr.*) to dress up (slightly ironical) (Wehr 113a) 443

Swahili (J)	juha	idiot, simpleton, ignoramus

jadd grandfather; ancestor, forefather (Wehr 113a) 445

Digo (MN&Z)	jadi	custom, tradition, precedent (via Swahili)
Swahili (J)	jadi	an ancestor, descent, origin, pedigree, genealogy, lineage

jadda (*v.*) to be new; to be or become serious (II) to renew (Wehr 113a) 446

Swahili (J)	jadi, mjadi	exertion, seriousness, strong desire

jadala (*v.*) to twist tight (III) to quarrel; to argue, debate; to dispute, contest (Wehr 115a) 451

Swahili (J)	-jadili (*v.*)	question, ask, inquire, argue

jadwal table, schedule (Wehr 115b) 453

Swahili (J)	jedwali	a table, i.e. timetable, table of imports, exports

jaḏb attraction; gravitation; enticement, captivation (Wehr 116a) 453a

Malagasy (Gue)	ĵadìḇa, ĵadhìba	ecstasy that sometimes occurs during mystical rituals

juḏām leprosy (Wehr 117a) 455

Swahili (J)	jethamu, jedhamu	elephantiasis, leprosy

jarrār tractor; tugboat, towing launch (Wehr 117b) 457

Swahili (J)	jarari	halyard, a rope running through a pulley (*abedari*) on deck, and another (*gofia*) attached to the thicker rope (*henza*), by which the mainyard and the sail of a native vessel are hoisted

jarraba (*v.*) (II) to try; to attempt (Wehr 118a) 458

Digo (MN&Z)	-jaribu	to taste, tempt, try (via Swahili)
Swahili (J)	-jaribu (*v.*)	experience, make trial of, test

jirāb travelling bag (Wehr 118a); **jurâb / jurâbât** large leather bag (JdP 672b) **459**

Bari (Mu)	jurak	bag; wallet
Swahili (J)	jaluba	small ornamental metal box for chewing mixture

jaraḥa (*v.*) to wound; to injure (Wehr 119a) **463**

Malagasy (Gue)	ĵaràha	injury
Swahili (J)	jeraha	a wound, sore, ulcer

majrūḥ injured (Wehr 119a) **464**

Swahili (J)	majeruhi	a wounded person

jarīda newspaper (Wehr 119b) **465**

Dinka (Id)	jarida	press (newspaper)
Swahili R	jarida	newspaper

jardal bucket, pail (Wehr 120a); **jardal / jarâdil** bucket (JdP 648b). Borrowed from Turkish *kardal* (Qāsim) **465a**

Acooli (Mu)	jɛrdɛ	bucket
Bari (Mu)	jɛrdɛk	bucket
Dinka (Id)	jerdak, jerdel	bucket
Lotuxo (Mu)	ajɛrdɛ	bucket

jarrāfa rake; harrow (Wehr 120a) **465b**

Malagasy (Gue)	ĵarìfa	fish net
Swahili (J)	jarife	drag-net

majran watercourse; course (of events), progress, passage (Wehr 122b) **469**

Swahili (J)	majira	time, period, season; course of a ship

juz' part, portion; the 30th part of the Qur'an (Wehr 123a) 471

Swahili (J)	juzuu	division, section, chapter of a book, esp. of the Qur'an

ajzā'īya, ajzāḫānā pharmacy (Wehr 123a) 471a

Madi (Bla)	àzàkánà	clinic; pharmacy

juzdān, jizdān wallet; change purse (Wehr 123a); **juzulân / juzâlîn** wallet, note-case, purse (JdP 674b); **ǧuzlān** wallet (RL 92a) 472

Madi (Bla)	jòjòlánɨ	purse, esp. one used by women

jazma, jizam (pair of) shoes, (pair of) boots (Wehr 124b); **jizma** shoe (S&A 117b) 475a

Dinka (Id)	jesma	shoe
Madi (Bla)	gɨ́zīmà	shoes

jazā (*v.*) to recompense (Wehr 124b) 476

Swahili (J)	-jaza, -jazi (*v.*)	reward, make a present to, grant a favor to

jāsūs spy (Wehr 125a) 478

Swahili (J)	jasusi, majasusi	a spy, traitor, sly person

jasara (*v.*) to span, traverse; to venture, risk, have courage (Wehr 125b) 479

Swahili (J)	-jasiri (*v.*)	to be bold, audacious, dare, venture, risk, make a brave [move, choice]

jiṣṣ gypsum; plaster of Paris (Wehr 126b) 480

Swahili (J)	jasi	a kind of soft friable stone rubbed on the fingers when plaiting mats; also sometimes used to soften the face and skin

jaʿala (*v.*) to make; to effect; to give, grant (Wehr 127a) **484**

Malagasy (Gue)	koĵaʿalìa	to be propitious, that is propitious (speaking of God)
Swahili (J)	-jalia (*v.*)	grant (to), give power (opportunity) to, enable

jafāʾ roughness, harshness; antipathy (Wehr 128b) **486**

Swahili (J)	jefule	violence, roughness, tyranny, brutality

jalāl loftiness, sublimity, augustness; glory (Wehr 129a); **jalāla** loftiness, sublimity, majesty (Wehr 129a) **490**

Swahili (J)	jalali	the Glorious One, a Muslim name of God

jallāb importer, trader (Wehr 129b); **ğellāba** caravan; party of merchants (RL 95a) **492a**

Dinka (Id)	jalaba, jellaap	northern (Sudanese) merchant/trader
Ndogo (Po)	Jala'ba	Ar. refers to the good "nomadic merchant," (usu. Arab). In *Baḥr al-ghazal* this designation is applicable without distinction to all Arabs.

gallābīya galabia (Wehr 129b) **493**

Bari (Mu)	jelabia	tunic
Dinka (Id)	jelabiya	clothes, dress
Madi (Bla)	jɛ̀lɛ̀bíà	cassock

juljulān, jiljilān sesame (Wehr 130a) **494**

Swahili (J)	gilgilani	coriander seed (Coriandrum sativum), used in curry powder

jalada (*v.*) to whip, flog (II) to bind (a book) (Wehr 130a) **495**

Swahili (J)	jalada	cover of a book, binding

jald flogging; staunch, steadfast; strong, sturdy (Wehr 130a) **496**

Swahili (J)	mjeledi	whip (of leather), thong, strap

jalīd staunch, steadfast; strong, sturdy (Wehr 130b) **497**

Swahili (J)	-jalidi (*v.*)	to bind a book; whip, scourge

jalīd ice (Wehr 130b) **498**

Swahili (J)	jalidi	black frost

majlis council (Wehr 131a) **500**

Swahili (J)	majilisi	reception room

galōn gallon (*eg.*) (Wehr 132b); **jalon** gallon (S&A 115b) **500a**

Acooli (Mu)	jolon	gallon
Bari (Mu)	jölun, jölunyön	gallon
Lotuxo (Mu)	ajʊlɔn	gallon

(*eg.*) **gumruk** customs; customhouse (Wehr 134b) **503a**

Madi (Bla)	jɔ́mɔ̄rɔ̀	customs

jamʿ gathering (*gram.*) plural (Wehr 135a); **jami** together (Z&T 129) **506**

Digo (MN&Z)	jamaa	society, family (via Swahili)
Swahili (J)	jamii	society
	ujamaa	relationship, kin

jumʿa Friday (Wehr 135a) 507

Bari (Mu)	jıma'	week
Digo (MN&Z)	Ijamaa	Friday
	juma	day (use is limited to questions and answers about which day of the week it is) (via Swahili)
Gikuyu (Ben)	njuma	Saturday (via Swahili)
Haya (Ka)	eilimânsi	week (via Swahili)
Kiw'oso (K&O)	-íjumaa	Friday
	í-jumaa	week
Kuria (MMR)	Ichumaa	Friday
Malagasy (Ade)	zomà	Friday
(Gue)	ĵomà, ĵomàʿa (in kiantal[3]) ĵòma	
Matengo (Yo)	ijûma	Friday
	jûma	week
Rendille (P&G)	Gumaá'd	Friday
Swahili (J)	ijumaa	Friday
	juma	week

jamʿīya association (Wehr 135a) 510

Swahili (J)	jumuiya	a society, association, community

jamīʿ total; whole, entire; all; entirety (Wehr 135b) 511

Swahili (J)	jamia, jamii	a collection of objects, group, company, total, sum

ajmaʿ entire; whole; all (Wehr 135b) 512a

Swahili (Bo)	ajmaina	all, whole, every

3 A sub-dialect of Malagasy spoken in Mayotte (Gueunier 1986: iv).

jamāʿa community (Wehr 135b) 513

Malagasy (Gue)	ĵamàʿa, ĵamà	parents, family, relatives
Swahili (J)	jamaa	a number of persons gathered or collected together, family, assembly, gathering, meeting

jāmiʿ general, universal; collector; typesetter; mosque (Wehr 136b) 515

Swahili (J)	jaamati	a mosque, place of meeting

jumla totality (Wehr 137a) 517

Digo (MN&Z)	jumula	total (via Swahili)
	ujumla	total number
Gikuyu (Ben)	njamura	wholesale; all together, in mass (via Swahili)
Malagasy (Gue)	ĵomòla, ĵòmla	all, all together
Swahili (J)	jumla	sum, total, a lot

jamāl beauty (Wehr 137b) 518

Swahili (J)	jumla	courtesy, good manners, beauty

tajmīl embellishment; cosmetics (Wehr 137b) 520

Swahili (J)	tajamala	a favor

jumhūrīya republic (Wehr 138a) 522

Digo (MN&Z)	jamhuri	republic (via Swahili)
Kuria (MMR)	chamuhuri	Republic Day (national holiday) (via Swahili)
Swahili (J)	jamhuri	a meeting; a republic

jinn (*coll.*) jinn, demons (Wehr 138a); **jānn** jinn, demons (Wehr 138b); **ğinn** genie; demon (RL 99a) 523

Malagasy (Gue)	ĵìny, gìny	spirit, jinn (mentioned in the Qur'an)

Rendille (P&G)	gínna	evil spirit, demon
Swahili (J)	jini	a spirit, genie

janna garden, paradise (Wehr 138a); **jinêne** garden (JdP 664b); **ǧanna** paradise (RL 99a) **524**

Swahili (Sacl)	dyanna	paradise (according to Muslims, in the fourth sky)

junaina little garden; garden (Wehr 138b); **jineena** garden (S&A 117b) **524a**

Dinka (Id)	janina	garden
Ndogo (Po)	jenina	vegetable garden

majnūn crazy; foolish; fool (Wehr 138b) **525**

Swahili (J)	majununi, majnun	buffoon, jester; madman; foolish conversation which causes amusement or ridicule

janaba (*v.*) to avert, ward off (VIII) to be at side of, run side by side with, run alongside, skirt, flank (Wehr 138b) **526**

Swahili (J)	-jitanibu (*v.*)	move from one place to another; show off, vaunt oneself

janāb (title of respect) approx.: Right Honorable (Wehr 139a) **527**

Swahili (J)	jenabu	a title of respect, used only in letters written in the Arabic fashion

janāba major ritual impurity (Wehr 139a) **528**

Malagasy (Gue)	ĵanàḇa	impurity contracted by s.o. who has had sex
Swahili (J)	janaba	pollution, defilement

jānib side; sidepiece; flank (Wehr 139a) **529**

Swahili (J)	janibu	locality, place, side, flank

junāḥ misdemeanor (*jur.*); sin (Wehr 140a) **531**

Swahili (J)	janaa, janaha	shame, disgrace

janāza, pl. **janā'iz** bier; funeral procession (Wehr 141a) **534**

Swahili (J)	jeneza	a bier

jinzīr chain (Wehr 141a) *cf.* **zinjīr** chain (Wehr 383a); **jinzir** chain (Daf 69); **jinzîr** chain (JdP 665a); **ǰinzīr** big chain (Kaye 45a); **ğinzir** chain (RL 100a); **janzîr** chain (Dfa 27) **535**

Ndogo (Po)	ganjir	chain

jins sort, species, class, genus; category; sex (male, female); gender (*gram.*); race; nation (Wehr 141a) **536**

Swahili (J)	jinsi (*n.* + *conj.*)	sort, kind

jinsīya nationality, citizenship (Wehr 141b) **536a**

Madi (Bla)	jìnìsíà	nationality

jināya perpetration of a crime; felony, capital offense (Wehr 142a) **541**

Swahili (J)	jinai (*n.* + *adj.*)	crime, criminal

ginēh, gunaih [Br. guinea] pound (*eg.*) (Wehr 142a) **542**

Acooli (Mu)	ginee	pound (sterling), sterling
Bari (Mu)	gine, ginejin	pound (sterling), sterling
Dinka (Id)	dzene, jene	pound (sterling), sterling
Lotuxo (Mu)	aginie	pound (sterling), sterling
Ndogo (Po)	jinia	pound (sterling), sterling

jahada (*v.*) to endeavor, strive (Wehr 142b) 543

Malagasy (Gue)	mikotahìdy	to strive
Swahili (J)	-jitahidi (*v.*)	make an effort

jahd, pl. **juhūd** effort; pains (on behalf of, or for the sake of s.th.) 544
(Wehr 142b)

Digo (MN&Z)	juhudi	effort (via Swahili)
Swahili (J)	juhudi	effort, exertion, strain, ardor, zeal, agony

ijtihād effort (Wehr 143a) 546

Malagasy (Gue)	ĵitihàdy	effort, application, zeal
Swahili (J)	jitihada, jitihadi	effort, endeavor

jahāz equipment, outfit; utensil (Wehr 143b) 547

Swahili (J)	jahazi	ship, dhow, vessel of any description

jāhiz ready, prepared (Wehr 144a); **jahizu** (*v.*) to prepare, make 547a
ready (S&A 115a)

Madi (Bla)	ɪ̄jāɪ̄sɔ̀ (*v.*)	to get ready; to be ready; to set ready

jāhil, pl. **juhhal** ignorant (Wehr 144b) 548

Swahili (J)	jahili	ignorant

jahannam hell (Wehr 144b) 551

Digo (MN&Z)	jahanamu	hell (via Swahili)
Swahili (J)	Jahanum	Gehenna, Hell, first [level] of the hells [according to Islam]

jāba (*v.*) (III) to reply (Wehr 145a); **jawāb** answer (Wehr 145b) 552

Digo (MN&Z)	-jibu	to answer (via Swahili)
Lega (Bot)	i.gyibu	reply (via Swahili)
Malagasy (Gue)	ĵaoàḇo	reply
	mikoĵìḇo, mikoĵìbo	to reply
Swahili (J)	jawabu	reply
	jibio, jibu	

jūḫ broadcloth (Wehr 146a) 555

Luganda (Sno)	\`jjòwô	woollen material; flannel (via Swahili)
Malagasy (Gue)	ĵôho	large caftan or long ceremonial dress, usu. in black cloth and embroidered
Swahili (J)	joho	woollen cloth

jawād openhanded, liberal, generous; racehorse (Wehr 146b); **ǰuwād** horse (Kaye 45b); **ǧawād** horse (RL 108a); **jawa:d** horse (Z&T 130) 557

Ndogo (Po)	juadi	horse

jaur injustice; oppression, tyranny; outrage (Wehr 147a) 558

Swahili (J)	jeuri	violence, outrage, brutality, assault, injustice, oppression

jār, pl. **jīrān** neighbor; refugee; protégé, charge (Wehr 147a) 559

Madi (Bla)	jìrání	neighbor
Malagasy (Gue)	ĵiràny	neighbor
Swahili (J)	jirani	neighbor, one living near; anything near, adjacent

jāza (*v.*) to pass; to be allowed, permitted (Wehr 147a) 561

Swahili (J)	-juzu (*v.*)	be permissible, be allowable, be suitable, be fitting for, be right for, be duty of

jā'iza reward (Wehr 148a) 563

Swahili (J)	jaza	a gift, reward, favor

jauz walnut (Wehr 148a) 564

Swahili (J)	jozi (?)	a pair, couple (of anything)

jauš chest; middle (of the human body); middle, heart of the night; trip overnight (Kazim: I, 356a) 565

Swahili (J)	joshi (?)	windward or weather side, in navigation

gonella (It. *gonnella*) (woman's) skirt (*eg.*) (Wehr 149b); **guniila** petticoat (S&A 108b) 569a

Madi (Bla)	gònílà	petticoat, lingerie

jauharī substantial; intrinsic, essential; jeweler (Wehr 150a) 570

Swahili (J)	johari	a jewel, a gem; nature, essence

jaib pocket (Wehr 150b); **jêb** pocket (JdP 659a) 571

Acooli (Cra)	jébà	pocket
Bari (Mu)	jeba	pocket (in clothes)
Dholuo (Odo)	jepa / (sometimes) jeba	pocket on a pair of trousers, coat or dress (via Swahili)
Lotuxo (Mu)	ajap	pocket (in clothes)
Madi (Bla)	jɛ́bà / jábà	pocket
Ndogo (Po)	jele	pocket

jaiš army, troops (Wehr 150b) 572

Dinka (Id)	deec, jec	army
Madi (Bla)	jésì	army
	jēsì	soldiership
Nyakyusa (Fel)	ilíjesí	army, military (via Swahili)
Swahili (J)	jeshi	a great company, assemblage, troop, army

Ḥā'

ḥabba (*v.*) to love (II) to awake love or a liking (X) to like; to deem desirable (Wehr 151a) 577

Swahili (J)	-hebu (*v.*)	like, be pleased with, take a fancy to
	-stahabu (*v.*)	like, prefer, be pleased (with); deserve
	haba	love, friendship

ḥubb love; affection (Wehr 151b) 578

Swahili (J)	huba	love, friendship

ḥabīb beloved, sweetheart (Wehr 152a) 579

Swahili (J)	hababi	master, my Lord, sir

maḥabba love; affection, attachment (Wehr 152a) 580

Swahili (J)	mahaba, mahuba	love, friendship

muḥibb loving; lover; amateur; friend (Wehr 152a) 581

Swahili (J)	muhebi	beloved, friend, dear

ḥabb grains; seed (Wehr 152b) 583

Swahili (J)	haba (*adj.*)	little (in quantity), few; rare; scarce, not enough, too little, short (in amount)

ḥabba ṣaudā' black caraway (L. Nigella sativa) (Wehr 152b) 583a

Swahili (Bo)	abasodi	cumin

maḥbūs imprisoned; prisoner (Wehr 154a); **mahbûs / mahâbîs** prisoner, in custody, locked up, reclusive (JdP 805a) 586

Acooli (Cra)	búùc, màbúùc	prison
(Mu)	mabuc	prisoner
Dholuo (Odo)	mabuc	prison (via Swahili)
Dinka (Id)	maabuuth	prisoner
Gikuyu (Ben)	*mũ*mabuthu, mabuthu	prisoner, convict, the accused (via Swahili)
Swahili (J)	mahabusi	a prisoner awaiting trial, and the place where such prisoners are kept

ḥattā until (Wehr 155a); **ẖatta** until (Dfa 74) 590

Digo (MN&Z)	hata	even, so that, until, then, not so (via Swahili)
Malagasy (Gue)	atà, attà, hatà, ttà, tà	until
Pokomo (Wü)	hatta	up to (time and place)
Swahili (J)	hata (*prep.* + *conj.* + *adv.*)	until; then

ḥajj hajj, the official Muslim pilgrimage to Mecca (Wehr 156a); **ḥiǰǰ** hajj (pilgrimage to Mecca) (Kaye 39b) 592

Swahili (J)	haji	pilgrimage to Mecca

ḥujja argument (Wehr 156a) 594

Swahili (J)	hoja, huja	want, need; argument

ḥājj pilgrim; honorific title of one who has performed the pilgrimage to Mecca (Wehr 156b) 595

Malagasy (Gue)	hàĵy	hajj, person who made the pilgrimage to Mecca, honorary title
Swahili (Sacl)	hadyi	pilgrim
(Bo)	alhaji	

ḥajar stone (Wehr 157b); **hojaar** battery (S&A 112b) **599**

Madi (Bla)	òjárɨ̀	battery

ḥadd, pl. **ḥudūd** border; boundary; limit; legal punishment (Wehr 159b); **hadd** limit, border (Kaye 36a) **603**

Madi (Bla)	ùdúdù	boundary, border
Swahili (J)	hadi (*prep.* + *conj.* + *adv.*)	until; then

ḥadīṯ hadith, narrative relating deeds and utterances of the Prophet and his Companions (Wehr 161b) **607**

Digo (MN&Z)	adisi / hadisi	story, tale (via Swahili)
Malagasy (Gue)	hadìsy, hadìthy	story (that we tell)
Swahili (J)	hadithi	story, tale; hadith, traditions relating to the Prophet
(FKM)	adisi / arishi	history, story, tale
	-adisiya (*v.*)	tell

ḥaḏira (*v.*) to be cautious, wary, to beware (III) to watch out, be careful (Wehr 163b); **ḥaḏāri** beware! watch out! be careful! (Wehr 164a); **ḥadder** to warn; to be careful (RL 111b) **611**

Swahili (J)	-tahadhari (*v.*)	be cautious, be careful
	hadhari (*n.* + *v.*)	caution, care

ḥarr heat (Wehr 165a) **614**

Swahili (J)	hari	fervor; heat in general

ḥurr noble, free-born; freeman (Wehr 165a); **ḥorr** free, noble, good quality (RL 112b) **615**

Swahili (J)	huri, huria, huru (*n.* + *adj.*)	a freeman, a person who is not a slave, free born or emancipated

ḥurrīya freedom; independence (Wehr 165a) **616**

Swahili (J)	huria	freedom, i.e. in the sense of being able to do what one wishes

ḥarīr silk (Wehr 165a) **617**

Dholuo (Odo)	aridi	silk
Digo (MN&Z)	hariri	silk (via Swahili)
Dinka (Id)	kharir	silk
Luganda (Sno)	àliìri, liìri	silk (via Swahili)
Malagasy (Gue)	harìry	silk, fabric imported from Arabia, highly valued
Swahili (J)	hariri	silk

ḥarāra heat; warmth; temperature (Wehr 165a) **619**

Madi (Bla)	hàrárà	temperature
Swahili (J)	harara	heat, warmth

miḥrāba a recess in a mosque indicating the direction of prayer, mihrab (Wehr 166a) **620**

Swahili (J)	mhirabu	the niche of a mosque, which shows the direction of Mecca

ḥirz amulet (Wehr 167b) **621**

Gikuyu (Ben)	gĩthitũ	amulet (via Swahili)
Luganda (Sno)	èyìrizì	phylacteries (via Swahili)
Malagasy (Gue)	hirìzy	talisman (objects wrapped in cloth, worn on oneself, etc.)
Swahili (J)	hirizi	charm, amulet

ḥaras watch; guard, escort; bodyguard (Wehr 167b) **621a**

Madi (Bla)	àrásà	custody; being locked up in custody

ḥarf, pl. **ḥurūf** letter of the alphabet (Wehr 169a) 623

Bende (Abe)	heelúfi	character, letter
Digo (MN&Z)	arufu	letter of the alphabet (via Swahili)
Kiw'oso (K&O)	e-r`ufi	character, letter
Malagasy (Gue)	haròfo	letter (of the alphabet), Arabic letters
Matengo (Yo)	helûpi	character, letter
Swahili (J)	herufi	a letter of the alphabet

ḥarāfa acridity (taste) (Wehr 169b) 625

Digo (MN&Z)	harufu	smell (via Swahili)
Malagasy (Gue)	haròfo	odor
Swahili (J)	harufu	scent, smell, odor of any kind (good or bad)

ḥaraka movement; vowel (Wehr 170b) 627

Digo (MN&Z)	haraka	(1) hurry (2) quickly (via Swahili)
Pokomo (Wü)	-haraka	to do quickly
Swahili (J)	haraka	haste, hurry, bustle, excitement

taḥarruk movement; forward motion; departure (Wehr 171a) 628

Swahili (J)	-taharaki, -taharuki (*v.*)	be in a hurry, be bustled, be excited (by any strong emotion)

ḥaram interdicted; sacred object (Wehr 171b); **alḥarram** respect (RL 115b) 629

Malagasy (Gue)	haràmo	religious prohibition of Islam; illicit thing
Swahili (J)	haramu (*adj.*)	forbidden, unlawful

ḥarām interdict, unlawful (Wehr 171b); **ḥaram** defended, prohibited, unlawful (RL 115b) 632

Swahili (J)	haramu (*adj.*)	forbidden, unlawful

ḥarīm, pl. **ḥurum** a sacred, inviolable place (Wehr 172a) 633

Swahili (J)	harimu (+ *v.*)	person or thing forbidden
	hirimu	age, period of life, and esp. of youth, from 10 to 25

ḥarāmī thief, robber, bandit (Wehr 172a); **ḫarâmi** malefactor (Daf 58); **ḥarāmī** bastard, natural child or adulterine (Kazim: I, 415a) 634

Swahili (J)	haramia	an outlaw, pirate, brigand

iḥrām garments (worn by) pilgrims to Mecca (Wehr 172a) 635

Swahili (J)	ihramu	clothes worn by Muslims doing the pilgrimage

muḥarram name of the first Islamic month (Wehr 172b) 637

Swahili (J)	muharamu	the fourth month of the Islamic year

ḥizām belt; girth (Wehr 173b) 639

Swahili (J)	hazama	a nose ornament, nose ring or
	hazamu	pendant, girdle

ḥuzn sadness (Wehr 174a) 640

Digo (MN&Z)	huzuni	sorrow (via Swahili)
Swahili (J)	huzuni	grief, calamity

ḥiss sensory perception, sensation; sense; voice; sound; noise (Wehr 174b); **hiss** voice, cry (JdP 584b); **ḥiss** noise, voice (RL 116b) 643

Swahili (J)	-hisi (*v.*)	feel, recognize, perceive, sense

ḥisāb arithmetic, calculus (Wehr 176a); **ḥisābī** arithmetical, mathematical, computational (Wehr 176a) 645

Digo (MN&Z)	-isabu	to count, consider (via Swahili)
Gikuyu (Ben)	ithabu	sum, bill, account; arithmetic (via Swahili)
Madi (Bla)	ìsábò	total, sum
Swahili (J)	hesabu, hisabu	reckoning, calculation; arithmetic

ḥasad envy (Wehr 176b); **ḥāsid**, pl. **ḥussād** envious; envier, grudger (Wehr 176b); **hasad** envy, to be jealous, envious (JdP 565b); **ḥasad** envy (RL 117a) 646

Swahili (J)	hasidi (+ *v.*)	a jealous person, enemy

ḥasūd, pl. **ḥusud** envious (Wehr 176b) 647

Digo (MN&Z)	husuda	envy (via Swahili)
Swahili (J)	husuda	envy, jealousy

ḥasuna (*v.*) to be handsome (IV) to do right (Wehr 177b); **aḥsanta** well (done)! bravo! (Wehr 178a) 649

Digo (MN&Z)	asanta (asantani)	thank you (via Swahili)
Swahili (J)	asante, ahasante, ahsante	used as an expression of thanks, gratitude, approval. Thank you

ḥasana good deed, benefaction; charity, alms (Wehr 178b) 650

Swahili (J)	hasanati	kindness, favor

iḥsān beneficence (Wehr 178b) 651

Swahili (J)	hisani, ihsani	kindness, favor

ḥašīš herbs; hemp (Cannabis sativa), hashish, cannabis (Wehr 179a) 651a

Acooli (Mu)	acic	hashish
Bari (Mu)	baŋgi	hashish
Lotuxo (Mu)	abaŋi	hashish

ḥišma shame, bashfulness; modesty, decency (Wehr 179b) 652

Bende (Abe)	-heesímú (*v.*)	honor; to pay homage
Digo (MN&Z)	ishima	respect, honor (via Swahili)
Malagasy (Gue)	hiŝìma	honor, part of honor, mark of honor, present offered in tribute
Matengo (Yo)	isîma	honor
Pokomo (Wü)	heshima	honor
Swahili (J)	heshima	honor, dignity, position, rank; modesty

ḥašw that with which s.th. is stuffed or filled; dressing, stuffing (Wehr 180a) 653

Swahili (J)	hasho	a piece of wood used as a patch, let in or fixed on, to close a hole

ḥāšā except, save (Wehr 180a); **ḥāšākum** without offending you 654

Malagasy (Gue)	hàsa, àsa	I do not know, perhaps, by chance, no doubt
Swahili (J)	hasha! (*interj.*)	certainly not! by no means! impossible! God forbid! A very emphatic negative
	ashakum, hashakum	pardon me for what I am about to say

ḥiṣṣa share, portion (Wehr 180b) 656

Malagasy (Gue)	hìsoa	share, due, share in a share
Swahili (J)	hisa	part, portion; in arithmetic, quotient

ḥaṣara (*v.*) encircle; to enclose (Wehr 181a); **ḥaṣira** (*v.*) to be in a fix, to be in a dilemma (Wehr 181b) 657

Digo (MN&Z)	hasira	rage (via Swahili)
Malagasy (Gue)	hasìra	anger
Swahili (J)	hasira	anger, wrath, passion

ḥuṣr retention (of urine); constipation (Wehr 181b) 658

Swahili (J)	-husuru (*v.*)	reduce to straits, oppress, besiege

ḥiṣn fortress, fort, castle (Wehr 183a) 661

Swahili (J)	husuni	fortress, fort, castle

ḥiṣān horse (Wehr 183a) 661a

Madi (Bla)	kòsánɨ̀	horse

ḥaḍara (*v.*) to be present; to attend (Wehr 183b); **hidir / yahdar** (*v.*) to attend, be present (JdP 578a) 662

Malagasy (Gue)	mikodhohorìa	to meet (for a solemn occasion)
Swahili (J)	-hudhuri (*v.*)	be present at a meeting

ḥaḍra presence (Wehr 184b) 663

Swahili (J)	hadhara (*adv.*)	in front of, in the presence of, before

ḥuḍūr presence; visit (Wehr 184b) 664

Swahili (J)	hudhurio	attendance

ḥāḍir present (Wehr 185a, Kaye 36b) 665

Swahili (J)	-hadhiri (*v.*)	make public, show before people

maḥaṭṭ place at which s.th. is put down or deposited; stop; fermata (Wehr 186a) 667

Swahili (J)	mahati	a carpenter's gauge for marking lines (Sacl, *trusquin*). Also a marking cord, ruddle

maḥṭūṭ low, depressed, (s.th.) which is not salient (Kazim: I, 451a) **668**

Swahili (J)	mahututi, hututi (*adj.*)	serious, difficult, used of distresses, illness

ḥaẓẓ part; fate, destiny; good luck, good fortune (Wehr 187a) **670**

Swahili (J)	hadhi	comfortable circumstances, position of respect, honor, circumstances befitting

ḥifẓ preservation; protection, guarding (Wehr 189a) **671**

Swahili (J)	hifadhi	guard, careful watch

muḥāfiẓ supervisory; governor (Wehr 190a) **671a**

Dinka (Id)	maapath	governor

ḥaqqa (*v.*) to be true; to be obligatory (X) to be entitled; to claim; to merit; to require (Wehr 191a) **673**

Swahili (J)	-stahika (*v.*)	be worthy, respected
	-stahiki (*v.* + *adj.*)	be fitting, be obligatory on, be a duty

ḥaqq one's due; duty; right (Wehr 192a); **haggá** portion, share (Kaye 36b) **674**

Kuria (MMR)	ehaki	share, one's due (via Swahili)
Malagasy (Gue)	hàky	justice, fairness, entitlement, s.th. which one must fairly attribute to s.o.
Swahili (J)	haki	justice, right, lawfulness

ḥaqīqa truth (Wehr 192b) **677**

Digo (MN&Z)	hakika	(1) certainty (2) certainly, surely (via Swahili)
Swahili (J)	hakika	certainty, reality, truth

ḥaqīr low; despised; contemptible (Wehr 194a) 680

Swahili (J)	-hakiri (*v.*)	treat with contempt, despise, abase

ḥaqn injection (Wehr 194b); **ḥuqna** injection (Wehr 194b); **hogna** syringe (S&A 112b) 680a

Acooli (Mu)	ogúna	injection
Bari (Mu)	uguna	injection
Lotuxo (Mu)	uguna	injection
Madi (Bla)	ógōnà	syringe

ḥakama (*v.*) to pass judgment, judge; to pass a verdict; to govern, dominate; to command (Wehr 195a); **hakam / yahkim** (*v.*) to govern, direct, judge, punish, fine (JdP 539b) 683

Swahili (J)	hakamu	judicial act; fine, punishment

ḥukm judgment, decision; condemnation; power; government (Wehr 196a) 684

Bende (Abe)	-húkúmú (*v.*)	judge
Digo (MN&Z)	hukumu	judgment, sentence (via Swahili)
Gikuyu (Ben)	ũkũmũ	sentence, verdict, judgment; insubordination; punishment, correction (via Swahili)
Malagasy (Gue)	hokòma	judgment, special arrangement, arbitration between spouses in case of dispute
Swahili (J)	hukumu (*n.* + *v.*)	judgment; make an official statement

ḥikma wisdom; sagacity (Wehr 196b) 686

Malagasy (Gue)	hikìma	wisdom
Swahili (J)	hekima	wisdom, knowledge, judgment

ḥakama bit (of a horse's bridle) (Wehr 196b) **686a**

Swahili (M.A.M.)	hakania	bridle

ḥakīm wise; sage; doctor (Wehr 196b) **686b**

Acooli (Cra)	àkíîm	medical man, doctor
Bari (Mu)	akim	doctor
Dinka (Id)	akiim, akim	doctor
Lotuxo (Mu)	akim	doctor
Madi (Bla)	àkɨ́mò	doctor, medical personnel

ḥukūma government (Wehr 196b); **hâkûma / hâkûmât** government, state authorities, authorities of the administration (JdP 541a); **ḥakūma** government (RL 123a) **687**

Dinka (Id)	akuma	government
Ndogo (Po)	akuma	government

maḥkama court, tribunal (Wehr 196b) **688**

Swahili (J)	mahakma	place of judgment

ḥākim ruler, sovereign; governor; judge (Wehr 197b) **689**

Bende (Abe)	hákímú	judge
Haya (M&L)	hakimu	judge (via Swahili)
Swahili (J)	hakimu	judge, ruler, chief

ḥikāya story, tale, narrative (Wehr 198a) **691**

Swahili (J)	hekaya	history, anecdote; remarkable incident

ḥalla (*v.*) to solve; to be allowed; to be due (IV) to release; to declare lawful, permit (X) to regard as permissible or lawful (Wehr 198a); **halla / yihill** (*v.*) to untie, detach, solve (JdP 544b) **692**

Swahili (J)	stahili (*v.* + *adj.*) astahili	merit, dignity

ḥilla way station, stop (Wehr 199a); **hille** village, city, district (JdP 580b); **ḥillé** village (RL 124a); **hille(t)** village (Z&T 128) 693

Madi (Bla)	ɨ́là	a residential area, usu. in an urban place

ḥalāl legal (Wehr 199a) 694

Swahili (J)	halali	legal

maḥall place; (place of) residence (Wehr 199b) 695

Malagasy (Gue)	mahàla	place
Swahili (J)	mahali	place, position, situation

ḥulqūm throat, gullet (Wehr 202b) 701

Swahili (J)	halkumu	jugular vein

ḥilya decoration, embellishment, finery; ornament (Wehr 203a) 701a

Malagasy (Gue)	holìa	jewel
Swahili (Gue)	hulia[4]	jewel

ḥalwā, pl. **ḥalāwā** candy (Wehr 203a) 702

Bari (Mu)	kalawa, kalawajin	sweet
Dinka (Id)	halawa, alawa	sweets
Lotuxo (Mu)	alawa, alawaxyen	sweet
Madi (Bla)	àláwà	sweets
Ndogo (Po)	alawa	sweet
Swahili (J)	halua	common sweetmeat made of flour, eggs, sugar, ghee; Turkish delight

4 Quoted by Gueunier (1986: 106a), probably Comorian Swahili.

ḥumma fever (Wehr 203b) 705

Bende (Abe)	hóma	fever
Digo (MN&Z)	homa	fever, sickness, used as a general term but also for malaria (via Swahili)
Gikuyu (Ben)	homa	cold (via Swahili)
Kiw'oso (K&O)	homâ	fever
Malagasy (Gue)	hôma	fever
Swahili (J)	homa	fever, any sickness with a high temperature

ḥamām dove, pigeon (Wehr 204a); **ḥamāmá** domestic pigeon (Kaye 37b) 706

Acooli (Cra)	àmáàm	dove
(Mu)	amam	domestic pigeon
Bari (Mu)	amam	domestic pigeon
Lotuxo (Mu)	amam	domestic pigeon
Madi (Bla)	àmámò	dove
Ndogo (Po)	amam	dove; pigeon

ḥammām bath; swimming pool; spa, watering place (Wehr 204a) 707

Madi (Bla)	àmámò	bathe; bathing shelter; bathroom
Swahili (J)	hamamu	a public bath, bathing establishment

ḥamd praise, laudation (Wehr 204b) 709

Swahili (J)	hamdu, himdu, himidi (+ *v.*)	praise

al-ḥamdu lillāh praise be to God! (Wehr 204b) 710

Macua (PP)	alihamutilila / alihamtilila	obliged! (via Swahili)
Malagasy (Gue)	alihamòdo, alihàmdo	name given to the first surah of the Qur'an
Swahili (J)	alhamdulillahi! (*interj.*)	praise be to God!

aḥmar red (Wehr 205a) 710a

Swahili (M.A.M.)	ahamaru (*adj.*)	red

ḥamiqa and **ḥamuqa** (*v.*) to be stupid; to become angry or furious (Wehr 206a) 716

Swahili (J)	hamaki (+ *v.*)	sudden anger, violent sudden burst of temper

ḥiml, ḥaml cargo, load, burden (Wehr 207a) 717

Swahili (J)	himila	load, burden; pregnancy

ḥamalī ambulant water vendor (Wehr 207a) 718

Swahili (J)	hamali	porter, carrier, coolie – only in coastal towns (Zanzibar, Mombasa)

ḥamala (*v.*) to become or be pregnant (Wehr 208a); **hâmil / hawâmil** pregnant woman (JdP 551a) 720

Malagasy (Gue)	hamìly	pregnancy
Swahili (M.A.M.)	-hamili (*v.*)	conceive; become pregnant

ḥamā (*v.*) to defend, guard, protect (Wehr 208b) 723

Swahili (J)	-hami (*v.*)	protect, defend

ḥimāya protection, patronage (Wehr 209a) 724

Swahili (J)	himaya	protection, guardianship

ḥinnā' henna (Wehr 209b) 727

Malagasy (Gue)	moìna	henna
Swahili (J)	hina	henna

ḥana (*v.*) to commiserate, feel compassion, pity (Wehr 210b) 729

Swahili (J)	-hani (*v.*)	mourn (with), pay a visit of condolence (to)

ḥanw bending, deflection, curving, turning (Wehr 211a) 730

Swahili (J)	hanamu (*n.* + *adj.*)	oblique, aslant, sideways

ḥawwāʾ Eve (Wehr 211b) 731

Malagasy (Gue)	Hàoa	Eve, the first woman
Swahili (J)	Hawa	Eve

ḥāja necessity; object of need or desire; business; thing, object; necessities (Wehr 211b); **hâja** need, necessary thing, business, luggage (JdP 535b); **hāǰa** thing; something (Kaye 36b); **ḥāǧa** thing; object. In North Africa it is commonly said: *ma'andi hayya*, i.e., I have nothing (RL 129b) 734

Malagasy (Gue)	hàĵa	request, claim
Swahili (J)	haja	need; reason, cause

ḥāra quarter, section (of a city) (Wehr 212b) 735

Swahili (J)	hara	district of town (seldom used except with locative)

ḥauz possession, tenure (Wehr 213a) 741

Swahili (J)	hozi, hodhi (+ *v.*)	possession

ḥauḍ basin; water basin; cistern, reservoir, container (Wehr 214a) 742

Swahili (J)	hodhi	a bath, large vessel for holding water, boiler, tank (of cement or metal)

ḥāl condition, state; status (Wehr 216b) 745

Digo (MN&Z)	hali	condition, state (via Swahili)
Malagasy (Gue)	hàly	state, health
Swahili (J)	hali	state, condition

ḥālan presently, immediately, right away (Wehr 217a) 746

Swahili (J)	halahala, alaala (*interj.*)	immediately! at once!

la ḥaula expression of disgust (the complete Arabic sentence is: *lā ḥaula wa-lā qūwata illā bi-llāh*, i.e. there is no power and no strength save in God) (Wehr 217b) 749

Swahili (J)	lahaula (*n. + interj.*)	blasphemy; well never! what next!

ḥīla stratagem, trick; device (Wehr 217b) 750

Malagasy (Gue)	hìla	difficulties, trouble (s.o. is blamed)
Swahili (J)	hila	cunning, device, trick, craft, deceit

ḥawāla bill of exchange, check, draft (Wehr 218a) 751

Swahili (J)	hawala	money order, check

muḥāl inconceivable, unthinkable, impossible, absurd (Wehr 219a) 752

Swahili (J)	muhali	anything difficult, impossible, absurd

ḥayy living, live (Wehr 220a) 754

Malagasy (Gue)	haiàny[5]	living
Swahili (J)	hai (*adj.*)	alive, living

5 With the Bantu locative suffix -ni (Gueunier 1986: 90b).

ḥayya come (Wehr 220a) 754a

Malagasy (Gue)	hàia, hà (*interj.*)	go, let's go, go ahead, let's go together
Swahili (M.A.M.)	haya (*interj.*)	Come on! Step out! Make haste!

ḥayāʾ shame, timidity; shyness (Wehr 220b) 755

Swahili (J)	haya	shame, modesty, bashfulness; disgrace; humility

ḥayāh life; liveliness (Wehr 220b) 756

Malagasy (Gue)	ohaiàty	life, existence
Swahili (J)	hayati	departed, deceased

ḥayawān animal, beast (Wehr 220b) 757

Swahili (J)	hayawani	brute, beast

taḥīya salutation (Wehr 220b) 758

Swahili (J)	tahyati	long life (to you) – only used in salutations

ḥaiḍ menstruation (Wehr 222b) 760

Swahili (J)	hedhi	menses, menstruation

Ḫāʾ

ḫabīṯ bad, evil, wicked; malicious (Wehr 225a) 761

Swahili (J)	habithi	a cruel, corrupt, malicious, evil person; cruelty

ḫabar, pl. **aḫbār** news (Wehr 225a); **xabar** news (RL 134a); **xaber** tale; story (RL 134a) 762

Bende (Abe)	habhaáli	news
Malagasy (Ade)	kabàry	speech
(Gue)	zehabàry[6]	news
	kabàro, kabàry	news, affair, thing, thing done to s.o., a wrong, stories, what happens
Matengo (Yo)	habâli	news
Swahili (J)	habari	news, report
(FKM)	abari	news, history
	hubiri (+ *v.*)	message, sermon

ḫābūr peg; pin; wedge (Wehr 225b) 763

Swahili (J)	kabari	a wedge (of wood or iron)

ḫabl, ḫabal confusion; mental disorder, insanity (Wehr 226b) 765

Swahili (J)	habali (*v.*)	irresponsible, irascible, hot-tempered (seldom used)
	hobelahobela (*adv.*)	anyhow, without arrangement, without skill

ḫātam, ḫātim, pl. **ḫawātim** seal ring; ring; seal; stamp (Wehr 227a); **xâtim / xawâtim** ring, seal (JdP 1302a); **xātem** bushing; ring (RL 135b) 766

Bari (Mu)	katiman	ring
Lotuxo (Mu)	akatim	ring

ḫitām sealing wax; end, conclusion (Wehr 227b) 767

Swahili (J)	hitima	a Muslim service, or office, at the conclusion of some event (a funeral service, a housewarming, feast)

6 With the prefix of class 10, defined value (Gueunier 1986: 89a).

ḫātima end, conclusion (Wehr 227b) 768

Swahili (J)	hatima	end, conclusion

miḫadda pillow (Wehr 228b) 769a

Dinka (Id)	mikadda	pillow (cotton)

ḫadaʿa (*v.*) to cheat; to deceive, mislead (Wehr 229a) 771

Swahili (J)	hadaa (+ *v.*)	deception, cunning, trickery

ḫadam servants, attendants (Wehr 229b) 771a

Dinka (Id)	khadan	servant
Madi (Bla)	kàdámɨ̀	maid, servant

ḫādim, pl. **ḫuddām** domestic servant; employee (Wehr 230a); **xādum** servant (Kaye 85a) 773

Malagasy (Gue)	mikohodòmo	to care, maintain
Swahili (J)	hadimu, mhadimu	servant, attendant, slave
	huduma, humuma (+ *v.*)	service

ḫaraba (*v.*) to destroy (Wehr 231a) 774

Swahili (J)	harabu (+ *v.*)	a destructive person, a spoiler, a ruffian, a vandal

ḫarib destroyed, devasted; ruined (Wehr 231a) 775

Swahili (J)	-haribu (*v.*)	injure, destroy, spoil, damage, demoralize

ḫurj saddlebag, portmanteau (Wehr 232b) 777

Swahili (J)	horji	a padded quilt for putting on top of a donkey's saddle

ẖarāj land tax (Wehr 233a) 778

Swahili (J)	haraja	expense, outlay (of money)

ẖardal mustard seeds; mustard (Wehr 234a) 780

Gikuyu (Ben)	*ka*ratarĩ	(bib.) mustard seed (via Swahili)
Swahili (J)	haradali	mustard

miẖraz, pl. **maẖāriz** awl; punch (Wehr 234a) 781

Swahili (J)	maharazi	a shoemaker's awl

ẖarṭūš, ẖarṭūša cartridge (Wehr 235a); **karṭūs** cartridge (RT 413b); **xarṭūša**, pl. **xarṭūš** cartridge (RT 138b); **kartuush** shotgun (S&A 121a) 782a

Madi (Bla)	kàràtúsì	shotgun; hose

al-ẖarṭūm Khartoum (Wehr 235a) 782b

Dinka (Id)	Kartum	Khartoum

muẖarram perforated; done in open work, in filigree (Wehr 236b) 783

Swahili (J)	mharuma	a colored woollen shawl, sometimes worn as a turban

ẖaizurān cane, reed; rattan, bamboo (Wehr 236b) 785

Swahili (J)	henzanani, henzerani	a cane

ẖazna treasure house; safe, coffer; locker (Wehr 237b) 785a

Madi (Bla)	káz̄īnà	cash box; safe

ẖazīna treasure house (Wehr 237b) 786

Swahili (J)	hazina	treasure, deposit of money, exchequer, privy purse

ḫaziya (*v.*) to be or become vile, despicable (X) to be ashamed (Wehr 238a) 787

Swahili (J)	-stihizai (*v.*) (rare)	dishonor, insult, inflict punishment

ḫizi, ḫazan shame, disgrace, ignominy (Wehr 238a) 788

Swahili (J)	-hizi (*v.*)	dishonor, insult, inflict punishment

ḫasāra loss, damage (Wehr 239a); **xasâra** loss, damage, bankruptcy, destruction (JdP 1297b) 789

Madi (Bla)	kàsárà / kòsárà	in vain; to come to no productive end
Malagasy (Gue)	hasàra	misfortune
Swahili (J)	hasara	loss, damage, injury
	-hasiri (*v.*)	injure, damage, hurt, inflict loss on

ḫašaba piece of wood; a timber (Wehr 239b) 790

Swahili (J)	kashabu	a wooden rod which draws the threads of the web apart in native weaving

ḫašm mouth (Wehr 240a) and **bait** house (Wehr 84b); **xacum bêt / xucûm buyût** (lit., house entrance) clan (JdP 1275b) 791a

Ndogo (Po)	kasim bet	title given by locals to group leaders

ḫuṣūṣ specialness (Wehr 241a) 793

Swahili (J)	-husu (*v.*)	give a share (to); assign as a person's share

ḫuṣūṣan especially, in particular, specifically (Wehr 241a) 794

Swahili (J)	hususa (*adv.* + *adj.*)	expressly, exactly, entirely; particular, special, exact

ḫāṣṣ special, particular, specific (Wehr 241b) 795

Swahili (J)	hasa (*adv.*)	expressly, exactly, entirely

maḫṣūṣ special (Wehr 242a) 796

Swahili (J)	mahsusi (*adj.*)	particular, special, exact

muḫtaṣar shortened, abridged; summary, abstract, compendium (Wehr 242b) 797

Swahili (J)	muhtasari, mutasari	abridgement, abstract, summary, précis

ḫaṣama (*v.*) to defeat (III) to argue, quarrel (Wehr 242b); **xâsam** (*v.*) (III) to no longer speak, ignore s.o., despise, discredit s.o., take the lead at a time, consider s.o. his enemy (JdP 1297b) 798

Swahili (J)	hasama	antagonist, rival, adversary, opponent

ḫaṣīm adversary, antagonist, opponent (Wehr 243a); **xasîm** / **xusmân** (*adj.*) enemy, opponent (JdP 1298b) 799

Swahili (J)	hasimu (+ *v.*)	antagonist, rival, adversary, opponent

ḫuṣūma quarrel, dispute; lawsuit (Wehr 243a) 800

Swahili (J)	husuma	enmity, antipathy, antagonism, quarrel, dispute

ḫaṣīy a castrate, eunuch (Wehr 243a) 802

Swahili (J)	-hasi (*v.*)	castrate, geld

ḫuṣya, pl. **ḫuṣan** testicle (Wehr 243a) 803

Swahili (J)	hasua	testicles

maḫṣīy castrated, emasculated (Wehr 243a) 804

Swahili (J)	maksai, mahsai	a castrated animal, bullock, gelding

aḫḍar green (Wehr 243b) 804a

Swahili (M.A.M.)	ahadharau (*adj.*)	green

ḫaṭṭ line; handwriting; writing, script (Wehr 244b) 805

Digo (MN&Z)	hati	document (via Swahili)
Swahili (J)	hati	written note, memorandum, document, certificate

ḫaṭṭ al-istiwāʾ equator (Wehr 244b) 806

Swahili (J)	istiwai	equator

ḫāṭiʾ wrong, incorrect, erroneous (Wehr 245b) 808

Swahili (J)	hatia	fault, transgression, crime, sin; guilt, culpability

ḫuṭba public address; speech; sermon, specif., Friday Muslim sermon (Wehr 246a) 809

Digo (MN&Z)	hotuba	speech
	-hutuba	to give a speech (via Swahili)
Jita (Ka)g	utibia	speech (via Swahili)
Swahili (J)	hutuba, hotuba	a reading of the Qur'an, a sermon, address, homily

ḫaṭīb (public) speaker; orator; lecturer; preacher (Wehr 246b) 810

Swahili (J)	hatibu	a preacher

ḫaṭar danger, peril; risk (Wehr 247a) **812**

Haya (Ka)	latâ:li	dangerous (via Swahili)
Kiw'oso (K&O)	atarí	danger
Kuria (MMR)	-hataari	dangerous
Madi (Bla)	kátārɨ̀	dangerous
Malagasy (Gue)	hatoàry	danger, accident
Swahili (J)	hatari	danger, peril, risk

ḫaṭm nose, muzzle (of an animal) (Wehr 248a) **813**

Gikuyu (Ben)	*ma*tamu	bit, bridle, and reins (via Swahili)
Swahili (J)	hatamu	bridle

ḫaṭwa, ḫuṭwa step, stride (Wehr 248b) **814**

Madi (Bla)	kátōwà	pace, stride; stride as unit of measurement
Swahili (J)	hatua	step, pace in walking; progress; opportunity, time

ḫafīf light (of weight); slight, little, insignificant (Wehr 249b) **816**

Swahili (J)	hafifu (*adj.*)	insignificant, poor in quality

taḫfīf lessening, decrease, diminution; reduction (Wehr 249b) **817**

Swahili (J)	tahafifu (*adj.*)	insignificant, poor in quality

ḫalal crack; rupture, fissure; damage, injury (Wehr 252a) **818**

Swahili (J)	halula	an abscess, boil
	haluli	a purgative medicine

ḫalāṣ liberation, deliverance; payment, liquidation (of bill) (Wehr 254b); **xalâs** invar. completed, finished, stop, point!, finally, that's enough, it's enough (JdP 1282b); **xelās** finished (RL 145a); **xala:s**! good! it's over! (Z&T 124) 821

Dinka (Id)	kalas	enough
Madi (Bla)	kàlásɨ̀ (*adv.*)	ready; already; finished
Ndogo (Po)	kalase; kelase; lisa	not yet
Swahili (J)	halasa	profit in trade

ḫāliṣ pure, clear, unmixed (Wehr 255a) 823

Digo (MN&Z)	halisi	real (via Swahili)
Malagasy (Gue)	halìsy	a lot, very
Swahili (J)	halisi (*adj.* + *adv.* + *v.*)	real, genuine, true; exactly, perfectly, really

ḫalafa (*v.*) to be the successor (III) to be contradictory, contrary (Wehr 257a) 825

Swahili (J)	halafa (*adv.*)	opposition, difference
	halifu (*adj.* + *v.*)	rebel, disobedient

ḫalfu back; successors (Wehr 257b); **ḫalfu**, **min ḫalfu** (*adv.*) at the back, in the rear (Wehr 257b) 826

Digo (MN&Z)	halafu / alafu	then, afterwards, later (via Swahili)
Kiw'oso (K&O)	alafû	then, after that (via Swahili)
Malagasy (Gue)	alàfo	then
Swahili (J)	halafu (*adv.*)	after a bit, afterward
	-halifu (*v.*)	leave behind, esp. at death

ḫilāf difference, disparity; divergence; contrast, conflict; disagreement, difference of opinion (Wehr 258a) 828

Swahili (J)	hilafu	opposition, difference

iḫtilāf dissimilarity, controversy (Wehr 258a) 829

Swahili (J)	hitilafu (+ *v.*), ihtilafu	difference, discord; defect, blemish

ḫulq, ḫuluq innate pecularity; character (Wehr 258b) 831

Malagasy (Gue)	koholòko	[that] which is created
Swahili (J)	hulka	state, natural condition
	-huluku (*v.*)	create, [for] creation of the world by God

ḫalīqa the creation; natural disposition; pl. **ḫalā'iq** creatures (Wehr 259b) 832

Swahili (J)	halaiki, ahlaki	much (of), many, abundance, collection, crowd

maḫlūq created; pl. **maḫālīq** creature (Wehr 259b) 833

Swahili (J)	mahluki, mahluku	a human being

ḫalā (*v.*) to be empty (II) **ḫallā** to vacate; to leave (Wehr 259b) 834

Swahili (J)	-hulu (*v.*)	stop doing an action, leave off

ḫamīra leaven; ferment; yeast (Wehr 261b) 839

Swahili (J)	hamira	leaven, yeast, made by mixing flour and water and leaving them to turn sour

ḫums one-fifth (Wehr 262a) 840

Swahili (J)	humusi	a fifth part

ḫamsa five (Wehr 262a); **xamsa** five (JdP 1288a) 841

Swahili (J)	hamsa (*n.* + *adj.*)	five (rarely used alone)

ḫamsa five (Wehr 262a) and **ʿišrīn** twenty (Wehr 614b) 842

Swahili (J)	hamsauishirini (*n.* + *adj.*)	twenty-five

ḫamsata ʿašara fifteen (Wehr 262a) 844

Swahili (J)	hamstashara (*n.* + *adj.*)	fifteen

ḫamsūn fifty (Wehr 262a), (*acc.*) **ḫamsīn** 845

Digo (MN&Z)	hamsini	fifty (via Swahili)
Kiw'oso (K&O)	-ámusiní	fifty
Swahili (J)	hamsini (*n.* + *adj.*)	fifty

ḫamīs Thursday (Wehr 262a) 846

Digo (MN&Z)	Alamisi	Thursday (via Swahili)
Kiw'oso (K&O)	nyálaamísi	Thursday
Kuria (MMR)	Aramisi	Thursday (via Swahili)
Macua (PP)	alhamisi / aluhamisi	Thursday
Malagasy (Ade)	alakamìsy	Thursday
(Gue)	lahamìsy	
Matengo (Yo)	halamîsi	Thursday
Rendille (P&G)	Khamiís	Thursday
Swahili (J)	alhamisi	Thursday

muḫmal velvet-like fabric, velvet (Wehr 262b) 847

Swahili (J)	mahameli, bahameli	velvet

ḫanit̲ effeminate (Wehr 263a) 848

Swahili (J)	hanithi	impotent man (sexually), sodomite

ḫunt̲ā hermaphrodite (Wehr 263a) 849

Swahili (J)	huntha	hermaphrodite

ẖanjar dagger (Wehr 263a) 851

Swahili (J)	hanjari	a scimitar
	hanzua (?)	a kind of sword dance

ẖandaq ditch; trench (Wehr 263a) 852

Lega (Bot)	n.daki	pond for fish farming (via Swahili)
Swahili (J)	handaki	ditch, trench, channel (artificial)

ẖinzīr pig (Wehr 263a); **xanzīr** domestic hog (RL 149a) 853

Swahili (J)	hanziri	a pig, for the common nguruwe

ẖawāja sir, Mr. (Wehr 264a); **kawaaja** European (S&A 122a) 854a

Acooli (Mu)	kawaja	trader
Bari (Mu)	kawaj	trader
Dinka (Id)	kawaja	trader

ẖaur inlet, bay (Wehr 264b) 855

Swahili (J)	hori	creek, inlet, gulf

ẖauf fear, dread (Wehr 265a) 857

Swahili (J)	hofu, hawafu	fear, apprehension, awe; danger

maẖāfa fear, dread (Wehr 265a) 858

Swahili (J)	afa, mwafa	disaster, damage; calamity

ẖiyāna betrayal; deception (Wehr 266a) 859

Malagasy (Gue)	ohaìnyȁ	injustice, perfidy
Swahili (Sacl)	uhiana	perfidy, disloyalty, deceit, treason, felony

ḫāʾin faithless; traitor (Wehr 266a) **860**

Malagasy (Gue)	mohaìny	unfair, envious
Swahili (J)	haini	traitor, betrayer

ḫair good; benefit, advantage; welfare (Wehr 266b); **xêr** good, happiness (JdP 1309a); **xēr** advantage (RL 151a); **xeir** advantage; fortune; peace (RL 151a) **862**

Digo (MN&Z)	heri	happiness, joy (via Swahili)
Malagasy (Gue)	haìry	well
Swahili (J)	heri	happiness, success

ṣabāḥ al-ḫair good morning! (Wehr 267a) **864**

Swahili (J)	sabalkheri	good morning

ḫiyār choice; option (Wehr 267a) **866**

Swahili (J)	hiari (+ *v.*)	choice, option

iḫtiyār choice; election; selection (Wehr 267a) **867**

Swahili (J)	hitiari, ihtiari	choice, selection
	-hitari (*v.*)	choose, select

ḫaiṭ, pl. **ḫuyūṭ** thread; twine, cord (Wehr 267b); **xêt / xuyût** sewing thread (JdP 1309a) **868**

Acooli (Mu)	kɛt	thread
Bari (Mu)	kɛt	thread
Lotuxo (Mu)	akaɛt	thread
Ndogo (Po)	keti	thread

ḫaima tent (Wehr 269a) **869**

Ateso (Kit)	ewema	tent
Dholuo (Gor)	hema, hembe	tent
(Odo)	kema	
Digo (MN&Z)	hema	tent (via Swahili)

Gikuyu (Ben)	hema	tent (via Swahili)
Kamba (Mbi)	ĩema, ĩeema[7]	tent (via Swahili)
Kuria (MMR)	irihema	tent
Lingala (Ev)	yéma	tent (via Swahili)
Luganda (Sno)	weemà	tent (via Swahili)
(Mo)	`ewe:m`a	
Lunyankole (Dav)	ihema	tent
Lunyoro (Dav)	ehema	tent
Madi (Bla)	kɛ́mà	tent
Matengo Häf	hema	tent (via Swahili)
Rendille (P&G)	eéma	tent (via Swahili)
Sukuma (Ri)	héema	tent (via Swahili)
Swahili (J)	hema	tent

Dāl

da'da'a (*v.*) run at full speed; shake (Kazim: I, 659b) 870

Swahili (J)	-taataa (*v.*)	move restlessly, move about

dārṣīny Cinnamomum zeylanicum (Gh: II, no. 17 468) 871

Gikuyu (Ben)	*mũ*tarathini, ndarathini	cinnamon (via Swahili)
Swahili (J)	mdalasini	cinnamon tree, Cinnamomum zeylanicum

dāya wet nurse; midwife (Wehr 269b) 872a

Madi (Bla)	dáyà	midwife

dubb bear (Wehr 269b) 874

Gikuyu (Ben)	nduba	bear (via Swahili)
Luganda (Sno)	`ddubù	bear (via Swahili)
Swahili (J)	dubu	bear

7 Mbiti gives *Mks* that is, "Machakos (for words used more commonly in Machakos than in Kitui)."

dabbāba armored car (Wehr 270a); **dabaaba** tank (S&A 96a) 874a

Madi (Bla)	dàbábà	assault tank

dībāja brocade; introductory verses or lines, preamble (Wehr 270a) 877

Swahili (J)	dibaji	good style in writing; preamble

dabra turn (of fate) (Wehr 270b) 880

Swahili (J)	mdubira	a person who always appears to have bad luck

tadbīr planning, organization (Wehr 270b) 882

Swahili (J)	-tadhibiri, -tadubiri (*v.*)	put right a wrong; search

dabelān, dabalān calico (RL 155a) 882a

Madi (Bla)	dà'bùlánì	cotton material used as a bedsheet

daẖl income; revenue, returns (Wehr 273b) 882b

Swahili (J)	dahili	income, revenue, returns

duẖūl entry; penetration; first coition in marriage (Wehr 274a) 886

Malagasy (Gue)	kodoholìa	we attack

madẖūl revenue, receipts, returns (Wehr 274b) 888

Swahili (J)	maduhuli	income, wages, revenue

duẖān smoke, vapor (Wehr 275a) 889

Swahili (J)	dohani	smoke; a chimney

durra a variety of parrot (L. Psittacus alexandri) (Wehr 275b) 890

Swahili (J)	dura	a parrot

darb narrow mountain pass (Wehr 276a); **darb** door, especially big (Kazim: I, 684a) 891

Swahili (J)	tarabe	used to describe a door or window consisting of a double door

durj drawer; desk (Wehr 276b); **duruj / adrâj** drawer (JdP 404 a) 892

Madi (Bla)	dúrōjì / dùrówà	drawer

daraja rank (Wehr 277a) 893

Digo (MN&Z)	daraja	bridge (via Swahili)
Gikuyu (Ben)	ndaraca	bridge (via Swahili)
Malagasy (Gue)	daràĵa	bridge, staircase, passage
Pokot (Cra)	tàrácà	bridge (via Swahili)
Rendille (P&G)	daraánja / daraáncha	bridge; culvert (conduit for water pipe or drain under a road) (via Swahili)
Swahili (J)	daraja	step, bridge; degree, rank

dars, pl. **durūs** lesson, chapter (Wehr 278a) 899

Digo (MN&Z)	darasa	class (via Swahili)
Swahili (J)	darasa	class, meeting for reading or study
	durusi (*v.*)	study a book

madrasa madrasah; school (Wehr 278b) 900

Ndogo (Po)	madrasa	school
	vi madrasa	student
Swahili (J)	darasa	class, meeting
	madarasa	school, academy

dir' coat of mail, hauberk; (suit of) plate armor; armor; armature (Wehr 278b); **daraga** screen, shelter, shield, protection (JdP 367b); **daraga / derga** shield (RL 160a) 901

Swahili (J)	deraya	armor, coat of mail, cuirass

DRK (*v.*) (II) to last (III) to reach (IV) to attain (VI) to take steps to prevent; to make amends (Wehr 279a); **daraka** (*v.*) to follow s.o.; to understand, know the meaning, the scope of (Kazim: I, 691a) 902

Swahili (J)	daraka	an arrangement, appointment

dirham, pl. **darāhim** dirhem, drachma (Wehr 280a) 904

Nyakyusa (Fel)	indalama	money
Swahili (M.A.M.)	dirhamu, darahamu dirhamu, darahimu	currency used in Arab states like Dubai, Abu Dhabi, and Yemen money, currency

dist kettle, boiler (Wehr 281a) 905

Swahili (J)	deste	a vessel in which to store halua, Turkish delight

dustūr constitution (Wehr 281a) 906

Digo (MN&Z)	desturi	custom (via Swahili)
Malagasy (Gue)	dastòry	bowsprit
Swahili (J)	desturi	custom

da'ib joking; playful (Wehr 281b) 907

Swahili (J)	daba	a fool, simpleton

daʿā (*v.*) to call; to invite; to invoke (Wehr 282b); **daʿa / yadʿi** (*v.*) to invoke, pray, invite (JdP 337b) 908

Malagasy (Gue)	mikodày	to complain, require, claim
Swahili (J)	dai	legal process

daʿwā allegation; lawsuit, legal proceedings (*Isl. law*) (Wehr 283a) 909

Swahili (J)	daawa	legal process, civil suit

duʿāʾ prayer (Wehr 283b) 910

For Swahili Knappert (1970: 71) explains: "*Dua* – 'prayer' – but not one of the five daily ritual prayers, called, *sala* ou *salati* (also *swala, swalati*). The *dua* has a fixed text in Arabic or Swahili, and it is performed at given times, after the *salati* or after other rites. *Ombi* is an individual prayer, a request."

Malagasy (Gue)	d̠òa, d̠òã, dòa	prayer, prayer to ask for s.th., prayer or magic formula
Swahili (J)	dua	prayer

daġdaġa (*v.*) to tickle; to crush; to chew, munch (Wehr 284a) 911

Swahili (J)	-daghadagha (*v.*)	taunt, state in an uncertain manner; be uncertain

daff tambourine (Wehr 284b) 912

Swahili (J)	dafi	tambourine

daftar booklet; daybook; register (Wehr 285a), borrowed from Persian 913

Swahili (J)	daftari	an account book, ledger, catalogue, register

dufʿa time, instance (Wehr 286a); **dufʿa / dufʿât** group together (JdP 398b) **914**

Madi (Bla)	dúfà	colleague; age-mate; belonging to the same military etc. graduating batch
Swahili (J)	defa	time, occasion

dafīna hidden treasure, treasure-trove (Wehr 287a) **917**

Swahili (J)	dafina	hidden treasure, treasure trove; treasure

bi-diqqa exactly, accurately (Wehr 287b) **918**

Swahili (J)	dike, tike (*adv.*)	exactly, just so, in the same way

daqīq flour, meal (Wehr 288a); **dagîg** flour, powder (JdP 351b) **920a**

Madi (Bla)	dègíì	flour; flour for making beer; fermented beer flour

daqīqa minute (time unit) (Wehr 288a) **921**

Bende (Abe)	dakíkeé	minute
Dholuo (Gor)	dakika, dakike	minute
Digo (MN&Z)	dakika	minute (via Swahili)
Gikuyu (Ben)	ndagĩka, ndakinga	a minute (via Swahili)
Haya (Ka)	edá:ki:ka	minute (via Swahili)
Kiw'oso (K&O)	-dakíka	minute
Kuria (MMR)	etagika	a minute
Luganda (Sno)	\`ddakiika	minute (via Swahili)
(Mo)	\`e\`ddaki:ka	
Madi (Bla)	dákíkà	minute; one minute; a moment (via Swahili)
Malagasy (Gue)	dakìka	minute
Ndogo (Po)	dagigi	minute
Rendille (P&G)	dekeéka	minute (via Swahili)
Runyankore (Ka)	edaki:ka	minute (via Swahili)
Swahili (J)	dakika	a minute, but often used as any small division of time

dukkān bench; store, shop (Wehr 288b) 925

Acooli (Cra)	dokà	merchant's shop
(Mu)	dʊkan	shop (via Swahili)
Bari (Mu)	dukan	shop
Bende (Abe)	iiduúka	shop
Dholuo (Gor)	duka, dukni	shop
(Odo)	duka	merchant's shop (via Swahili)
Dinka (Id)	dukaan, dukan, dukän	shop
Gikuyu (Ben)	nduka, matuka	shop (via Swahili)
Ik (Schr)	ɗʉkán (ɗʉkánì-) ɲáɗʉkán (ɲáɗʉkánì-)	kiosk, shop, store
Jita (Kag)	duuka	shop (via Swahili)
Kinyarwanda (CAT)	i-duka	store, shop (via Swahili)
Kiw'oso (K&O)	-dúka	shop
Lotuxo (Mu)	adukan	shop
Luganda (Mo)	\`e\`ddu:k^a	shop (via Swahili)
	\`ek\`idu:k^a	small shop (via Swahili kiduka)
Madi (Bla)	dòkánɨ	shop (via Swahili)
Malagasy (Gue)	dòka, dokàny	shop, store, trade
Matengo (Yo)	lilûka	shop, store
Ndogo (Po)	dukan	store
Pokot (Cra)	'dúkà	shop (via Swahili)
Rendille (P&G)	iltukáan / ildukáan	shop; store; commercial counter (via Swahili)
Runyankore (Ka)	edú:ka	shop; store (via Swahili)
Swahili (J)	duka	shop, stall

midakk ramrod; tamper rammer (Wehr 288b) 926

Swahili (J)	mdeki	a ramrod

duktūr, pl. **dakātira** doctor (Wehr 288b) **926a**

Digo (MN&Z)	dakitari	doctor (via Swahili)
Kamba (Whi)	ndakitá:lĩ	doctor (via Swahili)
Luganda (Mo)	`ddakit^a:ri	doctor (via Swahili)
Madi (Bla)	dàkɨtárɨ̀	medical personnel (doctors, nurses etc.); hospital; health center, etc. (via Swahili)
Matengo (Yo)	dakitâli	doctor
Rendille (P&G)	ilkitárri	doctor (via Swahili)
Swahili (J)	daktari	a doctor of medicine

dalla (*v.*) to show (II) to sell or put up at auction (Wehr 289a) **927a**

Madi (Bla)	ɨ̄dālà (*v.*)	to show off
	ɨ̄dālālà (*v.*)	to auction, put on sale

dalīl indication; sign; proof (Wehr 289b) **928**

Digo (MN&Z)	dalili	sign (via Swahili)
Malagasy (Gue)	dalìly	proof
Swahili (J)	dalili	sign

dallāl broker (Wehr 289b) **930**

Swahili (J)	dalali	an auctioneer, broker

dilāla auction (Wehr 289b) **931**

Ndogo (Po)	dalala	auction

dam blood (Wehr 291b) **937**

Digo (MN&Z)	damu	blood (via Swahili)
Ngh'wele (Leg)	damu	blood (via Swahili)
Swahili (J)	damu	blood

damara (*v.*) to perish, be destroyed (Wehr 292a) **937a**

Swahili (M.A.M.)	damiri (*v.*)	spoil, ruin, destroy

duniyā world (Wehr 295a); **dunia** this lowly world (Daf 32); **dunya** earthly life, earthly world, earth (JdP 402a); **dunia** world (RL 171b) **944**

Bende (Abe)	dunía	world
Digo (MN&Z)	dunia	world, earth (via Swahili)
Malagasy (Gue)	donìa	this world, the profane world; the universe; a crowd, a lot of people
Matengo (Häf)	dunia	world (via Swahili)
Swahili (J)	dunia	the world, universe, earth

dahr time; age; eternity (Wehr 295b) **945**

Swahili (J)	dahari (*adv.* + *n.*)	always, constantly; time, age

dahn oiling, greasing; painting, daubing (Wehr 296b) **946**

Swahili (J)	deheni	a water-proofing mixture of lime and fat, used on the bottoms of native vessels

dūd worm; maggot; larva; caterpillar (Wehr 297b); **dūd** insects; vermin; worms (RL 173a) **949**

Swahili (J)	dudu	large insect

dār house; building; region; land, country (Wehr 299a); **dār** country; district; kingdom (RL 173b) **951**

Malagasy (Gue)	dàry	floor of a house, a multi-storied house, palace
Swahili (J)	dari	upper floor, upper story, roof, esp. of a flat roof

daur round (of a patrol; in sports); part; stage role (Wehr 299b) 952

Swahili (J)	duara	a wheel, circle, flat round object; any machine of which the principal feature is a wheel
	duru	turn in a round of drinks

daurīya patrol, round; reconnaissance squad (Wehr 300a) 953

Swahili (J)	doria	the advance guard of an army, an outpost, spy, patrol

idāra department (Wehr 300b) 954

Digo (MN&Z)	idara	department (via Swahili)
Swahili (J)	idara	in Zanzibar, a department

dā'ira circle; compass (Wehr 301a) 955

Luganda (Sno)	\`ddiirâ	compass (via Swahili)
Malagasy (Gue)	daìra	religious dance, mystic
Swahili (J)	dira	compass

mudīr head, director; governor (Wehr 301a); **mudiir** director, manager (S&A 134a) 956a

Dinka (Id)	madiir	director
	mudir	governor

daula power (Wehr 302b); **dōle** must (Kaye 25b) 957

Malagasy (Gue)	d̠aula, d̠ôla	royalty, royal power (in a traditional context), state (modern)
Swahili (J)	daulati, dola	government

dūlāb gears, wheels; cabinet, cupboard (Wehr 303a); **dolâb** cabinet, cupboard, furniture (JdP 394b) **958a**

Dinka (Id)	doolaap	cabinet
Ndogo (Po)	dulab	cabinet
Swahili (M.A.M.)	dulabu	spindle; a thin pointed rod used for spinning wool into thread by hand

dāma (*v.*) to last (Wehr 303a); factitive **dawwama** **959**

Swahili (J)	dawamu (*adv.*)	perpetually

mā dāma as long as; inasmuch as, because; while he is …, when he is … (Wehr 303a) **960**

Malagasy (Gue)	madàma	when
Swahili (J)	maadan (*conj.*)	when, while, since that; since, if, because

dawām duration (Wehr 303a) **961**

Swahili (J)	-dumu (*v.*)	remain, continue, endure, abide

dā'im lasting; enduring, eternal; continued, continuous (Wehr 303b); **dā'imī** lasting; enduring, eternal; continued, continuous (Wehr 303b); **dāim** permanent; lasting; constant (RL 175b) **963**

Malagasy (Gue)	daìma	always
Swahili (J)	daima (*adv.*)	perpetually, permanently, constantly, continually, always

dīwān account books of the treasury; divan; council of state; government (Wehr 303b) **965**

Malagasy (Gue)	doàny	sacred place, pagan holy place
Swahili (J)	diwani	councilor; the court or council chamber of a king; a book of poetry

dūn low, lowly; bad, inferior (Wehr 304a) 966

Swahili (J)	duni (*adj.*)	inferior, low, worthless

dawāh inkwell (Wehr 304b); **dawāyá** inkwell (Kaye 24b) 968

Swahili (J)	dawati	writing desk, writing case

dawāʾ remedy, medicine (Wehr 304b); **dawa** medicine (RL 176b, Z&T 122) 969

Acooli (Cra)	dawà	medicine
Dholuo (Odo)	dawa	medicine (via Swahili)
Digo (MN&Z)	dawa	medicine (via Swahili)
Gikuyu (Ben)	ndawa	medicine, cure (via Swahili)
Kiw'oso (K&O)	-dáwa	agricultural chemicals, medicine for human beings (via Swahili)
Matengo (Yo)	òtěla	medicine
Ngh'wele (Leg)	dawa	medicine, remedy (via Swahili)
Rendille (P&G)	ildáwa	medicine, ointment; treatment (for illness) (via Swahili)
Swahili (J)	dawa	medicine, medicament; charm, talisman
Zulu (Kna 1972–73: 295)	ndawa	medicine (via Swahili)

dain debt; obligation (Wehr 305b) 972

Lega (Bot)	i.dέni	debt (via Swahili)
Malagasy (Gue)	d̠èny	debt
Ndogo (Po)	deni	debt
Swahili (J)	deni	a debt, loan, money obligation

dīn religion (Wehr 306a) 973

Acooli (Cra)	dinì	religion
Dholuo (Gor) (Odo)	dini	religion
Digo (MN&Z)	dini	religion (via Swahili)
Gikuyu (Ben)	ndini	religion (via Swahili)

Kuria (MMR)	idiini	a religion, religious instruction
	itiini	religion
Luganda (Sno)	\`ddiìni	religion; creed (via Swahili)
Madi (Bla)	dínì	religion (via Swahili)
Malagasy (Gue)	dìny	religion, in general; esp. Islam
Runyankore (Ka)	edî:ni	religion (via Swahili)
Swahili (J)	dini	religion, creed, worship

dīnār dinar (Wehr 306b). 974
The word is in the Qur'an (< Latin *denarius*), but we do not know if it means 'gold coin'; in any case, the word only takes on this meaning after 685, with 'Abd al-Malik.

Kinyarwanda (CAT)	i-denariyo	denarius (Roman coin)
Swahili (J)	dinari	gold coin (found only in stories of Arabic origin)

Ḏāl

ḏabaḥa to kill (by slitting the throat) (Wehr 307a); **dabah / yadbah** (*v.*) slaughter, immolate (JdP 338b); **debaḥ** to slay (RL 153b) 977

Swahili (J)	madhabahu madhabuha	place of sacrifice; an abattoir, public slaughterhouse a thing sacrificed, victim, offering in a sacrifice

ḏabīḥa, pl. **ḏabā'iḥ** slaughter animal; sacrificial victim; sacrifice (Wehr 307b) 979

Swahili (J)	dhahibu (*n.* + *v.*)	a sacrifice, a thing offered or animal killed for an offering to God, or spirits

ḏabḏaba (*v.*) to set into a swinging motion, swing (Wehr 307b) 980

Swahili (J)	mdhabidhabina	liar, cheat, deceitful person, one who spreads evil or false reports

ḏurrīya descendants (Wehr 308b) 983

Swahili (J)	dhuria	descendants

ḏirāʿ arm; forearm; cubit (Wehr 309a) 984

Swahili (J)	dhiraa	a cubit (measure of length, from elbow to fingertip)

ḏura durra, a variety of sorghum (Wehr 309a); **dura** name of a cultivated plant, red sorghum, white sorghum, Sorghum Durra (JdP 402b) 984a

Madi (Bla)	dɔ́rà	durrah

ḏikr mention of the Lord's name (Wehr 310a) 985

Swahili (J)	dhikiri	s.o. who mentions the name of God
	dhukuru (*v.*)	remember, think, consider

ḏakar penis (Wehr 310b) 986

Swahili (J)	dhakari	penis

taḏkira, mostly pronounced **taḏkara** message, note; paper, pass; ticket (Wehr 310b); **tazkara** ticket (S&A 152b) 986a

madi (Bla)	tɛ́sɨ́kārɨ̀	ticket for a train, bus, plane etc.

ḏalla (*v.*) to be low (Wehr 311b) 988

Malagasy (Gue)	mikodìly, mikodhìly	to annoy, to treat with contempt, to mistreat, to make suffer

ḏull lowness; humility (Wehr 311b) 989

Swahili (J)	dhila, dhili (*n.* + *adj.* + *v.*)	mean condition, abasement, low state

ḏalīl low; contemptible; humble, submissive, abject, servile (Wehr 311b) 991

Swahili (J)	dhahili (*adj.*)	low, humbled, poor, abject, wretched, contemptible, meek, submissive, obsequious

ḏanb, pl. **ḏunūb** offense, sin (Wehr 312b) 995

Malagasy (Gue)	ḏàmby	sin, fault against religion
Swahili (J)	dhambi	sin, crime

ḏahab gold (Wehr 313b); **dahab** gold (JdP 352b, (Kaye 23a); **dab**, **deheb** gold (RL 153a) 996

Acooli (Mu)	dab	gold
Bari (Mu)	dakap	gold
Dholuo (Gor)	dhahabu	gold
Digo (MN&Z)	zahabu	gold (via Swahili)
Dinka (Id)	zab	gold
Gikuyu (Ben)	thahabu	gold (via Swahili)
Haya (Ka)	ezaábu	gold (via Swahili)
Lega (Bot)	zahábu	gold (via Swahili)
Luganda (Sno)	zaabù	gold (via Swahili)
Madi (Bla)	dá'bò	gold
Malagasy (Gue)	dahàbo, dhahàbo	gold
Ndogo (Po)	dahab	gold
Nyakyusa (Fel)	sahabu	gold (via Swahili)
Rendille (P&G)	'dáhab	gold (via Swahili)
Runyankore (Ka)	ezá:bu	gold (via Swahili)
Swahili (J)	dhahabu	gold

maḏhab, pl. **maḏāhib** opinion; doctrine; school; orthodox rite of fiqh (*Isl. law*); religious creed, faith, denomination (Wehr 313b) 997

Swahili (J)	madhehebu	customs, ideas, tenets, usages; sect, denomination, party, persuasion

ḏāt being, essence, nature; self (Wehr 314b); **zāt** same; self (RL 209b); **ẓāt** same; the very same (RL 213b) 998

Swahili (J)	dhati	essence, innermost self

ḏāqa (*v.*) to taste; to try, try out (Wehr 315b) 999

Swahili (J)	-dhuku (*v.*)	taste, try the taste of

ḏail tail; border (of a garment); train (of a skirt) (Wehr 316b) 1000

Swahili (J)	deuli	a waistband of silk, cloth, shawl, or scarf worn round the waist on top of a jambia; a pall, cloth for covering a bier

Rāʾ

rādiyō radio (Wehr 317a); **râdyo / rawâdi** (French loanword), radio, transistor (JdP 1036a); **radiyoo** radio (S&A 139a) 1001a

Dinka (Id)	raadi	radio

raʾraʾa (*v.*) to roll one's eyes (Wehr 317b) 1002

Swahili (J)	-riaria (*v.*)	seek, watch

raʾs head; chief; summit; promontory, cape (Wehr 317b) 1003

Malagasy (Gue)	ràsy	cape, mountain peninsula, promontory
Swahili (J)	rasi	cape, head, promontory

raʾīs head; chief (Wehr 318a) 1004

Digo (MN&Z)	raisi	president (via Swahili)
Dinka (Id)	reeth	president
Rendille (P&G)	Raáyis	president (via Swahili)
Swahili (R)	rais, mrais	president

ra'ūf merciful, compassionate; kind, benevolent; gracious (Wehr 318b) 1005

Swahili (J)	raufu (*adj.*)	gentle

ra'y opinion, view, suggestion (Wehr 319b); **târi** maybe, or, that's it (JdP 1188a); **rāy** view (RL 181a) 1006

Swahili (J)	rai (*n.* + *v.*)	opinion, thinking; suggestion

ru'yā vision; dream (Wehr 320a) 1008

Swahili (J)	ruya	vision, dream

mir'āh, pl. **marā'in** mirror (Wehr 320a); **mirāya** mirror (Wehr 320a) 1010

Dholuo (Odo)	madara	mirror, spectacles
Dinka (Id)	madara[8]	mirror
Madi (Bla)	màráyà / nàdárà / mɨ̀ráyà	mirror; car screen; sunglass, spectacles

rabb lord; master (Wehr 320a); **rebb** master; Lord (RL 181b); **rābbanā** God (RL 181b) 1013

Swahili (J)	rabi	master, lord (used by Muslims referring to God, and some Christians referring to God or Jesus Christ)

rubbān captain (Wehr 320b) 1015

Swahili (J)	rubani	a guide, pilot, helmsman

rabṭa ribbon; parcel, package (Wehr 322a) 1018

Swahili (J)	robota	packet, parcel, bundle, bale

8 The words in Dholuo and Dinka may be derived from the Arabic word *maẓhar* 'appearance; look(s), sight view' (Wehr 584b), as suggested by Idris, the author of the Dinka dictionary, under 1767.

rubʿ, pl. **arbāʿ** quarter, fourth part; a dry measure (Wehr 322b) 1020

Gikuyu (Ben)	warobo	one shilling and fifty cents (via Swahili)
Madi (Bla)	rǒ'bò	one-quarter, esp. in time-telling
Swahili (J)	robo	one-fourth part, quarter

arbaʿa four (Wehr 323a) 1023

Madi (Bla)	árōbà	four, in time-telling

arbaʿūn forty (Wehr 323a), (*acc.*) **arbaʿīn** 1025

Digo (MN&Z)	arubaini	forty (via Swahili)
Kiw'oso (K&O)	-árubeéni	forty
Swahili (J)	arobaini	forty; forty days after a woman has given birth, during which period she is considered to be unclean

al-arbāʿāʾ Wednesday (Wehr 323a) 1026

Malagasy (Ade)	alorobìa	Wednesday
(Gue)	robìa	
Rendille (P&G)	Arbáh	Wednesday

murabbaʿ fourfold, quadruple; square; quadrangle; a square (Wehr 323b) 1028

Malagasy (Gue)	moràba, mràba	enclosure, yard, fence of a yard
Swahili (J)	mraba	what is fourfold, square, a square, rectangle, a right angle

riban interest; usury (Wehr 324a), unlawful under Islamic law, unlike **ribḥ** (Wehr 321a) interest (on money), legal 1031

Swahili (J)	riba	usury, interest on money or property

murabban jam, preserved fruit (Wehr 324b); **mirabba** (*eg.*) jam, preserved fruit (Wehr 320b) 1033

Madi (Bla)	mɔ̀rábà	jam (food)
Swahili (J)	mraba	jam, preserve

RTB (*v.*) (II) to arrange; to put into proper order (Wehr 324b) 1034

Swahili (J)	-ratibu (*v.*)	arrange, put in order

tartīb order (Wehr 325a) 1036

Ndogo (Po)	tartīb	status, ordinance
Swahili (J)	taratibu	sketch, pattern, design

rajab the seventh month of the Islamic calendar (Wehr 326b) 1038

Swahili (J)	rajabu	the seventh month of the Islamic calendar

rajaʿa (*v.*) to come back, return (Wehr 327b) 1041

Swahili (J)	-rejea (*v.*)	go back, return
	rejeo (*n.*)	return

rajul, pl. **rijāl** man (Wehr 329b) 1044

Swahili (J)	rijali	a man (seldom used except in the sene of implying real manliness)

mirjal, pl. **marājil** cooking kettle, caldron; boiler (Wehr 329b) 1045

Swahili (J)	marigedi (?)	a large cooking pot of copper

rajama (*v.*) to stone; to curse, damn (Wehr 329b) 1046

Swahili (J)	rajamu	mark, stamp, trademark

rajm stoning (Wehr 329b) 1047

Swahili (J)	rujumu (*v.*)	stone, kill by stoning

rajā (*v.*) to hope; to expect (V) to hope (Wehr 330a); **riji / yarja** (*v.*) to wait, hope (JdP 1063a); **raǧa** to expect; to hope (RL 185b) 1048

Malagasy (Gue)	mikotaraĵìa	to invite
Swahili (J)	-rajua (*v.*)	change the mind

marḥaban bika you're welcome! (Wehr 330b) 1050

Digo (MN&Z)	marahaba	the correct reply to the greeting *shikamoo* from a younger person or person of lesser status (via Swahili)
Malagasy (Gue)	marahàba	thank you
Swahili (J)	marahaba (*interj.*)	used as a common rejoinder to the salute of an inferior, dependent, or younger person

raḥma pity, compassion; mercy (Wehr 332a) 1053

Digo (MN&Z)	huruma	kindness, mercy, pity (via Swahili)
Malagasy (Gue)	rehèma	grace, blessing (of God, who is al-Rahman)
Swahili (J)	rehema	mercy, pity
	huruma (?)	mercy, pity, compassion

raḥīm merciful, compassionate (Wehr 332a) 1054

Swahili (J)	rahimu (*adj.*)	an attribute of God in the sense of His mercifulness, used commonly when some request or need has not yet been fulfilled

marḥūm deceased, late (Wehr 332a) 1055

Swahili (J)	marehemu (*n.* + *adj.*)	one who has found mercy, used as a euphemistic term of reference for a deceased person, the late, the defunct

ruḫḫ rok, name of a fabulous giant bird (Wehr 332a) 1056

Swahili (J)	Rok	the gigantic bird of eastern tales (i.e., Arabian Nights)

raḫuṣa (*v.*) to be cheap (Wehr 332a); **ruḫṣ** cheapness (Wehr 332b); **raḫīṣ** cheap (Wehr 332b); **raxīṣ** cheap (RL 187a) 1057

Digo (MN&Z)	rahisi	easy, cheap (via Swahili)
Pokot (Cra)	ràíis (*adj.*)	cheap (via Swahili)
Swahili (J)	rahisi (*adj.* + *v.*)	cheap, easy

ruḫṣa permission; authorization; permit (Wehr 332b) 1058

Dholuo (Odo)	rukca	a permission, absence from work (via Swahili)
Digo (MN&Z)	-ruhusa	to give permission (via Swahili)
Luganda (Sno)	lùkusà	permission; leave (via Swahili)
Madi (Bla)	rúkūsà	allowed; permission
Malagasy (Gue)	rohòsa	permission
Swahili (J)	ruhusa, ruksa	leave, permission, liberty, holiday

radd return; reimbursement (Wehr 334a) 1060

Swahili (J)	rada	punishment, but esp. an evil action recoiling on one

ridda apostasy (Wehr 334a) 1061

Swahili (J)	-ritadi	apostasize, change one's religion

taraddud frequent coming and going; hesitation, indecision; reluctance (Wehr 334b) 1062

Swahili (J)	-taradadi (*v.* + *n.*)	waver, hesitate, fluctuate, go here and there, wander about; turn over and over in the mind. S.t. as noun, indecision, weakness of intellect

mardūd yield, return(s) (Wehr 334b) 1063

Swahili (J)	mardudi	repudiation, rejection; the second time of doing a thing

ridf rear man; one who or that which is subsequent (Wehr 335a) 1064

Swahili (J)	-rudufu (*v.*)	double

ruzz rice (Wehr 336a); **rizz** rice, Oryza barthii, Oriza sativa (JdP 1067a) 1065

Acooli (Cra)	rúùc	rice
(Mu)	ruc	
Bari (Mu)	rus	rice
Lotuxo (Mu)	arus	rice

razza staple, U bolt; ring screw; joint pin (Wehr 336b) 1066

Swahili (J)	riza, liza	a door chain

razaḥa (*v.*) to succumb, collapse (III) to suffer (Wehr 336b) 1068

Swahili (J)	-ruzu (*v.*)	become poverty stricken, give up hope, be in difficulties

rizq, pl. **arzāq** livelihood, subsistence; blessing (of God) (Wehr 336b) 1069

Digo (MN&Z)	riziki	means of subsistence, necessities of life (via Swahili)
Swahili (J)	riziki	necessities of life, means of subsistence, food, maintenance; fate, destiny

razuna (*v.*) to be grave, serious, staid, calm, self-possessed (Wehr 337a) 1071

Swahili (J)	ruzuna (?)	a medicine which is a native mixture supposed to cure madness, or children's cough

rasūl envoy (Wehr 338b) 1073

Swahili (J)	rasuli	prophet, apostle, messenger, envoy

risāla shipment; message (Wehr 338b) 1074

Swahili (J)	risala	message, occasionally used to mean messenger

rasm drawing; trace, impression (Wehr 339b) 1076

Swahili (J)	rasimu	a drawing, plan, design

rasmī official (Wehr 339b) 1077

Digo (MN&Z)	rasmi	official (via Swahili)
Madi (Bla)	résīmú	officially
Swahili (J)	rasmi	official

rašš sprinkling; splattering (Wehr 340b) 1078

Swahili (J)	-rasha (*v.*)	daub on, paint, whitewash; do anything superficially

rašḥ secretion (of a fluid); perspiration, sweating (Wehr 340b) 1079

Swahili (J)	-rishai (*v.*)	be wet, moist, cool; exude moisture

rušd integrity of (one's) actions; maturity (of the mind) (Wehr 341a) 1080

Swahili (J)	rushd	used in the courts of Zanzibar to mean 'maturity'

rišwa, rušwa, rašwa bribe (Wehr 342a) 1082

Kinyarwanda (CAT)	ru-swa	bribe (via Swahili)
Madi (Bla)	résūà	bribe
Nyakyusa (Fel)	uluswa	bribe (via Swahili)
Swahili (J)	rushwa	bribe

raṣāṣ[9] lead; bullets (Wehr 342b); **raṣāṣa** bullet (Wehr 342b) 1083

Acooli (Cra)	ràcáàc	bullet
Alur (Kna 297)	risasi	lead
Ankole (Kna 297)	rusasi	lead
Bari (Mu)	rasas	lead
Bende (Abe)	iisaáse	bullet; steel
Dholuo (Odo)	racac	bullet
Digo (MN&Z)	risasi	bullet (via Swahili)
Dinka (Id)	rasas	bullet
Gikuyu (Ben)	rithathi, rĩthathi	bullet; ball-bearing; soldering-iron (via Swahili)
Jita (Kag)	ri-saási	bullet (via Swahili)
kiluba (Kna 297)	disashi	lead
Kinyarwanda (Kna 297)	isâsu	bullet
Kiw'oso (K&O)	í-r`isao	bullet (? via Swahili)
Lingala (Kna 297)	masási	lead
Lotuxo (Mu)	arryas	lead
Luganda (Sno)	`ssasì	lead; solder; bullet (via Swahili)

9 Knappert (1972–73: 297) states, "… which is ultimately from Babylonian *raṣâṣ*."

Matengo (Yo)	lisâsi	lead
Nyakyusa (Fel)	ilísasí	bullet (via Swahili)
Runyankore (Ka)	i:sási / amasási	bullet (via Swahili)
	kisási	gun (? via Swahili risasi)
Sango (Kna 297)	lichasi	bullet, cartridge; lead
Swahili (J)	risasi, lisasi	lead, solder, tin, bullet
	-rasisi (*v.*)	plate with tin
Zande (Kna 297)	lisasi	bullet (via Swahili)

riḍan contentment; pleasure (Wehr 344b) 1085

Swahili (J)	-ridhi (*v.*)	please, content

raḍīy satisfied, content; agreeing (Wehr 344b) 1086

Digo (MN&Z)	radhi	indulgence (via Swahili)
Malagasy (Gue)	ràdy, ràdhy (*adj.*)	convinced, who recognizes his wrongs
Swahili (J)	radhi (*n.* + *adj.*)	pardon, apology, contentment, acquiescence; blessing

riḍwān good will, favor; pleasure, delight (Wehr 344b) 1087

Swahili (J)	maridhawa (*adj.*)	in abundance, plenty, sufficient

tarḍiya satisfaction, gratification (Wehr 344b) 1088

Swahili (J)	-taradhia (*v.*)	desire

riḍā' contentment; agreement, acceptance (Wehr 344b) 1089

Swahili (J)	ridhaa	acceptance, agreement

ruṭūba moisture, dampness (Wehr 345a) 1091

Swahili (J)	rutuba	dampness, moisture

raṭl rotl, a weight (Wehr 345a) 1092

Dholuo (Gor)	ratil	pound (lb.)
(Odo)	ratili	weight (via Swahili)
Gikuyu (Ben)	ratiri	pound weight; scales, balance (via Swahili)
Madi (Bla)	ràtìlì / ròtōlò	pound, the weight (via Swahili)
Runyankore (Ka)	era:tiri	pound (via Swahili)
Swahili (J)	ratli, ratili	sixteen wakia, one pound

raʿaba (*v.*) to be alarmed, terrified (Wehr 345b); **tarʿāb** (Kazim: I, 878b), infinitive of IInd form 1093

Swahili (J)	-taraba (*v.*)	rule by violence

raʿd thunder (Wehr 345b) 1094

Swahili (J)	radi	clap of thunder

raʿīya subjects (Wehr 346b) 1095

Gikuyu (Ben)	raiya	citizen, civilian; subject (via Swahili)
Swahili (J)	raia	a subject, the condition or state of being a subject

raff shelf; rack; ledge (Wehr 348b) 1097

Swahili (J)	rafu	shelf, wall at the back of a recess

rafaʿa (*v.*) to lift (III) to act as defense counsel, defend, plead s.o.'s cause (Wehr 349b) 1098

Swahili (J)	rufani	appeal (legal)

rafīq friend (Wehr 351a) 1102

Swahili (J)	rafiki	friend

raqaʿa (*v.*) to patch (a garment) (Wehr 354b); **ragaɛ** to repair; piece (RT 193b); **ruga** patch (S&A 141a) 1106

Madi (Bla)	rʊ́gà ɨ̄rōgà (*v.*)	piece on or for a bicycle or car tire, clothing, etc. to mend, patch
Ndogo (Po)	ruga	piece, fabric
Swahili (J)	raka	a piece, spot, a patch different from the rest or the surroundings, color in spots or patches

tarqīm pointing; numbering, numeration (Wehr 355a) 1107

Swahili (J)	tarakimu	written numeral, figure

raqiya (*v.*) to rise (in rank), advance, be promoted (II) to promote, advance (Wehr 355a); **ruga-u** (*v.*) promote (S&A 141a) 1107a

Madi (Bla)	ɨ̄rōgà (*v.*)	promote (in the police, the army, etc.)

râkûba / **rawâkîb** shelter, awning, shed, small shed (JdP 1047b); **rakuuba** shelter (S&A 139b) 1109a

Madi (Bla)	ròkúbà	makeshift shelter, used mostly as kitchen

markab ship, boat, vessel (Wehr 357a); **markaba** canoe, boat, ship (Kaye 56a) 1110

Gikuyu (Ben)	merikebu, marikabu	ship, steamer (via Swahili)
Lingala (Ev)	masúwa (?)	boat, ship, vessel
Luganda (Sno)	màlèkebù	ship (via Swahili)
Ndogo (Po)	murkapa	boat
Swahili (J)	merikebu	a ship, esp. of foreign construction, as contr. with the native vessel chombo

tarkīb fitting in, insertion; installation; composition; manufacturing; structure (Wehr 357a) 1111

Swahili (J)	tarakibu	sketch, pattern, design

rākib riding, on horseback; horseman (Wehr 357a) 1112

Swahili (J)	rakibu (*n.* + *v.*)	a good rider (man); mount, ride

markūb red leather shoes (Wehr 357a); **markûb** / **marâkîb** pair of sandals, pair of shoes, pair of footgear (JdP 832b); **markūb** savate (RL 194b), in Egyptian and Syrian Arabic, the word means mount. 1113

Dinka (Id)	markuup, markup, markub	shoes made locally

rakaḍa (*v.*) to rush, run (Wehr 358b) 1114

Swahili (J)	-rukudhu (*v.*)	run into with evil intent, trespass

rakʿa a bending of the torso from an upright position, followed by two prostrations (in Muslim prayer) (Wehr 358b) 1115

Swahili (J)	rakaa	the act of bowing with the hands on the knees during the Muslim prayers

ramaḍān the ninth month of the Islamic calendar (Wehr 360a) 1121

Dholuo (Gor)	ramadhani	Ramadan
Gikuyu (Gor)	ramathani	Ramadan
Swahili (J)	ramadhani	the last month of the Islamic calendar

raml sand (Wehr 360b) 1122

Swahili (J)	ramli	soothsaying from figures in sand

ramya to throw, fling; to shoot (Wehr 361a) **1124**

Swahili (J)	ramia	a ballet

rāhiba nun (Chr.) (Wehr 362a) **1127a**

Ndogo (Po)	rabati	sister

marham ointment (Wehr 363a) **1128**

Swahili (J)	marhamu, marahamu makuru	ointment, plaster, glue ointment, sticking plaster

rahn pledge; mortgage (Wehr 363a) **1129**

Swahili (J)	rehani	pledge, security, mortgage

raub curdled milk, curds (Wehr 363b); **ruwâba** buttermilk, curd (JdP 1073a) **1130**

Swahili (J)	robu	used only in the expression, *maziwa ya robu curds*

rīḥ wind; fart; odor (Wehr 364b); **rîhe** strong smell, strong perfume (JdP 1062b) **1131**

Bari (Mu)	ria	perfume
Madi (Bla)	ríà	perfume
Swahili (J)	riahi, rihi	gas in the stomach

rūḥ breath of life, soul; spirit (in all senses) (Wehr 365a); **rū(h)** spirit, -self (in reflexives) (Kaye 68b); **rūḥ** soul (RL 198a) **1132**

Digo (MN&Z)	roho	soul, spirit of person (via Swahili)
Gikuyu (Ben)	roho	soul, spirit (via Swahili)
Malagasy (Gue)	raohàny	noun of a kind of spirits likely to possess humans
Swahili (J)	roho	soul, spirit, life

rāḥa repose; comfort (Wehr 365a) **1133**

Swahili (J)	raha	rest, repose, peace, comfort

raiḥān sweet basil (Ocimum basilicum) (Wehr 365b) **1134**

Swahili (J)	rihani	sweet basil

ṣalāt al-tarāwīḥ prayer performed during the nights of Ramadan (Wehr 365b) **1136**

Swahili (J)	tarawehi	a long prayer said at *isha*, the hour of prayer after sunset, during the month of Ramadan

istirāḥa rest, repose, relaxation (Wehr 366a) **1137**

Malagasy (Gue)	kosterèhy, kosterèhe, kositerèhy, kostarèhy sterèhy, siterèhy, sterèhe	to be at ease, to be comfortably seated, to be carefree, quiet, not to worry thank you, please, stay seated, stay to your pleasure
Swahili (J)	-starehe (*v.*)	be at rest, live in peace and quietness

mustarīḥ resting, relaxing (Wehr 366a); **mustarah / mustarâhât** toilet, closet, W.C., latrines (JdP 953a) **1138**

Dinka (Id)	mustarah	latrine
Madi (Bla)	mòsòtòrâ	toilet; latrine; excrement
	nòsòtòráà	latrine, lavatory; excrement
Swahili (J)	mustarehe, mstarehe	state of rest, repose, calm

murīd novice (of a Sufi oder); aspirant; adherent, disciple (Wehr 366b) 1139a

Malagasy (Gue)	morìdy	disciple, member of a Muslim brotherhood

murād desired; intention (Wehr 366b) 1140

Malagasy (Gue)	almoràdy	anyway, in any event, in any case
Swahili (J)	mradi, muradi	intention, plan, resolve

rāza (*v.*) to examine; to consider (Wehr 367a) 1143

Swahili (J)	ruwaza	a pattern, sample

rāġa (*v.*) to turn off (III) **rāwaġa** to deal with in an underhanded, fraudulent manner, double-cross (Wehr 368a) 1145

Gikuyu (Ben)	raghaĩ	good-for-nothing, wastrel, scoundrel; (of a child) troublesome rascal; rubbish, worthless thing (via Swahili)
Madi (Bla)	īrōgà (*v.*)	to bewitch (via Swahili)
Swahili (J)	laghai (*adj.* + *v.*) ragai, mlaghai	deceitful, false, sly, dishonest

al-rūm the Byzantines (Wehr 369a) 1146

Swahili (J)	rum	Turkey

rūmī Romaeans, Byzantine (Wehr 369a) 1147

Gikuyu (Ben)	rami	tar (via Swahili)
Swahili (J)	rumi	Rome, Roman
	lami (?)	pitch, tar, and sometimes used for any dark viscous stuff

riyāl riyal, silver coin (Wehr 370a); **riyāl** thaler (RL 201b) **1149**

Digo (MN&Z)	riyale	four shillings, term heard in stories (via Swahili)
Dinka (Id)	rial	ten piastre coin
Swahili (J)	riale, riali, reale	a dollar (worth varying according to variety), now only heard in stories

raiʿ yield; returns, income; profit share (Wehr 371a) **1150**

Swahili (J)	rai	health, strength, good bodily condition

Zā᾽

ziʾbaq mercury (Wehr 372a) **1152**

Swahili (J)	zebaki	mercury

zubb penis (Wehr 372a) **1154**

Swahili (J)	zubu	penis
	zebe (?)	one who practises sapphism

zabīb raisins (Wehr 372b) **1155**

Gikuyu (Ben)	thabibũ	grapes (via Swahili)
Kinyarwanda	umu-zabibu	vines, grapes
(CAT)	uru-zabibu	vineyard (via Swahili)
Luganda (Sno)	mùzabbibù	vine; by extension, grape
(Mo)	\`om\`uzabbib\`u	vine (via Swahili *mzabibu*)
Swahili (J)	zabibu	raisin, grapes

zabad foam, froth; dross (Wehr 372b) **1155a**

Madi (Bla)	zàbádì	yoghurt

zabād civet (Wehr 372b); **zabat, zabād** civet (RL 202a) **1157**

Swahili (J)	zabadi	civet

zabūr Psalms, psalter (Wehr 372b) **1158**

Dholuo (Odo)	jabuli	psalms, the songs of David in the Bible
Digo (MN&Z)	zaburi	psalm (via Swahili)
Kinyarwanda (CAT)	Zaburi	Psalm (via Swahili)
Luganda (Sno)	zà`bbulì	psalm (via Swahili)
Lunyankole (Dav)	zabuli	psalm
Lunyoro (Dav)	zabuli	psalm
Nyakyusa (Fel)	sabuli	psalm (via Swahili)
Swahili (J)	zaburi	a psalm, the psalter

zabūn customer, buyer (Wehr 373a) **1160**

Swahili (J)	-zabuni (*v.*)	bid at an action

zibāna clientele, patronage, custom (Wehr 373a) **1160a**

Malagasy (Gue)	masoahàba	the companions (of the Prophet)
Swahili (Sacl)	zabani	soldiers

zaḥala (*v.*) to move away (Wehr 374b); **zaḥala** (*v.*) to be tired, weary and stay back (Kazim: I, 978b) **1162**

Swahili (J)	mzuhali	a lazy, unpunctual person, one who is always late

zuḥal Saturn (planet) (Wehr 374b) **1163**

Swahili (J)	zahali	planet Saturn

zaḥama (*v.*) to push, hustle, crowd, press (Wehr 374b) **1164**

Swahili (J)	zahama, zahimu	confusion, noise; oppression, distress

azrār, pl. of **zirr** button (Wehr 375a); **zarrâr** button of a garment (JdP 1343b) 1165

Acooli (Cra)	jàrarà	button
Dholuo (Odo)	jarara	button
Dinka (Id)	zerar	button
Madi (Bla)	jàrárà / zàrárà	buttons

zaraʿa (*v.*) to sow; to plant; to cultivate (Wehr 375b) 1169

Swahili (J)	zaraa	Arabic for kilimo, agriculture

zarā (*v.*) to rebuke, scold, find fault (Wehr 376b) 1170a

Malagasy (Gue)	madarào	nonsense, malice, effrontery; cheeky, disrespectful
Swahili (Sacl)	mazarao	contempt, disdain

zaʿfarān saffron (Wehr 377b) 1171

Swahili (J)	zafarani	saffron

zaġara (*v.*) to eye, leer (Wehr 378a) 1174

Swahili (J)	-zagaa (*v.*)	shine, glisten, give light, illuminate

zaġala (*v.*) to pour out (Wehr 378b) 1175

Swahili (J)	digali	the stem of a hookah tobacco pipe

zikka arms (Kazim: I, 1000a) 1179

Swahili (J)	zaka, dhiaka	a quiver for arrows

zakāh alms tax (*Isl. law*) (Wehr 379b) 1180

Swahili (J)	zaka, zakati	tithe, offering for religious purposes

zillīya sort of woolen carpet (Kazim: I, 1003a) **1181**

Swahili (J)	zulia	a carpet

zalāqa slipperiness (Wehr 381a) and **kanīf** water closet, toilet **1182**
(Wehr 843a)

Swahili (J)	msala (?)	a private place, bath, closet, lavatory

zamr, pl. **zumūr** a wind instrument resembling the oboe; horn **1185**
(of an automobile) (Wehr 381b)

Malagasy (Gue)	anjomàry	oboe
Swahili (J)	zomari, zumari	a musical wind instrument, a kind of pipe, flageolet, clarinet

zimmīr fishes (F: II, 1253a); **zimmīr** big fish following the ships **1186**
(Kazim: I, 1010b)

Swahili (J)	mzumire	a kind of fish not considered by Europeans as good to eat

izmīl chisel (Wehr 382a); **azmiil** chisel (S&A 92b) **1188a**

Dinka (Id)	zamil	chisel

zamān time (Wehr 382a) **1189**

Digo (MN&Z)	zamani	long ago (via Swahili)
Malagasy (Gue)	zamàny	formerly
Swahili (J)	zamani	time, period, epoch

zunjufr, **zinjafr** cinnabar (Wehr 383a) **1191**

Swahili (J)	zingefuri	cinnabar

zinjīr chain (Wehr 383a); *cf.* **jinzīr** chain (Wehr 141a); **ǰinzīr** large **1192**
chain (Kaye 45a)

Ndogo (Po)	ganjir	chain

zindīq unbeliever, freethinker, atheist (Wehr 383a) **1194**

Swahili (J)	-zandiki (*v.*)	to be a hypocrite, pretend to be what one is not

zunnār, zunnāra belt (Wehr 383a) **1195**

Swahili (J)	zinara	the boards at the end of a vessel; an embroidered belt

zink zinc (Wehr 383b) **1195a**

Acooli (Mu)	jiŋki	zinc (corrugated iron sheets)
Bari (Mu)	jiŋki	zinc (corrugated iron sheets)
Lotuxo (Mu)	ajiŋki	zinc (corrugated iron sheets)

zinā' adultery; fornication (Wehr 383b); **zina** adultery, impudicity, fornication (Daf 143) **1196**

Swahili (J)	zina, zinaa	adultery, fornication

zānin adulterer (Wehr 383b) **1197**

Malagasy (Gue)	mikozàny	to commit adultery, fornication

zāhid, pl. **zuhhād** abstemious; ascetic (Wehr 383b) **1197a**

Ndogo (Po)	zadu	viaticum

zuhara Venus (planet) (Wehr 384a) **1199**

Swahili (J)	Zuhura	planet Venus

Z W D (II) to enrich (Wehr 385b) **1201a**

Malagasy (Gue)	kozìdy (*conj.*)	more than
Swahili (J)	-zidi (*v.*)	become more (greater, larger, taller, longer, etc.), grow, increase, multiply, be more and more

zād provisions (Wehr 385b); **zâd** road supply (JdP 1333b); **zād** provisions for a journey (Kaye 89a; RL 209b) 1202

Haya (M&L)	ezawadi	gift (via Swahili)
Malagasy (Gue)	zaoàdy	gift
Ndogo (Po)	zadu	provisions
Swahili (J)	zawadi	present, gift, keepsake

zūr untruth; falsehood (Wehr 386a) 1203

Swahili (J)	zuri (+ *v.*), azur	perjury, false swearing (rarely heard)

zaura visit (Wehr 386a) 1205

Malagasy (Gue)	mikozòro	to visit a sacred place, pray to a sacred place
Swahili (J)	-zuru (*v.*)	visit, go on a visit to

ziyāra visit (Wehr 386a) 1206

Malagasy (Gue)	ziàra	pilgrimage to the tomb of a holy shaykh of Muslims
Swahili (J)	ziara	tomb, burial place; visit, pilgrimage

zām quarter (of all things) (Kazim: I, 1029a) 1210

Nyakyusa (Fel)	isamú	turn (via Swahili)
Malagasy (Gue)	zàmo	alternatively
Swahili (J)	zamu	properly, a six-hour spell of work, or watching; period of duty or occupation

zāwiyal small mosque, prayer room (Wehr 387b) 1210a

Malagasy (Gue)	zaoìa	chapel
Swahili (Gue)	zawiya[10]	small mosque, prayer room

10 The word is given by Gueunier (1986: 329a) and is not present in Swahili dictionaries.

zait oil (edible, fuel, motor oil, etc.) (Wehr 388a); **zêd / zuyûd** engine oil, engine grease, olive oil, lubricant (JdP 1347a) 1211

Swahili (J)	halzeti	olive oil

zaitūn olive tree; olive(s) (Wehr 388a); **zeytûn** olive, olive tree, name of an amber pearl (JdP 1348a) 1212

Luganda (Sno)	mùzeyituùni `zzeyituùni	olive tree (via Swahili mzeituni) olive (via Swahili zeituni)
Swahili (J)	zeituni	olive

zāda (*v.*) to become greater, become more, grow (Wehr 388b); **zâd / yizîd** (*v.*) increase, add, raise the price, give more, take more (JdP 1333b) 1213

Digo (MN&Z)	zaidi	more (via Swahili)
Swahili (J)	zaidi (+ *adv.*), zaidana	increase, addition, increment, bonus

zā'ida appendix (Wehr 389b) 1214a

Madi (Bla)	záīdà	appendix

zīq collar; border, hem (of a garment) (Wehr 390a) 1215

Swahili (J)	ziki *in* kanzu ya ziki	a kanzu with a collar

zāna (*v.*) to decorate, adorn (II) **zayyana** to adorn (Wehr 390b) 1216

Swahili (J)	zana (?)	fittings, apparatus, gadgets

Sīn

sāj Indian oak (Wehr 391a) 1218

Swahili (J)	msaji	teak tree (Tectona grandis)

sa'ira (*v.*) to remain (Wehr 391a) 1219

Swahili (J)	usiri (+ *v.*)	detention, delay, be late, lag behind

sā'il questioner; petitioner; beggar (Wehr 391b) 1223

Swahili (J)	-saili (*v.*)	to ask, question, examine

sabb abuse, vituperation, insults (Wehr 392a) 1225

Swahili (J)	-sibu (*v.*)	afflict, bring misfortune (ruin, damage) upon

sabab cause (Wehr 392a) 1226

Digo (MN&Z)	sababu	cause, reason, sake (via Swahili)
Malagasy (Gue)	sib̲àb̲o, sibàbo	reason, cause
Swahili (J)	sababu	reason, cause, motive

sibāb abuse, vituperation (Wehr 392b) 1229

Swahili (J)	-sibabi (*v.*)	revile, overwhelm with abuse; slander, calumniate

Sabt, pl. **Subūt** Saturday (Wehr 393a), *cf.* Hebrew sabbat 1230

Acooli (Mu)	sabit	week
Ateso (Kit)	Esabiti	Sunday
Dholuo (Odo)	cabit	Sunday
Gikuyu (Ben)	thabatũ (*bib.*)	the Sabbath (via Swahili sabato)
Lingala (Dz)	sabala	Sabbath, Saturday of the Jews
Lotuxo (Mu)	ɛsabit, ɛsabiti	week
Luganda (Sno)	Ssabbiìti	Sabbath; week
Malagasy (Ade)	asabòtsy	Saturday
Rendille (P&G)	Sáb'di	Saturday
Swahili (M.A.M.)	sabato	the Sabbath

tasbīḥ glorification of God (Wehr 393b) 1235

Malagasy (Gue)	tasbìhy, tasobìhy	Muslim rosary
Swahili (J)	tasbihi	praise; a Muslim rosary

sabʿa seven (Wehr 394b) 1236

Digo (MN&Z)	sabaa	seven (via Swahili)
Madi (Bla)	sá'bà (*num.*)	seven, used in time-telling
Swahili (J)	saba	seven

sabʿūn seventy (Wehr 394b), (*acc.*) **sabʿīn** 1238

Digo (MN&Z)	sabini	seventy (via Swahili)
Kiw'oso (K&O)	-sabiíni	seventy
Swahili (J)	sabini, sabaini (*n.* + *adj.*)	seventy

sābiq antecedent (Wehr 395b) 1239

Swahili (J)	sabiki (*n.* + *v.*)	cause, reason, precedent

sabīl way; means, expedient (Wehr 396a) 1240

Swahili (J)	sabili	permission, freedom

sabahlalan indifferently, aimlessly, haphazardly (Wehr 396b); 1241a
sambala (*adv.*) haphazardly (S&A 143b)

Madi (Bla)	sàmbālà (*adv.*)	indisputably; randomly; without others

satara (*v.*) to cover, veil (Wehr 397a); **sitr**, pl. **sutūr** veil (Wehr 397a); 1242
sitār, pl. **sutur** veil; screen; curtain; pretext, excuse (Wehr 397a);
sitâra / satâyir curtain, mainsail, hanging, screen (JdP 1138a)

Madi (Bla)	sɨ̀tárà	curtains

sitta six (Wehr 397a) **1243**

Gikuyu (Ben)	thita (*adj.*)	only used in conjunction with thaa, *q.v.* (via Swahili)
Madi (Bla)	sítà	six, used in time telling
Malagasy (Gue)	tŝòta	six
Swahili (J)	sita (*n.* + *adj.*)	six

sitta ʿašrata sixteen (Wehr 397a) **1244**

Gikuyu (Ben)	*mũ*thitacara (?)	(arch.) magazine rifle (via Swahili)
Swahili (J)	sitashara (*n.* + *adj.*)	sixteen

sittūn sixty (Wehr 397a) (*acc.*) **sittīn** **1245**

Digo (MN&Z)	sitini	sixty (via Swahili)
Kiw'oso (K&O)	-sitinî	sixty
Swahili (J)	sitini (*n.* + *adj.*)	sixty

sitt lady (Wehr 397a) **1246**

Swahili (J)	siti	lady, (in address) my lady, madam

sitr veil; curtain (Wehr 397a) **1247**

Swahili (J)	stara	covering, concealment, modesty

sigāra cigarette (Wehr 397b); **sijâra / sajâyir** cigarette, cigar (JdP 1132a) **1248a**

Acooli (Mu)	cigara	cigarette
Bari (Mu)	sigara	cigarette
Gikuyu (Ben)	thigara	cigarette (via Swahili)
Gwere (Kag)	sigala	cigarette (via Swahili)
Lotuxo (Mu)	asijara [asigara]	cigarette
Madi (Bla)	sìgárà	cigarette
Rendille (P&G)	sigaára	cigarette (via Swahili)
Runyankore (Ka)	sigára	cigarette (via Swahili)
Swahili Mer	sigara	cigarette

sajda prostration in prayer (Wehr 397b); **sijda** how to worship God, to bow down to God (Kazim: I, 1052b) 1249

Swahili (J)	sijida	a callosity made on the forehead by prostration in Muslim prayer

sujūd prostration (Wehr 397b) 1250

Swahili (J)	sujudu (*v.*)	bow down (to), prostrate oneself (before), adore, worship

masjid mosque (Wehr 397b); **meszid** mosque (TC1 963); Algerian dialectal **mesjed**, Mauritanian Berber **ms'id** place of worship, mosque (Nicolas 127) where we see the reduction of /j/. Swahili is influenced by Egyptian Arabic, where /j/ > /g/ 1252

Bende (Abe)	músikítí	mosque
Digo (MN&Z)	msikiti	mosque (via Swahili)
Gikuyu (Ben)	mũthigitibarĩ	church building; mosque (via Swahili)
Jita (Kag)	omu-sigíti / omu-sikíti	mosque (via Swahili)
Kiw'oso (K&O)	ń'-sikití	mosque
Luganda (Sno)	mùzigiti	mosque (via Swahili)
Malagasy (Ade)	mosikirìny	mosque
Runyankore (Ka)	omuzigiti / emizigiti	mosque (via Swahili)
Swahili (J)	msikiti	mosque

musajjil tape recorder (Wehr 398b) 1254a

Dinka (Id)	musajil	cassette recorder
Madi (Bla)	mòsɛ́jīlì	cassette recorder

sijn prison (Wehr 399a); **sijin / sujûn** prison (JdP 1132b) 1254b

Dinka (Id)	sidzin, sijin	prison

suḥba sail, cover (Kazim: I, 1057b) 1255

Swahili (J)	subaya, subahiya	outside covering of a bier, used in high class funerals, a pall

siḥr bewitchment; sorcery, magic (Wehr 400a); **sihir** magic 1257
(Kaye 71b)

Swahili (J)	sihiri (*n.* + *v.*)	witchcraft

sāḥil, pl. **sawāḥil** littoral, coast, seashore (Wehr 400b) 1260

Rendille (P&G)	Kisaayíli	Swahili
Swahili (J)	Swahili	Swahili coast

saḥna, saḥana (external), appearance, look(s) (Wehr 401a) 1261

Swahili (J)	sini	features, complexion

miṣḥā iron shovel to remove ashes, ball, etc. (Kazim: I, 1064b) 1262

Swahili (J)	msaha	an iron crowbar

masḫara object of ridicule, laughingstock; ridiculous (Wehr 401b) 1263

Swahili (J)	masihara	play, jest, light matter

saḫā saḫiya (*v.*) to be liberal, generous; to grant, confer (Wehr 402a) 1266

Swahili (J)	-sihia (*v.*), *sihia mali*	transfer ownership of property

sadda (*v.*) to plug up, close up (Wehr 402b); **sedd** to close; to butcher 1267
(RL 219a)

Swahili (J)	sodo (?)	cloth used by women when menstruating

sidr, pl. **sidar** a variety of Christ's thorn (Ziziphus spina Christi) (Wehr 403b) 1270

Swahili (J)	msidari	a species of lotus-tree

suds, **sudus** one-sixth (Wehr 403b) 1271

Swahili (J)	sudusu	a one-sixth part

sirr secret (Wehr 404b) 1272

Digo (MN&Z)	siri	secret (via Swahili)
Madi (Bla)	sɨ́rɨ́	spy, an informer
Malagasy (Gue)	sìry	secret
Swahili (J)	siri	a secret, hidden thing, mystery, puzzle, secrecy

sarāya palace (Wehr 405b); **sorōya** flat roofed mud house (RT 222b) 1273a

Madi (Bla)	sàràyà	floor, story [re. of a building]

sarāb mirage (Wehr 406a) 1274

Swahili (J)	sarabi	a mirage

sarj saddle (Wehr 406a); **serǧ** saddle (RL 220b); **serj** saddle (Z&T 135) 1275

Swahili (J)	saruji, seruji	saddle

sirāj lamp, light (Wehr 406a) 1276

Swahili (J)	siraji	a lamp, torch (seldom used)

sirwāl trousers, underpants (Wehr 408b); **sirwāl** ~ **sruwāl** pants, trousers (Kaye 72a); **sirwāl** trousers (RL 222a) 1282

Acooli (Cra)	còròwáàl	trousers
(Mu)	wal	
(Mu)	toroji	trousers (via Swahili)

Bende (Abe)	nsulubhále	trousers
Dholuo (Odo)	curuwal	a pair of trousers (via Swahili)
Digo (MN&Z)	suruwale	trousers (via Swahili)
Gikuyu (Ben)	thuruarĩ, thuraarĩ	trousers, knickers (via Swahili)
Haya (Ka)	esuluwâli	trousers (via Swahili)
Kiw'oso (K&O)	-súr`uwaale	long trousers
Kuria (MMR)	isuruali	short trousers
Lotuxo (Mu)	accuruwal	trousers
Luganda (Sno)	`sseruwalè	trousers (via Swahili)
Lunyankole (Dav)	seruwali	trousers
Lunyoro (Dav)	seruwali	trousers
Madi (Bla)	sòrùwálì	pair of shorts (via Swahili)
Malagasy (Gue)	soroàly, saroàly, saraoàly	trousers
Matengo (Yo)	lisulubâli	trousers
Nyakyusa (Fel)	isúlúbalí	pants (via Swahili)
Pokot (Cra)	súrwâl	trousers, shorts (via Swahili)
Swahili (J)	suruali	trousers

sarīya concubine (Kazim: I, 1086b) **1283**

Swahili (J)	suria	a concubine, strictly speaking one who is a slave

saṭḥ roof, terrace; deck (of a ship) (Wehr 409b) **1284**

Swahili (J)	sitaha	deck, of a vessel

misṭara ruler; underline (Wehr 410a) **1286**

Digo (MN&Z)	msitari	(1) line (e.g. of poetry) (2) verse (in the Bible) (via Swahili)
Gikuyu (Ben)	mũthitarĩ	line, row (via Swahili)
Haya (M&L)	omustari	line (via Swahili)
Madi (Bla)	másɨ́tārà	ruler, for measurement etc.
Matengo (Yo)	òsitâli	line
Runyankore (Ka)	omusita:ri / emisita:ri	line (via Swahili)
Shona (Dal)	mutsara	line (? via Swahili)
Swahili (J)	mstari	a line, a line ruled or marked, a row

saʿd, pl. **suʿūd** good luck, good fortune (Wehr 410b); **saʿîd / suʿâd** lucky, happy, s.o. who is in happiness, content, who brings luck (JdP 1077a) 1288

Swahili (J)	sudi	luck, fortune, success

saʿīd happy; lucky, auspicious (Wehr 410b) 1289

Digo (MN&Z)	-saidiya	to help (via Swahili)
Swahili (J)	-saidia (*v.*)	aid, help, assist, support, countenance, abet

saʿāda good fortune; success (Wehr 410b) 1290

Malagasy (Gue)	msàda, mosàda	help, mutual help
Swahili (J)	msaada	help, aid, assistance, support

musāʿid assistant (Wehr 411a) 1290a

Madi (Bla)	mòsáɨ̀ / màsáɨ̀ / màsáyɨ̀	assistant; assistant driver

musāʿid assistant (Wehr 411a) + **ḥakīm** doctor (Wehr 196b) 1290b

Madi (Bla)	mòsàīdò àkɨ́mò	medical assistant

saʿʿara (*v.*) (II) to set a price (Wehr 411a); **siʿr**, pl. **asʿār** price (Wehr 411a) 1291

Swahili (J)	saari	price, value; for this, common words in Swahili are *bei, thamani, kiasi*

saʿūṭ snuff (Wehr 411b) 1292a

Madi (Bla)	sàû / sàwúù	snuff

saffara (*v.*) (II) to send on a journey (III) to travel (Wehr 412b); **sâfar / yisâfir** (*v.*) (III) to travel, to set off on a journey (JdP 1087b); **safar** journey, trip (Wehr 413a) 1294

Digo (MN&Z)	safari	journey (via Swahili)
Gikuyu (Ben)	thabarĩ	expedition with porters, expedition; party bound on an expedition; followers, retainers (e.g. of chief) (*cf.* Swahili)
Kamba (Mbi)	savalĩ	journey (via Swahili)
Kuria (MMR)	esabuari	a safari, journey (via Swahili)
Luganda (Sno)	`ssà`ffaàli	journey; caravan of porters
(Mo)	`e`ss`a:ff^a:ri	(via Swahili)
Madi (Bla)	sàfárɨ̀	journey (via Swahili)
Malagasy (Gue)	safàry	trip; time
Matengo (Yo)	sapwâli	journey
Swahili (J)	safari	a journey, voyage, expedition

safīr mediator (between contending parties); ambassador (Wehr 413a) 1297

Swahili (J)	-safiri (*v.*)	travel, engage in a journey or expedition, sail, start

safala, safila (*v.*) to be low; to be below s.th. (Wehr 413b) 1298

Swahili (J)	sefule (*interj.*)	You vile person! Low fellow!

safīna ship, vessel, boat (Wehr 414a) 1299

Gikuyu (Ben)	thabina	Noah's ark; ship (via Swahili)
Swahili (J)	safina	a ship, a vessel, Noah's ark

safanj, sifanji sponge (Wehr 414a) 1300

Swahili (J)	sifongo, sifunja, sifonjo	sponge

safiha (*v.*) to be stupid, silly; to be impudent, insolent (Wehr 414a) (III) to treat s.o. like a fool, like an insane (person) (Kazim: I, 1103b) 1301

Swahili (J)	-safihi, -safii (*v.* + *adj.*)	abuse, treat in a scornful manner, be arrogant, impudent

saqf[11] roof; ceiling (Wehr 415b) 1304

Swahili (J)	sakafu	floor or roof of a flat roofed stone building, cement or concrete floor

saqīfa roofed passage; roofing, shelter (Wehr 415b) 1305

Swahili (J)	-sakifu (*v.*)	make a floor, roof, or pavement of concrete

saqīm sick (Wehr 416a) 1306

Swahili (J)	-sakimu (*v.*)	be ill (rarely heard)

istisqā' dropsy; **ṣalāt al-istisqā'** prayer for rain (Wehr 416b) 1307

Swahili (J)	istiska	a Muslim prayer for rain; a dropsy

sukūt silence; reticence (Wehr 417a) 1308

Swahili (J)	-sukutu (*v.*)	to be silent, still, quiet (seldom heard)

sakra, pl. **sakarāt** inebriety, drunkenness (Wehr 417b) 1311

Swahili (J)	-sakara (*v.*)	to be tired, worn out by thirst, heat; overeat, eat so much as to feel tired or faint

11 Knappert (1972–73: 287, n. 9) states: "This word too, may be of Roman origin Ar. *saqf*, pl. *suquf* roofing, cp. Italian *scuffione* awning."

sukkar sugar (Wehr 417b) 1314

In some languages, the word for "sugar" may come from French sucre or English sugar.

Acooli (Cra)	cúkaàrì	sugar
(Mu)	cukari	
Bari (Mu)	sukwar	sugar
Bende (Abe)	sukaáli	sugar
Ciluba (Kab)	nsùkaadì	sugar
Dholuo (Gor)	sukari	sugar
(Odo)	cukari	
Dinka (Id)	sukkar, thokär, thukar	sugar
Gikuyu (Ben)	cukarĩ	sugar (via Swahili)
Haya (Ka)	eshukâli	sugar (via Swahili)
Kamba (Whi)	suká:l'ĩ	sugar (via Swahili)
Kinyarwanda (CAT)	i-sukari	sugar (via Swahili)
Kiw'oso (K&O)	-súkari	sugar
Lingala (Ev)	sukáli	sugar; sugary; sweetness (via Portuguese or Swahili)
Lotuxo (Mu)	asukar	sugar
Luganda (Sno)	`ssùkaàli	sugar (via Swahili)
Luyia (K&B)	isukari	
Malagasy (Gue)	sokàry	sugar
Matengo (Yo)	sukâle	sugar
Meru (K&B)	sukari	
Nyakyusa (Fel)	isúkalí	sugar (via Swahili)
Pokot (Cra)	sùkáarìn	sugar (via Swahili)
Rundi (K&B)	isakari	
Runyankore (Ka)	shukâ:ri	sugar (via Swahili)
Swahili (J)	sukari	sugar

(maraḍ al-baul) sukkarī diabetes (Wehr 417b) 1314a

Madi (Bla)	sùkàríà	diabetes

sakina residence, home (Wehr 418b) 1316

Swahili (J)	-sakini (*v.*)	remain in a place, settle down and live in a place

sukkān rudder (Wehr 418b) 1317

Malagasy (Gue)	sokàny	rudder
Swahili (J)	usukani	rudder

maskan, maskin dwelling; residence; domicile (Wehr 418b) 1319

Swahili (J)	maskani	dwelling place, home

silāḥ arm; armor (Wehr 420b) 1323

Shona Han	chiraha	butchery (via Swahili)
Swahili (J)	silaha, selaha	a weapon, arms

salsala (*v.*) to link together; to enchain (Wehr 421b); **silsila**, pl. **salāsil** iron chain (Wehr 421b); **sirsir** chain (RL 221a) 1327

Swahili (J)	silsila	chains, bonds; for this, common words in Swahili are *mnyororo, pingu*

SLṬ (*v.*) (II) to give power or mastery, set up as overlord, establish as ruler; to impose, inflict (Wehr 422a) 1328

Malagasy (Gue)	mikosoalìty	to get s.o. to do s.th. by gossip
Swahili (J)	-saliti (*v.*)	be harsh, sarcastic

salaṭa, salaṭā salad (Wehr 422a) 1328a

Madi (Bla)	sálātà	salad

sul**ṭān** sultan; (absolute) ruler (Wehr 422b) 1329

Dinka (Id)	thultän	sultan
Swahili (J)	sultani	king, ruler, chief

salīqa inborn disposition, instinct (Wehr 423b) 1331

Swahili (J)	silika, sirika	character, disposition, instinct

silk thread; string (Wehr 424a); wire; telegraph (RL 230a); **silik** wire, grilling (JdP 1133b) 1332

Acooli (Cra)	cïlï̀	wire
(Mu)	silik	
Bari (Mu)	asilik	wire
Dinka (Id)	wel cilik	term for iron cables
Lotuxo (Mu)	cılı	wire
Madi (Bla)	sɨ́lɨ̄gɨ̀	wire; wiring; bicycle spoke; animal trap

salima (*v.*) be safe and sound (II) **sallama** to preserve, protect from harm; to deliver; to surrender; to submit; to greet (Wehr 424b); **sallam / yasallim** (*v.*) (II) to greet, give peace (JdP 1105a) 1333

Swahili (J)	-salimu (*v.*)	express good wishes to, greet, congratulate; hand over safely, consign, deliver, rescue; give up, surrender, yield, resign

aslama (*v.*) (IV) to become a Muslim (Wehr 425a) 1334

Gikuyu (Ben)	thirimithia (*v.t.*)	to convert to Islam (via Swahili)
Swahili (J)	-silimisha (*v.*)	make a Muslim

sullam ladder; (flight of) stairs, staircase; stair, step (Wehr 425a) 1337a

Dinka (Id)	sellim	ladder
Ndogo (Po)	silim	stair; staircase

salām peace; security; salutation; salute (Wehr 425b) 1338

Digo (MN&Z)	salama	peacefully (via Swahili)
Malagasy (Gue)	salàma	in good health
Swahili (J)	salamu, salama, salaam	greeting, good wishes, compliments

salāma well-being, safety, security (Wehr 425b) 1341

Malagasy (Ade)	salàma	in good health

salīm safe, secure; safe and sound (Wehr 426a) 1342

Swahili (J)	salimini (*adv.*)	in safety, safely

sulaimān Solomon (Wehr 426a) 1343

Zulu (Bry)	-Sulumani	Muslim, Arabic

taslīm handing over; presentation; extradition; delivery; submission; salutation (Wehr 426a) 1344

Swahili (J)	taslimu	direct delivery, prompt (cash) payment

islām the religion of Islam (Wehr 426a) 1345

Dinka (Id)	ithlam	Islam
Malagasy (Gue)	silàmo	Muslim; good, caring, charitable
Rendille (P&G)	Múslam	Muslim (via Swahili Mwislamu)
Runyankore (Ka)	omusirâ:mu	Muslim (via Swahili)
Swahili (J)	-silimu (*v.*)	become Muslim, be converted to Islam
	Mwislamu	a Muslim

muslim Muslim (Wehr 426b) 1346

Dinka (Id)	muthilimiin	Muslim
Kikongo (Swa)	Muzùlúma	Muslim

ism name (Wehr 427a) 1348

Swahili (J)	isimu, ismu	name; a person himself, or thing itself

bi-ismllāhi in the name of God (Wehr 427b) 1349

Malagasy (Gue)	simìla	pardon (to apologize for entering, to pass in front of)
Swahili (J)	bismillahi	in the name of God
	simile (*interj.*)	make way! out of the road! by your leave!

samm, pl. **samūm** poison (Wehr 427b); **samm** venom (Daf 116) 1350

Dholuo (Gor)	sum	poison
Digo (MN&Z)	sumu	poison (via Swahili)
Gikuyu (Ben)	thumu	(of snake or other wild animal) poison from a bite (via Swahili)
Lega (Bot)	súmu	poison (via Swahili)
Madi (Bla)	sɨ́mɔ́	poison
Swahili (J)	sumu (+ *v.*)	poison

samḥ magnanimity, generosity; liberality (Wehr 428b); **samḥ** magnanimous, generous (Wehr 428b); **sameh / samhîn** (*adj.*) good, beautiful, well (JdP 1107b) 1352

Digo (MN&Z)	-samehe	to forgive (via Swahili)
Malagasy (Gue)	kosoamìhy	to whom we forgive
Swahili (J)	-samehe (*v.*)	pardon, forgive, remit

samaḥa magnanimity; generosity; liberality (Wehr 428b) 1353

Malagasy (Gue)	msoamàha	sorry
Swahili (J)	samaha	generally employed, or pl., pardon

samīr entertainer (in general, with stories, songs, etc.) (Wehr 429a) 1354

Swahili (J)	-simulia (*v.*) (?)	to narrate, relate, report, give an account, tell a story

mismār nail (Wehr 429b); **musmâr / masâmîr** nail, tip (JdP 949b) 1355

Acooli (Cra)	mùcùmáàr	nail
(Mu)	mucumar	nail (iron)
Bari (Mu)	musumar	nail (iron)
Dholuo (Odo)	mucumar	nail
Dinka (Id)	mucmar	nail
Kinyarwanda (CAT)	umu-sumari	nail, pin
Kiw'oso (K&O)	n'-shimári	nail (via Swahili)
Kuria (MMR)	umusumaari	nail or bolt
Lotuxo (Mu)	agusumar	nail (iron)
Madi (Bla)	mɔ̀sɔ̀márɨ̀ / lɔ̀sɔ̀márɨ̀	nail, for fixing s.th.

Malagasy (Gue)	mŝimàry, moŝimàry	nail
Matengo (Yo)	òsúmali	nail
Ndogo (Po)	musmar	nail
Nyakyusa (Fel)	unsúmalí	nail (via Swahili)
Rendille (P&G)	ussumáar	metal nail (used in carpentry) (via Swahili)
Swahili (J)	msumari	a nail, large pin, or anything similar in appearance or use

simsim sesame (Wehr 430a); **sumsum** sesame (JdP 1147a); **sumsum** sesame, couscous (Kaye 72b) 1356

Swahili (J)	semsem	sesame

sumsum red ant (Kazim: I, 1138a) 1357

Swahili (J)	samesame (?)	a kind of red bead

samʿan wa-ṭāʿatan I hear and obey! at your service! very well! (Wehr 430b) 1358

Swahili (J)	semaa wa taa	an Arabic expression (not common) hear and obey, to hear is to obey

samak fish (Wehr 431a); **samakī** similar to fish (Wehr 431a) 1359

Digo (MN&Z)	samaki	fish (via Swahili)
Gikuyu (Ben)	thamaki	fish (via Swahili)
Kiw'oso (K&O)	-samakí	fish (via Swahili)
Swahili (J)	samaki	fish (in general)

samm clarified butter, cooking butter (Wehr 431b) 1361

Gikuyu (Ben)	thamuri	ghee, clarified butter (via Swahili)
Malagasy (Gue)	samòly	butter, clarified butter for cooking
Swahili (J)	samli	ghee, native butter

samāʾ, pl. **samāwāt** sky (Wehr 432b) 1362

Swahili (J)	samawati	sky

samāwī celestial; sky-blue, azure (Wehr 432b) 1363

Swahili (J)	samawi	sky

samīy sublime (Wehr 432b) 1364

Swahili (J)	somo (?)	confidential adviser or friend, a term of friendly or familiar address; a friend and namesake; an assistant at initiation rites

sana year (Wehr 433a) 1365

Swahili (J)	sanati	the year, only used in writing the date in Arabic letters, or in documents

sanna (*v.*) to sharpen; to shape; to prescribe, establish (Wehr 433a) 1366

Swahili (J)	-sana (*v.*)	forge, as of hoes, hammers, knives, and such

sinn tooth (Wehr 433a) 1367

Swahili (J)	sine	the gum of the teeth

sunna the Sunna (Wehr 433b) 1368

Swahili (J)	suna (*adj.*)	good, commendable, meritorious

sunnī Sunnitic; Sunnite (Wehr 433b) 1369

Swahili (J)	suni	used of what is good, commendable, meritorious, but not absolutely binding or necessary; a Sunni (Muslim)

sanad fabric (Kazim: I, 1150b) 1372

Swahili (J)	sanda	shroud, winding-sheet, burial cloth – commonly of thin white calico
	satini (?)	grey long-cloth, also a kind of striped material

sandarūs sandarac (a resine obtained from the sandarac tree, *sp. Callitris quadrivalvis*) (Wehr 435b) 1374

Swahili (J)	sandarusi	gum copal, from the msandarusi tree

sandiwic sandwich (JdP 1111b) 1374a

Madi (Bla)	sòndòwísì	sandwich

sanṭūr dulcimer (Wehr 435b) 1375

Swahili (J)	santuri, senturi	a musical box, gramophone

sanā makkī *senna (tree); senna leaflets* (Wehr 436a); *Cassia acutifolia, Cassia lanceolata, Senna alexandrina* (Gh: I, 11460) 1377

Swahili (J)	sanamaki	senna, a laxative, a purgative

sanā brilliance; sublimity, high rank (Wehr 436b) 1378

Swahili (J)	sana (*adv.*)	very much, in a high degree

sahula (*v.*) to be smooth; to be or become easy (Wehr 437a) 1380

Swahili (J)	sahala (*adj.*)	light, i.e. not heavy, easy

suhail Canopus (*astron.*) (Wehr 437b) 1380a

Malagasy (Gue)	sohilìny, soilìny	South
Swahili (Sacl)	suheli	South

tashīl facilitation (Wehr 437b) 1382

Swahili (J)	tasihili (*adv.* + *n.*)	quickly, with speed; a goodbye

mushil purgative, laxative (Wehr 437b) 1383

Swahili (J)	msahala	a purgative medicine, salts

sahm portion, share; share (of stock) (Wehr 438a) 1384

Bende (Abe)	sehému	place
Digo (MN&Z)	seemu / sehemu	part, region, area (via Swahili)
Swahili (J)	sehemu (+ *v.*)	part, portion, piece, share, fraction

sahā (*v.*) to be inattentive, distracted (Wehr 438a) 1385

Swahili (J)	sahau (+ *v.*)	forgetfulness, a lapse of memory

sawād black clothing, mourning (Wehr 440a) 1386

Swahili (J)	soda	lunacy, melancholia

sūdānī Sudanese (Wehr 440b) 1388a

Ndogo (Po)	sudani	Sudanese

sayyid master; lord; chief (Wehr 440b) 1389

Swahili (J)	saidi	lord, master

sayyida mistress; lady (Wehr 440b) 1390

Swahili (J)	saada, seyyida	lady, madam

sūra chapter of the Qur'an (Wehr 441a) 1392

Acooli (Cra)	cuurà	chapter
Dholuo (Odo)	cura	chapter
Digo (MN&Z)	sura	chapter (via Swahili)

Luganda (Sno)	`ssuula	chapter (via Swahili)
Malagasy (Gue)	sôra, sòra	sura, Qur'an chapter
Swahili (J)	sura	a chapter of a book

sūs woodworm, borer; mothworm (Wehr 441a) **1394**

Swahili (J)	susa	tartar (of teeth), decay (of teeth)

sūs licorice (Glycyrrhiza glabra) (Wehr 441a) **1395**

Swahili (J)	sus	liquorice (very little known)

siyāsa administration; policy (Wehr 441b) **1396**

Dholuo (Gor)	siasa	politics
Digo (MN&Z)	siasa	politics (via Swahili)
Kuria (MMR)	isiasa	politics
	umusiasa	politician
Madi (Bla)	sìyásà / sìásà	politics; manipulation, trick or persuasive charm; inveigle
Malagasy (Gue)	siàsa	political (mostly in a negative sense)
Swahili (J)	siasa (*n.* + *adv.*)	orderliness, gentleness, politics

siyâsî / siyâsîyîn (*adj.*) policy (JdP 1139b) **1396a**

Madi (Bla)	sìyásínì	politicians

sā'is stableman, groom; driver (primarily of animals) (Wehr 441b) **1397**

Swahili (J)	saisi	a groom, coachman

sā'a while; hour; clock (Wehr 441b) **1398**

Acooli (Cra)	cáà	watch; hour
(Mu)	caa	clock; hour; interval (of time); time; watch
Anywa (Reh)	càa	watch; time
Ateso (Kit)	esawa	hour, clock, watch

Bari (Mu)	saa, salan	clock; hour; time (of the day); watch
Bende (Abe)	nsá	hour
Dholuo (Gor)	sa	hour
Dinka (Id)	thaa	watch
Gikuyu (Ben)	thaa	clock, watch; hour (cf. Swahili)
Haya (Ka)	esâa	hour (via Swahili)
Kinyarwanda (CAT)	i-sāha, isāa	clock, watch, hour
Kiw'oso (K&O)	-sáa	hour
Kuria (MMR)	saa	o'clock (via Swahili)
Lingala (Ev)	sâ (sáa)	watch
Lotuxo (Mu)	asaa	clock; hour
	nasaa	interval (of time)
	asaa, asaxyen	time (of the day); watch
Luganda (Sno)	`ssaàwa	hour; watch; clock; time of day (via Swahili)
Lunyoro (Dav)	esaha	time (hour)
Madi (Bla)	sáà / sáwà	time; hour; period; clock, watch; hour (used in telling time, when Arabic numerals are used)
Malagasy (Gue)	sà, sàa, sàia	hour, moment
Ndogo (Po)	saa	hour; clock
Nyakyusa (Fel)	isala	hour, watch, clock (via Swahili)
Pokot (Cra)	sáà	watch, hour, time (via Swahili)
Runyankore (Ka)	eshâ:ha	hour (via Swahili)
Sango (Bou)	sáà	watch, clock; measuring tool (via Lingala)
Swahili (J)	saa	an hour; time

hassâ (*invar.*), contraction of **al-sâ'a** now, immediately (JdP 567a); **'assa** now (Z&T 120) 1399

Dinka (Id)	hasa	now

saf row of stones, bricks, in a wall (Kazim: I, 1166b) 1400

Malagasy (Gue)	sàfo	rank, group
Swahili (J)	safu (+ *v.*)	row, line, rank, series

sauq driving (of a car) (Wehr 443a) **1401a**

Madi (Bla)	sɔ̀ágɨ̀	driver

sūq market (Wehr 443a); **sûg / sawaga** market (JdP 1144a); **sūg** market (Kaye 49b), **su:g** market (Z&T 136) **1402**

Acooli (Cra)	cúùk	market
(Mu)	cuk	
Bari (Mu)	suk	market
Bende (Abe)	iisóko	market
Dholuo (Odo)	cuk	market
Digo (MN&Z)	soko	market (via Swahili)
Dinka (Id)	cuk, suuk, thuuk	market
Gikuyu (Ben)	thoko	market, marketplace (via Swahili)
Haya (Ka)	eishóko	permanent market
(M&L)	esoko	market (via Swahili)
Ik (Schr)	dzígwààwa (dzígwà-àwà-)	market
Kuria (MMR)	esokoni	market
Lega (Bot)	i.sɔkɔ	market (via Swahili)
Madi (Bla)	sókò / sû	market (via Swahili)
Matengo (Yo)	sôko	market
Pokot (Cra)	máak^{o}t	market (via Swahili)
Rendille (P&G)	sókko	marketplace (via Swahili)
Swahili (J)	soko	market

siwāk, pl. **sūk** a small stick (the tip of which is softened by chewing or beating) used for cleaning and polishing the teeth (Wehr 443b); **miswāk** [as above] (Wehr 443b) **1403**

Swahili (J)	mswaki	a toothbrush

SWL II to talk or argue s.o. into s.th. evil or fateful (Wehr 444a) **1403a**

Digo (MN&Z)	swali	a question (via Swahili)
Swahili (J)	swali	question, inquiry, interrogation, problem

sawiya (*v.*) to be equivalent (VIII) to mature (Wehr 444b); **wâsa / yiwâsi** (*v.*) to equalize, level, be level with, align (JdP 1258a) **1405**

Swahili (J)	-sitawi (*v.*)	to be in good condition, reach full development, flourish, succeed

sawāʾ equal; equality (Wehr 444b); **sawā** to be equal (RL 239b) **1407**

Digo (MN&Z)	sawa	the same (via Swahili)
Swahili (J)	sawa (*adj.* + *n.*)	like; alike; likeness, equality

sawīy straight; right, correct (Wehr 445a); **sawīyan** in common, together (Wehr 445a) **1408**

Swahili (J)	sawia (*adv.*)	then, at that time, just then, on the spot

sāra (*v.*) to move (on), get going; to travel (Wehr 446b); **sâr** (*v.*) to leave, move, leave a place, be moved (JdP 1114a) **1409**

Swahili (J)	-sairi (*v.*)	coast, hug the shore in a vessel

sayyār planet (Wehr 447a) **1411**

Swahili (J)	sayari	planet

sīn name of the letter س (Wehr 448b) **1413**

Swahili (J)	yasini	a certain chapter from the Qur'an

Šīn

šākūš, šakūš hammer (Wehr 449a); **sakuus** hammer (S&A 143a) **1413a**

Madi (Bla)	sákúsì	hammer

šāl shawl (Wehr 449a) 1414

Swahili (J)	shali	a shawl

aš-šām Syria (Wehr 449b) 1415

Swahili (J)	Sham	Syria

šu'm calamity, bad luck, misfortune; evil omen, portent (Wehr 449b) 1416

Swahili (J)	shume *paka shume* (used with this meaning and context)	a semi-wild cat, a large male cat

maš'ūm, mašūm inauspicious, ill-omened; unlucky (Wehr 449b) 1417

Swahili (J)	mashumushu	an evil occurrence; evil recoiling on a person, i.e. witchcraft s.o. employs

ša'n matter, affair, business; circumstances; nature, character; situation, state (Wehr 449b) 1418

Swahili (J)	shani	startling (rare, unexpected) thing or occurrence, a wonder, a novelty, a curiosity, an adventure, a sudden mishap, accident

šāwuš (*tun.*) sergeant (Wehr 451a) 1419

Acooli (Cra)	càwîc	sergeant
Swahili (J)	shaushi	corporal (via Turkish *onbaşı*)

šāy tea (Wehr 451a); **šāhī** tea (RL 259b); **šaï** tea (RL 262a) 1420

Acooli (Cra)	caáì	tea
Ateso (Kit)	ecai	tea
Bari (Mu)	sayı	tea
Bende (Abe)	chaái	tea
Dholuo (Odo)	cai	tea
Digo (MN&Z)	chai	tea, breakfast (via Swahili)
Dinka (Id)	cai	tea
Kinyarwanda (CAT)	icy-āyi	tea (via Swahili)
Kiw'oso (K&O)	-chái	tea (via Swahili)
Kuria (MMR)	ichaahe	tea
Lega (Bot)	chai	tea (via Swahili)
Lotuxo (Mu)	asyayı	tea
Luganda (Mo)	`cc^a:zyi	tea (via Swahili)
Madi (Bla)	cáì / sáì	tea; (informal) bribe
Matengo (Yo)	sâi	tea
Nyakyusa (Fel)	ikyaí (?)	tea (via Swahili ?)
Rendille (P&G)	cháay	tea (via Swahili)
Swahili (J)	chai	tea (from Persian or Hindi)

šabb alum (Wehr 451a) 1421

Swahili (J)	shabu	alum

šabāb youth (Wehr 451b) 1422

Malagasy (Gue)	ŝabàby	young man, young woman, young people
Swahili (J)	shababi	a youth

šābb youthful; youth, young man (Wehr 451b) 1423

Swahili (J)	mashobo	showiness of dress, character of showing off

šabaḥ, **šabḥ** blurred; apparition; phantom (Wehr 451b) **1424**

Digo (MN&Z)	shabaha	target, aim (via Swahili)
Gikuyu (Ben)	cabaa	shooting practice range; good shot, aim (in shooting) (via Swahili)
Luganda (Sno)	\`ssà\`bbaàwa	target; mark (via Swahili)
Swahili (J)	shabaha, shebaha	a target, aim, a mark to aim at; aim (with a weapon), sight (of a gun)

šibr span of the hand (Wehr 451b); **šiber** span (RL 243b) **1425**

Swahili (J)	shibiri	a span, from thumb to little finger of the open hand, about nine inches, half a cubit

šibʿ, **šibaʿ** s.th. that fills or satisfies the appetite, fill (Wehr 452b) **1427**

Swahili (J)	-shiba (*v.*)	to have enough to eat or drink, have a full meal, be satisfied with food

šabakī reticulate, reticular, net-like (Wehr 453a) **1429**

Swahili (J)	shabaki, shabuka	a quarrelsome, cross-grained person; a snare, fishing net

šubbāk netting, network; window (Wehr 453a); **cubbâk** window (JdP 333a) **1430**

Ndogo (Po)	subaki	window
Swahili (J)	shubaka	small window, light-hole, loop-hole, porthole, embrasure

šbh (*v.*) (ii) to make equal or similar; to compare (iii) to resemble (Wehr 453b); **šabah** resemblance; similarity, likeness; brass (Wehr 454a); **câbah / yicâbih** (*v.*) (iii) to look like (JdP 291a); **šāba** resemble (Kaye 73a); **šabah, šabih** to be like; to resemble (rl 244b); **sha:ba** to look like (Z&T 136) **1431**

Malagasy (Gue)	msobìhy	appearance
Swahili (J)	shabaha, shebaha (+ *v.*)	similarity, likeness

šabah resemblance; similarity, likeness; brass (Wehr 454a) **1431a**

Malagasy (Gue)	ŝàba	copper (or other metal?)
Swahili (J)	shaba	brass
	shaba nyekundu	copper

šabīh similar, like, resembling (Wehr 454a) **1432**

Swahili (J)	shabihi (+ *v.*)	form, outward appearance of a person, dignity

šatm abuse, vilification (Wehr 455a) **1435**

Swahili (J)	shutumu (+ *v.*)	reproach, railing, abuse, blame

šujāʿ, šijāʿ courageous [man], brave [person]; hero (Wehr 456a) **1438**

Swahili (J)	shujaa	a brave man, warrior, hero, champion

šaḥm fat, suet, grease; lard (Wehr 457b) **1440**

Swahili (J)	shahamu	fat, lard, grease

šaḥna cargo, lading, load, freight (Wehr 458a) **1441**

Swahili (J)	shehena	cargo, freight, load

šadda (*v.*) to be or become firm, solid, hard; to press (Wehr 459a) **1442**

Malagasy (Gue)	ŝìd̠a, ŝìdra	lazy (slow or bad, not incapacitated); tired
Swahili (J)	shudu mashudu	refuse of seed after it has been crushed for oil, oil-cake the remains of seed, after the oil has been pressed out

šadīd strong, powerful, vigorous (Wehr 460a) **1444**

Swahili (J)	-shadidi (*v.*)	hold fast to, fix, use influence, order, direct influence

tašdīd intensification, strengthening (Wehr 460b) **1445**

Swahili (J)	tashtiti	teasing, provocation, provocative, harsh

šarr evil; wickedness (Wehr 461b) **1448**

Malagasy (Gue)	ŝàry	evil
Swahili (J)	shari	evil, malice, disaster, adversity

šurrāb stocking, sock (Wehr 462a); **currâb / currâbât** (term used in Sudan) sock (JdP 335a) **1449a**

Bari (Mu)	suraf (sing. sarabat)	sock, stockings
Ndogo (Po)	sarabat	sock

šurba drink; potion (of a medicine) (Wehr 462b); **curba / curbât** (term used in Sudan) soup (JdP 335a); **šorba** soup (RT 247a); **shurba** soup (S&A 147b) **1449b**

Acooli (Mu)	curba	soup
Bari (Mu)	surba	soup
Madi (Bla)	súrūgbà	soup

šarāb beverage, drink; wine; sherbet (Wehr 462b) 1450

Swahili (J)	sharabu	an intoxicating drink

šārib, pl. **šawārib** mustache (Wehr 463a) 1451

Bende (Abe)	iisulúbhu	mustache
Swahili (J)	sharubu	mustache

šarābāt syrup (Kazim: I, 1210b) 1452

Swahili (J)	sharabeti, shebeti	sherbet

šurrāb stockings, sock (Wehr 463a) 1452a

Madi (Bla)	sàràbáì / sòròbɨ̀	socks

šaraḥa (*v.*) to cut in slices; to comment (VII) to be opened (heart); to be glad, happy (Wehr 463a) 1453

Swahili (J)	sherehe	show, pomp, display; demonstration, cheers, triumph

širās glue (Wehr 464b) 1455

Swahili (J)	sherisi, sheresi	glue

šarṭ condition; stipulation (of a contract) (Wehr 465a) 1456

Malagasy (Gue)	ŝàrty, ŝoròty, maŝaròty	condition, convention, stipulation
Swahili (J)	sharti	necessity

šarīṭ tape (Wehr 465a) 1456a

Dinka (Id)	carit	cassette

širāʿ sail; tent (Wehr 466a) 1458

Swahili (J)	shira	sail of a vessel, for the more common *tanga*

šarīʿa the Sharia (Wehr 466a); **cerî'e / carâye** justice, judgment, litigation, trial (JdP 324b); **šarīɛa** Islamic law (RL 248b); **gadiiya** lawsuit (S&A 104a) 1459

Bende (Abe)	syelía	law
Digo (MN&Z)	shariya	law (via Swahili)
Dinka (Id)	gediya	court (case)
Haya (M&L)	esheria	law (via Swahili)
Kiw'oso (K&O)	-shariâ	law
Madi (Bla)	sɛ̀ríà	Islamic sharia (law)
Matengo (Yo)	selîa	law
Swahili (J)	sheria, sharia	law

šāriʿ street (Wehr 466b); **šāriɛ** street (RL 248b) 1460

Madi (Bla)	sɛ̀rīà	a street woman

šarīf sherif, title of the descendants of Muhammad (Wehr 467a) 1463

Malagasy (Gue)	ŝarìfo	sherif; descendant of Prophet Muhammad
Swahili (J)	sharifu (*v.* + *adj.*) sherifu	honorable, respectable, noble

mašriq the Orient, the East (Wehr 468a) 1465

Swahili (J)	mashariki	the East

šarak net; trap (Wehr 468b); **carak / curkân** net, trap (JdP 310b); **sharak** net (Z&T 137) 1467

Swahili (J)	shalaka	a hole in the gunwale of a boat for securing the loop of rope (*kishwara*) used as a rowlock

širka, šarika partnership; business (Wehr 468b) 1468

Madi (Bla)	síríkà	factory, industry, company; band
Malagasy (Gue)	ŝirìka	society, association, indivision
Swahili (J)	shirika, sharika	partnership

šarmūṭa prostitute (Wehr 469b); **šarmūṭa** prostitute (RL 250a) 1471

Madi (Bla)	sàràmòtà	prostitute
Ndogo (Po)	sharmuta	prostitute

šaṭṭa a variety of pepper, Capsicum conicum Mey (Wehr 470b); **šitta** (chili) pepper (Kaye 75b); **šiṭṭa** pepper, used as a general term and more particularly for the small red chili; Capsicum frutescens (RL 250b) 1473

Bari (Mu)	kiteta	cayenne pepper
Lotuxo (Mu)	asitata	cayenne pepper

šaṭr partition, division (Wehr 471b) 1474

Gikuyu (Ben)	cotara	half-caste (via Swahili)
Swahili (J)	chotara (?)	a person of mixed race

šiṭranj, šaṭranj chess (Wehr 471b) 1475

Swahili (J)	sataranji	the game of chess

šaʿbān Shaban, name of the eighth month of the Islamic calendar (Wehr 473a) 1477

Swahili (J)	shabani, shaabani	the month of the Islamic calendar preceding Ramadan

al-šiʿrā Sirius, Dog Star (Wehr 474a) 1479

Swahili (J)	Shiraa	the dog star

šaʿīr barley (Wehr 474a) 1480

Gikuyu (Ben)	cairi	barley (via Swahili)
Luganda (Sno)	è`ssàyirì	barley (via Swahili)
Swahili (J)	shayiri	barley

šāʿir, pl. **šuʿarāʾ** poet (Wehr 474b) 1482

Swahili (J)	shairi	a song, a line of poetry

šauġara bag or basket made of palm leaves for storing dates (Kazim: I, 1224a) 1483

Swahili (J)	shogi, sogi	a pannier, a pack-saddle, a large matting bag slung over a donkey's back, and open across the middle

šuġl occupancy, activity; work, job; business, concern (Wehr 476b); **shoGol / shuGul** thing (Z&T 137) 1484

Digo (MN&Z)	shuhuli	business, activity, function (via Swahili)
Malagasy (Gue)	ŝogòly, ŝoghòly, ŝohòly	take care of (in active sense, always negatively)
Swahili (J)	shughuli	business, occupation; trouble, worry

šafʿ either part of a pair (Wehr 478a) 1486

Swahili (J)	shufwa	even number

šafāʿa mediation, intercession (Wehr 478b) 1487

Malagasy (Gue)	ŝifaʿy	savior
Swahili (Sacl)	shifai	intercessor

šafaqa compassion, pity (Wehr 478b) 1490

Swahili (J)	shufaka, shafaka	compassion, tenderness, pity

mašaqqa trouble, difficulty (Wehr 480b) **1493**

Kiw'oso (K&O)	ma-shakâ	doubt
Malagasy (Gue)	maŝàka	trouble, difficulties, pain, miseries
Matengo (Yo)	masâka	doubt
Swahili (J)	mashaka	trouble, difficulty
	shakawa	trouble, danger

šaqīy unlucky; scoundrel; naughty (Wehr 481b) **1495**

Swahili (J)	ushakii	bravery, courage

šakk doubt (Wehr 481b); **šakkak** doubt (*v.*) (Kaye 74a) **1497**

Bende (Abe)	syăka	doubt
Digo (MN&Z)	shaka	trouble, disaster, doubt (via Swahili)
Haya (M&L)	amashaka	suspicion (via Swahili)
Swahili (J)	shaka	doubt
	shuku (*n.* + *v.*)	doubt, perplexity, uncertainty

šukr thankfulness (Wehr 482a) **1500**

Digo (MN&Z)	-shukurani	to thank (via Swahili)
Malagasy (Gue)	mikoŝokòro	thank, give thanks; but generally used in the sense of resigning
Swahili (J)	shukrani	gratitude, thanksgiving, thanks
	-shukuru (*v.*)	thank

šakā (*v.*) to complain, make a complaint (Wehr 483b); **caka / yacki** (*v.*) to complain to, accuse (Wehr 300b) **1504**

Digo (MN&Z)	shitaka	accusation (via Swahili)
Malagasy (Gue)	mikoŝitàky, mikoŝtàky	to complain, accuse
Swahili (J)	shtaka	charges, accusations, reproaches

šikāya complaint; accusation (Wehr 483b) **1504a**

Madi (Bla)	sīkíà	accusation, complaint, legal suit

š m r (*v.*) (ii) to gather up, lift, roll up, turn up; to prepare, get ready (Wehr 485b) **1511**

Swahili (J)	-shamiri (*v.*)	load a gun; put together

šamar fennel (Wehr 486a) **1512**

Swahili (J)	shamari	fennel

šams, pl. **šumūs** sun (Wehr 486a); **šamš** sun (RL 257a) **1513**

Swahili (J)	shemshi	the sun, usu. *jua*
	shumusi	sunshine, brightness

šamsīya parasol; umbrella (Wehr 486a); **shemsiiya** umbrella (S&A 146b) **1514**

Acooli (Cra)	tàmciià	umbrella
Dholuo (Odo)	tamciya	an umbrella

šammās deacon (Wehr 486a) **1515**

Gikuyu (Ben)	mũcemathi	deacon (of the Anglican Church) (via Swahili)
Swahili (J)	shemasi	deacon

šamʿ, **šamaʿ** wax; (wax) candles (Wehr 486b); **šamʿa, šamaʿa** (wax) candle (Wehr 486b); **cam'e** wax, candle (JdP 305b) **1517**

Bari (Mu)	sama	candle
Dinka (Id)	shama	candle
Gikuyu (Ben)	mũcumaa	candle (via Swahili)
Ndogo (Po)	sama	candle
Swahili (J)	mshumaa	candle

mušammaʿ wax cloth (Wehr 486b); **mashaama** canvas (S&A 131b) **1517a**

Madi (Bla)	mòsɛ́mà	canvas

šamāl north; north wind (Wehr 487a) 1518

Swahili (J)	shemali	the left (hand); the north (quarter);
	mshemali	the north wind, mist, fog a northern Arab, i.e. from Mascat and the Persian Gulf

šanṭa suitcase; satchel; bag, traveling bag (Wehr 488a); **šanṭa** bag; suitcase; trunk; box (RT 258b); **shanta** bag (S&A 146a) 1520

Madi (Bla)	sándà	bag, box
Ndogo (Po)	shanta	suitcase
Swahili (J)	shanta	haversack, rucksack, knapsack

šahīd, pl. **šuhūd** witness; martyr, one killed in battle with infidels; one killed in action (Wehr 489a) 1522

Swahili (J)	shuhuda	testimony, evidence, witness

šahāda Muslim creed (Wehr 489a) 1523

Malagasy (Gue)	ŝahàda	profession of faith of Islam, which consists in saying “there is no god but God and Muhammad is the messenger of God”
Swahili (J)	shahada	covenant; the Muslim creed, confession of faith

šāhid witness (Wehr 489b); **câhid / cuhûd** eyewitness, present (JdP 299b); **šāhèd** witness (RL 259a) 1525

Acooli (Cra)	càdéèn, cadì	witness
(Mu)	caden	
Bari (Mu)	kadirin-te	witness
Dholuo (Odo)	caden	witness, testimony
Digo (MN&Z)	shahidi	witness (via Swahili)
Dinka (Id)	cäät	witness
Gikuyu (Ben)	caĩri	witness (via Swahili)
Madi (Bla)	sàdénì	witness; alibi
	sìádà	certificate
Malagasy (Gue)	ŝahìdy	witness
Swahili (J)	shahidi	witness, martyr

mušāhara monthly salary; pl. monthly payments, monthly allowances (Wehr 490b) 1528

Gikuyu (Ben)	mũcara	wages, salary (via Swahili)
Kiw'oso (K&O)	n`-shaára	wages, salary
Pokot (Cra)	mìsìárà	payment, salary (via Swahili)
Rendille (P&G)	macchaára	salary, wage (via Swahili)
Runyankore (Ka)	omushâ:ra / emishâ:ra	salary (via Swahili)
Swahili (J)	mshahara	monthly wages, regular salary

mašhūr well known, renowned, celebrated; notorious (Wehr 490b) 1529

Digo (MN&Z)	mashuhuri	famous, well known, notorious (via Swahili)
Swahili (J)	mashuhuri	famous, renowned

šahwa desire (Wehr 491a) 1530

Malagasy (Gue)	ŝahào	envy, desire (sexual)
Swahili (J)	shahawa	semen

šuwāl, šiwāl (large) sack (Wehr 491b); **cawâl / cawâwîl** sack (JdP 335b); **šuwāl** sack (Kaye 75b); **shuwa:l** sack (Z&T 154) 1532

Acooli (Mu)	cwal	sack
(Cra)	kìcàá	bag
Bari (Mu)	suar	sack
Dholuo (Odo)	kicaa	sack
Dinka (Id)	cuali	sack
Lotuxo (Mu)	asʊal	sack
Ndogo (Po)	swali	sack

šāwara (*v.*) (III) to ask s.o.'s advice (Wehr 492a); **côra** consultation, advice (JdP 332a); **šawwar** advice; consult (RL 260a) 1533

Digo (MN&Z)	shauri	decision, advice (via Swahili)
Gikuyu (Ben)	cauri	affair, business; discussion, dispute (via Swahili)
Malagasy (Gue)	ŝaoriŝaory	advice, idea, way (of doing s.th.)
Swahili (J)	(-)shauri (*n.* + *v.*)	plan; advice; counsel; ask counsel

išāra sign; signal; indication; allusion (Wehr 492b) 1534

Digo (MN&Z)	ishara	sign (via Swahili)
Swahili (J)	ishara	sign, signal, omen, indication, hint
	-ashiria (*v.*)	signal to, make a sign to

šāš muslin (Wehr 493a) 1535

Swahili (J)	shashi, bushashi	a kind of thin muslin

tašwīš confusion; derangement (Wehr 493b) 1536

Malagasy (Gue)	taŝaòŝy	annoyance, discomfort
Swahili (J)	tashwishi	doubt, perplexity, confusion

šāfa (*v.*) to see (word used in the Arabic of Syria and Egypt) (Kazim: I, 1288a) 1537

Swahili (J)	-shufu (*v.*)	perceive, see, look at

šauq desire (Wehr 494a) 1538a

Malagasy (Gue)	oŝôko	desire, will
Swahili (J)	shauku	eagerness, strong desire, sexual passion

šauk forks (Wehr 494a) 1539a

Dinka (Id)	shok	fork
Ndogo (Po)	soka	fork

šawwāl Shawwal, name of the tenth month of the Islamic calendar (Wehr 494b) 1541

Swahili (J)	shawali	the tenth month according to the Islamic calendar

in šā'a allāh God willing; it is to be hoped; I (we) hope so (Wehr 495b) 1543

Swahili (J)	inshallah (*adv.*)	Oh yes; certainly; of course

mâlêc expression, contraction of **mâlê l-ceyy**, it does not matter, never mind (JdP 815a); **maleesh** never mind (S&A 130a) **1543a**

Dinka (Id)	males	sorry

šaib grayness of the hair, gray or white hair; old age (Wehr 496a); **šāib** old (RL 262b) **1544**

Swahili (J)	shaibu	a very old man

šaiḫ shaykh; title of native scholars trained in the traditional sciences such as clerical dignitaries (Wehr 496b) **1546**

Malagasy (Gue)	ŝehoŝèho	a man who is a little shaykh, a devotee
Swahili (J)	sheik, sheki	elder, chief, ruler, teacher
	shaha, shehe, sheki	chef

šīša bottle of the narghile; narghile (Wehr 497a); pipe with persian, calioune, hocca (Kazim: I, 1297a) **1547**

Swahili (J)	shisha	a kind of sand-glass for measuring time, used in some native vessels

šaiṭān Satan, devil (Wehr 497b); **šī/ēṭān**(e) devil, Satan (Kaye 75b) **1548**

Ateso (Kit)	Satan	Satan
Digo (MN&Z)	Shetani	Satan (via Swahili)
Kamba (Mbi)	Satani	Satan, devil (via Swahili)
Madi (Bla)	sìtánì	Satan, devil
Malagasy (Gue)	ŝetoàny	devil, devils, spirits
Matengo (Yo)	lisetâni	Satan, spirit of the dead
Ndogo (Po)	sitani	demon; Satan
Ngh'wele Leg	shetani	bad spirit (via Swahili)
Nyakyusa (Fel)	setano	Satan, devil (via Swahili)
Swahili (J)	shetani	an evil spirit, demon, Satan

Ṣād

ṣubḥ dawn; morning (Wehr 500b); **sabah** east (JdP 1078b); **sab**(**ā**)(**h**) morning, east (Kaye 69a) **1552**

Swahili (J)	asubuhi	morning

ṣabāḥ al-ḫair good morning (Wehr 500b) **1553**

Swahili (J)	sabalkheri	common Arabic morning salutation

ṣabara (*v.*) to be patient (Wehr 501a); **ṣabr** patience (Wehr 501a); **sabar / yasbur** (*v.*) to wait, endure, expect, resign (JdP 1079a); **ṣabar** (*v.*) endure, be patient (Kaye 73a); **seber** to wait (RL 215a); **ṣeber** to wait (RL 265b) **1555**

Malagasy (Gue)	sab̲òry	hold on!
Swahili (J)	saburi, subira	patience
	saburi, subiri (*v.*)	be patient

ṣabir, ṣabr aloe (Wehr 501a) **1556**

Swahili (J)	subili	aloe

ṣābūn soap (Wehr 502a) < Greek loan σάπων **1557**

Acooli (Cra)	càbúùn	soap
(Mu)	cabun	
Ateso (Kit)	asabuni, esabuni	soap
Bari (Mu)	söbun, söbunyön	soap
Bende (Abe)	saabhúni	soap
Digo (MN&Z)	sabuni	soap (via Swahili)
Dinka (Id)	thaabuun, sabun, thabun	soap
Gikuyu (Ben)	thabuni	soap; cake of soap (via Swahili)
Gwere (Kag)	saabuuni	soap (via Swahili)
Haya (Ka)	esa:bûndi	soap (via Swahili)
Kamba (Mbi)	savunĩ	soap (via Swahili)
Kinyarwanda (CAT)	i-sabune	soap

Kiw'oso (K&O)	-sábuni	soap
Lotuxo (Mu)	asyebun	soap
Luganda (Sno)	`ssà`bbuùni	soap (via Swahili)
Lunyoro (Dav)	esabūni	soap
Madi (Bla)	sàbú	(short for) soap (via Swahili)
Matengo (Yo)	sabûni	soap
Ndogo (Po)	sabun	soap
Pokot (Cra)	sàpónìyɔ́n	soap (via Swahili)
Rendille (P&G)	saabbúun	soap (via Swahili)
Runyankore (Ka)	esa:bû:ni	soap (via Swahili)
Swahili (J)	sabuni	soap

ṣaḥḥa (*v.*) to be healthy (Wehr 503a); **ṣiḥḥa** health (Wehr 503b) 1560

Swahili (J)	siha	strength, health, good bodily condition

ṣiḥḥi wholesome, salubrious, healthy (Wehr 503b) 1561

Swahili (J)	-sihi (*v.*)	beg humbly, supplicate, beseech

ṣaḥīḥ veritable, real; authentic (Wehr 503b); **sahi** true, that's right, just, exact, is it not? (JdP 1096a); **sāhi** honest, candid, truthful (Kaye 69b); **ṣahi** true; it is true! (Z&T 136) 1562

Gikuyu (Ben)	thahihi	signature (via Swahili)
Swahili (J)	sahihi (*adj.* + *v.*)	attestation, guarantee, signature

ṣaḥāba Companions of the Prophet Muhammad (Wehr 504a) 1563

Malagasy (Gue)	masoahàba	the Companions (of the Prophet)
Swahili (J)	masahaba	the special friends and companions of Muhammad

ṣāḥib, pl. **ṣuḥba** companion, comrade, friend (Wehr 504a) 1565

Swahili (J)	suhuba, sahibu	a friend, for the common *rafiki*

ṣaḥīfa leaf (in a book or notebook), page (Wehr 505a) 1566

Malagasy (Gue)	msahàfo, msàfo	the holy book, the Qur'an
Swahili (J)	sahifa, sahifu	page of a book, leaf of a book, for the usu. *ukurasa*

ṣaḥn bowl, dish; phonograph record (Wehr 505a) 1567

Acooli (Cra)	caan	plate
Ateso (Kit)	asanit	plate, dish
Bari (Mu)	sani, saniat	dish
Bende (Abe)	iisahaáni	plate
Dholuo (Gor)	san	plate
(Odo)	can / cwan / cuwan	
Digo (MN&Z)	sahani	plate (via Swahili)
Dinka (Id)	thään	dish
Gikuyu (Ben)	thani	plate, saucer (via Swahili)
Kinyarwanda (CAT)	i-sahane	dish, plate
Lega (Bot)	i.sagáni	plate (via Swahili)
Luena (Vet)	disahányi	plate (adaptation of the Swahili word)
Luganda (Sno)	`ssàwaàni, `ssaani, `ssòwaàni	plate; dish (via Swahili)
Madi (Bla)	sàánì / sákānì	plate
	sákānì	record album
Malagasy (Gue)	sahàny	plate (most common word)
Matengo (Yo)	sahâni	plate, dish
Ndogo (Po)	saani	dish
Nyakyusa (Fel)	isahaní	plate (via Swahili)
Rendille (P&G)	saháni	plate (via Swahili)
Runyankore (Ka)	eshohá:ni	dish; plate (via Swahili)
Swahili (J)	sahani	dish, plate

ṣadrīya jacket, vest; chemisette (Kazim: I, 1319b); **ṣadrīya** by corruption **ṣidrīya** jacket (Dozy: I, 823a) 1568

Nyakyusa (Fel)	isíndililа	brassiere, bra (via Swahili)
Swahili (J)	sidiria	a cloth worn by some women just below the breasts to support them, also called *kanchiri*

ṣadaqa alms; charitable; legally prescribed alms tax (Wehr 509a); **sadaxa / sadaxât** alms, sacrifice (JdP 1085a); **sadaka** alms (not compulsory) (Kaye 69a); **sadaga** alms; charity; sacrifice (RL 219b) 1571

Digo (MN&Z)	sadaka	offering, sacrifice (via Swahili)
Malagasy (Gue)	sadàka	sacrifice
Rendille (P&G)	sadákha (?)	libation (of milk) (via Swahili)
Swahili (J)	sadaka	a religious offering, sacrifice, alms

ṣidq truth (Wehr 509a); **ṣādiq** true, sincere (Kazim: I, 1323b) 1573

Swahili (J)	-suduku (*v.*)	verify, ascertain, make sure, prove; accept, concur

ṣādiq true, sincere; reliable; faithful (Wehr 509b) 1575

Swahili (J)	-sadiki (*v.*)	believe, give credence to, accept as true (truthful)

ṣārūj quicklime; mixture of quicklime and arsenic (Kazim: I, 1328a) 1576

Swahili (J)	saruji, seruji	debris made up of lime (when a wall is demolished); concrete, cement, chalk, and sand mixture

ṣirāṭ way, path that spans hell, into which sinners fall (Wehr 511b) 1578

Swahili (J)	sirati	a way or road (used by some Muslims in reference to the way to heaven or hell)

ṣarf expense; spending; money changing (Wehr 513a) **1580**

Malagasy (Gue)	mikoĵisarìfo sarìfa	to serve yourself the necessary, maintenance (of the household, provided to a wife by a husband)
Swahili (J)	sarafu	coin, small change, money; exchange

ṣarfīyāt payments, disbursements (Wehr 513a); **ṣarfīye** wages; pay (RL 269b) **1581a**

Ndogo (Po)	sarafia	pledges; salary

ṣarrāf money changer; cashier (Wehr 513a) **1581b**

Madi (Bla)	sàráfò̀	cashier

maṣrūf expenses (Wehr 513b) **1583**

Swahili (J)	masarufu, masurufu	provisions taken on a journey

ṣarīn, ṣariya mast, pole (Wehr 514a) **1585**

Swahili (J)	mwashiri mhashiri	one of the longitudinal timbers that supports the mast a strong beam, to which the mast is secured in a native vessel

ṣaġīr small; young (Wehr 516a) **1586**

Swahili (J)	saghiri (*adj.*)	small, little, youngest (seldom heard)

ṣaġār impotence, weakness (Kazim: I, 1341b) 1587

Swahili (J)	shoga	a catamite; an impotent male person who associates with women, often as a servant

ṣaġw, ṣaġan inclination; affection, attachment (Wehr 516b) 1588

Swahili (J)	shoga	a term of endearment or familiarity between women

ṣafīḥa plate, sheet (of metal); tin plate (Wehr 517a); **safîhe / safâya** iron container (JdP 1090b); **safiiya** tin (S&A 142b) 1591a

Acooli (Mu)	safia	tin
Bari (Mu)	safia	large tin
Dinka (Id)	safia	tin
Lotuxo (Mu)	asufia	large tin
Ndogo (Po)	safia	tin

ṣafara (*v.*) to whistle (bird, person) (Wehr 517b); **saffar / yisaffir** (*v.*) (II) to whistle (JdP 1088b) 1592

Acooli (Mu)	cufara	metal whistle
Bari (Mu)	sufara	metal whistle
Lotuxo (Mu)	accʊfara	metal whistle
Madi (Bla)	sòfárɨ̀	whistle

ṣufr brass; money (Wehr 517b); **ṣufrīya** copper vase, cauldron (Dozy: I, 835b) 1593

Acooli (Cra)	cùpùriíà, cibìriíà	metal kitchen pot
Gikuyu (Ben)	thaburia, thuburia	open metal cooking pot, saucepan (via Swahili)
Haya (Ka)	ese:fulía	pan; pot (via Swahili)
Rendille (P&G)	subbúrya	metal cooking pot, *sufuria* (via Swahili)
Runyankore (Ka)	esoforíya	cooking pan; pot (via Swahili)
Swahili (J)	sufuria	metal cooking pot (of copper or iron), s.t. very large size

ṣafrā᾽ bile, gall (Wehr 518a) **1595**

Malagasy (Gue)	safòra	name of a disease (causes frequent fainting)
Swahili	safura	a disease causing a swollen or dropsical condition; ankylostomiasis

ṣifr zero (Wehr 518a) **1596**

Digo (MN&Z)	sifuri	zero (via Swahili)
Swahili (J)	sifuri	brass; cipher, naught, zero

ṣāfin clear, limpid; undiluted, pure (Wehr 520a) **1598**

Malagasy (Gue)	soàfy	beautiful and good, very, quite, really
Swahili (J)	safi (+ *v.*), swafi (*adj.*)	clean, pure, bright; honest

ṣaqīʿ frost; ice; hoarfrost (Wehr 520a) **1599**

Swahili (J)	sakitu	hoarfrost

ṣaluba, ṣaliba (*v.*) to be or become hard, solid or rigid (Wehr 521a) **1600**

Swahili (J)	sulubu, usulubu	firmness, strength, vigour

ṣalīb, pl. **ṣulbān, ṣulub** cross (Wehr 521b) **1601**

Gikuyu (Ben)	*mũ*tharaba	cross (for crucifixion) (via Swahili)
Matengo (Häf)	msalaba	cross (via Swahili)
Runyankore (Ka)	omusharába	cross (via Swahili)
Swahili (J)	-sulibi (*v.*)	crucify
	msalaba	a cross, anything in the form of cross

ṣulḥ peace, (re)conciliation (Wehr 522a) **1602**

Malagasy (Gue)	komasolàha	reconciliation (between spouses, arranged by notables)
Swahili (J)	suluhu (+ *v.*) -selehi, -suluhi (*v.*)	peace, agreement to leave off a quarrel, or to come to terms without quarrelling improve, make, agree (with)

ṣāliḥ good; pious (Wehr 523a) **1607**

Swahili	salihi (*adj.*)	good, sound, fitting

ṣalāh salat, the official Islamic prayer (Wehr 524a); **selāt** prayer (RL 231b) **1612**

Gikuyu (Ben)	thara	prayer, collect (via Swahili)
Luganda (Sno)	-saàla (*v.i.*)	pray in a set form, pray in Muslim way (via Swahili *sali*)
Malagasy (Gue)	kosoàly soalà	to perform the Muslim prayer, to do the five prayers of the day Muslim ritual prayer
Runyankore (Ka)	eshâ:ra	prayer (via Swahili)
Swahili (J)	sala	prayer

ṣamġ, pl. **ṣumūġ** gum; resin (Wehr 525b) **1616**

Swahili (J)	sumughu	gum arabic, gum

ṣandūq box (Wehr 526a) **1617**

Acooli (Cra)	càndúùk	box; trunk
(Mu)	canduku	
Ateso (Kit)	esaduku	box
Bari (Mu)	söntuk	box; trunk
Batéké (Cal)	sãnduku	hut
Bende (Abe)	iisandúku	box

Dholuo (Gor)	sanduk	box
(Odo)	canduk	box, trunk
Digo (MN&Z)	sanduku	box (via Swahili)
Dinka (Id)	sunduuk, sanduk, thanduk	box
Gbéa (Cal)	sanduku	hut
Gmbwaga (Cal)	sanduku	hut
Gikuyu (Ben)	*i*thandũkũ	box, locker; suitcase (via Swahili)
Haya (Ka)	eishandî:ko	coffin (via Swahili)
Kamba (Mbi)	ĩsandũkũ	box (via Swahili)
Kikongo (Lam)	sāndukù	crate, box; burden, trunk
Kinyarwanda (CAT)	i-sandugu, i-sanduku	box (via Swahili)
lhukonzo (Bal)	sanduko	box
Lingala (Ev)	sandúku	crate, trunk, chest (via Swahili)
Lotuxo (Mu)	asennúk, asennuxi	box; trunk
luena (Vet)	sandúku	hut
Luganda (Sno)	\`ssanduùko	box; chest (via Swahili)
Lunyankole (Dav)	sanduko	box, chest
Lunyoro (Dav)	sanduko	box, chest
Madi (Bla)	sàndúù / sàndúkù	suitcase; box; briefcase; coffin (via Swahili)
Ndogo (Po)	sanduk	hut
Ngombe (Rd)	sandúku	hut, trunk
Rendille (P&G)	sandúukh	large box, trunk (made of metal or wood, for storing or transporting goods) (via Swahili)
Runyankore (Ka)	esha:ndû:kye	hut (via Swahili)
Sango (Bou)	sàndúgù	hut, trunk, canteen
Swahili (J)	sanduku	box, trunk, case

ṣandal sandalwood (Wehr 526a) **1618**

Swahili (J)	sandali	sandalwood from the tree msandali

ṣunʿ benefit, favor (Wehr 526b) 1619

Swahili (J)	suna (*adj.*)	good, commendable, meritorious
	Suni	good traditions; one of the Sunni sect

ṣanʿa trade, occupation (Wehr 526b) 1620

Swahili (J)	sanaa (+ *v.*)	art, work of art, skilled handicraft

ṣanf, ṣinf kind, sort, specimen (Wehr 527a) 1621

Swahili (J)	-sanifu (*v.*)	to work with skill, compose, invent

ṣanam idol, image (Wehr 527b) 1622

Digo (MN&Z)	sanamu	image, likeness, idol (via Swahili)
Malagasy (Gue)	sanàmo	image, drawing, statue, idol
Swahili (J)	sanamu	idol, image

ṣanaubar stone pine (Pinus pinea) (Wehr 527b); pine (S, F, E) (Gh: II, 13337) 1623

Swahili (J)	sunobari	deal, pine wood of the tree msunobari

ṣāba (*v.*) to hit; to hold true, be to the point (II) to agree, consent, approve (Wehr 528a) 1624

Swahili (J)	-zaba (*v.*) (?)	hit, beat

ṣaub direction (Wehr 528b); rain (Kazim: I, 1381b) 1625

Swahili (J)	shumbi	deep water, depth; a heap

muṣība misfortune (Wehr 529a) 1627

Malagasy (Gue)	mosìba	mourning, misfortune
Swahili (J)	msiba	calamity, misfortune

ṣāta (*v.*) to ring (Wehr 529a); **ṣaut** sound; voice (Wehr 529a) 1628

Digo (MN&Z)	sauti	voice (via Swahili)
Malagasy (Gue)	saòty	voice
Swahili (J)	sauti	voice, sound, noise

ṣūra form; image, picture (Wehr 530a); **sûra** photo, image, illustration (JdP 1148b) 1629

Digo (MN&Z)	sura	appearance, face (via Swahili)
Dinka (Id)	sura, thura	picture
Malagasy (Gue)	sôra	visage, face, facial features
Ndogo (Po)	sura	effigy; drawing; board; portrait; statue
Swahili (J)	sura	form, appearance, look, expression, face, likeness

ṣūf wool (Wehr 531a) 1632

Swahili (J)	sufi, usufi, sufu, usufu	the fine soft silky cotton from the pods of the tree msufi; kapok

ṣūfī Islamic mystic, Sufi (Wehr 531a) 1633

Swahili (J)	sufii	a hermit, dervish; saint

ṣāma (*v.*) to abstain; to fast (Wehr 531b); **sam** (*v.*) to fast (JdP 1106a) 1634

Madi (Bla)	ɪ̄sāɪ̄mɔ̀ (*v.*)	to fast

al-ṣaum fasting during the month of Ramadan (Wehr 531b) 1635

Swahili (J)	tumu	fasting
	saumu (+ *v.*)	fasting

ṣiyām fasting (Wehr 531b) 1636

Madi (Bla)	sáɪ̄mɔ̀	fasting

ṣaiḥ crying, clamor (Wehr 532a) **1637**

Swahili (J)	-sihi (*v.*) siaha	beg humbly, supplicate, beseech, entreat a loud cry

ṣāra (*v.*) to become (Wehr 532b) **1638**

Swahili (J)	-siri (*v.*)	become, change into (seldom used)

ṣāʿa (*v.*) to disperse, disseminate; to frighten, to terrify, to strike with terror; to come unexpectedly on s.o. (Kazim: I, 1384b) **1639**

Swahili (J)	-sai (*v.*)	challenge a person to fight or compete in a game

ṣīnīya a large, round metal plate with raised rim, esp. one made of copper, used as baking tin, serving tray and table top (Wehr 533b); **siniiya** tray (S&A 148b) **1641**

Madi (Bla)	sὲníà	tray; roundabout
Ndogo (Po)	sania	tray
Swahili (J)	sinia	a tray – commonly a circular metal tray for carrying food

Ḍād

ḍāma checkers (Wehr 534a) **1642**

Swahili (J)	dhumma	dominoes, game of dice

ḍabaṭa (*v.*) to grab; to keep; to have under control; to do accurately (Wehr 534a) **1643**

Malagasy (Gue)	mikodhibìty	to worry about
Swahili (J)	-dhibiti (*v.*)	guard, protect against, manage (seldom used, probably because it sounds similar to *thabiti*)

ḍābiṭ officer (Wehr 534b); **dâbit / dubbât** officer (JdP 344b) **1643a**

Madi (Bla)	dábɨ̀	officer (police, military etc.)

maḍbūṭ exact, correct, right, precise (Wehr 535a) **1644**

Swahili (J)	madhubuti (*adj.*)	precise, accurate, trustworthy, honest, reliable, strong, firm, durable, resolute, solid

ḍiḥk laugh(ing) (Wehr 536a) **1645**

Swahili (J)	dhihaka	mockery, ridicule, scorn

ḍuḥan forenoon (Wehr 536b) **1646**

Swahili (J)	dhuha	the period between sunrise and noon

ḍurr, **ḍarr** damage, injury, hurt (Wehr 537b); **durr** deliberate wrong, revenge, nuisance, grudge (JdP 403b) **1651**

Swahili (J)	dhara	hurt, harm, violence
	-dhuru (*v.*)	hurt, damage, cause loss or injury to, harm

ḍarūra necessity, stress, constraint; distress, plight (Wehr 538a) **1652**

Swahili (J)	dharura	sudden unexpected happenings, commotion

ḍaraba (*v.*) to beat, strike (Wehr 538b) **1654**

Malagasy (Gue)	daròba, dharòba	cyclone, storm
Swahili (J)	dharuba	stroke, blow, rush – blow of an axe, sudden calamity; rarely, in arithmetic, multiplication

ḍarba blow; shock (Wehr 539b) 1655

Swahili (J)	dhoruba	a hurricane, storm of wind and rain, tempest

ḍawārib, pl. of **ḍārib** beating (Wehr 540b); **ḍawārib** birds of passage (Kazim: II, 18b) 1656

Swahili (J)	zawaridi	Java sparrow, Padda oryzivora

aḍraʿ humble, submissive (Kazim: II, 23b) 1657

Swahili (J)	dharau (+ *v.*) (?)	scorn, slight, despise

ḍaʿīf feeble; delicate, impotent (Wehr 542a) 1658

Swahili (J)	dhaifu (*adj.*)	weak, feeble, infirm, powerless; deficient, insignificant, mean, base, despicable

ḍamīr heart; mind; (independent or suffixed) personal pronoun (Wehr 545b) 1661

Malagasy (Gue)	mikodhamìry	to think
Swahili (J)	dhamira, dhamiri	real intention, secret thought, mind, resolution, inner consciousness, conscience

ḍamīn responsible; warrantor, guarantor (Wehr 546a) 1663

Swahili (J)	dhamini	trustee

ḍamāna guaranty, surety, warrant(y) (Wehr 546a) 1664

Malagasy (Gue)	dhoamàna	responsibility
Swahili (J)	dhamana	surety, guarantee, certificate

maḍmūn guaranteed, insured; meaning (Wehr 546a) 1665

Swahili (J)	madhumuni	intention, purpose

ḍai' loss (Wehr 547b) **1667**

Swahili (J)	-dhii (*v.*)	waste away, pine, be spoiled, be consumed; be hard driven, be ruined, be distressed

ḍīq narrowness; restriction; oppression, anguish; distress; anger, annoyance (Wehr 549a); **dîxe / dîxât** anxiety, torment, oppression, moral suffering (JdP 393b) **1670**

Swahili (J)	dhiki (+ *v.*)	narrowness, want of space, confinement; being pressed, annoyance, distress

Ṭā'

ṭābūr battalion; (*eg.*) line, single file (of soldiers, of persons walking one behind the other) (Wehr 550a) **1671a**

Madi (Bla)	tàbúrù	parade, marching

ṭāqīya white cotton skullcap (often worn under the tarboosh) (Wehr 550a); **tâgiye / tawâgi** hat, chechia, cap, calotte (JdP 1165a); **tāgiya** cap, skullcap, hairstyle (RL 75a); **ṭāgīyé** white cap (RL 289b); **tagiiya** hat (S&A 151a) **1672**

Dinka (Id)	takia	cap
Madi (Bla)	tɛ́gíà	hat
Ndogo (Po)	tagia	hat

ṭibb medicine (Wehr 550b) **1674**

Swahili (J)	tiba	medicine

ṭabīb doctor (Wehr 550b) **1675**

Swahili (J)	tabibu	doctor, medical man

ṭabīʿa nature; character (Wehr 552a) **1679**

Malagasy (Gue)	tabìa, toabìa	character, ways of behavior (always in negative sense), fault, sin, shame
Pokomo (Wü)	tabia	character
Swahili (J)	tabia	condition, state, nature

ṭabaq plate; dish, shallow bowl (Wehr 553a) **1682**

Madi (Bla)	tá'bāgà	a lid or cover; hat, head dress
Ndogo (Po)	tabaka	woven tray with colorful herbs

ṭabaqa layer; stratum (Wehr 553a); **tabge / tabgât** fold (JdP 1159a) **1683**

Swahili (J)	tabaka	anything laid on another – lid, cover, lining (of a dress), layer, row, stratum, stage, story (of a house)
	-tabiki (*v.*)	lie close to, stick to, line, cover, be attached to

ṭāḥūn, ṭāḥūna mill, grinder (Wehr 554b); **ṭahûna** mill (Daf 133); **tâhûna** mill (JdP 1167b); **tahuuna** grinding mill (S&A 151a); **ṭāḥūna** mill (RT 286a) **1689**

Dinka (Id)	tɔla	crusher

ṭarrār tambourine player (Wehr 554b) **1689a**

Malagasy (Gue)	tàry	single-skin tambourine
Swahili (J)	tari	a kind of small drum

ṭaraʿa (*v.*) to descend, break in, to happen unexpectedly; to occur (Wehr 554b) **1690**

Swahili (J)	taraa (*conj.*)	if

ṭarab joy, pleasure; music (Wehr 555a) 1691

Swahili (J)	tarabu	music of *gambusi, zeze*, accompanied by singers

muṭrib musician (Wehr 555a) 1692

Swahili (J)	mutribu	a player of the *gambusi, zeze*

ṭarbūš tarboosh (Wehr 555b) 1693

Dinka (Id)	tarbush	hat
Madi (Bla)	tèrèbúsì	hat, helmet
Swahili (J)	tarbushi	a tarboosh, a fez, red cap with tassel

ṭarz type, model, make, sort, kind; fashion, style (Wehr 557a) 1695

Swahili (J)	taraza, tarizo	border or edging, woven on to turbans or waistcloths, giving the effect of a narrow ornamental braid of silk

ṭaraf utmost part; **min ṭaraf** on behalf of (Wehr 558a) 1698

Swahili (J)	mintarafu (*conj.*)	concerning, with regard to, regarding, on behalf

ṭarīq way; road; path (Wehr 559a) 1701

Swahili (J)	tariki	road, path, way, usu. *njia*

ṭarīqa manner; method; faith, religion; religious brotherhood (Wehr 559a); **tarîxa / turux** way, brotherhood, sect (JdP 1189a) 1702

Malagasy (Gue)	toarìka	Muslim religious brotherhood

ṭurumba pump (Wehr 559b) 1702a

Dinka (Id)	turumba	gas station, pump
Madi (Bla)	tùrúmbà	bicycle pump; petrol station

ṭāʿūn pestilence (Wehr 560b) 1704

Swahili (J)	tauni	plague, pestilence, an epidemic (usu. refers to bubonic plague)

ṭafar crupper (of the saddle) (Wehr 562a) 1705

Swahili (J)	mtafura	crupper – the strap fastened to the saddle passing under the tail of a horse, donkey

ṭufāl[12] potter's clay; argil; clay, loam (Wehr 562b) 1707

Acooli (Cra)	mùtàfalì	brick (via Swahili)
Ciluba (Kab)	dìtàfwadì	brick (via Swahili)
Digo (MN&Z)	tofali	brick (via Swahili)
Dinka (Id)	tup	brick
Gikuyu (Ben)	ituBari, iturubarĩ	brick, cement block (via Swahili)
Runyankore (Ka)	i:tafâ:ri	brick (via Swahili)
Swahili (J)	tofali	brick, tile

ṭalaba (*v.*) to look, search (Wehr 563b); **tâlab / yitâlib** (*v.*) (III) to ask, claim, demand (JdP 1171b) 1707a

Madi (Bla)	ītālābò (*v.*)	to order a meal, car etc.; summon

maṭlūb wanted (in classified ads); desire (Wehr 564a) 1709

Swahili (J)	matilaba	desire, wish, purpose

12 Arabic and Persian *tufal* ("clay"), perhaps from Latin, *cf.* French *tuffeau* ("chalk") (Knappert 1972–73: 287 n. 8).

ṭilasm, ṭillasm, pl. **ṭalāsim** talisman, a seal, or the like, inscribed with mysterious words or characters; charm, magical combination of words (Wehr 564b) 1711

Swahili (J)	talasimu	talisman, charm, magic diagram

ṭalīʿa front row (Wehr 565b) 1711a

Malagasy (Gue)	talè	leader, the strongest

maṭlaʿ rise, time of rising (of celestial bodies); point of ascent (Wehr 565b) 1712

Swahili (J)	matlaa, matlai	sunrise, the east, east wind, morning wind

ṭāliʿ rising (Wehr 566a); **ṭāliʿ** s.o. who looks, who looks down; s.o. who examines, considers (Kazim: II, 98b) 1713

Malagasy (Gue)	mikotoàly	to study, learn (in a book)
Swahili (J)	-talii (*v.*)	inquire into, look into, examine

ṭalaqat (*v.*) to be divorced (II) to repudiate, divorce (Wehr 566a); **talag / yatlig** (*v.*) to release, detach, let go, liberate, give up (JdP 1172a); **tallag / yitallig** (*v.*) (II) to divorce from, repudiate a woman (JdP 1176a); **attâlago / yittâlago** (*v.*) (VI) to separate by divorcing, divorce (JdP 202b) 1714

Madi (Bla)	ītālà (*v.*)	to be away from home; be out
	ītālāgò (*v.*)	to divorce

ṭalāq divorce (Wehr 567a) 1715

Nyakyusa (Fel)	italaka	divorce (via Swahili)
Malagasy (Gue)	talàka, toalàka	repudiation
Ngh'wele (Leg)	talaka	divorce (via Swahili)
Swahili (J)	talaka	divorce

ṭalīq freed, released, set free (Wehr 567b) 1716

Swahili (J)	-taliki (*v.*)	divorce

ṭalā (*v.*) to paint, daub; to coat, overlay, plate (Wehr 568a) 1717

Swahili (J)	-taliza (*v.*)	smear, plaster – with clay or mortar, so as to give a smooth surface to the wall of a house

ṭimm large quantity; sea (Wehr 568a); **ṭimm** debris, garbage, litter that water rejects (Kazim: II, 105b) 1718

Swahili (J)	tama	dirt, rubbish, filth, dregs

ṭumāṭa tomato (Wehr 569a) 1720

Malagasy (Gue)	matimàty	tomato

ṭamiʿa (*v.*) to covet, desire (Wehr 569b) 1721

Digo (MN&Z)	tamaa	desire, lust, hope
	-tamani	to desire
	-tumaini	to hope, to expect (via Swahili)
Haya (M&L)	etamaa	desire (via Swahili)
Malagasy (Gue)	kotamàny	to desire
	tàma, tamà	hope, expectation
Swahili (J)	tamaa (*n.*)	desire, lust
	tumai (*v.*)	desire, covet
	tamani (*n.*)	desire, covetousness; also hope, trust
	-tumaini (*v.* + *n.* + *adj.*)	hope, trust, be confident, rely on

ṭahāra cleanness, purity; cultic purity (*Isl. law*); circumcision (Wehr 570b) 1724

Swahili (J)	tohara	purity, cleanness (esp. in a ceremonial sense); circumcision

ṭāhir clean, pure (Wehr 571a) 1725

Malagasy (Gue)	mikotahìry	to circumcise, to perform a ceremony of circumcision
Swahili (J)	tahiri (+ *v.*)	a ceremonially clean person

ṭūb brick(s) (Wehr 571b); **tûb** piece of brick, brick (JdP 1220a) 1726

Bari (Mu)	tup	brick
Dinka (Id)	tup	brick
Ndogo (Po)	tobo	brick

ṭāsa round, shallow drinking cup made of metal (Wehr 572b); **ṭāsa** general term for metal containers (RT 293a) 1728

Swahili (J)	tasa	cup, jug, mug

ṭayyiʿ obedient, compliant, submissive (Wehr 573a) 1730

Swahili (J)	-tii (*v.* + *adj.*)	obey, submit to, be docile

ṭāʿa obedience, submissiveness; pious deed (*Isl. law*) (Wehr 573a) 1731

Swahili (J)	taa	obedience
Swahili (M.A.M.)	taa (*adj.*)	exalted, sacred, holy

ṭāfa (*v.*) to [turn] about; to circumambulate (Wehr 573b); **tôb**, pl. **tîbân** cloth, fabric, roll of 6 meters of fabric (JdP 1217b); **ṭāfa** (*v.*) to turn around s.th. (Kazim: II, 120b); **ṭāf** s.th. that turns; neck wool (Kazim: II, 121a); **tōb**, pl. **tībān** men's clothing (RL 80a). Arabs of Sudan "dress with shirts (*tob, khaleg*) made from strips of cloth sewn together" (Baumann and Westermann: 307) 1733

Madi (Bla)	tó'bù	a sari-like northern Sudanese woman's dress

ṭauf round, circuit; wall, enclosure (Wehr 574a) 1734

Swahili (J)	tufe	a ball, a game of ball

ṭawwāfa patrol boat (Wehr 574a); torch that is used when walking the streets during the night (Dozy: II, 69b) 1736

Swahili (J)	tawafa	a candle; a candelabrum

ṭūfān inundation (Wehr 574a); hurricane, storm at sea, waterspout (Kazim: II, 121b) 1737

Swahili (J)	tufani	storm, hurricane

ṭāʾifa part; sect; party, faction; religious minority (Wehr 574b) 1738

Digo (MN&Z)	taifa	nation (via Swahili)
Swahili (J)	taifa	a nation, a tribe (generally *kabila*)

ṭāq kind of clothes (F: III, 80a) 1740

Swahili (J)	taka	a length of calico or cloth (in pieces of about 30 yards)

ṭāla (*v.*) to be or become long; to last long (II) to lengthen, grow longer (Wehr 575a); **ṭawāla, ṭiwāla** (*prep.*) during, throughout; along, alongside of (Wehr 576a); **tawwal** (*v.*) (II) to last, linger, stay long (JdP 1196a); **ṭāla** (*v.*) to be long, last a long time (II) to make longer, extend (Kazim: II, 123a); **tawaali** (*adv.*) immediately, straight away, directly (S&A 152b) 1742

Madi (Bla)	tɔ̀álì (*adv.*)	immediately

mustaṭīl long, oblong; a rectangle (Wehr 576b) 1744

Swahili (J)	mstatili	an oblong

ṭayyib good; well, in good health (Wehr 578a) 1746

Swahili (J)	-taibu (*v.* + *adv.*)	be good, be well

ṭīb goodness; perfume (Wehr 578a) 1747

Swahili (J)	tibu	perfume, scent made from ground sandalwood mixed with rose water and cloves

ṭāba a sort of game that is played by throwing four pieces of wood cut by hand from palm branches or other wood, such that one side is flat and white, and the other side has bark. To count the throws, a bin is divided into four ranks, each of which has nine boxes (Kazim: II, 127a) 1748

Swahili (J)	tiabu	a game played by throwing bits of a stick, and watching how they fall

ṭayyāra airplane, aircraft; kite (toy) (Wehr 579a); **ṭā'ira** airplane, aircraft (Wehr 579b); **ṭaiyāra** airplane; kite (toy) (RL 295b) 1751

Dinka (Id)	taiara	airplane
Madi (Bla)	tìárì	airplane
Swahili (J)	tiara	a kite (child's toy)

Ẓā'

ẓarīf elegant, graceful, charming (Wehr 581a) 1755

Swahili (J)	mdirifu (?)	a person in easy circumstances

ẓulm wrong; iniquity; injustice; oppression, tyranny (Wehr 582b); **dulum** injustice, wrong, fault, insult, crime (JdP 400b) 1757

Digo (MN&Z)	-zulumu	to oppress, to treat unjustly (via Swahili)
Malagasy (Gue)	kodolòmo, kodholòmo, dholòmo	to hurt, do evil, commit injustice, be tyrannical, deceive
Swahili (J)	dhulumu (+ *v.*)	injustice, fraud, oppression, violence

ẓālim tyrant, oppressor (Wehr 583a) 1759

Swahili (J)	dhalimu (*adj.* + *v.*)	oppressive, tyrannical

maẓlūm ill-treated, unjustly treated, tyrannized (Wehr 583a); **madelūm, maẕlūm, maẓlūm, maḏlūm** injured; having a claim to make (RL 168a) 1760

Dinka (Id)	madhuluum	an appeal, court (being cheated)

ẓann opinion, idea (Wehr 583a) 1762

Malagasy (Gue)	mikodhoàny	to think, believe
Swahili (J)	dhana	thought, idea, notion, suspicion
	mdhana	bad luck, a bad omen

ẓahara (*v.*) to be or become visible, clear, apparent (Wehr 583b) 1764

Swahili (J)	-dhahiri (+ *adj.*) -dhihiri (*v.*)	make clear, show, explain

zahari / zahariyîn blue, blue gray (JdP 1136b) 1765

Madi (Bla)	zákārì	blue (color); clothing whitener (trademark)

ẓuhr, pl. **aẓhār** midday prayer (Wehr 584b) 1766

Malagasy (Gue)	adohòry	the hour of the noon prayer
Swahili (J)	adhuhuri	noon, between noon and 2 PM, one of the hours of the Muslim prayer

maẓhar appearance, external make-up; bearer or object of a phenomenon (Wehr 584b) 1767

Swahili (J)	madahiro	elegance, gravity of gait

ʿAin

ʿabada (*v.*) to serve, adore (Wehr 586b); **abad / yaʿabid** (*v.*) to adore, love a lot (JdP 24a) 1769

Digo (MN&Z)	-abudu	to worship (via Swahili)
Malagasy (Gue)	koabòdo, koʿabòdo, koãbòdo	to worship (God)
Swahili (J)	-abudu (*v.*)	serve, adore, used only of religious worship and service

ʿabd slave, serf (Wehr 586b) 1770

Swahili (J)	abd	servant, slave (only used in such names as Abdallah, Abdul-Rahmani, etc.)

ʿibāda adoration (Wehr 586b) 1771

Swahili (J)	ibada	worship, divine service; regular service, habit, characteristics

maʿbad place of worship; house of God, temple (Wehr 586b) 1772

Swahili (J)	maabadi	a place of worship

maʿbūd worshiped; deity; idol (Wehr 587a) 1774

Swahili (J)	maabudu	worship; object of worship

ʿabara (*v.*) to cross (II) to determine the weight of a coin, weigh (Wehr 587a); **abbar / yiʿabbir** (*v.*) (II) to measure a surface (JdP 26a) 1775

Digo (MN&Z)	abiriya	passenger (via Swahili)
Swahili (J)	-abiri (*v.*)	pass over, cross over (i.e. a river, lake, sea); but also used for "travel as a passenger by any kind of conveyance"
	abiria	a passenger

ʿibra admonition (Wehr 587b) 1776

Swahili (J)	ibra, ibura	s.th. wonderful, a miracle, a very rare occurrence; stain, speck, blot

taʿbīr interpretation (of a dream) (Wehr 588a) 1777

Swahili (J)	-tabiri (*v.*)	interpret, explain, expound

iʿtibār respect, esteem (Wehr 588a) 1778

Swahili (J)	itibari	trust, faith, respect, esteem, respectability

ʿatb censure, blame, rebuke, reproof (Wehr 589a) 1779

Swahili (J)	-atibu (*v.*)	blame, reproach, find fault with

ʿajab astonishment (Wehr 591a); **ajab** amazing thing (JdP 71a); **'ejeb** amazing thing (Z&T 124) 1782

Digo (MN&Z)	ajabu	marvel, wonder, miracle (via Swahili)
Malagasy (Gue)	kotaʿaĵàbo, kotaĵàb̠o	to marvel at, marvel, wonder
Swahili (J)	ajabu (*v. + adj. + adv.*)	wonder, be astonished, feel surprise

ʿajīb wonderful, admirable (Wehr 591b) 1784

Swahili (J)	ajib, ajibu (*adj. + adv.*)	wonder, astonishment, admiration

uʿjūba wondrous thing; marvel, miracle (Wehr 591b) 1785

Swahili (J)	ujuba	fearlessness, violence, tyranny, oppression

muʿjib causing admiration, admirable (Wehr 591b) 1786

Swahili (J)	mjibu	an affable, pleasant, accessible person

ʿajūz old woman; old man (Wehr 592a) 1788

Dholuo (Odo)	ajuc	old man
Swahili (J)	ajuza	a very old woman

ʿājiz weak (Wehr 592b) 1789

Swahili (J)	ajizi	slackness, remissness, lateness

muʿjiza miracle (esp. one performed by a prophet) (Wehr 592b) 1790

Malagasy (Gue)	moĵòza, mĵòza, sometimes miĵoza	amazing thing, miracle, prodigy, wonder
Swahili (J)	mwujiza, muujiza	anything wonderful, extraordinary, supernatural, a wonder, a surprise, a miracle

ʿajam barbarians, non-Arabs; Persians (Wehr 593b); **al-ʿajam** Persian (Wehr 593b); **ʿajamī** barbaric, non-Arab; Persian (Wehr 593b); **ajami** ignorant, ignoramus, dazed (JdP 72a) 1796

Swahili (J)	Uajemi, Ajemi	Persia, Iran

maʿjūn paste, cream (cosmetics) (Wehr 594a) 1798

Swahili (J)	majuni	a preparation of opium, Indian hemp, etc. with sugar and other ingredients made up into a sweetmeat (strongly intoxicating)

ʿidda iddat, legally prescribed period of waiting during which a woman may not remarry after being widowed or divorced (*Isl. law*) (Wehr 595a) 1800

Swahili (J)	eda	time of customary ceremonial mourning, or seclusion of a woman after a death or divorce

ʿidād number (Wehr 595a) 1802

Malagasy (Gue)	indàdy, ʿidàdy, idàdy	number, large number, count
Swahili (J)	idadi	reckoning, counting, number from the point of view of magnitude, computation

mustaʿidd prepared; inclined; predisposed (Wehr 595b) 1804

Swahili (J)	stadi	an experienced, capable, skilled person

ʿadara (*v.*) to be bold; courageous (Kazim: II, 189a) 1805

Swahili (J)	hodari (*adj.*)	strong, firm, stable; active, energetic, brave, earnest

ʿadas lentil(s) (Wehr 595b) 1806

Madi (Bla)	ádɛ̄sɨ̀	lentil
Swahili (J)	adesi	lentils

ʿidl equal, tantamount, corresponding (Wehr 596b) 1809

Swahili (J)	idili	effort, enthusiasm, perseverance

ʿādil just, honest (Wehr 597a) 1813

Swahili (J)	adili (*adj.*)	right, righteous

ʿadīm not having, lacking; deprived (of) (Wehr 597b) **1814**

Swahili (J)	adimu (*adj.*)	rare, unobtainable

ʿadn Eden, Paradise; **ʿadan** Aden (city in southern Arabia) (Wehr 598a) **1816**

Swahili (J)	Aden	the garden of Eden; Aden, the port

maʿdin, pl. **maʿādin** mine; metal (Wehr 598a) **1817**

Swahili (J)	madini	metal (of any kind)

ʿadā (*v.*) to run; to pass; to engage in aggressive; to assail (Wehr 598a) **1818**

Swahili (J)	-adua (*v.*) (?)	make an offering to the spirits, or prepare an charm against the effects of the evil eye

ʿadūw enemy (Wehr 599a) **1819**

Digo (MN&Z)	adui	enemy (via Swahili)
Malagasy (Gue)	adòy, andòy	enemy
Swahili (J)	adui	enemy, opponent

maʿdiya ferry, ferryboat (Wehr 599b); **madiiya** ferry (S&A 128b) **1820a**

Madi (Bla)	màdíà	ferry

ʿaḏāb, pl. **aʿḏiba** pain, torment, torture; punishment (Wehr 600a) **1823**

Bende (Abe)	azaábhu	fine
	-azíbhu (*v.*)	punish
Malagasy (Gue)	adhàbo	punishment
Swahili (J)	adhabu	punishment
	-adhibu (*v.*)	punish

ʿuḏr, pl. **aʿḏār** excuse (Wehr 600a) 1824

Swahili (J)	udhuru (+ *v.*)	excuse, pretext, reason; need; opportunity

ʿ R B (*v.*) (II) to Arabicize; to translate into Arabic (X) to become an Arab (Wehr 601a) 1826

Gikuyu (Ben)	*ũ*thitarabu	civilization, culture (via Swahili)
Swahili (J)	-staarabu (*v.* + *adj.*)	to become understanding, wise, civilized

ʿarab (*coll.*) Arabs (Wehr 601a) 1827

Anywa (Reh)	ārābā	Arab person; small sharp knife for surgery
Gikuyu (Ben)	*Mw*arabu	an Arab (via Swahili)
Kikongo (Swa)	Mulábu, pl. Balábu	one of the Arabs; an old Arab slaveboy; Muslim
Kinyarwanda (CAT)	Umw-ārabu	Arab (via Swahili)
Luganda (Sno)	Mùwalabù	Arab (via Swahili)
Malagasy (Gue)	Aràbo	Arab, dignified man, well dressed, elegant
Nyakyusa (Fel)	umwalabu	Arab (via Swahili)
Swahili (J)	mwarabu	Arab

ʿarabīya carriage, vehicle (Wehr 601b); **arabiye / arabât** big car, vehicle, truck (JdP 178b); **arabiiya** car (S&A 89b) 1828a

Acooli (Mu)	arabiya	vehicle
Bari (Mu)	arabiya	vehicle
Dinka (Id)	arabia	car
	arabiya	cart
Lotuxo (Mu)	arabiya, arabiyaa'	vehicle
Madi (Bla)	àràbɨ́à	car; vehicles in general
Ndogo (Po)	arabia	wagon, truck, cart

iʿrāb manifestation; desinential inflection (Wehr 601b) **1829**

Swahili (J)	irabu	a vowel sign in writing Arabic

ʿurbūn, **ʿarabūn** earnest money; pledge (Wehr 602a) **1830**

Swahili (J)	arabuni	a deposit paid on an article in advance as a guarantee

ʿurs, **ʿurus** marriage; wedding, wedding feast (Wehr 602b); **iris** wedding party, marriage (JdP 611b) **1832a**

Madi (Bla)	írīsì	wedding

ʿarūs bridegroom (Wehr 602b) **1833**

Digo (MN&Z)	arusi / harusi	wedding (via Swahili)
Kiw'oso (K&O)	-ar'úsi	wedding
Malagasy (Gue)	haròsy, aròsy	weddings, wedding, solemn wedding, occasion of great festivities
Swahili (J)	arusi	nuptials, wedding

ʿaruḍa (*v.*) to be or become wide (Wehr 603a); **ʿaraḍa** (*v.*) to become visible, appear; to occur (II) to expose; to insinuate, allude (Wehr 603a) **1835**

Swahili (J)	-aridhia (*v.*)	explain, inform, set before

ʿarḍ, pl. **ʿurūḍ** breadth; presentation, demonstration; exhibition; merchandise (Wehr 603b) **1836**

Swahili (J)	gwaride	drill, parade

ʿarīf knowing; expert, specialist (Wehr 606a) **1839**

Swahili (J)	-arifu (*v.* + *adj.*)	inform, tell (esp. by letter)

maʿrifa knowledge, information (Wehr 606b) **1841**

Digo (MN&Z)	maarifwa	wisdom, knowledge, intelligence (via Swahili)
Swahili (J)	maarifa	knowledge, intelligence, information, news; a plan, means of getting over a difficulty

taʿrīf announcement, notification, information (Wehr 606b) **1842**

Swahili (J)	taarifu	a report, either written or spoken

taʿrīfa notification, information, apprising (Wehr 606b) **1843**

Digo (MN&Z)	taarifa	information (via Swahili)
Swahili (J)	taarifa	a report, either written or spoken

maʿrūf known, well-known; universally accepted (Wehr 607a) **1844**

Swahili (J)	maarufu	well-known, known, famous, well-informed

ʿaraq arrack, a strong colorless liquor maid of raisins, milky white when diluted with water (Wehr 607b); **argi** millet alcohol (JdP 183a); **ɛaragī** fermented drink made from dates (RT 307a) **1847**

Acooli (Cra)	àrɛgɛ̀	arrack
(Mu)	arɛgɛ	brandy (native); whiskey
Bari (Mu)	wörögi	brandy (native); whiskey
Lingala (Ev)	álɛgɛ	arrack, alcohol
Lotuxo (Mu)	awarigi	brandy (native); whiskey
Malagasy (Kna)	arafàna[13]	palmwine

13 Knappert (1999: 212) states: "The Malagasy word *arafàna* (palmwine) puzzled me for some time. It looks like a passive noun and could well be native from a morphophonological point of view. But it also looks deceptively like Arabic *ʿaraq*, Swahili *araki*, Malay *arak* (palmwine, gin) – but how to account for the *f*? Finally I found Malagasy passive forms like *doafana* (what has been beaten) from a basic form *doàka* (to beat). It follows that one can regard the Malagasy *aràfana* as a derivative from the presumed loanword **àraka* not now recorded in the language in that form."

Sango (Bou)	ɛ́rɛ́gɛ̀	alcohol distilled locally from a mixture of maize and cassava; imported alcohol
Swahili (J)	araka	arrack, used of any intoxicating liquor

ʿizza power; honor, glory (Wehr 609b) **1850**

Malagasy (Gue)	èzi, ièzi	power (royal, political), potency, order (of a king)
Swahili (J)	enzi (+ *v.*)	power, might, dominion
	ezi	might, power

ʿazīz respected, distinguished, notable; rare; precious, costly, valuable (Wehr 609b) **1851**

Swahili (J)	azizi (+ *adj.*)	a rarity, curiosity, costly thing, treasure

ʿazara (*v.*) to censure, rebuke, reprove (II) to censure (Wehr 610a) **1853**

Swahili (J)	-aziri (*v.*)	slander, disparage, bring into disrepute
	izara	disgrace, shame

ʿizrāʾīl Azrael, the angel of death (Wehr 610b) **1854**

Swahili (J)	Izraili, Israfil	the angel of death

ʿuzul unarmed, defenseless (Wehr 611a) **1855**

Swahili (J)	uzulu (+ *v.*)	abdication, discharge

ʿazīma determination, firm intention; resolution, decision; incantation (Wehr 611b) **1857**

Swahili (J)	azima, azimio	intention, resolve, purpose, scheme, plans, program
	azima	a charm, talisman

ʿuzhūl light and agile (Kazim: II, 247b) 1858

Swahili (J)	uzuhali	gentleness, slowness

taʿziya consolation; condolence (Wehr 612a) 1859

Swahili (J)	tanzia	news of a death, announcement of a funeral

ʿaskarī military, army (in compounds) (Wehr 613a) 1862

Acooli (Cra)	àcekèrè	soldier
	cȍrkaálî	
(Mu)	acɛkɛrɛ	
Bari (Mu)	asɛkɛr	soldier
Digo (MN&Z)	asikari	soldier, policeman, guard, watchman (via Swahili)
Dinka (Id)	alathker	soldier
Gikuyu (Ben)	thigari	soldiery, police; soldier, policeman; companionship, consorting together (*cf.* Swahili)
Lotuxo (Mu)	ɔl'ɔsɛŋɛr, ɔsɛŋɛr	soldier
Luganda (Sno)	mùserikalè (?)	soldier (via Swahili)
Madi (Bla)	àsɛ́kɛ̄rɛ̀ / àsɨ̀kárɨ̀	soldier (via Swahili)
Malagasy (Gue)	sikàry, asikàry[14]	soldiers
Matengo (Yo)	lisilíkali	soldier
Ndogo (Po)	askeri	military
Pokot (Cra)	sìrkáalìyɔ́n	soldier (via Swahili)
Rendille (P&G)	iskár	soldier(s); police; gamewarden(s) Refers to any uniformed officer(s) in a position of authority (via Swahili)
Swahili (J)	askari	soldier, guard, armed attendant

14 In Kiantal, one of the sub-dialects of Malagasy from Mayotte (Gueunier 1986: iv).

ʿasal honey (Wehr 613a); **ʿesel** honey (Z&T 124) 1863

Digo (MN&Z)	asali	honey (via Swahili)
Swahili (J)	asali	honey, syrup

ʿušr, pl **ʿušūr** one-tenth; tithe (Wehr 614a) 1865

Acooli (Cra)	mùcóòrò	tax, impost
(Mu)	mucoro	poll-tax
Bari (Mu)	ussur	poll-tax
Lotuxo (Mu)	amussɔrɔ	poll-tax
Luganda (Sno)	bùsuùlu	rent; property income
(Kna)	òkùsolooza[15]	collect the contribution, impose taxes (via Swahili)
Swahili (J)	ushuru	taxation, tax, customs duty, rate, rent

ʿašara ten (Wehr 614a) 1866

Madi (Bla)	ásārà	ten, used in time-telling or money counting
Swahili (J)	ashara (*n.* + *adj.*)	ten, rarely used except in the Arabic numerals

aḥad ʿašar eleven 1867

Madi (Bla)	ìdásārà numeral	eleven, used in time-telling
Swahili (J)	edashara	eleven

ʿišrūn twenty (Wehr 614b), (*acc.*) **ʿišrīn** 1869

Digo (MN&Z)	ishirini	twenty (via Swahili)
Kiw'oso (K&O)	í-shiriní	twenty
Swahili (J)	ishirini, asherini	twenty

ʿašīq lover (Wehr 614b) 1870

Swahili (J)	ashiki (+ *v.*)	strong desire, affection, wish

15 Knappert (1970: 83).

ʿišāʾ evening; evening prayer (Wehr 615a) **1872**

Malagasy (Gue)	alèŝa, aliʿèŝa, liʿ èŝa	hour of the night prayer
Swahili (J)	isha, esha	the Muslim prayers after sunset, during the period from about 6:30 PM to 8:30 PM[16]

ʿaṣr afternoon; afternoon prayer (Wehr 616a) **1874**

Malagasy (Gue)	alasìry, alasoìry, alaasìry	afternoon prayer time, afternoon
Swahili (J)	alasiri	afternoon; one of the regular Muslim times of prayer, from 3:30 PM to 4:30 PM[17]

ʿaṣan stick (Wehr 617b); **ʿaṣāh** stick, cane, wand (Wehr 618a) **1875**

Swahili (J)	wasa	used collectively for the small sticks or lathes which are put in to reduce the spaces between larger ones in the framework of the wall or roof of a native house

ʿāṣin disobedient; rebel (Wehr 618b) **1878**

Malagasy (Gue)	koʿàso, koå̂so	to sin, commit sin, disobey God
Swahili (J)	-asi, -aasi (*v.*)	disobey, fail to carry out instructions; fail to carry out duties or obligations; rebel (against), mutiny

ʿiṭr, pl. **ʿuṭūr** perfume, essence (Wehr 619b) **1879**

Swahili (J)	ituri, uturi	perfume

16 This prayer follows the sunset prayer by approximately 80 minutes.
17 This prayer falls between the noon prayer and the sunset prayer.

ʿaṭila (*v.*) to be destitute, be devoid, lack (II) to leave without care (Wehr 621b) 1883

Swahili (J)	-atilika (*v.*)	to be injured, deformed (as the result of an accident, illness)

ʿaṭīya gift, present (Wehr 622b) 1885

Swahili (J)	adia	a present

ʿaẓama majesty; pride; exaltedness (Wehr 623b) 1887

Swahili (J)	adhama	grandeur, glory, majesty, exaltation

ʿaẓīm powerful; magnificent (Wehr 623b) 1888

Swahili (J)	-adhimu (*v.* + *adj.*)	celebrate, honor, glorify, exalt, magnify

taʿẓīm aggrandizement, glorification; military salute (Wehr 624a) 1889

Swahili (J)	taadhima	honor, respect
(Bo)	adhimisho	celebration (solemnity), ceremony

ʿifrīt, pl. **ʿafārīt** malicious; demon, devil (Wehr 624b) 1891

Swahili (J)	afriti	an evil genius; an evilly disposed, wicked malevolent person

ʿafw pardon (Wehr 625b) 1893

Swahili (J)	afu, afua	deliverance from calamity

ʿāfiya (good) health (Wehr 625b) 1894

Digo (MN&Z)	afya	health (via Swahili)
Pokomo(Wü)	afia	health
Swahili (J)	afya, afia	good health

ʿaqīq carnelian (Wehr 626a) 1895

Swahili (J)	akiki	a kind of red stone, cornelian, used for putting in rings, earrings

ʿaqīqa sheep or any other animal that is slaughtered when the head of a male child is shaved for the first time (Kazim: II, 306b) 1896

Swahili (J)	akika	a feast made at the first hair-cutting of a child
	akiki	the goat slain at the feast of the first hair-cutting

ʿuqūba punishment, penalty (Wehr 627a) 1897

Swahili (J)	ukuba	a bad omen, misfortune, curse, evil fortune

ʿāqiba end, outcome, upshot; effect, result, consequence (Wehr 627a) 1898

Malagasy (Gue)	akìba	reserves, savings
Swahili (J)	akiba	store, reserve, stock, what is laid by for the future

ʿaqd knitting, tying; contract, agreement; legal act (Wehr 628a); **ɛugda** knot (RL 315a); **ʿged, yaʿged** (*v.*) to make a knot (TC1 1464) 1900

Swahili (Bo)	akidi	celebration of a marriage, marriage

ʿaqīd contracting party; a military rank (Wehr 628b) 1901

Swahili (J)	akida	formerly a leader / commander, esp. of soldiers, but in Tanganyika Territory only known as an Arab or native

iʿtiqād (firm) belief, confidence; (religious) faith (Wehr 628b) 1902

Swahili (J)	itikadi	faith, belief in a religion or tradition or custom handed down from father to son; perseverance, effort

ʿāqid legally competent to contract (Wehr 629a) 1903

Swahili (J)	-akidi (*v.*)	suffice (for), be enough (for); finish

ʿaqqār drug; medicament, remedy (Wehr 629b) 1904

Swahili (J)	akari	intoxicating liquor

ʿaqrab scorpion; hand (of a watch or clock) (Wehr 629b) 1905

Swahili (J)	akarabu	the hand of a watch or clock, but usu. *mkono* or *mshale*

ʿaql intelligence (Wehr 630a); **agil / ugûl** consciousness, reason, state of mind, intelligence, wisdom (JdP 67a) 1907

Digo (MN&Z)	achili	mind, intellect, understanding, reason, sense, intelligence, judgement (via Swahili)
Malagasy (Gue)	akìly, ankìly	intelligence, cunning, malice
Swahili (J)	akili	mind, intellect; judgement

ʿalla, laʿalla (*part.*) perhaps (Wehr 632b) 1911

Swahili (J)	lila na fila (?)	a saying: for good and bad, whether or not; 'perhaps' and 'actually' are not compatible

ʿilla deficiency, defect, weakness (Wehr 633a) 1913

Digo (MN&Z)	ila	defect, fault, blemish (via Swahili)
Swahili (J)	ila	defect, blemish, drawback, disgrace, stain, blot

ʿulba box, case (Wehr 633a); **ilba** box (S&A 113b) **1914a**

Dinka (Id)	elba	box

ʿaliqa (*v.*) to hang, be suspended; to be attached (V) to be attached; to be dependent (Wehr 634a); **allag / yiʿallig** (*v.*) (II) to hook, hang, suspend, upgrade (JdP 102b) **1915**

Swahili (J)	-aliki (*v.*)	hang, hang up, suspend, attach

ʿilm knowledge; science (Wehr 635b) **1917**

Digo (MN&Z)	ilimu	education (via Swahili)
Malagasy (Gue)	ilìmo, ʿilìmo, ĩlìmo	knowledge, knowing, especially when speaking of magical knowledge
Swahili (J)	elimu	knowledge, learning, wisdom, science

ʿalam flag (Wehr 636a) **1918**

Swahili (J)	alamu	flag, banner

al-ʿalīm the Omniscient (Wehr 636a) **1918a**

Swahili (M.A.M.)	aalam (*adj.*)	(of God) Omniscient

ʿalāma sign (Wehr 636a) **1920**

Bende (Abe)	haláma	sign
Digo (MN&Z)	alama	mark, sign, symbol (via Swahili)
Gikuyu (Ben)	rama	mark, sign (*cf.* Swahili)
Malagasy (Gue)	alàma, parfois halàma	mark, sign (to distinguish, recognize)
Matengo (Yo)	alâma	mark
Swahili (J)	alama	sign, mark, symbol

maʿlam place; trace; landmark, mark (Wehr 636b) 1921

Swahili (J)	mialamu, mwalamu	a mark, the marks of a fold; stripe, band of color, esp. in dress material

taʿallum learning, studying; education (Wehr 636b) 1922

Malagasy (Gue)	mikotalàmo	be updated
Swahili (J)	-taalamu (*v.* + *adj.*)	know, be learned in, be educated

ʿālim knowing; expert (Wehr 636b); **ɛālim** learned (RL 317b) 1923

Ndogo (Po)	alimi	student

maʿlūm known; fixed, determined, given (Wehr 637a) 1924

Digo (MN&Z)	maalumu / malumu	special, particular (via Swahili)
Swahili (J)	maalum (*adj.*)	recognized, known, particular, proper, special

muʿallim teacher (Wehr 637a); **muɛallim** teacher; schoolmaster (RL 318a) 1925

Bende (Abe)	mwalímu	teacher
Digo (MN&Z)	mwalimu	(a) teacher (via Swahili)
Kiw'oso (K&O)	m`-malimu	teacher
Lega (Bot)	mw.alímo	teacher (via Swahili)
Malagasy (Gue)	moalìmo	soothsayer, astrologer, magician, healer
Matengo (Häf)	mwalimu	teacher (via Swahili)
Rendille (P&G)	maalímo	teacher (via Swahili)
Swahili (J)	mwalimu	a learned man, a teacher, a schoolmaster

iʿlān proclamation; notice (Wehr 637b) 1927

Swahili (J)	ilani	a notice, proclamation

ʿAlī (EI: I, 392a) Ali (anthroponym) 1930

Dholuo (Odo)	Ali	man's name

aʿlā, pl. **aʿālin** higher, highest (Wehr 640a) 1931

Swahili (J)	aali (*adj.*)	good, superior, first rate

ʿamm father's brother, paternal uncle (Wehr 640b) 1933

Swahili (J)	ami	uncle, father's brother

ʿamada (*v.*) to support, prop; to intend, purpose; to take up (Wehr 641b) 1936

Swahili (J)	hamadi! (*interj.*) (?)	used frequently when a person stumbles

ʿamara (*v.*) to live long; to build (II) to load (a gun) (Wehr 643a); **ammar** (*v.*) to load the rifle (JdP 137b) 1939

Swahili (J)	-amiri (*v.*)	begin a thing

ʿumr life, duration of life (Wehr 643b) 1940

Digo (MN&Z)	umri	age (via Swahili)
Swahili (J)	umri	time of life, age

ʿimāra building, structure (Wehr 643b) 1942

Digo (MN&Z)	imara	strength, firmness, hardness (via Swahili)
Swahili (J)	imara (*n.* + *adj.*)	firmness, compactness, hardness, strength, stability, solidity (material and moral)

ʿamq, **ʿumq**, pl. **aʿmāq** depth; bottom (Wehr 644b) 1943

Swahili (J)	maki	thickness, stoutness

ʿamila (*v.*) to do, work; to make (VI) to trade (Wehr 644b) **1944**

Swahili (J)	-amili (*v.*)	manage, make, work, effect, bring about; s.t. used in the sense of taking part in an evil, base action or venture

ʿamal doing, acting, action; work; occupation, business (Wehr 645a) **1945**

Madi (Bla)	ɔ̀málɨ̀	menial laborer
Malagasy (Gue)	amàly, ʿamàla	business, occupation
Swahili (J)	amali	an act, action, thing done; business, occupation, practice; a kind of charm

ʿamalīya operation (Wehr 645b); **amaliye / amaliyât** surgery, operation (JdP 113b) **1945a**

Madi (Bla)	lɛ̀mɛ̀lɨ́à / àmɛ̀lɨ́à	surgical operation

ʿanbar ambergris (Wehr 647b); *cf.* Portuguese *alambra* **1952**

Swahili (J)	ambari	ambergris

ʿinād obstinacy (Wehr 648b) **1956**

Swahili (J)	inda	meanness of spirit, willfulness
	inadi	meanness of spirit, willfulness; provocation, perversity, obstinacy

ʿunwān address; title; sign (Wehr 650a) **1957**

Swahili (J)	anwani	address of a letter

yaʿanī that is, i.e. (Wehr 650a) **1958**

Bende (Abe)	yaáni (*conj.*)	manually
Digo (MN&Z)	yani	in other words, that is to say (via Swahili)
Malagasy (Gue)	iaàny, iaanỳ	that is to say, it means that
Swahili (J)	yaani (*conj.*)	that is, I mean

maʿnan sense, signification (Wehr 650b) 1959

Bende (Abe)	maána	meaning
Digo (MN&Z)	mana	meaning, reason (via Swahili)
Malagasy (Gue)	màna, maàna, maʿana	sense, signification
Swahili (J)	maana	cause, reason; meaning; sense

ʿahd promise; pact, agreement (Wehr 651b) 1960

Digo (MN&Z)	ahadi	promise, covenant
	-ahidi (*v.*)	to promise (via Swahili)
Malagasy (Gue)	oahàdi	vow, oath, promise
Swahili (J)	ahadi	promise, agreement

ʿāhira, pl. **ʿawāhir** adulteress; prostitute (Wehr 653a) 1961

Swahili (J)	hawara, hawaa	a paramour

ʿūd aloe (wood) (Wehr 654a) 1962

Swahili (J)	udi	aromatic aloe wood (used in fumigation)

ʿūd lute (Wehr 654a) 1963

Swahili (J)	udi	a musical instrument like a banjo

ʿāda habit, custom (Wehr 654b); **ādá** custom (Kaye 2b) 1964

Pokomo (Wü)	ada	custom
Swahili (J)	ada	custom, manner, habit

al-ʿāda commission (Wehr 654b) 1965

Swahili (J)	ada	commission or fee given on certain occasion

aʿūḏu bi-llāh God forbid! God save me from that! (Wehr 655b) 1966

Swahili (J)	audhubillahi! (*interj.*)	used as an expletive or expression of impatience, surprise. God preserve us! Botheration! Would you believe it! What next!

ʿ W N (*v.*) (III) to help, aid, assist, support (Wehr 659a); **âwan** (*v.*) (III) to help (JdP 204b) 1974

Swahili (J)	auni, muawana	aid, help
	-auni, -awini (*v.*)	assist, aid, help

ʿaib fault, defect, flaw; shame (Wehr 660b); **ʿêb** shame (FA no. 637); **êb / uyûb** shame, modesty, reserve, shyness, defect (JdP 407a); **ʿe:b** shame (Z&T 124) 1977

Malagasy (Gue)	aìbo, aìmbo	shame, dishonor
Swahili (J)	aibu	disgrace, shame

ʿīd feast, feast day (Wehr 661a) 1978

Malagasy (Gue)	ìdy, ʿìdy	Muslim religious holiday, especially the ʿīd al-fiṭr, considered the main holiday in Comoros[18]
Swahili (J)	idi	Muslim festival; a common male personal name

ʿār shame, dishonor, ignominy (Wehr 661a) 1979

Swahili (J)	ari	shame, reproach, dishonor

18 ʿĪd al-fiṭr, literally 'feast of interruption' [of fasting]) is the second most important religious holiday for Muslims; it is celebrated at the end of the lunar month of Ramaḍān (i.e., the 1st of Shawwal). The ʿīd al-kabīr literally, 'big feast' (after the pilgrimage), is considered the feast of sacrifice.

ʿayyār loafer, scoundrel, bum; vagabond; crane (machine) (Wehr 661b) 1981

Swahili (J)	ayari	a knave, rogue, impostor, impudent cheat

aʿyas of a dirty white color, yellowish white (camel) (Wehr 661b) 1982

Swahili (J)	yasi (?)	a yellow powder from India used by women as a cosmetic, more often called dalia

ʿāša (*v.*) to live, be alive (Wehr 661b) 1983

Swahili (J)	aushi (*n.* + *adj.*)	life, wear, durability, permanence, long lasting

ʿīša sort of life, life (Wehr 662a) 1985

Malagasy (Gue)	koèŝy	live
Swahili (J)	-ishi (*v.*)	last, endure, continue, live, remain

maʿīša life, way of living; subsistence (Wehr 662a) 1987

Bende (Abe)	maísya	life
Digo (MN&Z)	maisha	life (via Swahili)
Haya (M&L)	amaisha	life (via Swahili)
Kiw'oso (K&O)	ma-ísha	life
Malagasy (Gue)	maìŝa, maèŝa	life; in the sense of always
Swahili (J)	maisha	continuance, duration, permanence; life, period of living, mode of life

maʿīšī of or pertaining to the way of living (Wehr 662a) 1988

Pokomo (Wü)	maishi	age, length of life
Swahili (J)	maishilio	what one lives by, i.e. work, occupation, business

ʿayyina sample, specimen (Wehr 663b) 1993

Swahili (J)	aina	kind, class, genus, family, species, sort, sample

muʿāyana view(ing), examination, survey(ing); inspection; surveillance (Wehr 663b) 1994

Digo (MN&Z)	miwani	spectacles (via Swahili)
Gikuyu (Ben)	*mĩ*wani	spectacles, (eye)glasses (via Swahili)
Swahili (J)	miwani	a pair of spectacles

Ġain

ġubār dust; dust cloud (Wehr 664b) 1995

Swahili (J)	ghubari	a cloud of rain or dust

ġabn, **ġubn**, pl. **ġubūn** fraud, deceit (Wehr 665a) 1996

Swahili (J)	-rubuni (*v.*)	cheat, deceive, beguile, entice

ġarra (*v.*) to mislead, deceive (Wehr 667a) 2000

Swahili (J)	-ghuri (*v.*)	cheat, beguile, deceive

ġurūr deception; illusion; vanities (Wehr 667b) 2002

Swahili (J)	ghururi	arrogance, self-conceit, infatuation, vanity, folly, blindness, all terms refer to transitory things

ġarb west; occident (Wehr 668b); **xarib** west (JdP 1293b) 2004

Swahili (J)	ghurubu	the setting of the sun, sunset (usu. magharibi)

maġrib prayer at sunset (Wehr 669a); **maxrib / maxârib** sunset, dusk, dusk prayer (JdP 853a) 2006

Malagasy (Gue)	makarìby, maharìb̲y, maharìby	one of the hours of the day: the hour of evening prayer, at sunset
Pokomo (Wü)	magura	tomorrow
Swahili (J)	magharibi, mangharibi	time of sunset, Muslim evening prayers; place of sunset, the west

ġaraḍ aim, object (Wehr 670a) 2007

Swahili (J)	gharadhi	aim, object, intention (seldom used)

ġurfa upstairs room, room on an upper floor (Wehr 670b) 2009

Dholuo (Gor)	gorofa	store; upper rooms
Gikuyu (Ben)	ngorba	store; upper rooms
	ngoroba	upper story, story, upper flat, loft (via Swahili)
Kinyarwanda (CAT)	i-gorofa	story (of house)
Luganda (Sno)	`ggòloòfa	upper story, upstairs
(Mo)	`gg`oro:f`a	floor (via Swahili)
Swahili (J)	ghorofa, but usu. orofa	upper story, upper room

ġariqa (*v.*) to plunge, dive, sink (Wehr 671a) 2010

Malagasy (Gue)	koharìky, koarìky	perish, be lost; die
Swahili (J)	gharika	flood, deluge

ġarāma fine; indemnity, compensation (Wehr 671b) 2012

Digo (MN&Z)	garama	expenses, costs (via Swahili)
Malagasy (Gue)	haràma	necessary supplies, expenses (e.g. for a wedding)
Swahili (J)	gharama	expense, outlay, payment

ġasīl washed (Wehr 673b) 2018

Swahili (J)	dasili, ghasili	a powder made of the dried and pounded leaves of a tree, Ziziphus jujuba, used as a cleanser for a kind of skin disease

ġašš adulteration; fraud, deceit (Wehr 674a) 2019

Swahili (J)	ghashi	deceit, guile

ġaṣṣa (*v.*) to be choked; to choke; to be overcrowded, congested, jammed, packed (Wehr 675a) 2021

Swahili (J)	-ghasi (*v.*)	to cause confusion, confuse, complicate, bustle

ġaṣaba (*v.*) to take away by force or illegally, extort; to force, coerce; to violate (Wehr 675a) 2022

Swahili (J)	-ghusubu (*v.*)	compel, coerce, take away by force, violate

ġaḍab wrath, rage, fury; exasperation (Wehr 676a) 2024

Swahili (J)	ghadhabu	rage, fury, passion, anger, exasperation

ġafara (*v.*) to forgive (Wehr 677b), present imperfect **yaġfara** he forgives; **ġafr** pardon (Wehr 678a) 2027

Swahili (J)	ghofira	pardon, forgiveness of sins, absolution

ġafr pardon, forgiveness (Wehr 678a) 2030

Swahili (J)	ghofira	pardon, forgiveness of sins, absolution (used only of God)

ġafala (*v.*) to neglect (V) to surprise (Wehr 678a) 2032

Swahili (J)	-taghafali (*v.*)	be taken unawares, be surprised, be off one's guard; be unmindful (of), neglect to notice; take by surprise, make a sudden attack (or demand) on

ġafal negligence, inadvertence (Wehr 678b); **ġafla** negligence, inadvertence (Wehr 678b) 2033

Digo (MN&Z)	gafula	suddenly (via Swahili)
Swahili (J)	ghafula, ghafala	suddenness, sudden occurrence

ġāfil negligent, careless, unaware, inattentive (Wehr 679a) 2034

Malagasy (Gue)	mikoghafilìŝa	to surprise s.o.
Swahili (J)	-ghafilika (*v.*)	be thoughtless, neglectful, inattentive, imprudent; be taken unawares

ġalaba victory (Wehr 680a) 2037

Swahili (J)	mghalaba	competition, rivalry

aġlab majority (Wehr 680b) 2038

Swahili (J)	aghalabu, aghlabu (*adv.*)	usually, more often, chiefly, as a rule, mainly

ġālib (pre)dominant; most of, the majority of (Wehr 680b) 2039

Swahili (J)	-ghilibu, ghalibu (*v.*)	get the better of, beat, often used in the sense of getting the better of by cheating or by shrewd practices
	ghalibu (*adv.*)	usually, more often, chiefly, as a rule, mainly

ġalaṭ error, mistake (Wehr 681a) 2042

Malagasy (Gue)	mikohalàty	deceive
Swahili (J)	ghalati	lie, fault, mistake

ġulām boy, youth (Wehr 682b) 2043

Swahili (J)	ghulamu	a youth (male), a young man

ġālin expensive; costly (Wehr 683a) 2044

Swahili (J)	ghali (*adj.*)	scarce, rare, hard to get; dear, expensive, costly

ġamma (*v.*) to cover, veil, conceal (VIII) **iġtamma** to be distressed, be worried, be sad (Wehr 683a) 2046

Swahili (J)	jitimai	chagrin, affliction

ġamm grief, affliction, distress (Wehr 683a) 2047

Malagasy (Gue)	hàmo	pain, sorrow
Swahili (J)	ghamu	grief, sorrow, affliction

ġamā (*v.*) to provide with a roof, to roof; (*pass.*) **ġumiya** to faint (Wehr 685b) 2049

Swahili (J)	-ghumia (*v.*)	faint, lose consciousness; be astounded, dumbfounded

ġanīma booty (Wehr 686a) 2051

Swahili (J)	ghanima	good luck, prosperity

ġaniya (*v.*) to be free from want, be rich (II) to sing (Wehr 686a) 2052

Swahili (J)	ghani (+ *v.*)	a song

ġinā’ singing, song (Wehr 687a) 2053

Swahili (J)	guni	blank verse (as opposed to rhymed poetry)

ġār jealousy (Kazim: II, 516a) 2054

Swahili (J)	ghera	jealousy, zeal (usu. the effort made to avoid disgrace, dishonor, shame)

ġaib absence; hidden; divine secret (Wehr 689a) 2058

Swahili (J)	ghaibu	absence

ġāra (*v.*) to be jealous (II) **ġayyara** to alter, modify, change (Wehr 690a) 2060

Swahili (J)	-gairi (*v.*)	change one's mind, alter plan, annul

bi-ġairi, min ġairi without (Wehr 690b) 2062

Swahili (J)	baghairi, minghairi (*prep.*)	without, except, other than

ġaiẓ anger (Wehr 691a) 2064

Swahili (J)	ghaidhi	anger; determination, resolution, exertion

Fa’

fu’ād heart (Wehr 692a) 2068

Swahili (J)	fuadi	heart

fa's ax, hatchet; hoe (Wehr 692a); **fâs / fîsân** ax (JdP 442b); **fās** ax (Kaye 29b); **fa:s** ax (Z&T 125) 2070

Dinka (Id)	mapath	ax

fa'l good omen; auspice, sign (Wehr 692b) 2072

Swahili (J)	fali	an omen, either good or bad; chance

fānūs lantern (Wehr 692b) 2073

Swahili (J)	fanusi	lantern

futḥa, pl. **futaḥ** opening, aperture (Wehr 693b) 2076

Swahili (J)	futahi (+ *v.*)	good luck

miftāḥ key (Wehr 693b); **muftah / mafâtîh** key (JdP 897a) 2078

Bari (Mu)	mʊkʊta, mʊkʊtajin	key
Dinka (Id)	mufta	key
Lotuxo (Mu)	ammʊxʊtá	key
Madi (Bla)	mʊ̀fʊ̀tâ	key
Ndogo (Po)	mufti	key

al-fātiḥa name of the first sura [of the Qur'an] (Wehr 694a) 2077

Malagasy (Gue)	fatìha	title of the first sura of the Qur'an
Swahili (J)	fatiha	prelude (usu. the first chapter of the Qur'an)

F T Š (*v.*) (II) to examine (thoroughly), search, explore; to inquire (Wehr 694b); **fattac** (*v.*) (II) to search, look for (JdP 451a) 2079

Swahili (J)	-fatiisha (*v.*)	be inquisitive, search, pry into

taftiš examination, scrutiny, search; investigation; inquiry (Wehr 694b) 2080

Swahili (J)	-tafiti (*v.*)	pry into, be inquisitive, examine, criticize

mufattiš inspector, supervisor (Wehr 694b) 2080a

Dinka (Id)	mapatic	inspector

fatfata (*v.*) to speak secretly (Wehr 694b) 2081

Swahili (J)	mtafitafi	a blabber, go-between, tale-bearer

fatq tear, cleft, crack, slit (Wehr 695a) 2082

Lingala (Dz)	fatáki	rifle primer, shotgun (via Swahili)
Matengo (Häf)	fataki	percussion cap (via Swahili)
Swahili (J)	fataki (?)	gun cap

fitna intrigue; sedition, riot, discord, dissension (Wehr 696a) 2085

Digo (MN&Z)	fitina	discord (via Swahili)
Gikuyu (Ben)	bitina	false allegation, spite, conspiracy against a person, deliberate mischief; underhand dealing, discord, antagonism, mischief (via Swahili)
Madi (Bla)	fítīnà	envy, jealousy (via Swahili)
Malagasy (Gue)	fitìna	slander, betrayal
Swahili (J)	fitina	discord

fatwā futwa, formal legal opinion (Wehr 696b) 2086

Swahili (J)	fetwa (+ *v.*)	a legal decision

faj'atan suddenly (Wehr 697a) 2088

Swahili (J)	fajaa (+ *adv.*)	sudden death; suddenly, unawares

fajr dawn, daybreak (Wehr 697b) 2090

Macua (PP)	alfajiri / alifajiri / lifajiri	in the morning, in the early morning (via Swahili)
Malagasy (Gue)	alifagìry, alifaĵìry, alfagìry, alfaĵìry	the hour of dawn prayer
Swahili (J)	alfajiri	dawn, daybreak; one of the regular Muslim times of prayer (between first light and sunrise)

fujl radish (L. Raphanus sativus) (Wehr 698a) 2092

Swahili (J)	figili	a kind of radish, both root and leaves are used as vegetables

faḥl male (of large animals), stallion (Wehr 698b) 2094

Malagasy (Gue)	fahàly (?)	normal state, use
Swahili (J)	fahali	bull

faḫār glory, pride (Wehr 699b) 2095

Swahili (J)	fahari	grandeur, glory; ostentation

fidya ransom; redemption (from the omission of certain religious duties, by a material donation or a ritual act) (Wehr 701a) 2097

Swahili (J)	fidia	ransom, fine, money paid as composition or reparation

faraja (*v.*) to open; to comfort, [give] solace [to] (Wehr 702a) 2100

Swahili (J)	faraja	comfort, relief, cessation of pain, ease, consolation

farj opening, aperture, breach; pudendum of the female, vulva (Wehr 702a) 2101

Gikuyu (Ben)	*mũ*berethi	pipe, pipeline, tube (via Swahili)
Swahili (J)	mfereji	a ditch, water channel, trench dug for carrying off water or for irrigation
	fereji	a large ditch, channel

tafarruj inspection; observation (Wehr 702b) 2103

Swahili (J)	tafrija	enjoyment, rest, comfort, relaxation, amusement, pleasant, entertainment

faraḥ joy, gladness (Wehr 702b); **farha / afrâh** joy, rejoicing (JdP 434b) 2104

Digo (MN&Z)	raha	joy, happiness, pleasure
	-furahi	to be happy (via Swahili)
Swahili (J)	furaha	joy, pleasure, happiness, bliss, gladness
	-furahi	rejoice, be glad, feel pleasure, be happy, be pleased, enjoy oneself

farḫ, pl. **firāḫ** young bird; shoot, sprout (of a plant, of a tree) (Wehr 703a) 2106

Swahili (J)	mfarika	a young animal, goat, sheep, etc., grown but not yet breeding

farīd alone; lone (Wehr 703b) 2108

Swahili (J)	-firidi (*v.*)	to smell nice, pleasant

mufrad single (Wehr 704a) 2109

Swahili (J)	mfuradi	a verse of poetry

faras horse (Wehr 704b) 2112

Alur (Kna 298)	farasi	horse
Digo (MN&Z)	farasi	horse (via Swahili)
Gikuyu (Ben)	mbarathi	horse (via Swahili)
Jita (Kag)	i-faraási	horse (via Swahili)
Lingala (Ev)	farása	horse (via Swahili)
Luganda (Sno)	`mbalaàsi	horse (via Swahili)
Malagasy (Gue)	faràsy, faràŝy	horse, unknown animal (mare in the Comoros), but frequently mentioned in fairy tales
Matengo (Yo)	lipalâsi	horse
Ngh'wele (Leg)	farasi	horse (via Swahili)
Pokomo (Wü)	farazi	horse
Rendille (P&G)	fára'd (?)	horse
Runyankore (Ka)	embarâ:si	horse (via Swahili)
Swahili (J)	farasi	horse

firāsa perspicacity, acumen, discernment (Wehr 704b) 2113

Swahili (J)	farisi	expert, capable

farš mat, rug, carpet (Wehr 705a); **firāš**, pl. **furuš** cushion, pillow; blanket, cover; mattress; bed (Wehr 705a); **furâc** mattress, carpet, mat, blanket for horse (JdP 466a); **faraša** saddle cloth over saddle for horse (RL 347b) 2115

Dinka (Id)	farash	bed
Madi (Bla)	fórōsù	mattress
Swahili (J)	mfarishi	a kind of thin quilted mattress
	firashi, farisha,	a bed coverlet, quilt
	farishi	bundle, packet, package
	furushi	

furša brush; paintbrush (Wehr 705b) 2116a

Ndogo (Po)	fursa	paintbrush; brush

firṣād mulberry; mulberry tree (Wehr 705b) **2117**

Swahili (J)	forosadi, forsadi	mulberry, fruit of the mforosadi, Morus alba

farḍ religious duty (Wehr 706a) **2118**

Swahili (J)	faradhi, faridhi	necessity, obligation, prescribed duty

furḍa notch; opening; seaport (Wehr 706a) **2119**

Swahili (J)	forodha	customs house

farāġ void; leisure (Wehr 707b) **2125**

Malagasy (Gue)	faràha	secret parties, purses, testicles
Swahili (J)	faragha	privacy, seclusion, leisure, retirement
	-faragua (*v.*) (?)	to show off, vaunt oneself

faraqa (*v.*) to separate; to distinguish (Wehr 708a); **farrag / yifarrig** (*v.*) (II) to separate, divide (Wehr 439b) **2129**

Swahili (J)	rufuku (+ *v.*) (?)	interdiction, refuse
	faraka	a comb-like instrument for keeping threads apart, part of a weaver's loom; a division, sect

firqa band (Wehr 708b) **2130a**

Madi (Bla)	fírīkà	a jazz band

al-furqān the Qur'an (Wehr 709a); [Title of the holy book of Islam: al-Qur'ān wa-huwa al-furqān] **2131**

Swahili (J)	Furkani	a name of the Qur'an

farmala brake (of a wheel, etc.) (Wehr 710a); **farmala / farâmil** brake (JdP 438a); **farmala** brake (RL 350a) 2132a

Dinka (Id)	fermala	brake
Madi (Bla)	fàrámīlà / fōrómīlà / bòrέkì	brakes
Ndogo (Po)	fermala	brake

faransā France (Wehr 710b) 2136

Gikuyu (Ben)	Baranja	France (via Swahili)
Malagasy (Gue)	Faràntsa, Faransa	France
Swahili (J)	-faransa (*adj.*)	French

farwa fur, pelt; skin (Wehr 710b) 2137

Swahili (J)	mfuria	an Arab garment, a sort of loose cloth coat, with a collar, but no sleeves

fazaʿ fear, terror, alarm, panic (Wehr 711b) 2138a

Malagasy (Gue)	fàza	coward, cowardice
Swahili (Sacl)	fazaa	anxiety, worry, domestic disturbance, alarm, agitation, perplexity; fear, fright

fasaḫa (*v.*) to dislocate; (*jur.*) to cancel (Wehr 712a) 2140

Swahili (J)	-fusahi (*v.*)	annul, sometimes used in the sense of make poor

fasada (*v.*) to be or become bad, rotten, be spoiled (Wehr 712b) 2141

Swahili (J)	fisadi, mfisadi	a corrupter, esp. s.o. who corrupts women, a seducer, immoral person

fassara (*v.*) (II) to explain, interpret, comment (Wehr 713a); **fassar / yifassir** (*v.*) (II) to explain, clarify, comment (JdP 446b) **2143**

Malagasy (Gue)	fasoìry	translation, explanation
Swahili (J)	-fasiri (*v.*)	explain, interpret, translate

tafsīr commentary (esp. on the Qur'an) (Wehr 713a) **2144**

Swahili (J)	tafsiri (+ *v.*)	an explanation, translation

fāsiq sinful, dissolute; offender (Wehr 713b) **2146**

Swahili (J)	fasiki	an immoral (person), profligate, dissolute (person)

faṣṣ, pl. **fuṣūṣ** stone of a ring (Wehr 714b) **2148**

Swahili (J)	fususi	a gem, a precious stone

faṣīḥ skillful in using the correct literary (expression); eloquent (Wehr 714b) **2149**

Swahili (J)	fasihi (*adj.*)	correct, pure, elegant, lucid (in taste or style)

faṣāḥa purity of the language; fluency, eloquence (Wehr 715a) **2150**

Swahili (J)	fasaha (*adj.*)	correct, pure, elegant, lucid (in taste or style)

fiḍḍa silver (Wehr 717a); **fuḏḏa** silver (metal) (Daf 41); **fuḏḏā** silver (metal) (Dfa 41) **2154**

Acooli (Cra)	pɛcà	old copper coin
(Mu)	pɛca	money
Bende (Abe)	iihéla	money
Dholuo (Gor)	pesa	money
Digo (MN&Z)	feza	money (via Swahili)
	pesa	

Dinka (Id)	fadda	money
Gikuyu (Ben)	betha	money (via Swahili)
Kinyarwanda (CAT)	i-fēza	money, silver (via Swahili)
Kiw'oso (K&O)	m'besâ	money
Luganda (Sno)	`ffeezà	silver (via Swahili)
(Mo)	`ppeesà	button; coin
	`e`ffe:z`a	silver, money (via Swahili)
Malagasy (Gue)	fèda, fèdha	money (metal)
Matengo (Häf)	fetha	money (via Swahili)
Nyakyusa (Fel)	fesa	money (via Swahili)
Swahili (J)	fedha	silver; money, coin, cash (in general)

faḍaḥa (*v.*) to shame, dishonor (Wehr 717a) **2155**

Swahili (J)	fedheha	disgrace, a disgraceful thing, shame, scandal

faḍḥ exposure, humiliation, degradation (Wehr 717b) **2156**

Swahili (J)	fadhaa	dismay, confusion, perplexity, trouble, agitation

faḍala (*v.*) to be surplus, be left (over), remain (Wehr 717b) **2156a**

Malagasy (Gue)	mikofodhòly, mikofodòly	make fun, disrespect
Swahili (J)	fudhali	arrogant

tafaḍḍal (*imperative*) please! (Wehr 718a) **2157**

Digo (MN&Z)	tafadhali	please (via Swahili)
Malagasy (Gue)	tafadàly, tafadhàly	please, if you please!, I beg you
Swahili (J)	-tafadhali (*v.*)	please, do a kindness to, be good to

faḍl, pl. **fuḍūl** surplus; overplus; grace, favor (Wehr 718a) **2158**

Madi (Bla)	fádōlù	welcome; come in; do join us, me etc.
Malagasy (Gue)	fodhòly, fodòly	mockery, presumptuous behavior
Swahili (J)	fadhili (+ *v.*)	favor, kindness, benefit, privilege
	fidhuli, -fidhuli (*adj.*)	arrogant, insulting, officious, self-asserting

afḍal better; more excellent (Wehr 718b) **2162**

Swahili (J)	afadhali (*adv.*)	rather, better

faṭr, pl. **fuṭūr** crack, fissure, rift, rupture (Wehr 719b) **2164**

Swahili (J)	futari	first meal in the evening after a day's fast

fiṭr fast breaking (Wehr 719b) **2165**

Swahili (J)	fitiri	alms given at the end of Ramadan; an offering of grain

faṭūr breakfast (Wehr 720a); **faṭar**, **fuṭūr** breakfast (RL 354a) **2165a**

Dinka (Id)	futur	breakfast
Madi (Bla)	fòtúrù	breakfast
	īfōtūrù (*v.*)	to have breakfast

fuṭa table napkin; handkerchief; towel (RT 354b) **2166a**

Madi (Bla)	fótà	table cloth

fiʿl activity, doing, action; verb (Wehr 721a) **2167**

Malagasy (Gue)	fèly, fèʿly	bad action, malice, defect, vice
Swahili (J)	feli (+ *v.*), fiili	act, deed, way of acting; misdeed

F ʿ Y (*v.*) (V) **tafaʿʿan** (derived from **afʿan**) to be or be as mean as a viper (Kazim: II, 615b); **afʿan** viper (Wehr 722a) 2169

Swahili (J)	fii	discord, quarreling, evil intention, trouble

afʿā' pl. good smells, scents (Kazim: II, 616a) 2170

Swahili (J)	afu	blossoms of the wild jasmine (mwafu), used for perfume

faqr poverty; need, lack (Wehr 722b) 2171

Madi (Bla)	fógūrù (*adj.*)	(said of a person or thing) likely to cause embarrassment

faqīr, pl. **fuqāra'** poor; mendicant dervish, Sufi mendicant (Wehr 723a); **fagri / fagâra** poor, helpless (JdP 417b); **faqīr** pious man; scholar (RL 356a) 2172

Malagasy (Gue)	fokàra	poor, needy, miserable
Swahili (J)	fakiri, fukara	a poor person, beggar

fuqqāʿ beer, prepared barley drink (Kazim: II 621b) 2173a

Malagasy (Gue)	fòka	decoction with lots of ginger and/or pepper; given to women who have just given birth
Swahili (J)	fuka	a kind of thin porridge (of rice flour, with sugar, honey, spice, etc.) served to guests at an entertainment or festival; a thin kind of gruel flavored with much pepper and cardamom, given to women after childbirth, said to clean the stomach

fakka (*v.*) (*eg.*) to change (money) (Wehr 723b); **fakka** change (coin) (RL 356b) 2175a

Madi (Bla)	fákà	change; changeable

fikr thinking (Wehr 724b) 2177

Gikuyu (Ben)	thikiri, bikiri	thoughts, meditations, brooding (via Swahili)
Malagasy (Gue)	kofikìry	think, reflect
Swahili (J)	-fikiri (*v.*)	think (about), ponder (over), meditate (upon), consider

fikra thought (Wehr 724b) 2178

Malagasy (Gue)	fikìra	thought, idea
Swahili (J)	fikira, fikara	thought, thoughtfulness, meditation, consideration, reflection

tafakkur thinking, reflection (Wehr 725a) 2179

Swahili (J)	-tafakari (*v.*)	think (about), ponder (over), meditate (upon), reflect (about)

falata (*v.*) to escape; to be freed, be released; to let escape (Wehr 725b) 2180

Swahili (J)	-feleti (*v.*)	let go, discharge, release; run away, abscond

fālūḏ a kind of sweetness composed of starch, water and honey (Kazim: II, 629b) 2183

Swahili (J)	faluda	gruel made of milk and maize flour

F L S (*v.*) (II) to declare bankrupt or insolvent (IV) to be or become bankrupt or insolvent, to fail; to be ruined (Wehr 726b) 2184

Swahili (J)	-filisi (*v.*)	to sell a person's goods for debt, declare bankrupt

fals, pl. **fulūs** fels, a small coin, in Iraq and Jordan (Wehr 726b) 2185

Swahili (J)	fulusi	money, cash, a general term

muflis bankrupt, insolvent (Wehr 726b) 2187

Swahili (J)	mfilisika	a bankrupt, a ruined person

filfil pepper (Wehr 727a) 2189

Kiw'oso (K&O)	bilibíli	pepper
Luganda (Sno)	`ppiripiri	pepper (via Swahili)
Madi (Bla)	pìlìpílì	hot pepper (via Swahili)
Ndogo (Po)	filfil	pepper
Pokot (Cra)	pìlìpíl	pepper (via Swahili)
Swahili (J)	pilipili	pepper, seeds and pods
	felefele	an inferior kind of millet

falak celestial sphere (Wehr 727b) 2191

Malagasy (Gue)	falàky	what is in the sky; hence the astrological fate
Swahili (J)	falaki	astronomy, astrology

fulk ship (Wehr 727b) 2192

Ndogo (Po)	ta feluka (*v.*)	navigate
Swahili (J)	falka (?)	the hold of a ship

fulān, fulāna so-and-so (Wehr 727b); **fulānī** (*adj.*) such (Wehr 727b) 2193

Digo (MN&Z)	fulani	such a person, a certain one, so-and-so, such and such (things), alluding indefinitely to persons or things for reference only (via Swahili)
Swahili (J)	fulani	such a person, a certain one, so-and-so

fann kind, specimen, variety (Wehr 728a) 2196

Swahili (J)	fununu	a rumor, s.th. which is not known for certain, or only partly known

fani', **fanī'** who got rich (Kazim: II, 638b) 2201

Swahili (J)	fani (*adj.*)	worthy, fitting, prosperous

F N Q (*v.*) (V) to live in ease and affluence (Wehr 729a) 2202

Swahili (J)	fanaka	prosperity, success, benefit, favor, comfort

fanîle / fanâyil loanword (F., Eng.) "flanelle" [flaenl], also used in Arabic sweater, pullover (JdP 427b); **faniila** vest (S&A 101b); **fānellā** jersey (from flannel) (RT 360b) 2202a

Dinka (Id)	paniina	undershirt (via a language of Moro-Madi or Bongo-Bagirmi groups)
Madi (Bla)	fàlànì / fòlànì / fènílà	vest, flannel

fahrasa (*v.*) to compile an index, to index (Wehr 730a) 2203

Swahili (J)	faharasa, fahirisi	table of contents of a book, index

fahm comprehension (Wehr 730a) 2206

Malagasy (Gue)	fahàmo	watch out, take care
Swahili (J)	-fahamu (*v.*)	know, perceive

tafāwut difference, dissimilarity, contrast; disharmony (Wehr 731a) 2209

Digo (MN&Z)	tafauti	difference (via Swahili)
Swahili (J)	tofauti	difference, discrepancy, interval (of space or time)

fauz success, triumph, victory (Wehr 732a) 2210

Swahili (J)	-fuzu (*v.*)	succeed, win, as in a competition, game, or examination

fauqa (*prep.*) above, over; more than (Wehr 733a) **2212**

Swahili (J)	fauka, foko (*adv.*)	more

fāqa poverty, neediness, indigence (Wehr 733a) **2213**

Swahili (J)	ufuke	poverty, necessity, need

fūl bean(s) (Wehr 733b); **fûl** groundnut; peanut (*Arachis hypogaea*) (JdP 464b) **2214**

Madi (Bla)	fùlù másīrɨ̀	broad beans

fī (*prep.*) in; at; on; with; as to (Wehr 734a) **2215**

Swahili (J)	fi (*prep.*)	on, with, in such phrases as *saba fi saba* (seven by seven)

fā'ida utility, benefit; profit; interest (on money) (Wehr 735a); **fāyde** use, usefulness, advantage, benefit (Kaye 30a) **2216**

Digo (MN&Z)	fwaida	profit (via Swahili)
Gikuyu (Ben)	baita	profit (via Swahili)
Swahili (J)	faida	profit, interest

fairūz turquoise (Wehr 735a; (Kazim: II, 653a) **2217**

Swahili (J)	feruzi	turquoise

Qāf

qabr tomb (Wehr 738a) **2223**

Bende (Abe)	kabhúli	tomb
Dholuo (Gor)	kaburini	cemetery (via Swahili)
Gikuyu (Ben)	*ka*buri	graveyard (via Swahili)
Kiw'oso (K&O)	-kaburî	grave
Malagasy (Gue)	kab̠òry, kabòry	tomb
Swahili (J)	kaburi	grave, tomb

maqbar tomb; cemetery (Wehr 738a); **maxbara / maxâbir** graveyard (JdP 852a) 2223a

Madi (Bla)	mògábīrì	cemetery

qabaḍa (*v.*) to seize (Wehr 738b); **qabaḍa** (*v.*) taking possession of the property of another (Kazim: II, 662a); **qabḍ** seizure; hold, handful (Wehr 738b) 2224

Malagasy (Gue)	kotakabadhìňa	to whom we entrust, (those) to whom we put s.th. into the hands of
Swahili (J)	kabidhi (*v.* + *adj.*)	charge, care, guardianship
	stakabadhi (+ *v.*)	a receipt; earnest money
	-takabadhi (*v.*)	receive, hold, keep

qabala (*v.*) to accept; to receive (kindly, hospitality) (Wehr 739b) 2228

Malagasy (Gue)	kobab̲ìly	approach, go to meet
Swahili (J)	-kabili	be in front, be opposite

qabla (*prep.*) before, prior to (Wehr 740b) 2229

Bende (Abe)	kabhúla	before
Digo (MN&Z)	kabla	before (in time) (via Swahili)
Malagasy (Gue)	kabòla, kàbla	before, until
Matengo (Yo)	kábula ja ~	before ~
Swahili (J)	kabla	before

qibla kiblah, direction to which Muslims turn in prayer (toward the Kaaba) (Wehr 740b) 2231

Malagasy (Gue)	kibolàny, kiblàny	in the direction of Mecca; to the north
Swahili (J)	kibla	the direction of Mecca

qabūl, qubūl (friendly) reception; acceptance (Wehr 740b) 2232

Malagasy (Gue)	kob̲àly, kobàly	accept, agree
Swahili (J)	kabuli, kibali, ikibali, ukubali	acceptance, sanction, favor, assent

qabīla tribe (Wehr 741a) 2233

Bende (Abe)	kabhíla	tribe
Digo (MN&Z)	kabila	tribe (via Swahili)
Gikuyu (Ben)	kabira	sort, kind, breed (via Swahili)
Haya (M&L)	ekabila	tribe (via Swahili)
Malagasy (Gue)	kaba'ìla kabìla	noble, aristocrat; who claims to descend from an Arab tribe race, tribe, species
Matengo (Yo)	likabîla	tribe
Swahili (J)	kabila	tribe, clan

taqabbul receptivity, susceptibility, sensibility (Wehr 741b) 2235

Swahili (J)	-takabali (*v.*)	accept, approve, acknowledge, assent (to)

qābilīya faculty, power, capacity (Wehr 741b) 2236

Swahili (J)	kabaila	an important man, a man of high birth

muqābil facing, opposite (Wehr 741b) 2238

Swahili (J)	mkabala (*adv.*)	mostly in (*prep.*) phrase, *mkabala wa*, in front of, opposite

qaḥba prostitute (Wehr 743b) 2241

Digo (MN&Z)	ukaaba	prostitute (via Swahili)
Swahili (J)	kahaba, mkahaba	prostitute

qiḥf, pl. **aqḥāf** skull; cranium (Wehr 744a) 2242

Swahili (J)	kahafi	the top center piece of a white skull-cap such as are worn by some natives, the other part is called *mshazari*

qadda (*v.*) to cut lengthwise, cut into strips (Wehr 744b); **gadda / yigidd** (*v.*) pierce, to make a hole, perforate (JdP 475b); **qadda, biqaddi** (*v.*) have breakfast or lunch (together) (Kaye 64a) **2242a**

Madi (Bla)	gádà	lunch
	ɪ̄gādà (*v.*)	to have lunch

qadr value, standing, rank; divine decree (Wehr 745b) **2246**

Malagasy (Gue)	kadìry	approximately, say, about
Swahili (J)	kadiri (*v.* + *adv.* + *conj.*)	amount, measure, extent, capacity, value, rank; moderation, self-control, temperance

al-qurʾān the Qurʾan (Wehr 753b) **2261**

Malagasy (Gue)	koràny, koroàny	Qurʾan
Swahili (J)	korani, kurani	the holy book of Muslims, the Qurʾan

qarīb near (in place and time), nearby, close at hand; relative, relation (Wehr 754b) **2264**

Luganda (Sno)	kàribù (*interj.*)	come in! (via Swahili)
Malagasy (Gue)	karìb̠ò, karìbo	close, near; come in, answer to *hôd̠y*
Swahili (J)	karibu (*adv.* + *prep.*)	near relation, kinsman; near, close to; shortly; nearly

aqrab nearer; pl. relatives (Wehr 755a) **2265**

Swahili (J)	akraba	kinsman (used of near relationship only)

angarêb / anâgrib rope bed (JdP 163b); **anggreb** bed (S&A 89a) **2266a**

Acooli (Cra)	làŋgɛ̀rɛ́ɛ̀, làŋgɛ̀rı́ı̀ŋ	bedstead
Dholuo (Odo)	laŋgere	a bedstead made of leather with wooden legs

Dinka (Id)	angareb	bed (of strings)
Madi (Bla)	lènggèrí	bed

qirš, pl. **qurūš** piaster (Wehr 756a); **gursaé**, **gursaya** thaler (RT 374a); **gurus** money; dollars; cash; change (RT 374a); **girš**, **giriš** (pl. **gurūš**) piaster (RT 374a).; Maybe from German "Groschen." 2267

Bari (Mu)	gurus	money
Dinka (Id)	girceen	two piastre coin
	giric	half-piastre
	gric	piece of money
Lotuxo (Mu)	agurusi	money
Madi (Bla)	gírīsì	money; pence
Ndogo (Po)	gurusu	money; change

qarḍ loan (Wehr 757a) 2269

Swahili (J)	karadha	money on loan, advance, credit, but without interest being charged

qirṭās paper (Wehr 757b); **qarṭas** paper (Wehr 757b); **katkat** paper, ticket (JdP 715b) 2270

Acooli (Cra)	kàrtacì	sheet of paper
Anywa (Reh)	wàràkàtá	paper; book; letter
Bende (Abe)	kalataási	paper
Dholuo (Gor)	kalatas, kalatase	paper
(Odo)	karatac	a sheet of paper (via Swahili)
Digo (MN&Z)	karatasi	paper (via Swahili)
Gikuyu (Ben)	*ka*rata	playing card; card game, gambling
(Gor)	iratathi	piece of paper, paper
	karatathi	paper (via Swahili)
Haya (Ka)	olukaratâ:si	paper (via Swahili)
Kamba (Mbi)	kalatasi	paper (via Swahili)
Kiw'oso (K&O)	-karitási	paper

Kuria (MMR)	ekarataasi, iritarataasi	paper, a piece of paper
Malagasy (Ade)	taratàsy	paper; letter
(Gue)	karatàsy, kiritàsy, taratàsy	
Matengo (Yo)	likalatâsi	paper
Ngh'wele Leg	kalatasi	paper (via Swahili)
Swahili (J)	karatasi	paper, a piece of paper

qara'a (*v.*) to knock VIII to vote (Wehr 757b); **angara' / yingari'** (*v.*) (VII) to be careful, heed, beware of, stop (JdP 163a) **2271a**

Gikuyu (Ben)	kura	vote (via Swahili)
Rendille (P&G)	kúra	election (via Swahili)
Swahili (J)	kura	a lot, i.e. in casting lots

qarqūša (*eg.*) a kind of crisp cookies (Wehr 759a) **2274a**

Madi (Bla)	gòrògósì	dried bread

qarn century (Wehr 760a) **2276**

Digo (MN&Z)	karina	century (via Swahili)
Swahili (J)	karini, karne, karni	a century

maqran yoke to which the oxen are (attached) (Kazim: II, 729a) **2278**

Swahili (J)	mangrini (?)	a knot tied in the rope of the anchor of a native boat
	mangili (?)	a kind of cathead or cross-piece for securing a cable, anchor, or rope to the bow of a native vessel

qaranful carnation; clove (Wehr 760b) **2280**

Swahili (J)	karafuu	cloves, the flower bud of the *mkarafuu*

qizāz (*eg.*) glass (Wehr 761b); **qizāza, qizā'iz** (*eg.*) bottle (Wehr 761b); **gazzāzá** bottle, glass (Kaye 34b); **gazza:za**(**t**) bottle (Z&T 126); **gazāz** bottle (RT 377b) 2282

Dinka (Id)	gidhaath	bottle
Ndogo (Po)	gizaza	bottle

qissīs priest, minister, pastor (Wehr 762a) 2283

Gikuyu (Ben)	*mũ*gathithi	priest, presbyter (via Swahili)
Swahili (J)	kasisi	a priest

qasr force, coercion, constraint (Wehr 762a) 2284

Swahili (J)	-kusuru (*v.*)	accomplish by effort, difficulty, self-denial, deny oneself s.th. in order to gain an object

qasama (*v.*) to divide; to distribute (II) to divide; to distribute (Wehr 762b) 2285

Swahili (J)	kasama, mkasama	a division, part, portion; division (in mathematics)

qasam oath (Wehr 763a) 2287

Swahili (J)	kasama	an oath

qišṭa (*eg.*), **qašṭa** (*syr.*), cream (Wehr 764b) 2289

Swahili (J)	kashata	a kind of confectionery, boiled sugar with grated coconut, coconut cream

qiṣṣa narrative, tale, story (Wehr 765b) 2290

Swahili (J)	kisa mkasa	story, account, report, history, narrative; statement of case, reason alleged, cause; affair, business, subject of report an event, happening, news (either good or bad)

miqaṣṣ, pl. **al-maqāṣṣ** scissors (Wehr 766a); **magaṣṣ** scissors (Z&T 126) 2291

Acooli (Mu)	magac	scissors
Ateso (Kit)	amakasi	scissors
Bari (Mu)	magas	scissors
Bemba (WF)	makashi	scissors
Digo (MN&Z)	makasi	scissors (via Swahili)
Dinka (Id)	magas	scissors
Gikuyu (Ben)	*ma*gathĩ	scissors, shears (via Swahili)
Kiw'oso (K&O)	ma-akási	scissors (via Swahili)
Kuria (MMR)	irigasi	a pair of scissors
	amagasi	a pair of scissors; a pincer-like instrument for castrating bullocks
Lingala (Ev)	makási	scissors, shears (via Swahili)
Lomongo (Hul)	bokátsi	scissors (< via Swahili)
Luganda (Sno)	màkânsi	scissors (via Swahili)
Madi (Bla)	màgásɨ / màkásɨ	scissors
Malagasy (Gue)	makàsy	scissors (of seamstress)
Matengo (Yo)	òkâse	scissors
Ndogo (Po)	magas	scissors
Pokot (Cra)	màkásò	scissors (via Swahili)
Runyankore (Ka)	makâ:nsi	scissors (via Swahili)
Swahili (J)	mkasi, makasi	a pair of scissors

qiṣāṣ requital, reprisal; punishment, chastisement (Wehr 766a) 2292

Malagasy (Gue)	kìsoa	grudge, revenge
Swahili (J)	kisasi	vengeance

qaṣṣaba (*v.*) (II) to curl; to embroider with gold and silver thread (Wehr 766a); **qaṣab** gold and silver thread, gold and silver embroidery; brocade (Wehr 766a) 2293

Swahili (J)	kasabu	gold cloth, cloth thread embroidery

qaṣaba cane, reed; kassabah, a linear measure (Wehr 766b) 2294

Swahili (J)	kasiba	barrel (of a gun)
	kashabu	a kind of colored bead, often of silver or gold, hollow, and of very thin glass

qaṣada (*v.*) to go or proceed straightaway; to intend (Wehr 766b) 2295

Malagasy (Gue)	kosòdy, koŝòdy, kasìdy, makosòdy, makosòdo	expressly for, with intent, serious thing, that has a good reason
Swahili (J)	kusudi (*v.* + *adv.*)	intention, purpose, aim, object, end

qaṣīda kasida (Wehr 767a) 2296

Malagasy (Gue)	kasoìda	Muslim religious poem that is sung in ceremonies, during which people dance the *daira*
Swahili (Bo)	kasida	a religious poem

iqtiṣād economization; economy (Wehr 767a) 2297

Swahili (J)	iktisadi	economy, thrift

quṣūr insufficiency; deficiency, lack (Wehr 768b) 2302

Swahili (J)	-kusuru (*v.*)	shorten, e.g. as of a Muslim combining the prescribed prayers

quṣairā term, last limit (Kazim: II, 752a) 2303

Swahili (J)	kasiri	end

taqṣīr defect, fault (Wehr 768b) 2304

Swahili (J)	taksiri	fault, defect, offense, deficit, crime

qaḍīya (legal) case, cause; affair (Wehr 772b); **gadiiya** lawsuit (S&A 104a) 2306

Madi (Bla)	gɛ̀dɨ́yà	legal case
Swahili (J)	kadhia	affairs, things which happen

qāḍin judge (Wehr 772b); *cf.* Portuguese *alcaide*, French *alcade* 2307

Dinka (Id)	gaadit	judge
Madi (Bla)	gádì	judge, magistrate; lawyer
Malagasy (Gue)	kadhy	cadi, Muslim judge; presides over the registration of legal marriages, shares, etc.
Swahili (J)	kadhi	judge

qaṯr (rail route) train (Wehr 774a); **gatar** train (S&A 105b) 2309a

Dinka (Id)	gatar, gatta	train

miqṭara stocks (device for punishment) (Wehr 774b) 2310

Swahili (J)	mkatale	stocks, instruments for confining a prisoner or demented man by the feet

qiṭʿa piece, fragment; part (Wehr 776b) 2312

Gikuyu (Ben)	gata (*v. t.* ?)	cut (via Swahili)
Swahili (J)	kataa	a cutting, piece, part, portion, section, fraction

ḏū al-qaʿda name of the eleventh month of the Islamic calendar (Wehr 779b) 2316

Swahili (J)	kaida	the second month after Ramadan

qāʿida, pl. **qawāʿid** foundation; fundament; pedestal; rule, principle; method (Wehr 780a) 2318

Digo (MN&Z)	kawaida	usual (via Swahili)
Haya (Ka)	kawaída	normal; regular; common (via Swahili)
Swahili (J)	kawaida, kaida	regulative principle, fundamental rule, usage, custom, system

qufl padlock (Wehr 782a) 2322

Dinka (Id)	gifl	padlock
Ndogo (Po)	kulul	lock

qāfila caravan; column; convoy (Wehr 782a) 2323

Swahili (J)	kafila	a caravan (rarely heard, used for *msafara* and *safari*, but only by Muslims)

aqall less (Wehr 783b) 2327

Swahili (J)	akali (+ *adj.*)	a few of, some

qālab, **qālib** form; mold; model; matrix (Wehr 785a); **qālb** mold; sugar loaf, soap (Beau 559b) 2331

Swahili (J)	kalibu	a mold, e.g. for bullets; a mold for casting concrete, such as for drainpipes, sections for wells; a heating pot or furnace

inqilāb revolution, bouleversement (Wehr 785b); **ingilâb / ingilâbat** coup d'etat, putsch (JdP 608b) 2331a

Madi (Bla)	ɨ̀nggɨ̀lá'bò̀	coup

qalāš small, picked up, chunky (Kazim: II, 801b) 2332

Swahili (J)	kalasha (?)	tusk of ivory, smaller than buri

qalfaṭa (*v.*) to caulk (a ship) (Wehr 787a) **2334**

Swahili (J)	kalafati (+ *v.*)	caulking material (usu. cotton and grease)

qalam pen (Wehr 788a) **2335**

The Arabic word is itself a borrowing from Greek κάλαμος "reed; reed calamus, stylus," *cf.* Latin *calamus* "reed."

Acooli (Cra)	kàláàm	pencil
(Mu)	kalam	pen, pencil
Dholuo (Gor)	kalama, kalambe	pen
(Odo)	kalam	
Digo (MN&Z)	kalamu	pen (via Swahili)
Dinka (Id)	galam	pen, pencil
Gikuyu (Ben)	*ka*ramu	pen, pencil (via Swahili)
Haya (Ka)	ekalâ:mu	a pen or pencil (via Swahili)
Kinyarwanda (CAT)	i-karamu	pencil (via Swahili)
Kuria (MMR)	ekaraamu	a pen or pencil (via Swahili)
Lega (Bot)	ka.lámo	pencil (via Swahili)
Luganda (Mo)	\`e\`kk\`ar^a:mu	pencil, pen (via Swahili)
Madi (Bla)	gálámò, kàlámò	pen
Malagasy (Gue)	kalàmo	pen to write, reed, especially in a religious context; pen, pencil
Ndogo (Po)	galam	pencil
Runyankore (Ka)	ekarâ:mu	pencil (via Swahili)
Swahili (J)	kalamu	pen or pencil

iqlīm region; province (Wehr 788b) **2336**

Madi (Bla)	ɨ̀kɨ̀lɨ́mɨ̀	regional autonomy

qamḥ wheat (Wehr 789a); **gameh** corn, Triticum sp. (JdP 484b) **2337**

Madi (Bla)	gɛ́mɛ̀	wheat

qamara (*v.*) to gamble (Wehr 789b); **qimār** gambling; bet (Wehr 789b); **gumâr** gambling, gamble game, poker (JdP 515b); **gumaar** gambling (S&A 108a) 2339

Acooli (Mu)	jaará	gambling
Lotuxo (Mu)	agʊmar	gambling
Madi (Bla)	gòmárɨ̀	gambling

qāmūs dictionary (Wehr 790a) 2340

Swahili (J)	kamusi	a lexicon, a dictionary

qamīṣ shirt; dress (Wehr 790b); **gamīs** gown (Kaye 33a); **gumâj** cloth, shirt, coat (Daf 47); **gumâji / gumâjiyât** long dress, dress, boubou (JdP 515b); **angumâji / angumâjiyât** clothing, long dress, dress, boubou (JdP 164b); **gumāš** cotton canvas (RT 391a) 2341

Ciluba (Kab)	nkanzu	dress (via Swahili)
Dinka (Id)	gomith, gamish	shirt
Kinyarwanda (CAT)	i-kanzu	gown, dress (via Swahili)
Lega (Bot)	(n.) kánzú	dress (via Swahili)
Luganda (Sno)	\`kkanzù	long dress, reaching the feet; surplice (via Swahili)
Malagasy (Ade)	akànjo	clothes (via Comorian *nkandzu* 'standard dress worn by Muslim men')
Ndogo (Po)	kamis	shirt
Runyankore (Ka)	eká:nju	dress (via Swahili)
Swahili (J)	kanzu	formerly the usual outer garment of men (via lingua franca)

qaml louse (Wehr 791a); **gamul** louse (JdP 486a) 2341a

Madi (Bla)	gómōrò	clothing lice

qānūn canon; law (Wehr 791a) 2342

Malagasy (Gue)	kanòny	rule, law
Swahili (J)	kanuni	that which is regular (necessary, indispensable), a fundamental rule, a necessary condition, general law governing the treatment of a subject, a canon

qindīl lamp; candlestick; candelabrum (Wehr 792a) 2345

Swahili (J)	kandili	lantern

qanṭara arched bridge, stone bridge (Wehr 793a) 2346

Swahili (J)	kantara	a bridge (rarely heard)

qahwa coffee (Wehr 795a) 2350

Acooli (Mu)	gawa	coffee
Bari (Mu)	gawa	coffee
Bende (Abe)	kaháwa	coffee nut
Dholuo (Gor)	kahawa	coffee
Digo (MN&Z)	kahawa	coffee (via Swahili)
Gikuyu (Ben)	kahũa	coffee; coffee plants
	*mũ*kawa	coffee shop, restaurant, hotel (via Swahili)
Kinyarwanda (CAT)	i-kāwa	coffee (tree, or drink)
Kiw'oso (K&O)	kaáwa	coffee nut, coffee plant, coffee
Lega (Bot)	k.ábwa	coffee (via Swahili)
Lotuxo (Mu)	agawa	coffee
Luganda (Sno)	kaawà	coffee (via Swahili)
Madi (Bla)	gáwà / káwà	coffee
Malagasy (Gue)	gahàoa	coffee; tea, infusion prepared in large pots to distribute to assistants during religious ceremonies
Ndogo (Po)	gawa	coffee
Nyakyusa (Fel)	ikahabwa	coffee (via Swahili)
Pokot (Cra)	káawèn	coffee (via Swahili)

Rendille (P&G)	gaáwo	coffee (via Swahili)
Runyankore (Ka)	káiwa	coffee (via Swahili)
Sango (Bou)	káwà	coffee (via Lingala)
Swahili (J)	kahawa	coffee

qawwād pander, pimp, procurer (Wehr 795b) 2351

Swahili (J)	kawadi, kuwadi	a procurer, a pander, a pimp

qaula remark, word; pronouncement, dictum (Wehr 797b) 2358

Malagasy (Gue)	kaòly	speech
Swahili (J)	kauli	sentence; opinion, advice

maqāla article; treatise (Wehr 798a) 2359

Swahili (J)	makala	a written article, treatise

qaum fellow tribesmen, kinsfolk; tribe, race, people, nation; people (Wehr 800a) 2359a

Malagasy (Gue)	kaòmo	group (of people), generation; ethnicity, race
Swahili (J)	kaumu	a crowd

qīma value; price (Wehr 800a) 2360

Malagasy (Gue)	kìma	price (of s.th. to sell)
Swahili (J)	kima	price, value

qiyāma resurrection (Wehr 800b) 2361

Malagasy (Gue)	kiàma	last day, day of general resurrection, last judgment, late, last
Swahili (J)	kiyama	the general resurrection of the dead, as conceived by Muslims

taqwīm setting up; calendar; chronology (Wehr 801a) 2364

Swahili (J)	takwimu	a calendar

qāsa (*v.*) to measure; to weigh (Wehr 804b); **gâwas / yigâwis** (*v.*) (III) to measure, take the measure, try a garment (JdP 499a) 2370

Swahili (J)	kasi (+ *adv.*) *in* -tia (-piga) ~	apply force, tighten

qiyās analogy (Wehr 804b) 2371

Malagasy (Gue)	kiàsy	enough, sufficiency, what is good, compliance
Swahili (J)	kiasi (+ *adv.*)	a measure; moderation, self-control

Kāf

ka-ḏā so; such and such (Wehr 807a); **ka-ḏā wa-ka-ḏā** so and so (Wehr 807a) 2376

Digo (MN&Z)	kadhaa	various, a certain (small) number (via Swahili)
Malagasy (Gue)	kadhà, kadà	this or that (not to pronounce the exact word)
Swahili (J)	kadha wa kadha (*adj.* + *adv.*)	thus and thus, etc.

ka-ḏālika so, like this (Wehr 807a) 2377

Digo (MN&Z)	kadhalika	likewise (via Swahili)
Swahili (J)	kadhalika (*adv.*)	in like manner, likewise, similarly

ka-mā as, just as, as also; also well (Wehr 807a) **2378**

Digo (MN&Z)	kama	(1) like, such as (2) if (via Swahili)
Swahili (J)	kama (*conj.*)	as, such as, like, as if; like, almost, about; rather than, and not

ka's cup (Wehr 808a); **kās** cup (Wehr 846a) **2379**

Madi (Bla)	kásɨ̀	cup, as ornamental prize

kabid, kabd, kibd center (Wehr 809b) **2383**

Swahili (J)	gubeti	prow of a native vessel; head, figure-head of prow

takbīr the exclamation **Allāhu akbar** (Wehr 810b) **2389**

Malagasy (Gue)	mikotakabìry	say "God is great," glorify God
Swahili (J)	-takbira (*v.*)	repeat the Muslim formula: **Allāhu akbar**, God is great

kibrīt sulfur; matches (Wehr 811a) **2391**

Acooli (Mu)	kibirit	match (fire stick)
Bari (Mu)	kibirit	match (fire stick)
Dholuo (Gor)	kibrit	match
Gikuyu (Gor)	kibiriti	match
Haya (Ka)	ekibilíti	matchbox (via Swahili)
Kamba (Whi)	kĩvĩlĩtĩ (Machakos) kĩla:víti (Ikutha, Kitui)	match (via Swahili)
Kinyarwanda (CAT)	iki-biriti	box of matches (via Swahili)
Lotuxo (Mu)	akibirit	match
Luganda (Sno)	kìbiriiti	match (fire stick) (via Swahili)

Madi (Bla)	kìbìrítì / tìbìrítì	matches; matchbox (via Swahili)
Ndogo (Po)	kabrit	match
Pokot (Cra)	kìpìríitᵓ̀	match (via Swahili)
Runyankore (Ka)	ekibíri:ti / ebiríri:ti	matchbox (via Swahili)
Swahili (J)	kiberiti, kibiriti	sulphur, a match

kubrī (Tk. *köprü*) bridge; deck (Wehr 811a); **kubri** bridge (JdP 737b), Turkish loanword 2391a

Dinka (Id)	kubra, kumbur	bridge
Madi (Bla)	kú'bīrì	bridge

kabsa raid, surprise attack (Wehr 811b) 2392

Swahili (J)	kamsa	a fire alarm, or escape of a prisoner

kibēg round bowl (earthenware) (RT 405a) 2394a

Madi (Bla)	kóbáyà	cup, mug

kitāb, pl. **kutub** book (Wehr 812b); **al-kitāb** Qur'an; Bible (Wehr 812b) 2396

Acooli (Cra)	kìtabù	book
Ateso (Kit)	ekitabo	book
Dholuo (Gor)	kitabu, kitape	book
(Odo)	kitabu	
Digo (MN&Z)	chitabu	book (via Swahili)
Dinka (Id)	kitab	book
Gikuyu (Ben)	*gĩ*tabu	book; pamphlet, exercise or notebook, magazine (via Swahili)
Kinyarwanda (CAT)	igi-tabo	book
Kiw'oso (K&O)	kí-tabu	book
Lega (Bot)	ke.rábɔ	book (via Swahili)
Luganda (Sno)	kìtabo	book (via Swahili)
(Mo)	\`ekitabo	
Madi (Bla)	kɨ̀tá'bò	book (via Swahili)
Matengo (Yo)	kitâbu	book

Nyakyusa (Fel)	ikitabu	book (via Swahili)
Runyankore (Ka)	ekitabo / ebitabo	book (via Swahili)
Swahili (J)	kitabu	book

maktab office; bureau (Wehr 813a) 2397a

Acooli (Cra)	mákátàp	office; court
Dinka (Id)	mäktäp	office

kātib scribe (Wehr 813b) 2398

Dinka (Id)	katib	clerk
Swahili (J)	katibu (*n.* + *v.*)	a writer, clerk; write

maktūb written; letter (Wehr 813b; Z&T 126) 2399

Malagasy (Gue)	mkatàb̲aə	treaty (in writing)

kattān (**kittān**) linen (Wehr 815a) 2401

Gikuyu (Ben)	*ga*tani	flax, linen (via Swahili)
Swahili (J)	katani	hemp, sisal fibre, coarse sacking, rope
	mkatani	the sisal hemp plant (Agave sisalana)

aḫtar more; oftener, more frequently; most (Wehr 815b) 2401a

Swahili (Bo)	akthari	a lot, large quantity

kuḥl antimony; kohl, a preparation of pulverized antimony used for darkening (the edges of) the eyelids (Wehr 816b) 2402

Swahili (J)	kohl	antimony used to beautify the eyes

kadîs / **kadâyis** cat (JdP 683b); **kadīs** cat (RL 409b) 2404a

Lotuxo (Mu)	akedus	cat

kaḏḏāb liar (Wehr 818a); **kaddâb** liar (JdP 682b) 2407

Swahili (J)	kadhabu	liar (seldom used)

karra (*v.*) to turn around and attack (II) to repeat, reiterate (Wehr 818b) 2408

Swahili (J)	-kariri (*v.*)	repeat, say over and over again, recite, rehearse

kurbāj, kirbāj whip, riding whip, *kurbash* (Wehr 819b); **kurbağ** jet knife (RL 411b); **kurbāč** whip; jet knife (RL 412a); **kurbai** whip (S&A 125a) 2414

Madi (Bla)	kórùbáɨ̀	whip
Ndogo (Po)	kurbaci	whiplash

kirbāl teasing bow (for combing or carding cotton); coarse sieve (Wehr 819b); **karbōl** type of sowing stick without footrest (RL 412a) 2414a

Ndogo (Po)	kurbal, kurbala	sieve

kursī chair; throne (Wehr 820a); **karâsi** chair; sultan's envoy (JdP 745b) 2415

Acooli (Cra)	kuur(u)cùk	lying chair
(Mu)	kurcuk	easy chair
Bari (Mu)	kursi'	easy chair
Dholuo (Odo)	kurucuk	a chair to lie down
Ik (Schr)	kàràtsa (kàràtsì-)	chair, seat, stool
Lotuxo (Mu)	akursi	easy chair
Swahili (Sacl)	kurusi, kursi	seat

kurrāsa quire; booklet; notebook, copy book; fascicle (of a book) (Wehr 820b) 2416

Gikuyu (Ben)	ũkuratha, mokuratha; ũkaratha, mokaratha	page (via Swahili)
Swahili (J)	ukurasa	sheet or strip of paper, leaf or page of a book

karkadê name of a drink, drink made from hibiscus flower (JdP 705a); **karkadē** sorrel; red appearance; sabdariffa (RT 414b) 2417a

Madi (Bla)	kɛ̀'dɛ̀kɛ̀'dɛ́	a plant with a mild sour leaf that can be boiled as tea or taken chilled as a soft drink; the boiled leaves can be made into tea or a hot drink

karuma (*v.*) to be noble, generous (II) to honor (Wehr 821b); **karam** noble nature; generosity, magnanimity (Wehr 821b); **karāma** generosity; miracle (worked by a saint) (Wehr 822a); **karâma / karâmât** nobility, generosity, magnanimity (JdP 701b); **karram** respect, honor, be generous to, give almsgiving (JdP 708b); **karram** to be generous; to support; to honor; to respect (RT 415a) 2419

Acooli (Cra)	kàraamà	feast with much food and beer
(Mu)	karama	banquet; wedding feast
Dholuo (Odo)	karama	a feast with much food and drink, now refers to Christmas
Digo (MN&Z)	karamu	party, feast (via Swahili)
Malagasy (Gue)	karàma	special graces, miracles,
	karàmo	mystical or ascetic exploits, fakirism
		great treat, party with meals (like a big wedding)
Swahili (J)	karama	an honor, privilege; gracious gift, talent, accomplishment
	karamu	a feast, banquet, festive entertainment

karāma liberality, munificence (Wehr 822a) 2419a

Malagasy (Gue)	karàma	salary, wages, rent

karīm generous (Wehr 822a) 2420

Swahili (J)	karimu (*adj.*)	liberal, generous

akram nobler, more distinguished; more precious (Wehr 822a) 2421

Swahili (J)	akram, el akram	honored, respected (only used in the complimentary introduction of letters written in Arabic style)

takrīm, takrima honoring, tribute, honor (Wehr 822b) 2422

Swahili (J)	takaramu (*n.* + *v.*)	an honor; generous behavior

kariha (*v.*) to feel disgust, be disgusted (Wehr 823a) 2424

Swahili (J)	-kirihi (*v.*)	loathe, abhor, hate; give offense, provoke, insult, disgust, treat disrespectfully

karāha hatred; aversion; abhorrence, disgust (Wehr 823a) 2425

Swahili (J)	karaha	aversion, disgust, abhorrence

ikrāhī compulsory, coercion, forced, enforced (Wehr 823b) 2427

Swahili (J)	kirahi (sometimes heard as ikirahi or ikrahi)	being offended, disgust, causing offense, provocation, insult, abhorrence

makrūh detested, abhorred, hated, disgusting, unpleasant (Wehr 823b) 2428

Swahili (J)	makuruhi, makeruhi (*adj.*)	offensive, in bad taste, wrong, abhorrent

kura globe, sphere; ball (Wehr 823b) 2429

Madi (Bla)	kúrà	bowl
Ndogo (Po)	kura	ball

kirā' rent (Wehr 824a) 2430

Swahili (J)	karo	fee, honorarium, a present

kurēk (Tk. *körek*) shovel (Wehr 824b); **koreek** shovel, spade (S&A 124a) **2430a**

Bari (Mu)	koret	shovel

kustubān, pl. **kasātibīn** thimble (Wehr 825b) **2432**

Swahili (J)	kastabini, kustabani	a thimble

kisra, pl. **kisar** fragment; a small piece; chunk (of bread); slice (of bread) (Wehr 826b); **kisra**, pl. **kisâr** pancakes (Daf 75); **kisâr** pancake, galette (JdP 729a); **kisra** very thin crepe pancake (RL 419a) **2435**

Ndogo (Po)	kesra	Arabic word for a kind of *piada*,[19] very long, thin like puff pastry

kāšif uncovering, revealing (Wehr 829b) **2443**

Swahili (J)	kashifa	slander, false statements
	Inkishafi	"The revelations," name of a poem by Sayyid ʿAbdallāh b. ʿAlī b. Nāṣir

mikʿab shoe that does not cover the heel (Dozy: II, 474a) **2445**

Swahili (J)	makubazi (?)	leather sandals with ornamentation

19 The (Italian) Romagnolo name of a focaccia made of flour mixed with water, salt, and lard, without yeast, round and flattened, cooked on a disk of refractory earth (called *testo* in Italian), it is red-hot when burned with wood, or on a stone slab; in the Rimini area, a lard-free type is widespread; this is thinner and more crisp. The term is from the medieval Latin *plàdena* or *plàtena*, from *plathana*, in turn from the Greek *πλάθανον* "long dish, pan."

kufr, kufrān unbelief, infidelity (Wehr 833a) 2451

Malagasy (Gue)	kofòro	cruelty, bad trick, malice
Swahili (J)	-kufuru (*v.*)	treat with mockery or contempt, revile, curse; become an unbeliever, apostatize, blaspheme, commit sacrilege

kaffāra penance; reparation; expiations (Wehr 833a) 2452

Swahili (J)	kafara	an offering, a charm, a sacrifice made to avert evil

kāfir infidel (Wehr 833a) 2453

Acooli (Mu)	lakafir	heathen
Luganda (Mo)	\`om\`uka:f^i:ri	heathen (via Swahili)
Madi (Bla)	kàfɨ́rɨ̀	heathen
Malagasy (Gue)	kafìry	unfaithful, heathen, impious, cruel
Swahili (J)	kafiri	an infidel, an unbeliever

kafana (*v.*) to cover with a winding sheet, to shroud, dress for the grave (II) to wrap, cover (Wehr 834a); **kafan** shroud (Wehr 834a). The extension of the same word through very different languages lends itself to the idea of a common origin. Burial in a shroud is a Muslim custom: apart from Islam, the dead are buried either naked or with their clothes, sometimes rolled in a mat. The passage from one fricative to another (from [f] *kafan*, to [s] *kasan*) is found in other occasions, *cf. safande* or *fafande* 'soap' under **ṣābūn 1557**. 2455

Swahili (J)	-kafini (*v.*)	cover up, wrap (i.e. of a corpse in a shroud)

kalb dog (Wehr 836a) 2465

Swahili (J)	kelb	dog (seldom heard and then only as a term of abuse)

kalab rabies, hydrophobia; burning thirst; greed (Wehr 836a) 2466

Swahili (J)	kalab	rabies, hydrophobia

kalifa (*v.*) to become brownish red (face); to become covered with freckles (II) **kallafa** to commission, charge, assign (Wehr 836b); **taklīf** charges; taxes, imposts (Wehr 836b) 2467

Swahili (J)	takalifu (*n.* + *v.*)	discomfort, annoyance, trouble, worry

kalima word (Wehr 838a) 2472

Swahili (J)	kalima	word

kalmānī, **kalamānī**, **killimānī** eloquent; fluent speaker (Wehr 838b) 2474

Swahili (J)	mkalimani	interpreter

kamala, **kamula**, **kamila** (*v.*) to be or become whole, complete; to be finished (II) and (IV) to finish, conclude (VI) and (VIII) to be or become complete (Wehr 840b) 2480

Swahili (J)	-takamali (*v.*)	complete, finish

kāmil perfect; complete (Wehr 841a); **kāmil** absolutely, positively (Kaye 47a) 2481

Malagasy (Gue)	kamìly	all, in whole, completely, entirely, perfectly
Swahili (J)	kamili (*adj.* + *v.*)	complete, perfect, whole, entire, unimpaired

kānūn stove (Wehr 842a); **gânûn** stove with embers (Daf 44); **kanuun** stove, brazier (S&A 120b) 2483

Madi (Bla)	kònúnù	charcoal stove

kinbār rope made of coconut fiber (Kazim: II, 933b) 2484

Gikuyu (Ben)	*i*kamba, kamba	sisal tow (rope); rope, cord (via Swahili)
Swahili (J)	kamba (?)	cord, rope (the most generic term)

kanz treasure (Wehr 842b) 2485

Swahili (J)	kanzi	treasure, hoard

kanīsa church (Wehr 842b) 2486

Ateso (Kit)	ekanisa	church
Bari (Mu)	kanisa	church
Dholuo (Gor)	kanisa, kanise	church
(Odo)	kanica	
Gikuyu (Gor)	kanitha	church
Jita (Kag)	ri-kanísa	church (via Swahili)
Kamba (Mbi)	ĩkanisa	cathedral, church
	kakanisa	chapel (via Swahili)
Kiw'oso (K&O)	-kanisâ	church
Kuria (MMR)	ekanisa	a church (via Swahili)
Luganda (Sno)	`kkànisà	church (via Swahili)
Madi (Bla)	kànísà	church
Matengo (Yo)	kanisa-kanisa	church
Pokot (Cra)	kànísà	church (via Swahili)
Rendille (P&G)	kaníssa	church (via Swahili)
Runyankore (Ka)	ekanísa	church (via Swahili)
Swahili (J)	kanisa	church

kahraba electricity (Wehr 843b); **kahrabāʾī, kahrabī** electric(al); electrician (Wehr 844a) 2488

Swahili (J)	karabai	a pressure lamp, either for petrol or kerosene, also used of an acetylene lamp

kāhin diviner; priest (Wehr 844b) 2489

Swahili (J)	kahini, kuhani	word used in the Bible for a priest under the Jewish dispensation (*kasisi* is used of a Christian priest); soothsayer; deceiver, swindler

kūb drinking glass (Wehr 845a); **kôb** box (Daf 75) 2490

Gikuyu (Ben)	*mũ*kebe	tin, tin can (via Swahili)
Swahili (J)	mkebe (?)	pot, can, canister, mug

kūra ball (Wehr 845b) 2495

Acooli (Mu)	kura	ball; football
Bari (Mu)	kura	ball; football
Dinka (Id)	kuura	ball
Lotuxo (Mu)	akura	ball; football
Madi (Bla)	kúrà	football, football match

kūz small jug of clay or tin; mug, tankard (Wehr 846a) 2496

Dinka (Id)	kɔɔth, kɔɔc	cup
Malagasy (Gue)	kòĵo	calabash (without collar, round shape)
Swahili (J)	kuzi	an earthenware pitcher or jug, with handle or handles and a narrow neck

kūfīya kaffiyeh, square kerchief (Wehr 846b) 2497

Acooli (Cra)	kòfíà	tarboosh
Dholuo (Odo)	kopia	kofia, a hat that is conical in shape, which used to be worn by police and Muslims
Gikuyu (Ben)	ngũbia, ngobia	cap, hat; tilde, diacritical mark over vowel (via Swahili)
Gwere (Kag)	énkófwíilá	cap (via Swahili)
Haya (Ka)	eko:fî:la	hat; cap (via Swahili)

Kiw'oso (K&O)	-kofyâ	hat
Malagasy (Gue)	kofìa, kôfìa, koafìa	cap, embroidered hat worn by men
Matengo (Yo)	kopîa	hat; cap
Runyankore (Ka)	enkofì:ra	cap; hat (via Swahili)
Swahili (J)	kofia	cap (usu. a fez of red cloth)

makān place where one is or stands; place (Wehr 847b) 2498

Swahili (J)	makani	place, dwelling place, residence, home

makwan ironing establishment (Wehr 848b); **makwa** iron (S&A 130a) 2500a

Dinka (Id)	makua	iron
Madi (Bla)	mákwà	iron plate

kaid ruse, artifice; slyness; deception (Wehr 849a) 2501

Malagasy (Gue)	mkaìdy	stubborn, obstinate
Swahili (J)	-kaidi (*v.* + *adj.*)	be obstinate, rebel, refuse to obey
	gaidi	plunderer, thief

kīs sack; bag; purse (Wehr 849a) 2503a

Lotuxo (Mu)	akis	bag
Ndogo (Po)	kisi	pocket

kaifa how? how …! (Wehr 849b); **ke:f ?** how? (Z&T 122) 2504

Dinka (Id)	kep	how (are you)?

kīnīn quinine (Wehr 850b); **kīna** quinine (RL 436b) 2507a

Acooli (Mu)	kina	quinine
Bari (Mu)	kina	quinine
Lotuxo (Mu)	akina	quinine

Lām

li (*prep.*) for; in favor of (Wehr 851a) **2509**

Swahili (J)	ili (*conj.*)	in order that, that

lā not; no! (Wehr 851b) **2511**

Malagasy (Gue)	là	no
Swahili (J)	la! (*interj.*)	no! not so! by no means!

wa-lā nor; not even (Wehr 852a) **2513**

Digo (MN&Z)	wala	nor (via Swahili)
Malagasy (Gue)	oalà	and not
Ndogo (Po)	wala (*adv.*)	or
Swahili (J)	wala (*conj.*)	nor

lākin however, but (Wehr 852b) **2515**

Digo (MN&Z)	lakini	but (via Swahili)
Dinka (Id)	laakin	but
Lega (Bot)	alakíni (*conj.*)	but (via Swahili)
Malagasy (Gue)	lakìny	but
Pokomo (Wü)	lakini	but, however
Swahili (J)	lakini (*conj.*)	but, yet, however, nevertheless

lu'lu' pearls (Wehr 852b) **2516**

Ateso (Kit)	elulu	pearl
Kamba (Mbi)	lũlũ (?)	jewel (via Swahili)
Luganda (Sno)	luùlu, èruùlu	pearl (via Swahili)
Malagasy (Gue)	lòlo, lôlo	pearl, necklace of large pearls, esp. necklace worn on the occasion of the wedding
Swahili (J)	lulu	pearl

labīb understanding, reasonable, sensible, intelligent (Wehr 854a) **2518**

Swahili (J)	ulabibu	perseverance, sustained effort

libās clothes; (*eg.*, *syr.*) (men's) drawers (Wehr 855b) 2521

Bari (Mu)	libas	trousers
Madi (Bla)	lɨ̀básɨ̀	knickers, underwear
Swahili (J)	lebasi, libasi	clothes

talbīs clothing; wall plaster (Wehr 855b) 2522

Swahili (J)	talibisi	a mat fastened round the sides of a heavily laden dhow to prevent the waves from washing in

lubān frankincense (Wehr 856b) 2524

Gikuyu (Ben)	ubani	frankincense (via Swahili)
Malagasy (Gue)	oḇàny	the incense of the Orient
Swahili (J)	ubani	frankincense

labbaika here I am! at your service! (Wehr 857a) 2526

Malagasy (Gue)	labè, abè, bè	Yes? Here I am! (in polite response to a call, esp. from a child to his parents, or to other adults, from a wife to her husband)
Swahili (J)	labeka!, lebeka!	at your service! yes sir / madam!

lijām bridle (Wehr 858b) 2527

Swahili (J)	lijamu	bit

laḥama (*v.*) to mend, patch, solder (Wehr 861a) 2531

Swahili (J)	lehemu, lahamu, lihamu, lihimu (*n.* + *v.*)	solder

laḏḏa joy; pleasure, delectation (Wehr 863b) 2533

Malagasy (Gue)	làda, làdha	pleasure, enjoyment, esp. sexual pleasure
Swahili (J)	ladha, ludha	the taste or flavor of anything, whether pleasant or unpleasant

lazima (*v.*) to attend; to be imperative (Wehr 864b) 2534

Gikuyu (Ben)	rathima, *dans* wĩra wa ~	compulsory labor (via Swahili)
Haya (Ka)	lá:zima (*invar.*)	necessary (via Swahili)
Malagasy (Gue)	kolazìmo lazìma	it must, it should
Swahili (J)	lazima	necessity, obligation, surety, bail, responsibility

lastik, **lastīk** rubber; eraser (Wehr 866a); **lastik** elastic (S&A 126b) 2537a

Madi (Bla)	lɨ́sītɨ̀	elastic material

lisān tongue; language (Wehr 866a) 2538

Swahili (J)	lisani	used for the flap under the opening of a *kanzu*,[20] in the front

laṭīf delicate; gentle (Wehr 868a) 2540

Swahili (J)	latifu	goodness, gentleness

laʿb game; joke (Wehr 869a) 2542

Swahili (J)	-laabu (*v.*)	play with, entertain with

20 A *kanzu* is the usual outer garment worn by men; it is a long-sleeved calico gown.

laʿba game; trick (Wehr 869a) 2543

Swahili (J)	leba	deceit, untruthfulness, slyness with intent to deceive

milʿaqa, pl. **malāʿiq** spoon (Wehr 869b); **malaga** spoon (S&A 130a) 2543a

Acooli (Cra)	malagà	spoon
Dholuo (Odo)	malaga	a spoon
Dinka (Id)	maalaga	spoon
Ndogo (Po)	malaga	spoon

laʿana (*v.*) to curse (Wehr 870a); **laʿna** curse; execration, imprecation (Wehr 870a) 2544

Swahili (J)	laana	a curse, imprecation, oath

luġa language; idiom (Wehr 870b) 2547

Bende (Abe)	luúgha	language
Swahili (J)	lugha	language, speech

lifāfa envelope; cloth covering (Wehr 871b); **laffay** / **laffâfi** mainsail (JdP 754b) 2548

Swahili (J)	alfafa	the dressing put on the wound after circumcision to hold it in place

lafẓ pronunciation (Wehr 873a) 2552

Swahili (J)	lafudhi, lafidhi	accent, pronunciation

luqma mouthful; little piece, morsel (Wehr 874b) 2556

Swahili (J)	lukuma	food, sometimes used in the sense of a bribe

talqīn instruction, direction; suborning of a witness (Wehr 875a) 2557

Swahili (J)	talakim	the Muslim prayers recited at burials

laqiya (*v.*) to encounter (III) to come to meet (Wehr 875a); **lâga / yilâgi** (*v.*) (III) to meet, go to meet, welcome (JdP 755b) 2558

Swahili (J)	-laki (*v.*)	meet, go to meet

lakan basin, copper basin (Wehr 877a) 2559

Swahili (J)	legeni	a large metal vessel used for cooking *mkate wa kumimina*

lamba lamp; tube (radio) (Wehr 878a); **lampa** oil lamp (JdP 763a) 2561a

Dinka (Id)	lamba	lamp
Ndogo (Po)	lampa	fire; torch; lamp; lantern

laulā if not (Wehr 881b) 2566

Swahili (J)	laula *in* l. kama	if not, unless (rarely used)

lauḥ, lauḥa board; slate (Wehr 882b) 2567

Ndogo (Po)	lo	axis
Swahili (J)	laha	a sheet of paper

lauz almond(s) (Wehr 883a) 2568

Gikuyu (Ben)	njothi	nut; almond (*cf.* Swahili)
Swahili (J)	lozi	an almond, fruit of the *mlozi*

lūṭī sodomite, pederast (Wehr 883b) 2570

Swahili (J)	-lawiti (*v.*)	commit sodomy

lūf luffa, dishcloth gourd (Luffa cylindrica Roem) (Wehr 883b) 2570a

Dinka (Id)	lifa	sponge
Madi (Bla)	lífà	vegetable sponge, used for bathing (Luffa Cylindrica)

laum, lauma censure, reproof, blame, reproach (Wehr 884a) 2571

Swahili (J)	laumu (*n.* + *v.*), usu. lawama	reproach, charge, blame, reproof, guilt

laun color; kind, sort (Wehr 884b) 2573

Swahili (J)	launi	likeness, kind, shape, color, esp. of countenance (very rarely used)

luwwa aloe, fragrant wood that is burned as incense (Kazim: II, 1046b) 2574

Swahili (J)	liwa	a sweet-scented wood of the Spirostachys africana tree, a kind of sandalwood

laita, yā laita would God! if only …! (Wehr 886a) 2576

Swahili (J)	laiti! (*interj.*)	oh that, if only (esp. of regret for what is past or impossible)

līf fibers, fibrils (Wehr 886b) 2577

Swahili (J)	difu	the fibre binding the young leaves of the coconut around the growing stem

lāqa (*v.*) to befit, become, be proper (Wehr 886b) 2578

Swahili (J)	laiki (*n.* + *v.*)	what is becoming, fitness, fitting, proper

laila night (Wehr 886b) 2579

Swahili (J)	lela	a night (seldom used, usu. *usiku*)

laimun lemon (Wehr 887b); **lêmûn** lime, lemon (JdP 770a) 2581

Acooli (Mu)	lemun	lemon
Bari (Mu)	lemun, lemunyön	lemon
Dinka (Id)	leemuun	lemon
Kiw'oso (K&O)	-ndimû	lemon, lime (introduced) (via Swahili)
Kuria (MMR)	indiimu	lemon
Lega (Bot)	lo.ndímo	orange (via Swahili)
Lotuxo (Mu)	allemuny, allemunyi	lemon
Matengo (Yo)	lindìmu	lemon
Ndogo (Po)	lemuna	lemon
Runyankore (Ka)	endɨmu	lemon (via Swahili)
Swahili (J)	mndimu	the lime tree (Citrus aurantifolia)

layyin soft; flabby, feeble; gentle; flexible, pliable (Wehr 887b) 2582

Swahili (J)	laini (*n.* + *v.*) -lainifu (*adj.*)	(of things) smooth, supple, soft, flexible, pliable; (of persons) facile, gentle, good-humored

Mīm

māhīya salary, income; pay (*mil.*) (Wehr 889b); **mahiiya** salary (S&A 129b) 2583b

Madi (Bla)	màyíà	salary, wages

mi'a, pl. **mi'ūn**, **mi'āt** hundred (Wehr 889b); **miya** hundred, five hundred franc [of the Financial Community of Africa] (JdP 864b); **mīya** hundred (RL 476a) 2584

Acooli (Cra)	miíâ	hundred (via Swahili)
Bari (Mu)	mia	hundred
Dholuo (Gor) (Odo)	miya	hundred (via Swahili)

Digo (MN&Z)	mia	hundred (via Swahili)
Kiw'oso (K&O)	-miâ	hundred
Kuria (MMR)	mia	hundred (via Swahili)
Luena (Vet)	mía	hundred (via Swahili)
Madi (Bla)	míà	hundred
Swahili (J)	mia (*n.* + *adj.*)	hundred
	miteen (*n.* + *adj.*)	two hundred

mitr meter (measure of length) (Wehr 890a); **mitr** meter (RL 453b) **2584a**

Ndogo (Po)	mitri	meter

mit̠l resemblance, similarity (Wehr 891b) **2588**

Swahili (J)	mithali, methali, mizali, midhali, misili, mizili	a likeness, resemblance, emblem, similitude, parable, proverb, allegory

mat̠al likeness; metaphor, simile (Wehr 892a) **2590**

Swahili (J)	madhali (*conj.*)	while, when, since; since, if, seeing that, because

mat̠alan for example (Wehr 892a) **2591**

Swahili (J)	mathalan, methalan(i), mazalani	for example

mit̠āl example (Wehr 892a) **2592**

Swahili (J)	mithali, methali	a likeness, resemblance, emblem, similitude, parable, proverb, allegory

majūs Magi, adherent of Mazdaism (Wehr 894b) **2594**

Swahili (J)	majusi	astrologer

maḥḍ of pure descent (Wehr 894b) 2595

Dinka (Id)	määdi	Mahdi

mudda period, space of time, interval; while; limited or appointed time (Wehr 897a) 2600

Digo (MN&Z)	muda	period of time (via Swahili)
Swahili (J)	muda	space of time, period, set term, fixed interval

madîde / **madâyid** porridge (JdP 794a); **madiida** porridge (S&A 128b) 2601a

Dinka (Id)	madida	(a kind of liquid) boiled

tamaddun civilization; refinement of social culture (Wehr 899a) 2605

Swahili (J)	-tamaduni (*v.*)	become civilized

madiyy sperm emitted only as a result of contact with a woman (Kazim: II, 1082b) 2606

Swahili (J)	madhii	the clear viscid discharge of the male organ when sexually excited

marra time, turn (Wehr 900b) 2607

Bende (Abe)	mála	time
Digo (MN&Z)	mara	time, sometimes (via Swahili)
Jita (Kag)	mara	time (via Swahili)
Malagasy (Gue)	màra	time
Swahili (J)	mara (*n.* + *adv.*)	a time, a single time, a turn, an occasion, an occurrence; immediately

mamarr transition; passage (Wehr 901a); **mumariiya** journey (S&A 38b) 2608a

Madi (Bla)	mòmòríà	trip

maraʾa, mariʾa, maruʾa (*v.*) to be wholesome, healthful, palatable (food) (Wehr 901b) 2611

Swahili (J)	murua	nice, pleasing, beautiful, elegant

murūʾa, murūwa the ideal of manhood, comprising all knightly virtues, esp. manliness, valor, chivalry, generosity, sense of honor (Wehr 902a) 2612

Malagasy (Gue)	moròa	elegant, beautiful
Swahili (J)	mrua	pleasant person; pleasing manners, honor, respect

marjānī coral red (Wehr 902a) 2614

Swahili (J)	marijani	red coral

marasa rope, cord, line; cable, hawser (Wehr 903b) 2617

Swahili (J)	maarasi	a pole with a load

maraḍ malady; sickness (Wehr 903b) 2620

Swahili (J)	maradhi	sickness, disease

marṭīs kind of blue stone (Dozy: II, 583a) 2622

Swahili (J)	mrututu (?)	sulphate of copper, bluestone, blue vitriol, often used as a caustic for sores

marmar marble (Wehr 905a) 2624

Swahili (J)	marmar	marble

mazzāḥ; māziḥ joker, jester, buffoon, wag (Wehr 906a) 2627

Swahili (J)	mzaha	fun, joke, ridicule, derision

massa (*v.*) to feel, finger, handle, palpate (III) to touch (Wehr 906b) **2628**

Swahili (Me)	-tomasa (*v.*) (?)	press, feel

al-masīḥ the Messiah, Christ (Wehr 907b) **2630**

Swahili (J)	Masiya	Christ

al-masīḥīya Christendom; Christianity, the Christian faith (Wehr 907b) **2631**

Swahili (J)	masihiya, mmasihiya	a Christian

misk musk (Wehr 909a) **2632**

Swahili (J)	miski	musk, or similar perfume

miskīn poor (Wehr 909b) **2633**

Gwere (Ka)g	ó-masikíiní	beggar (via Swahili)
Kamba (Mbi)	masĩkinĩ	beggar (via Swahili)
Malagasy (Gue)	masikìny, maskìny	poor, miserable, for whom we have pity
Rendille (P&G)	miksíin / miskíin	poor person (via Swahili)
Runyankore (Ka)	masikî:ni	beggar (via Swahili)
Swahili (J)	maskini	a poor man, beggar

masāʾ al-ḫair good evening! (Wehr 910a) **2634**

Swahili (J)	masalkheri	good evening

mušṭ comb (Wehr 910a) **2635a**

Madi (Bla)	mísītì	comb

miṣr, (*colloq.*) **maṣr** Egypt; Cairo (Wehr 911b) **2637**

Dholuo (Odo)	Miciri	Egypt, an old name for it, found in the Bible [Old Testament]
Luganda (Sno)	Mùmisìri	Egyptian (via Swahili)
Lunyankole (Dav)	Misiri	Egypt
Lunyoro (Dav)	Misiri	Egypt
Ndogo (Po)	Masri	Egypt
Swahili (J)	Misri	Egypt

muṭrān, maṭrān, miṭrān metropolitan, archbishop (Wehr 914a) **2639a**

Dinka (Id)	mutran	archbishop
Ndogo (Po)	mutran	bishop

maġar, muġra reddish, russet color (Wehr 916a); **maġar** okra (RT 467a) **2639b**

Madi (Bla)	mòláà	okra; lady finger

makka Mecca (Wehr 917a) **2640**

Malagasy (Gue)	Màka	Mecca
Swahili (J)	Maka	Mecca

makuna (*v.*) to be or become strong (Wehr 917b); **makīn** strong, firm, solid (Wehr 918a) **2644**

Swahili (J)	makini (*n. + adj.*)	strength of character, dignity; quiet, calm, amenable, gentle

makina, mākīna machine (Wehr 918b); **makana / makanât** machine, engine (JdP 810a); **mákina** machine (RL 468b) **2645**

Acooli (Mu)	makana	machine
Bari (Mu)	makana, makanajin	machine
Dinka (Id)	makana	engine
Lotuxo (Mu)	amakana	machine
Ndogo (Po)	makana	machine

milla religious community; faith (Wehr 918b) 2646

Digo (MN&Z)	mila	custom, tradition (via Swahili)
Swahili (J)	mila	custom, habit, usage

malāla weariness, boredom; ennui (Wehr 919a) 2647

Swahili (J)	malale	sleeping sickness

mala'a (*v.*) to fill, fill up (Wehr 919a) 2648

Swahili (J)	milele (*n.* + *adv.*) (?)	eternity, perpetuity

malāriyā malaria (Wehr 920a); **milârya** malaria, paludism (JdP 859a); **malāryā** malaria (RL 469b) 2648a

Acooli (Mu)	malarya	malaria
Bari (Mu)	malarya	malaria
Lotuxo (Mu)	amalarya	malaria
Kinyarwanda (CAT)	malariya	malaria

milḥ salt (Wehr 920a); **mileh** cooking salt (JdP 859a); **mili/eh** salt (Kaye 57b); **mile** salt (S&A 132b) 2649

Dinka (Id)	mela, melh	salt
Shilluk (Koh)	omɛllo	salt

milk property, possessions, wealth (Wehr 922b) 2654

Digo (MN&Z)	milki	possession (via Swahili)
Swahili (J)	milki	possession, property, dominion, kingdom

malik king, sovereign, monarch (Wehr 922b) 2655

Swahili (J)	maliki, malki	a king, ruler, sovereign

mal'ak, pl. **malā'ika** angel (Wehr 922b) 2657

Ateso (Kit)	emalaika	angel
Dholuo (Gor)	malaika, malaike	angel
(Odo)	lamaraika	angel (an old name, now called
	lumalaika/	lamalaika) (via Swahili)
	lumaraika	angels
Digo (MN&Z)	malaika	angel (via Swahili)
Gikuyu (Ben)	*mũ*raika	angel (via Swahili)
Kamba (Mbi)	mũlaika	angel (via Swahili)
Kuria (MMR)	omomalaika / omomaraika	angel
Luganda (Sno)	màlayìka	angel (via Swahili)
Madi (Bla)	màlááīkà	angel (via Swahili)
Malagasy (Gue)	malaìka	angel
Matengo (Häf)	malaika	angel (via Swahili)
Swahili (J)	malaika	messenger, angel, a good spirit

mulkī civil (as opposed to military) (Wehr 922b); **malakī** civil (not military) (RT 470b); **melaki** civil (S&A 132a) 2657a

Madi (Bla)	màlàkíà	civilian residential area
	mélēkì	of or related to civil life; civilian

mamlaka kingdom, empire, state; sovereignty (Wehr 923a) 2658

Digo (MN&Z)	mamlaka	authority (via Swahili)
Swahili (J)	mamlaka	authority, dominion, rule, rights of ownership; property, possession

tamalluk taking possession; domination, control, mastery (Wehr 923a) 2659

Swahili (J)	matamalaki	rule

imlā' dictation (Wehr 924a) 2662

Swahili (J)	imla	dictation

milāya wrap worn by Egyptian women; bed sheet (Wehr 924a) **2662a**

Dinka (Id)	malaya	bed sheet

malīya, pl. **malāyā** (*tun.*) garment of Bedouin women (Wehr 924a) **2663**

Acooli (Cra)	màlayà	harlot
	mùlayà	Europe; harlot (via Swahili)
Dholuo (Odo)	malaya	harlot, prostitute (via Swahili)
Digo (MN&Z)	malaya	prostitute (via Swahili)
Luganda (Sno)	màlaàyà	harlot; banana on Entebe peninsula (via Swahili)
Madi (Bla)	màláyà	prostitute
Pokot (Cra)	cè-màláyán	prostitute (via Swahili)
Swahili (J)	malaya	a prostitute, either male or female (< Pers.); a short garment worn by some women

min (*prep.*) of; some, some of, (a) part of; belonging to, from among (Wehr 924a) **2664**

Swahili (J)	min (*prep.*)	in Arabic, used in such words as *min ghayri, min tarafu, min ajili*

mannān kind; benign; **al-mannān** (one of the attributes of God) the Benefactor (Wehr 925b) **2665**

Swahili (J)	Manani	a title of God, the Beneficient

mandīl, mindīl kerchief; handkerchief (Wehr 926a); **mindîl** small shawl, scarf, handkerchief (JdP 860b); **mandīl** handkerchief (RL 483b) **2666**

Madi (Bla)	mèndílì	handkerchief; head scarf; table cloth
Ndogo (Po)	mandili	handkerchief

manan, manīya fate; death (Wehr 928a); **manan** death, pl. **maniyy** two pounds weight (Kazim: II, 1158b) **2670**

Swahili (J)	mani	a weight, about three pounds

minan semen, sperm (Wehr 928a) 2671

Digo (MN&Z)	minya	sperm (via Swahili)
Swahili (J)	manii	sperm

mahd bed; cradle (Wehr 928b) 2673

Swahili (J)	mahdi	cradle, a bed (rarely heard)
	mede	a small bedstead, used as a seat for guests

mahr dower; price, stake (Wehr 929a) 2674

Malagasy (Gue)	mahàri	matrimonial compensation, dower paid according to Muslim law by the husband to his wife
Swahili (J)	mahari	marriage settlement, money or property paid to the wife's relations, or settled on the wife, dowry

māhir skillful, adroit, expert, experienced (Wehr 929a) 2675

Swahili (J)	mahiri (*adj.*)	skillful, clever, quick, adept, adroit, artful

muhr seal, signet; stamp (Wehr 929a) 2676

Swahili (J)	muhuri	seal, signet, crest, armorial bearing

muhla respite, delay; time limit for a decision, time to think s.th. (Wehr 929b) 2677

Swahili (J)	muhula	space of time, period, interval

maut death (Wehr 930a) 2678

Digo (MN&Z)	mauti	death of a person (via Swahili)
Swahili (J)	mauti	death

mayyit, mait lifeless, deceased (Wehr 930a); **maita** corpse, carcass, carrion; meat of an animal not slaughtered in accordance with ritual requirements (*Isl. law*) (Wehr 930b) 2679

Malagasy (Gue)	maìty	corpse
Ngh'wele Leg	maiti	body, corpse (via Swahili)
Swahili (J)	maiti	a dead body, corpse (usu. human body only; a dead person)

mauj billows, seas; waves; **mauja** billow, sea, breaker; wave (Wehr 930b) 2680

Swahili (J)	mauja, muuya, mwuja	agitation, danger, misfortune; a wave

mauz banana (Wehr 931b) 2681

Swahili (J)	mazu	kind of banana

mūsīqā music (Wehr 931b); **musîxa** music (JdP 949a); **mizzīga** music (RL 461b) 2683a

Dinka (Id)	musica	music
Ndogo (Po)	muzika	music

māl goods; wealth; money; goods (Wehr 931b); **ma:l** money, wealth (Z&T 132) 2684

Acooli (Cra)	määlî	goods, wealth
Dholuo (Odo)	mali	wealth; used often in the 1920s and 1930s
Digo (MN&Z)	mali	possessions, wealth, brideprice (via Swahili)
Haya (Ka)	emá:lsi	property; material possession (via Swahili)
Ila (Smi)	Madi	money
Khoi-Khoin (Krö)	maríb (?)	money
Luganda (Sno)	\`mmaàli	possessions; money; wealth (via Swahili)
Malagasy (Gue)	màly	wealth, fortune

Ndogo (Po)	mali	money with which one pays the bride; wealth
Ndonga (Tir)	oshi/maliwa	coin, money, finance
Shona (Dal)	mari	money (cash) (via Swahili)
Swahili (J)	mali	property, goods, wealth
Xhosa (Fis)	imali	money (? via Swahili)
Zulu (Bry)	mali	money, cash

Nūn

nāmūs law; rule; honor (Wehr 936b) **2690**

Swahili (J)	nemsi	good name, honor (rarely heard)

nabīḏ wine (Wehr 938b); **nabīt** wine (RT 478a) and **nabīḍ** wine (RT 478b); **nabiiz** wine (S&A 135b) **2691a**

Ndogo (Po)	nebit	wine

nibr, **anbār** barn, shed, warehouse (Wehr 938b); **ambar** ward (S&A 88b) **2691b**

Madi (Bla)	ámbārà	hospital ward

minbar minbar; pulpit (Wehr 939a) **2692**

Swahili (J)	mimbari	a pulpit (in a mosque)

nabl arrows (Wehr 940a); **nible** catapult, slingshot (JdP 1008a); **nibla** catapult (RL 479a) **2693a**

Ndogo (Po)	nibla	slingshot

nabiha (*v.*) to mind, note, observe (V) to perceive; to be alerted (Wehr 940b) **2694**

Swahili (J)	-nabihi (*v.*)	remember, perceive

tanabbuh awakening, wakefulness, alertness (Wehr 941a) 2696

Malagasy (Gue)	kotanabày	realize
Swahili (J)	-tanabahi (*v.*)	be awake to, give attention (to), turn the mind to, carefully notice and consider, form a conclusion (about); be on the alert, be ready; understand

nabīy prophet (Wehr 941b) 2697

Ateso (Kit)	enabi	prophet
Bari (Mu)	nebi	prophet
Dholuo (Odo)	lanebi s. lunebi pl.	prophet
Digo (MN&Z)	nabii	prophet (via Swahili)
Gikuyu (Ben)	*mũ*nabii	prophet (via Swahili)
Kuria (MMR)	omonaabi	prophet
	enaabi / obonaabi	prophecy
Swahili (J)	nabii	a prophet, a preacher of righteousness, one who foretells the future

najjār carpenter (Wehr 944a); **najjâr / najjârîn** sculptor, carpenter (JdP 944b) 2697a

Dinka (Id)	najar	carpenter
Madi (Bla)	nàjárɨ̀	carpenter

najis impure, unclean (Wehr 945a) 2699

Digo (MN&Z)	najisi	unclean in a religious sense, defiled, profane (via Swahili)
Swahili (J)	-najisi (*v.* + *adj.*)	defile, contaminate, pollute, cause ceremonial uncleanness

najm, pl. **nujūm** celestial body; star; lucky star (Wehr 945b) 2700

Swahili (J)	jumu, nujumu	fortune, luck

najjām, **munajjim** astrologer (Wehr 945b) 2701

Swahili (J)	mnajimu	an astrologer

naḥs, pl. **nuḥūs** misfortune, calamity, disaster (Wehr 947a) 2703

Swahili (J)	nuksani, nuksi, nuhusi	bad luck, a quarrel, a mischievous action

naḥw grammar; syntax (Wehr 948b) 2706

Swahili (J)	nahau	explanation; grammar, syntax

nāḫuḏā boss of a boat, captain of a ship (Kazim: II, 1220a) 2708

Malagasy (Gue)	nahòda	boss, captain of a boat; in a boat where there are only two men; marine
Swahili (J)	nahodha	captain (of a vessel); a name for the Heron

nadra rarity, rareness (Wehr 951b) 2712

Swahili (J)	nadra (*adj.*)	uncommon, rare

nadā (*v.*) to call together (III) to shout; to proclaim, announce (Wehr 952b) 2715

Swahili (J)	-nadi (*v.*)	call, summon, announce publicly, proclaim; hold a sale (or public auction), hawk about the streets

naḏīr consecrated to God; vowed, solemnly pledged (Wehr 953b) 2716

Malagasy (Gue)	nadàra	vow that one makes to God (or to a sacred place)
Swahili (J)	nadhiri	vow, solemn promise, dedication of s.th. to God

naḏl low, mean, vile, despicable, debased (Wehr 953b) 2717

Swahili (J)	anzali	an abject, despised person

narjis, nirjis narcissus (*bot.*) (Wehr 954a) 2718

Swahili (J)	nargisi	a bulb plant rather like an onion with white flowers, also its flowers

nazr, nazīr little; insignificant (Wehr 954b) 2719

Swahili (J)	nusura (*adv.*)	almost, nearly, within a little

naza'a (*v.*) to extract (III) to fight, struggle, dispute (Wehr 954b) 2720

Swahili (J)	nazaa (*n.* + *v.*)	a quarrel, contention, noise, confusion, feud

manzila degree; position; dignity (Wehr 958a) 2721

Swahili (J)	manzili, menzili	circumstances, position (as given by God)

nasab lineage, descent; kinship, relationship by marriage (Wehr 960a) 2724

Swahili (J)	nasaba	pedigree, genealogy, lineage

nāsūr fistula (Wehr 961b) 2727

Swahili (J)	nasuri	a fistula

nusāla fibrous waste, thrums (Wehr 962b) 2729

Swahili (J)	mansuli	a kind of woollen material, used for dress and as a coverlet

inšā' creation; composition, writing; essay (Wehr 964a) 2731

Swahili (J)	insha	an essay, composition

nušādir ammonia (Wehr 965a) 2733

Swahili (J)	shazasi	sal-ammoniac

nišān, nīšān sign; mark, medal (Wehr 967b) 2736

Swahili (J)	nishani	a medal, decoration, badge

našā' starch, cornstarch (Wehr 967b) 2738

Swahili (J)	nisha, nishaa	starch (rarely heard)

naṣīb luck; chance; fate (Wehr 969a) 2741

Swahili (J)	nasibu	chance, fortune, accident, destiny

naṣīḥa sincere advice; friendly admonition (Wehr 970a) 2742

Swahili (J)	nasiha	a sincere friend, faithful counselor, wise adviser

nuṣra aid, assistance (Wehr 970a) 2746

Malagasy (Gue)	nosòra	relief, help
Swahili (J)	nusura, nusra	aid, help

naṣāra, pl. of **naṣrānī** Christian (Wehr 970a) 2747

Swahili (J)	mnasara	Nazarene, used of Christians by Muslims

niṣf, nuṣf half (Wehr 971a); **nuss** half (Kaye 62b) 2748

Acooli (Cra)	nùcù	half (a shilling)
(Mu)	nucu	half
Bari (Mu)	nusu	half
Dholuo (Gor)	nus, nuse	half
(Odo)	nucu	
Gikuyu (Ben)	nuthu	half; 50-cent piece; portion more or less than one-half (via Swahili)
Kinyarwanda (CAT)	nusu	half (via Swahili)
Kuria (MMR)	enoso	half
Lotuxo (Mu)	nanus	half
Luganda (Sno)	`nnusù	half (via Swahili)
Madi (Bla)	núsù / nùsù	half
Malagasy (Gue)	nòso	half
Ndogo (Po)	nusu	half
Rendille (P&G)	nyúus	half (via Swahili)
Swahili (J)	nusu	a half, a part, a portion, a bit

naṭrūn, aṭrūn natron (Wehr 973b) < Greek νίτρον; **atrôn** natron, sodium salt (JdP 201a; RL 21a) 2751

Madi (Bla)	àtùrúnì	sodium bicarbonate (via Swahili **aturun**)

naẓar vision; look, glance; study; consideration (Wehr 975b) 2754

Swahili (J)	nadhari	look, glance; attention, consideration; choice, discretion, judgment, common sense

naẓẓāra binocular; telescope, spyglass; (pair of) eyeglasses (Wehr 976b); **naddâra / naddârât** pair of glasses (JdP 981a); **nadaara** glasses, spectacles (S&A 135b) 2754a

Acooli (Cra)	maádaàrà	mirror; (pair of) glasses
(Mu)	maddara	
Bari (Mu)	mandara	mirror; (pair of) glasses

Dholuo (Odo)	mandara	looking glas4s
Dinka (Id)	mandhara	mirror
Lotuxo (Mu)	amannara	mirror; (pair of) glasses
Ndogo (Po)	mandara	mirror; window

manẓar view; appearance, aspect (Wehr 977a) 2755

Swahili (J)	mandhari	appearance, aspect, landscape, prospect, view, scene, show

minẓār telescope, spyglass; magnifying glass; mirror (Wehr 977a) 2756

Dinka (Id)	mandhara	mirror

nāẓir supervisor; director, chief (Wehr 977a) 2757a

Dinka (Id)	naajir	director

naẓīf clean, neat (Wehr 977b) 2759

Swahili (J)	nadhifu (*adj.*)	clean, neat, well kept

naʿam yes (Wehr 980a) 2763

Digo (MN&Z)	naam	yes (via Swahili)
Malagasy (Gue)	nàam	yes ?
Swahili (J)	naam!	yes, certainly

naʿma life of ease; prosperity; happiness (Wehr 980b); **niʿma** benefit, blessing (Wehr 980b) 2764

Luganda (Mo)	\`e\`nne^e:ma	grace, blessing (via Swahili)
Swahili (J)	neema	ease, affluence; favor, grace

naʿām ostrich (Wehr 980b); **naʿâm** ostrich, *Struthio camelus* (JdP 976a) 2764a

Ndogo (Po)	naam	ostrich

na'na', **na'nā'** mint; peppermint (*bot.*) (Wehr 981a) 2766

Malagasy (Gue)	nàna	mint
Swahili (J)	nanaa	mint

minfāḫ bellows; air pump, tire pump (Wehr 982b) 2767a

Dinka (Id)	mafak	pump

nafīr band, party, group (Wehr 984b); working group, mutual aid, collective help (JdP 986a); sound; call of trumpet (RL 493b) 2769

Ndogo (Po)	nafir	trumpet

nafs soul; mind; human being; desire (Wehr 985a); **nafsân** / **nafsânîn** greedy, selfish, sponger, parasite (JdP 986b). 2770

Digo (MN&Z)	nafsi	person, self, soul (via Swahili)
Malagasy (Gue)	nafòsy	the body, the person
Swahili (J)	nafsi	vital spirit, breath, soul, self, person, individuality, essence

nafas breath; puff (from a smoking pipe, from a cigarette); swallow (Wehr 985b) 2772

Digo (MN&Z)	nafwasi	(1) opportunity, occasion (2) space (via Swahili)
Malagasy (Gue)	nafàsy	opportunity, time, leisure (to do s.th.); ease, tranquility
Swahili (J)	nafasi	breathing time, space, room, opportunity, leisure, relief, spare time; interval

tanaffus respiration (Wehr 986a) 2773

Swahili (J)	-tanafusi (*v.*)	breathe, draw breath, recover breath

nafaḍa (*v.*) to recover (Wehr 986b); **nafaḍa** (*v.*) to be cured, restored from illness (Kazim: II, 1312a) 2774

Swahili (J)	-nafidhi (*v.*)	save, help

naf‘ advantage, profit (Wehr 987a); **nafū‘** very useful, of good use (Wehr 987a); **nâfi** useful, effective (Daf 100) 2775

Swahili (J)	nafuu	profit, advantage

manfa‘a use, benefit; advantage, profit, gain (Wehr 987a) 2775a

Malagasy (Gue)	manofà	utility, profit, importance
Swahili (J)	manufaa	useful things, provisions

nafaqa cost of living (Wehr 987b) 2776

Swahili (J)	nafaka	corn, grain

munāfiq hypocrite (Wehr 988a) 2777

Digo (MN&Z)	mnafiki	hypocrite (via Swahili)
Malagasy (Gue)	monfìky, mnafìky	liar, curious and malicious, reporter, informer, whistleblower
Swahili (J)	mnafiki	a hypocrite, pretender, impostor, liar

naqdī monetary; cash (*adj.*) (Wehr 990a) 2781

Swahili (J)	nakidi, nakudi	cash, ready money, payment on the spot

naqš sculpture (Wehr 991b) 2783

Swahili (J)	nakshi (*n.* + *v.*)	carving, carved ornament

naqṣ defect, fault (Wehr 992a) 2785

Swahili (J)	nakisi	reduction, deficit, blemish

nuqṭa point (Wehr 993a); **nugta / nugat** point, drop (JdP 1015b) 2788

Luganda (Sno)	`nnukùta	letter of the alphabet
(Mo)	`e`nnuk`uta	(via Swahili)
Madi (Bla)	nɔ́kɔ̄tà	an important point to be made; full stop, period; a small trading post; a police station
Malagasy (Gue)	nakòta	point (on a letter)
Swahili (J)	nukta	a dot, point, mark, spot, vowel sign; a second (of time)

naqala (*v.*) to move; to transfer; to copy (Wehr 994a); **nagal / yangul** (*v.*) to carry (JdP 988b); **nanggalu** (*v.*) copy, transfer (S&A 136b) 2789

Malagasy (Gue)	mikotanakalìha	be changed into, transformed into
Madi (Bla)	ɪ̄nggɔ̄lɔ̀ (*v.*)	copy the work of another; transfer
Swahili (Sacl)	-tanakali (*v.*)	to move or be transported elsewhere, transferred

naql transport; translation, transcription, copy; tradition (Wehr 995a) 2790

Swahili (J)	nakili, nakula (*n.* + *v.*) nakala	a copy, an imitation, a translation, duplicate

naqāwa, **nuqāwa** purity (Wehr 996b) 2791

Swahili (J)	nakawa (*adj.*)	clear, good-looking, in sound condition, of fine quality (of persons and things)

naqīy pure, clean (Wehr 997a) 2792

Swahili (J)	-jinaki (*v.*)	(used only as a reflex. verb form), to consider oneself pure, be proud

nikāḥ marriage (Wehr 997b) 2793

Swahili (J)	nikaha, nikahi	marriage

munkar one of the angels of death (Wehr 998b), see **nakīr** 2797

Swahili (J)	munkari	a wicked, bad, malevolent person

numra, **nimra** number, numero (Wehr 1000b) 2802a

Madi (Bla)	nìmìrà	number

nāmūsīya mosquito net (Wehr 1000b); **nāmūsīye** mosquito net (Kaye 61b); **namliiya** mosquito wire (S&A 136b) 2803

Madi (Bla)	lɛ̀mɛ̀síà	mosquito net
	lɛ̀mɛ̀líà / àmɛ̀líà	sieve; wire net

namā (*v.*) to grow; to increase (Wehr 1001b) 2805

Swahili (J)	nomi (*adv.*)	full up to the brim

nā'ib substitute (Wehr 1008a) 2810

Swahili (J)	naibu	deputy

nūbī (*adj.* and *n.*) Nubian (Wehr 1008a); **Nûba** Nubian (-enne), Black (JdP 1014b); **nubāï** who is not Arab and who is not a fetishist (RL 501b) 2811

Swahili (J)	Mnubi	Nubian

nūr light; ray of light; glow (Wehr 1009a) 2814

Bari (Mu)	anur	lamp
Bende (Abe)	nuúlu	light
Lotuxo (Mu)	anur	lamp
Swahili (J)	nuru	light, brightness

manār, **manāra** lighthouse; minaret (Wehr 1009b) 2815

Digo (MN&Z)	mnara	lampstand, lighthouse (via Swahili)
Malagasy (Gue)	monàra	tower, esp. mosque minaret
Swahili (J)	mnara	a lighthouse; tower, minaret, steeple

naulūn, **nāwulūn** freightage, freight (Wehr 1012b) 2818

Nyakyusa (Fel)	inaulí	(e.g. bus) fare (via Swahili)
Swahili (J)	nauli (*n.* + *v.*)	fare, charge for freight (or conveyance), passage money

nawā (*v.*) to intend, propose, plan, have in mind, make up one's mind (Wehr 1013b) 2821

Swahili (J)	-nuia (*v.*)	have in mind, consider, purpose, intend

nīya intention (Wehr 1013b) 2822

Malagasy (Gue)	konìa	intend to
Swahili (J)	nia	intention, purpose

nīr yoke (Wehr 1014a) 2823

Swahili (J)	nira	a yoke (for oxen)

nīl, **nīla** indigo plant, indigo (Wehr 1015a) 2825

Swahili (J)	nili	indigo

Hā'

habba (*v.*) to get in motion, start moving (Wehr 1016a) 2826

Swahili (J)	hobe! (*interj.*)	go! clear off!

hataka (*v.*) to tear apart; to disgrace (Wehr 1018a) 2829

Swahili (J)	-hatiki (*v.*)	trouble, annoy (seldom used)

hajara (*v.*) to emigrate; to separate (Wehr 1019a) 2830

Swahili (J)	-hajiri, -hujuru (*v.*)	remove (from), leave, emigrate, move house

hudhud hoopoe (*zoo.*) (Wehr 1023a) 2836

Swahili (J)	hudhud	hoopoe

hadā (*v.*) to lead on the right way, guide (Wehr 1023a); **haddây / haddâyîn** counselor (JdP 529b); **hady** advice (Wehr 1023b) 2837

Swahili (J)	-hidi (*v.*)	convert, lead aright

hadīya, pl. **hadāyā᾽** gift, present (Wehr 1024a); **hdiya** (*n.* + *v.*) present, gift (Harrell 53b); **hadiye** present, gift (JdP 531a) 2838

Madi (Bla)	àdíà	gift; present
Malagasy (Gue)	hidàia	present, gift especially of God (precious and unexpected)
Swahili (J)	hedaya, hidaya	gift, present

haram, pl. **ahrām** pyramid (Wehr 1026a) 2841

Swahili (J)	haram, ihramu	the Pyramids

hurmān understanding, reason, spirit (Kazim: II, 1415b) 2842

Swahili (J)	-hirimia (*v.*)	purpose, decide, intend

huss hush! quiet! silence! (Wehr 1028b) 2843

Swahili (J)	huss! (*interj.*)	make less noise! be quite! silence!

hilāl new moon (Wehr 1030b) 2847

Swahili (J)	hilali	a crescent

tahlīl utterance of the formula *lā ilāha illā llāh* (Wehr 1030b) 2848

Swahili (J)	tahlili	funeral song, dirge, coronach (esp. of the recitation of the Muslim creed at a funeral)

halaka (*v.*) to perish; to die; to be destroyed (Wehr 1031b) 2849

Swahili (J)	-hiliki (*v.*)	be lost, destroyed, be ruined, perish

hamm anxiety; worry, care; sorrow, affliction (Wehr 1033a) 2851

Swahili (J)	hamu	longing, yearning, anxiety, love, desire for s.th. (either good or bad)

himma endeavor; ardor (Wehr 1033a) 2852

Swahili (J)	hima (*n.* + *adv.*)	energy, urgency, importance

muhimm important, significant (Wehr 1033b) 2853

Swahili (J)	muhimu (*adj.*)	important, special, significant, urgent

ahwan easy; comfortable (Wehr 1039b) 2861

Swahili (J)	ahueni	better condition regarding health

hawan love; affection; passion; desire, longing (Wehr 1040a) 2862

Swahili (J)	hawa	longing, strong inclination, passionate desire, passion

hawāʾ air; atmosphere; wind (Wehr 1040a) **2863**

Digo (MN&Z)	hurum	air (via Swahili)
Haya (M&L)	ehewa	air (via Swahili)
Kiw'oso (K&O)	hewâ	air
Malagasy (Gue)	hàoa	the air (we breathe)
Matengo (Yo)	hégwa	air
Swahili (J)	hewa	air, atmosphere

istihwāʾ fascination, captivation; enchantment; seduction (Wehr 1040b) **2863b**

Malagasy (Gue)	kostô, kostôo	well dressed, well decorated
Swahili (J)	-stahi (*v.*)	give honor to

hayyā (*interj.*) up! come on! let's go! (Wehr 1041a) **2865**

Gikuyu (Ben)	haya, heya (*interj.*)	1. surprise; there, didn't I tell you so? 2. encouragement; well done! come on! (via Swahili)
Swahili (J)	haya!	(used to call to action or effort) come on! now then! work away! step out! make haste!

hayyā (*interj.*) up! come on! let's go! (Wehr 1041a) + **nafsi** myself (Z&T 133): **hayyā** + **ti**+ **nafsi** "let's go myself!" **2866**

Swahili (J)	hatinafsi, hayatinafsi	used of a person taking an action without consulting anyone because he thinks they may try to persuade him not to do it; going one's own way without asking advice

haiba fear; respect; dignity; prestige (Wehr 1042a) **2867**

Swahili (J)	haiba, heba	beauty of countenance, appearance, but esp. of character

haikal temple (Wehr 1043b) 2869

Ateso (Kit)	eyekalu	temple
Dholuo (Gor)	hekalu	temple
Gikuyu (Gor)	hekaru	temple
Swahili (J)	hekalu	a temple, the temple at Jerusalem

Wāw

wa and; and also, and … too (Wehr 1044a) 2870

Madi (Bla)	wɔ̀ (*conj.*)	and, especially used in time-telling

wa-llāh by God! (Wehr 1044a) 2871

Swahili (J)	wallahi!, wallai!	by God!

wa-illā (and if not), otherwise (Wehr 1044a); **wallâ** or?, or else?, is? (JdP 1251a) 2872

Swahili (J)	wala (*conj.*)	or

wa-in even if, although (Wehr 1044b) 2873

Swahili (J)	waima, waina (*conj.*)	if not, otherwise

wa-lākin, wa-lakinna but, however (Wehr 1044b) 2874

Swahili (J)	walakini (*conj.*)	but, however, nevertheless, notwithstanding

wabaʾ, **wabāʾ** infectious disease; epidemic (Wehr 1045b); **wabaʾ** plague, epidemic disease (Kazim: II, 1475a) 2877

Swahili (J)	waba	cholera

wabr, pl. **wibār** daman (Hyrax syriaca) (Wehr 1045b) 2878

Swahili (J)	wibari	a hyrax, rock-rabbit

wabīl unhealthy, unwholesome (climate, food) (Wehr 1046a) 2879

Swahili (J)	-wapilia (*v.*)	smell strongly of scent, be heavily scented

watr, witr odd (number) (Wehr 1046b) 2881

Swahili (J)	witiri, wituri	odd (of a number)

watar, pl. **autār** string (of a bow, of a musical instrument); chord (*geom.*) (Wehr 1046b) 2882

Swahili (J)	utari	string of an instrument, leather thong, cord, rope

wājib incumbent; duty, obligation (Wehr 1049a) 2886

Swahili (J)	wajibu	what is right, suitable

mūjib obligating, necessitating (Wehr 1049b) 2887

Swahili (J)	mujibu, muujibu	duty, obligation, due courtesy

wajāḥ sail, curtain; stone with a smooth and smooth surface (Kazim: II, 1489a) 2888

Swahili (J)	barawaji (?)	a cloth (rarely used now), like a silk shawl, worn round the waist

wajuha (*v.*) to be a man of distinction, belong to the notables (III) to be opposite s.th.; to meet, counter; to envisage (Wehr 1051b) 2891

Swahili (J)	-ajihi (*v.*)	visit a person living at a distance

wajh front, face; appearance; direction (Wehr 1052a); **wijih / wujûh** visage, figure, face (JdP 1265b) 2893

Swahili (J)	wajihi (*n.* + *v.*)	form, appearance

wāḥid one (numeral); someone; sole, only (Wehr 1055b) 2895

Madi (Bla)	wáyì (*num.*)	one, used in time-telling
Swahili (J)	wahedi (*n.* + *adj.*)	one (the numeral)
	wahedu (*adv.*)	alone, only

waḥā (*v.*) to inspire; to reveal (Wehr 1056b); (*v.*) to hurry, go fast (Kazim: II, 1502b) 2898

Swahili (J)	-wahi (*v.*)	be in time, be prompt (ready, forward)

wadaʿa (*v.*) to put down, lodge, deposit (Wehr 1058a) (III) to reconcile, make peace, make amends with s.o. (Kazim: II, 1509a) 2902

Swahili (J)	-adi (*v.*)	accompany a person part of his way, as a polite attention
	edaha	a sacrifice or offering made for some special object

diya blood money; indemnity for body injury (Wehr 1059b); **dîya** blood price (Daf 31) 2906

Swahili (J)	dia	money paid for a life, fine for murder, ransom

wādin valley; river bed (Wehr 1059b) 2907

Swahili (J)	wadi	watercourse, bed of a torrent, ravine (seldom used)

wariṯa (*v.*) to be heir (Wehr 1060a) 2908

Digo (MN&Z)	urisi	inheritance (via Swahili)
Malagasy (Gue)	koarisìna, koarithìna	which one inherits
Swahili (J)	-rithi (*v.*)	inherit
	urithi	inheritance, legacy

warīṯ heir (Wehr 1060a) 2911

Swahili (J)	warithi	an heir

mīrāṯ heritage, inheritance (Wehr 1060a) **2912**

Malagasy (Gue)	moaràta, moaràtha	heritage
Swahili (J)	mirathi	inheritance, heritage

wird, pl. **aurād** specified time of day or night devoted to private worship (in addition to prescribed prayers) (Wehr 1060b); litany of the Sufi brotherhood (Clarke 1982: 264) **2914**

Swahili (J)	uradhi, auradi	prayers said at a Muslim burial

ward rose(s) (Wehr 1061b); **wardī** roseate (Wehr 1061b) **2916**

Swahili (J)	waridi	a rose

warša workshop (Wehr 1061b) **2916a**

Dinka (Id)	warca	workshop

waraq foliage, leaves; paper (Wehr 1062a); **waraqa** sheet of paper (Wehr 1062b); **waragá** leaf; paper; leather amulet worn around the neck, containing excerpts from Qur'an (Kaye 83a) **2917**

Acooli (Cra)	waragà	paper, book, etc.
Bari (Mu)	waraga, waragat	card; cardboard; paper
Dholuo (Odo)	waraga	paper, letter, epistle
Dinka (Id)	waragak	paper, book
Lotuxo (Mu)	awaraga, awaragaa', agagar	card; letter (written message); paper
Madi (Bla)	wárāgà	paper; newspaper; letter
Ndogo (Po)	waraga	letter; mail
Swahili (J)	waraka	a letter (of correspondence), document; a cigarette paper

wazīr vizier (Wehr 1064a) **2922**

Digo (MN&Z)	waziri	government minister (via Swahili)
Madi (Bla)	ɔ̀zárà	ministry
	òzírì	(government) minister

Malagasy (Gue)	oazìry	vizier, an ancient title of the hierarchy of the Comorian kingdoms
Swahili (J)	waziri	prime minister

waza'a (*v.*) to curb, restrain (II) to distribute, allot (Wehr 1064b) 2923

Swahili (J)	-awadha, -awaza (*v.*)	allot, arrange, dispose (seldom heard)

mīzān balance (Wehr 1065b); **mîzân / mawâzîn** balance (JdP 865a) 2924

Acooli (Cra)	màjáàn	balance, weighing machine
Dholuo (Odo)	majan	a balance, weighing scale
Dinka (Id)	mizam	scales (weight)
Luganda (Sno)	mìnzaàni	scales for weighing; spring balance (via Swahili)
Swahili (J)	mizani	balance; clock, watch

wasaḫ, pl. **ausāḫ** dirt; squalor (Wehr 1066a); **wasax** dirt, junk (JdP 1258b); **wasxân / wasxânîn** (*adj.*) dirty (JdP 1261b) 2925

Swahili (J)	usaha	pus, discharge

wasṭānī middle, central; medium (Wehr 1067a) 2928

Swahili (J)	wastani (*n.* + *adj.*)	middling, average, medium, between extremes

wasa' vastness, vast space (Wehr 1068b) 2931

Swahili (J)	wasaa	room, space, freedom, means, leisure, opportunity

mausim time of the year, season; festive season (Wehr 1070a) 2934

Swahili (J)	msimu, musimu	the northeast monsoon; a season

waswās devilish insinuation; doubt (Wehr 1070b) 2935

Digo (MN&Z)	wasi-wasi	worry, fear; doubt, uncertainty (via Swahili)
Swahili (J)	wasiwasi	doubt, perplexity, scruple

waṣafa (*v.*) to describe; to praise (Wehr 1072a); **wassaf** / **yiwassif** (*v.*) (II) to show, indicate (JdP 1260a) 2938

Malagasy (Gue)	mikosifìa	describe, rent
Swahili (J)	-wasifu (*v.*)	describe, explain
	-tawasifu (*v.*)	give information
	tawasifu	moderation, temperance, good character

ṣifa quality, property; attribute; adjective (*gram.*); way, manner (Wehr 1072a) 2939

Malagasy (Gue)	sìfa	reputation
Swahili (J)	sifa	praise, commendation, flattery, applause; character, reputation, fame, characteristic; an adjective

waṣala (*v.*) to unite; to arrive; to come; to reach (Wehr 1072b) 2940

Swahili (J)	wasili (+ *v.*)	receipt, income, credit side of cash account; arrive, reach, come to

W Ṣ Y (*v.*) (II) to order, charge; to give s.o. an order for; to will (Wehr 1075a); **wassa** / **yiwassi** (*v.*) (II) to advise (JdP 1259b); **waṣāh** advice (Wehr 1075b); **wasiye** / **wasâya** advice, recommendation, order (JdP 1259a) 2943

Swahili (J)	-asa (*v.*)	forbid, warn
	-wasa (*v.*)	

waṣīy executor; trustee (Wehr 1075a) 2944

Malagasy (Gue)	koôsy	to whom we leave our last wishes
Swahili (J)	wasii	executor, trustee

waṣīya direction; exhortation; will, testament; legacy (Wehr 1075a) 2945

Digo (MN&Z)	wasiya	will, testament, final instructions (via Swahili)
Malagasy (Gue)	oasìa	last wishes, last words, recommendations, sentence, wisdom advice
Swahili (J)	usia (+ *v.*)	solemn charge, last will and testament, warning, exhortation, commission
	wosia (+ *v.*)	sometimes heard for *usia*; last will and testament

wuḍūʾ purity; ritual ablution before prayer (Wehr 1075b) 2947

Swahili (J)	udhu	state of ceremonial purity

tawaḍḍuʾ ritual ablution (Wehr 1076a) 2948

Malagasy (Gue)	mikotaoàza	do his ablutions (rituals, before prayer)
Swahili (J)	-tawadha (*v.*)	perform ceremonial ablution (esp. as to the feet: *-tawadha miguu*)

muwāṭin compatriot, fellow citizen (Wehr 1080a); **muwâtin** / **muwâtinîn** citizen (JdP 965b) 2951a

Madi (Bla)	mὸátīnɨ̀	citizen

waʿd promise (Wehr 1081a) 2954

Swahili (J)	wadi (+ *v.*)	appointed time

mīʿād promise; appointment (Wehr 1081a) 2955

Swahili (J)	miadi	a promise, esp. with reference to a particular time or date

waʿẓ, waʿẓa admonition; warning; sermon (Wehr 1082a) 2956

Swahili (J)	waadhi	a sermon, solemn exhortation

mauʿiẓa religious exhortation, spiritual counsel; exhortation (Wehr 1082a) 2957

Swahili (J)	mauidha, maowidha, mauwidha	good advice, teachings, exhortations

wiʿāʾ vessel, container, receptacle (Wehr 1082b) 2959

Swahili (J)	waya	an earthen dish for baking cakes in

wafiqa (*v.*) to be right, proper, suitable (v) to be favored (by God) (viii) **ittafaqa** to agree (Wehr 1084b) 2961

Malagasy (Gue)	koafiky	to get along, agree, trust
Swahili (J)	-afiki (*v.*)	agree with, accord with, correspond to, be same as, fit (seldom used)

taufīq success (granted by God), prosperity, successfulness (Wehr 1085b) 2962

Swahili (J)	taufiki	guidance and grace of God, fulfilment of one's wishes, success, prosperity

muwāfaqa agreement; correspondence; approval (Wehr 1085b) 2964

Swahili (J)	mwafaka	agreement, bargain, pact, conspiracy, plot

ittifāq coincidence; agreement (Wehr 1085b) **2966**

Swahili (J)	itifaki	agreement, concord, harmony

waqt time (Wehr 1087a); **waqa/it** time (Kaye 83a); **wakit / awkât** time, moment (JdP 1249b) **2970**

Digo (MN&Z)	wakati	time, season, period (via Swahili)
Luganda (Sno)	wàkàtî (*adv.*)	in the middle; midway (via Swahili)
Malagasy (Gue)	oakàty, kàty	moment, time
Swahili (J)	wakati	time, season

waqaʿa (*v.*) to happen, befall (Wehr 1089a) **2971**

Swahili (J)	wakaa	time, a single time

waqafa (*v.*) to stop; to get up; (*pass.*) **wuqifa** to institute a religious endowment or *waqf* (Wehr 1091a) **2973**

Swahili (J)	-wakifu, -akifu (*v.*)	stand, stop; be priced at, cause expense
	-akifia (*v.*)	entrust with (property, money)

waqf stop; pause (*gram.*); religious endowment, *waqf*, "habous" (*Isl. law*) (Wehr 1093a) **2974**

Swahili (J)	wakf	s.th. set apart for religious purposes, consecrated, devoted to a holy use, esp. of land or other gifts assigned to a mosque for its expenses, pay of the minister, or land left by will for use as burial ground

wiqīya a weight (Wehr 1095a) 2976

Swahili (J)	wakia	an ounce (weight) (formerly reckoned in Zanzibar as the weight of an Austrian silver dollar piece, *thaler*)

muttakaʾ cushion, pad (Wehr 1095a) 2978

Swahili (J)	takia	a large cushion

wakala (*v.*) to entrust (Wehr 1096a) 2979

Malagasy (Gue)	oakàla	the woman's proxy for the engagement of a marriage; wedding witness
Swahili (J)	wakala	agency, commission

wakīl authorized representative (Wehr 1096a) 2980

Digo (MN&Z)	wakili	advocate, attorney (via Swahili)
Madi (Bla)	òkílì	assistant, deputy; a person who acts as a deputy for another
Swahili (J)	wakili	agent, steward, representative

wakāla representation; agency (Wehr 1096b) 2981

Swahili (J)	wakala	agency, appointment, commission, power of attorney

taukīl authorization (Wehr 1096b) 2981a

Madi (Bla)	tòkílì	proxy

tawakkul trust, confidence; trust in God (Wehr 1096b) 2981b

Malagasy (Gue)	mikotanakalìha	to be changed into, transformed into
Swahili (J)	-tawakali (*v.*)	put trust in

walad, pl. **aulād** descendant; child; son; boy (Wehr 1097b) 2982

Swahili (J)	wadi	son of
	uledi	cabin boy

walad al-nās people's son (Wehr 1097b) 2983

Swahili (J)	wadinasi	a man of good birth

maulid birthday (Wehr 1097b) 2984

Digo (MN&Z)	maulidi	anniversary, Muslim ceremony of remembrance (e.g. forty days after a death) (via Swahili)
Swahili (J)	maulidi	birthday celebration, esp. of Muhammad

waliya (*v.*) to be close **V** to be in charge; to come into power (Wehr 1099b) 2986a

Malagasy (Gue)	kotaoàla	to rule, govern
Swahili (J)	-tawala (*v.*)	become ruler, govern, rule

walīy close associate; curator; holy man (Wehr 1100b); **wali / wilyân** (*adj.*) protector, friend, godfather, godmother (JdP 1250b) 2987

Swahili (J)	walii	a holy person, a saint, a dervish, a calender[21]

wilāya sovereignty; administrative district headed by a *vali*, *vilayet* (formerly, under the Ottoman Empire), province (Wehr 1100b) 2990

Digo (MN&Z)	Ulaya	Europe (via Swahili)
Dholuo (Odo)	Ulaya	Europe (via Swahili)
	Mulaya	Europe, generally called Bulaya, the latter is preferred
Gikuyu (Ben)	Rũraya, Ũraya	Europe (via Swahili)
Nyakyusa (Fel)	iwílaja	district (via Swahili)

21 That is, a Qalendar, a type of Sufi or dervish who has renounced the world and roams about like a vagabond.

Swahili (J)	wilaya	parish, district, province
	ulaya	country; Europe; district
	ulayiti, ulaiti	European fabric, said to be a very light, off-white, cotton fabric

aulā better suited, more suitable, more adequate (Wehr 1101a) 2991

Swahili (J)	aula (*adj.*)	better, superior, more deserving, fitting

maulan master, lord (Wehr 1101a) 2992

Swahili (J)	Mola	a title of God, 'Lord,' used chiefly by Muslims

maulānā form of address to a sovereign (Wehr 1101a) 2993

Swahili (J)	Maulana	Lord, sir, a title of God

wālin governor, vali; prefect (administrative officer) (Wehr 1101b) 2995

Swahili (J)	liwali, wali	a headman, usu. an Arab, appointed by the government to deal with the affairs of the Muslim community

hiba gift, present, donation, grant (Wehr 1102b) 2997

Swahili (J)	hiba	gift, present, souvenir; bequest, legacy

tawahhum suspicion; imagination (Wehr 1103b) 3003

Swahili (J)	tuhuma	suspicion, accusation

wēka (*eg.*) okra, gumbo (Abelmoschus esculentus) (Wehr 1104b); **wêke** sauce, meat for the sauce (JdP 1264a); **weike** sauce with food; soup (RT 538a) 3005a

Dinka (Id)	weeka	dry okra
Madi (Bla)	wɛ́kà	dry okra pounded into powder; a dish made from it

wail affliction, distress, woe; woe! (Wehr 1104b) 3006

Swahili (J)	ole	exclamation of woe, pity

Yā'

yā (*voc.* + *excl.*) O, oh (Wehr 1104a) 3008

Madi (Bla)	yábà	elder; a title of respect for a man (see **ab 10**)
Swahili (J)	yaa (*interj.*)	*esp.* yaa Rabi! Oh God!

yā-llāh what a calamity is …! (Wehr 1104a); **yalla!** go! let's go! (Z&T 140) 3009

Dinka (Id)	yela	so what
Malagasy (Gue)	alahàla[22] (*excl.*)	really! warning!

yā' name of the letter ي (Wehr 1104b) and **sīn** name of the letter س (Wehr 448b); name of Surah 37 of the Qur'an, which starts with these letters 3011

Swahili (J)	yasini	a certain chapter from the Qur'an, used in making charms

yāqa collar (Wehr 1105a); **liyaaga** collar (S&A 127b) 3013a

Madi (Bla)	líāgà	collar; necklace

yāqūt sapphire (Wehr 1105a) < Greek loanword: ὑάκινθος 3014

Digo (MN&Z)	yakuti	sapphire (via Swahili)
Swahili (J)	yakuti	ruby, sapphire

22 Gueunier (1986: 13a) says: "sw. du village de Marodoka (Madagascar) *haḻḻahaḻḻa* même sens, peut-être de l'ar."

yābis dry, arid (Wehr 1105b) 3015

Swahili (J)	yabisi, yabis	dry, hard

yatīm orphan (Wehr 1105b) 3017

Malagasy (Gue)	itìma, hitìma	orphan
Swahili (J)	yatima	a fatherless, motherless, or orphan child

yājūj Yajuj, name of a barbarian people spoken of in the Qur'an and who, with **mājūj** Majouj, corresponds to Gog and Magog from the Bible (Kazim: 11, 1623a; Qur'an: 18:94; Qur'an: 21:96; *cf.* Genesis 10:2; Ezekiel 38:2–3 and 39:1; Apocalypse 20:8) 3018

Swahili (J)	Juju	Gog and Magog

yasmīn jasmine (Wehr 1108a) 3019

Swahili (J)	yasmini	a cultivated kind of jasmine, Jasminum Sambae

yaqīn certainty, conviction (Wehr 1108b) 3022

Swahili (J)	yakini (*adj.* + *v.*)	truth, proof

yamīn oath (Wehr 1109b) 3025

Malagasy (Gue)	iamìny	oath
Swahili (J)	yamini	right hand; solemn oath sworn with the right hand on the Qur'an

yahūdī Jewish; Jew (Wehr 1109b) 3027

Kamba (Mbi)	Mũyuti	Jewish (via Swahili)
Swahili (J)	yahudi	a Jew, Hebrew

yaum, pl. **ayyām** day (Wehr 1110a); **yôm** day (JdP 1328b) 3030

Malagasy (Gue)	(in kiantal)[23] ĵòma	day of the week, composed by adding a number to the word for *juma* (Friday), in the Swahili system
Swahili (J)	ayami in siku ~	many days (seldom used)

al-yūnān Greeks; Greece (Wehr 1110b) 3032

Luganda (Sno)	Mùyonaàni	a Greek (via Swahili)
Swahili (J)	Myunani	an ancient Greek

23 A sub-dialect of Malagasy from Mayotte (Gueunier 1986: iv).

Addenda

Words of non-Arabic origin sometimes given for Arabic

jamal camel (Wehr 138a); **jamal / jumâl** camel, name of a constellation (JdP 640a); **ğemel** camel (RL 98a) It has the same Semitic root JML, which gave the Greek *κάμηλος*, the Latin *camelus*. The loanwords below come from Berber l-ɣ-m (see Tourneux 1987: 167–205).

Kinyarwanda (CAT)	in-gamiya	camel
Runyankore (Ka)	engamɨra	camel (via Swahili)
Swahili (J)	ngamia	camel

manā (*v.*) to put to the test, afflict; to undergo (Wehr 927b); **munya**, **minya** wish, desire; object of desire (Wehr 928a)

Haya (M&L)	omwoyo	heart
Ngh'wele (Leg)	moyo	heart (via Swahili)
Swahili (J)	moyo	the heart; courage, resolution

 | DOI:10.1163/9789004438484_004

Bibliography

Abe, Yuko. 2006. *A Bende Vocabulary* (Bantu Vocabulary Series 13). Tokyo University of Foreign Studies. Research Institute for Languages and Cultures of Asia and Africa (ILCAA), 146 pp.

Adelaar, Alexander. 2009. "Malagasy Vocabulary," in Haspelmath, Martin & Tadmor, Uri (eds.), *World Loanword Database*. Leipzig. Max Planck Institute for Evolutionary Anthropology, 1680 entries. (Available online at http://wold.clld.org/vocabulary/28, Accessed on 26 Feb. 2018.)

Armitage, Peter B. 1966. "Some Common Arabic Words in Hausa and Swahili": 14–32 in Margaret Gœrner, Yousef Salman and Peter B. Armitage, *Two Essays on Arabic Loanwords in Hausa*. (Occasional Paper 7). Zaria. Ahmadu Bello University, ii–32 pp.

Baldi, Sergio. 1988. *A First Ethnolinguistic Comparison of Arabic Loanwords Common to Hausa and Swahili*, Supplément n° 57 à *AION*, XXXXVIII (4), 83 pp.

Baldi, Sergio. 1995. "Sur la création d'une banque des emprunts arabes dans le cadre de la base de données lexicales et dialectologiques sahélo-saharienne gérée par MARIAMA": 289–306 in *Cinquième Colloque de Linguistique Nilo-Saharienne / Fifth Nilo-Saharan Linguistics Colloquium. Nice, 24–29 août 1992. Actes / Proceedings*. Ed. par Robert Nicolaï et Franz Rottland (NiloSaharan Vol. 10). Köln. Rüdiger Köppe, 429 pp.

Baldi, Sergio. 2005. "L'influence de la langue arabe en Afrique," *Lingua Posnaniensis* XLVII: 7–19.

Baldi, Sergio. 2008. "Arabic Loanwords in Swahili: Addenda," in *Lingua Posnaniensis* L: 9–22.

Baldi, Sergio. 2008. *Dictionnaire des emprunts arabes dans les langues de l'Afrique de l'Ouest et en Swahili* (Dictionnaires et Langues). Paris. Karthala, 616 pp.

Baldi, Sergio. 2009. "Hausa and Swahili: A Common Arabic Heritage": 69–81 in *Proceedings of the 2nd International Conference on Hausa Studies: African and European Perspectives*, edited by Sergio Baldi and Hafizu Miko Yakasai (Studi Africanistici; Serie Ciado-Sudanese 3). Napoli. Università degli Studi di Napoli: "L'Orientale," Dipartimento di Studi e Ricerche su Africa e Paesi Arabi, 108 pp.

Baldi, Sergio. 2009. "Swahili": 381–387 in *Encyclopedia of Arabic Language and Linguistics*, vol. IV (Q–Z). Leiden. Brill.

Baldi, Sergio. 2015. "Les emprunts arabes en Digo via Swahili," *Faits de langue et société*, N° 1 (Mélanges en l'honneur de Miloud Taifi, éditées par Nadia Kaaouas & Mourad Mawhoub): 241–252.

Baldi, Sergio. 2017. "Arabic Loans in Some Nilo-Saharan Languages," in *Folia Orientalia* 54: 35–51, paper presented at *12 Nilo-Saharan Linguistics Colloquium 2015* (Nairobi, 1–4 September 2015).

Baldi, Sergio and Maddalena Toscano. 2015. "Arabic Grammatical Loans in Contemporary Swahili Prose Texts": 5–52 in *Studies of the Department of African Languages and Cultures*, no. 49, University of Warsaw.

Balinandi, Kambale. 2006. *Lhukonzo-English. English Lhukonzo Dictionary*. Kampala. Fountain Publishers, xvi–320 pp. [www.fountainpublishers.co.ug].

Baumann, Hermann and Westermann, Dietrich. 1948. *Les Peuples et les civilisations de l'Afrique, suivi de Les langues et l'éducation* (traduction française par L. Homburger). Paris. Payot, 605 pp.

Baumer, Michel, 1975. *Noms vernaculaires soudanais utiles à l'écologiste*. Paris. Éditions du Centre national de la recherche scientifique.

Beaussier, Marcelin. 1887. *Dictionnaire pratique arabe-français*. Alger. Librarie Adolphe Jourdan, Imprimeur-Éditeur, 764–8 pp.

Benson, Thomas Godfrey. 1964. *Kikuyu-English Dictionary*. Oxford. Clarendon Press, xlix–562 pp.

Bertoncini-Zúbková, Elena. 1996. *Vamps and Victims: Women in Modern Swahili Literature*. Köln. Rüdiger Köppe, 314 pp.

Blackings, Mairi John. 2000. *Madi-English Dictionary* (Languages of the World/ Dictionaries 25). Muenchen. Lincom Europa, 126 pp.

Bosha, Ibrahim. 1993. *Taathira za kiarabu katika kiSwahili pamoja na kamusi thulathiya – The Influence of Arabic Language on KiSwahili with a Trilingual Dictionary* (*Swahili–Arabic–English*). Dar es Salaam. Dar es Salaam University Press, 268 pp.

Botne, Robert. 1994. *A Lega and English Dictionary with an Index to Proto-Bantu Roots* (East African languages and Dialecta, volume 3). Köln. Rüdiger Köppe, xviii–138 pp.

Bouquiaux, Luc et al. 1978. *Dictionnaire sango-français et lexique français-sango* (Langues et civilisations à tradition orale, 29). Paris. SELAF, 663 pp.

Bryant, Alfred Thomas. 1905. *A Zulu-English dictionary with notes on pronunciation, a revised orthography and derivations and cognate words from many languages, including also a vocabulary of Hlonipa words, tribal-names, etc., a synopsis of Zulu grammar and a concise history of the Zulu people from the most ancient times*. Durban & Pietermaritzburg. Marianhill Press, 778 pp.

Calloc'h, Jean-René. 1911. *Vocabulaire Français-Gbéa: précédé d'éléments de grammaire*. Paris. Paul Geuthner, 170 pp.

Calloc'h, Jean-René. 1911. *Vocabulaire Français-Gmbwaga-Gbanziri-Monjombo: précédé d'éléments de grammaire*. Paris. Paul Geuthner, 204 pp.

Clarke, Mary Lale. 1922. *A Limba-English Dictionary*. New York. Houghton, 150 pp. [Reprinted in 1971 by Gregg International, Farnborough, Hants].

Cox, Betty Ellen; Myra Adamson and Muriel Teusink. [n.d.]. *Dictionary Kinyarwanda-English English-Kinyarwanda*, 128 pp. [fmcusa.org/…/06/Dictionary_LoRes_Kinyarwanda-English-English-Kinyarwanda.pdf].

Crazzolara, Josef Pascal. 1955^2. *A Study of the Acooli Language. Grammar and Vocabulary*. London. Oxford University Press for the International Institute of African Languages & Cultures, xix–434.

Crazzolara, Josef Pascal. 1978. *A Study of the Pokot (Suk) Language. Grammar and Vocabulary*. Bologna. Editrice Missionaria Italiana, 372 pp.

Dale, Desmond. 1987. *A Basic English-Shona Dictionary*. Gweru (Zimbabwe). Mambo Press, xii–212 pp.

Davis, Margaret Beatrice. 1952. *A Lunyoro-Lunyankole-English and English-Lunyoro-Lunyankole Dictionary*. Kampala. Uganda Book Shop; London. Macmillan and Co. Limited, xi–332 pp.

Dictionnaire arabe-français (dialecte du Tchad). 1960. N'Djaména, Tchad. [La Bonne nouvelle, Mulhouse]. B.P. 127, 155 pp.

Dictionnaire français-arabe (dialecte du Tchad). 1964. Fort-Lamy. [Assemblées chrétiennes du Tchad]. B.P. 10, 134 pp.

Dozy, Reinhart. 1845. *Dictionnaire détaillé des noms des vêtements chez les Arabes*. Amsterdam. Jean Müller, viii–444 pp.

Dozy, Reinhart. 1881. *Supplément aux dictionnaires arabes*. Leyde. Brill (tome 1: xxxii–864 pp.; tome 2: 855 pp.).

Dzokanga, Adolphe. 1979. *Dictionnaire lingala-français, suivi d'une grammaire lingala*. Leipzig. VEB Verlag Enzyklopädie, 304 pp.

Encyclopaedia of Islam. Second edition. 1960–2004. Edited by P.J. Bearman, Th. Bianquis, C.E. Bosworth, E. van Donzel, and W.P. Heinrichs. Leiden. Brill.

van Everbroeck, René. 1985. *Dictionnaire lingála-français et français-lingála*. Limete (Kinshasa). Éditions l'Épiphanie, ix–358 pp.

al-Farâ'id. 1971. *Dictionnaire arabe-français*. Beirut. Dar el-Mashreq Publishers, 1012 pp.

Faure, Pierre. 1969. *Introduction au parler arabe de l'est du Tchad*. Lyon. Afrique et Langage; Fort-Lamy. Librairie N.D., B.P. 456, 92–50 pp.

Felberg, Knut. 1996. *Nyakyusa-English-Swahili and English-Nyakyusa Dictionary*. Dar es Salaam. Mkuti na Nyota Publishers Limited, Kariakoo, xxii–222 pp.

Ferrari, Aurélia; Marcel Kalunga et Georges Mulumbwa. 2014. *Le swahili de Lubumbashi. Grammaire, Textes, Lexique*. Paris. Karthala, 226 pp.

Fischer, Arnold. 1985. *English-Xhosa Dictionary*. Cape Town. Oxford University Press, 738 pp.

Freytag, Georg Wilhelm. 1830–35. *Lexicon arabico-latinum*. Halis Saxonum. C.A. Schwetschke et Filium, 2 vols.

Gasselin, Edouard. 1880–86. *Dictionnaire français-arabe (arabe vulgare-arabe grammatical)*. Paris. Ernest Leroux [volume I (1880), xxix–975 pp.; II (1886), 960 pp.].

Ghaleb, Edouard. 1966. *Dictionnaire des sciences de la nature*. Beyrouth. Édition de l'imprimerie catholique (vol. I, 19–589 pp.; vol. II, 15–662 pp.; vol. III, 388 pp.).

Gorman, Thomas Patrick (ed.). 1972. *A Glossary in English, KiSwahili, Kikuyu and Dholuo*. London. Cassell & Company, vi–111 pp.

Gueunier, Noël J. 1986. *Lexique du dialecte Malgache de Mayotte (Comores)* (Études Océan Indien, 7 numéro spécial, Dico-Langues'O). Paris. Institut National des Langues et Civilisations Orientales, Centre Océan Indien Occidental, iv–369 pp.

Häflinger, Johannes. 1909. "KiMatengo-Wörterbuch," *Mitteilungen des Instituts für orietalische Sprachen* XII Abt 3: 131–214 [Published by LINCOM, Muenchen 2015].

Hannan, Michael. 1968. *Standard Shona Dictionary*. London. MacMillan & Co., xix–825 pp.

Harrell, Richard Slade (ed.). 1966. *A Dictionary of Moroccan Arabic: Moroccan-English* (The Richard Slade Harrell Arabic Series). Washington. Georgetown University Press, xxi–268–228 pp.

Hulstaert, Gustaaf. 1952. *Dictionnaire français-lomongo (lonkundo)*. Tervuren. Annales du Musée Royal du Congo Belge. Sciences de l'Homme, Linguistique, Volume 2, xxxii–466 pp.

Hulstaert, Gustaaf. 1957. *Dictionnaire lɔmɔ́ngɔ-français*. Tervuren. Annales du Musée Royal du Congo Belge. Sciences de l'Homme, Linguistique, Volume 16: Tome I (A–J), xxxi–917 pp.; Tome II (K–Z), ix–919–1948 pp.

Idris, Hélène Fatima. 2004. *Modern Developments in the Dinka Language* (Göteborg Africana Informal Series – NO 3). Göteborg. Institutionen för orientaliska och afrikanska spark, Göteborg universitet, 77 pp.

Johnson, Frederick. 1939. *A Standard Swahili-English Dictionary*. London-Oxford. O.U.P., x–548 pp.

Jullien de Pommerol, Patrice. 1999. *Dictionnaire arabe tchadien-français suivi d'un index français-arabe et d'un index des racines arabes*. Paris. Karthala, 1640 pp.

Kabuta, Ngo Semzara. 1998. "Loanwords in Cilubà," *Lexikos*, v. 8: 37–64.

Kagaya, Ryohei. 2005. *A Jita Vocabulary* (Asian and African Lexicon 47). Tokyo University of Foreign Studies. Research Institute for Languages and Cultures of Asia and Africa (ILCAA), xxi–482 pp.

Kagaya, Ryohei. 2006. *A Gwere Vocabulary* (Asian and African Lexicon 48). Tokyo University of Foreign Studies. Research Institute for Languages and Cultures of Asia and Africa (ILCAA), xi–485 pp.

Kagaya, Ryohei & Olomi, Rogati. 2006. *A Kiw'oso Vocabulary*. (Bantu Vocabulary Series 14). Tokyo University of Foreign Studies. Research Institute for Languages and Cultures of Asia and Africa (ILCAA), ix–414 pp.

Kaji, Shigeki. 2000. *A Haya Vocabulary*. (Asian and African lexicon No. 37). Tokyo University of Foreign Studies. Research Institute for the Study of Languages and Cultures of Asia and Africa (ILCAA), 532 pp.

Kaji, Shigeki. 2004. *A Runyankore Vocabulary*. (Asian and African lexicon No. 44). Tokyo University of Foreign Studies. Research Institute for Languages and Cultures of Asia and Africa (ILCAA), xxxiii–603 pp.

Kaye, Alan Stewart. 1986. *A Dictionary of Nigerian Arabic* (Bibliotheca Afroasiatica, vol. 2). Malibu. Undena Publications, ix–90 pp.

Kazimirski, Albert de Biberstein. 1860. *Dictionnaire arabe-français*. Paris. Maisonneuve et Cie (tome 1: 1392 pp.; tome 2: 1638 pp.).

Kazimirski, Albert de Biberstein. 1875. *Dictionnaire arabe-français*, revu et corrigé par Abed Gallab. Le Caire. Imprimerie V.R. égyptienne (tome 1: ii–838 pp.; tome 2: 917 pp.; tome 3: 1079 pp.; tome 4: 999 pp.).

Kiraithe, Jacqueline M. & Nancy T. Baden. 1976. "Portuguese influences in East African languages": 3–31, *African Studies*, 35:1.

Kitching, Arthur Leonard. 1915. *A Handbook of the Ateso Language*. London. Society for Promoting Christian Knowledge, ix–144 pp.

Knappert, Jan. 1970. "Contribution from the Study of Loanwords to the Cultural History of Africa": 78–88 in *Language and History in Africa*, a volume of collected papers presented to the London Seminar on Language and History in Africa (Held at the School of Oriental and African Studies, 1967–69). Ed. by David Dalby. London. Frank Cass & Co. Ltd., xvii–159 pp.

Knappert, Jan. 1970. "Swahili Religious Terms," *Journal of Religion in Africa*, III, 1: 67–80.

Knappert, Jan. 1972–1973. "The Study of Loan Words in African languages," *Afrika und Übersee*, LVI, 4: 283–308.

Knappert, Jan. 1999. "Loanwords in African Languages": 203–220 in Rosalie Finlayson (ed.). *African Mosaic* (*Festschrift for J.A. Mosaic*). Pretoria. Unisa Press, University of South Africa, xx–417 pp.

Kohnen, Bernardo. 1994. *Dizionario shilluk*, a cura di Manuela Brovarone (Biblioteca Africana, N. 7; Museum Combonianum, N. 49). Trieste (Università di Trieste. Scuola Superiore di Lingue Moderne Interpreti e Traduttori) e Roma (Missionari Comboniani), xii–226 pp.

Krapf, Johann Ludwig. 1850. *Vocabulary of Six East African Languages: Kisuaheli, Kinika, Kikamba, Kipokomo, Kihiau, Kigalla*. Tübingen. Lud Fries Fues, x–64 pp.

Krönlein, Johann Georg. 1889. *Wortschatz der Khoi-Khoin* (*Namaqua-Hottentotten*). Berlin. Deutsche Kolonialgesellschaft in Kommission bei Carl Heymanns Verlag, vi–350 pp. [Republished in 1971 by Gregg International Publishers Limited, Westmead, Farnborough, Hants, England].

Laman, Karl Edvard. 1936. *Dictionnaire kikongo-français avec une étude phonétique décrivant les dialectes les plus importants de la langue dite kikongo*. Republished in 1964 by Gregg Press Incorporated, Ridgewood, New Jersey, 2 vols., xciv–1183 pp. [numérotation continue].

Legère, Karsten. 2003. *Trilingual Ngh'wele-Swahili-English and Swahili-Ngh'wele-English wordlist*. Dept. of Oriental and African Languages, Göteborg University, 81 pp. [www.african.gu.se/research/nghwele.html].

Lethem, G.L. 1920. *Colloquial Arabic, Shuwa Dialect of Bornu, Nigeria and of the Region of Lake Tchad*. London. Published for the Government of Nigeria by the Crown Agents for the Colonies, xv–487 pp.

Luffin, Xavier. 2003–2004. *Un créole arabe: le kinubi de Mombasa. Étude descriptive.* Faculté de Philosophie et Lettres, Université Libre de Bruxelles, thèse de Doctorat (publié en "Studies in Pidgin & Creole Linguistics 07" par Lincom. Muenchen 2005, 200 pp.).

Maʿlūf, Luwīs. 1975. *al-Munjid fī-al-lughah wa-l-aʿlām.* Dār al-Mashriq, 1813 pp.

Maho, Jouni Filip; Lodhi, Abdulaziz Yusuf. 2004. *Ten unannotated Haya wordlists from Tanzania.* Göteborg africana informal series, #4. Dept. of Oriental and African Languages, Göteborg University, 126 pp. [www.african.gu.se/gais.html].

Mbiti, John S. 1959. *English-Kamba Vocabulary* (Eagle Language Study Series). Kampala, Nairobi, Dar es Salaam. East African Literature Bureau, iv–52 pp.

Mertens, Georges. 2006. *Dictionnaire kiswahili-français et français-kiswahili.* Paris. Karthala, 285 pp.

Mohamed, Mohamed A. 2011. *Comprehensive Swahili-English Dictionary.* Nairobi, Kampala, Dar es Salaam, Kigali. Eastern African Educational Publishers, xxxii–891 pp.

Mosha, M. 1971. "Loan-Words in Luganda: A Search for Guides in the Adaptation of African Languages to Modern Conditions": 288–308 in Wilfred H. Whiteley (ed.), *Language Use and Social Change. Problems of Multilingualism with Special Reference to Eastern Africa.* London. Oxford University Press for International African Institute, x–406 pp.

Muniko, S.M., Muita oMagige, B. & Ruel, M.J. (eds.). 1996. *Kuria-English Dictionary* (Monographs from the International African Institute). Hamburg. Lit Verlag, x–137 pp.

Muratori, Carlo. 1948. *English Bari-Lotuxo-Acoli Vocabulary.* Okaru. Catholic Mission Printing Press, vii–270 pp.

Muraz, G. 1926. *Vocabulaire du patois arabe tchadien ou "Tourkou" et des dialectes sara-madjingaye et sara-m'baye; suivi de conversations et d'un essai de classification des tribus Sara (S.-O. du Tchad).* Paris, Limoges, Nancy. Charles Lavauzelle et Cie, 322 pp.

Mwalonya, Joseph; Nicolle, Alison; Nicolle, Steve & Zimbu, Juma. 2004. *Mgombato. Digo-English-Swahili Dictionary.* Nairobi. Digo Language and Literacy Project, x–216 pp.

Nicolas, Francis. 1953. *La Langue berbère de Mauritanie* (Mémoires de l'Institut français d'Afrique noire, n° 33). Dakar. IFAN, 475 pp.

Odonga, Alexander. 2005. *Lwo-English Dictionary.* Kampala. Fountain Publishers, xix–283 pp.

Pillinger, Steve and Galboran, Letiwa. 1999. *A Rendille Dictionary. Including a Grammatical Outline and an English-Rendille Index* (Kuschitische Sprachstudien; Bd. 14). Köln. Rüdiger Köppe Verlag, 414 pp.

Pires Prata, António. 1990. *Dicionário Macua-Português.* Lisboa. Ministério do Planeamento e da Administração doTerritório. Secreteria da Estado da Ciência e Tecnologia. Istituto de Investigação Científica Tropical, xxii–508 pp.

Pozzati, Aurelio (a cura di Vera Carnielli con la collaborazione di Stefano Santandrea). 1987. *Vocabolario Ndogo-italiano-Ndogo* (Bibliotheca Africana n. 2; Museum Combonianum n. 42). Trieste. Università di Trieste; Roma. Missionari Comboniani, 447 pp.

Prost, André. 1983. *Inventaire des mots d'origine arabe passés dans diverses langues de l'Afrique de l'Ouest*. Paris. L'Auteur, 190 pp. (multigraphié).

Qāsim, ʿAw al-Sharīf. 1985. *Qāmūs al-lahjat al-ʿammiya fī l-Sudān*. Cairo. Al-Maktab al-Masrī al-Ḥadīth, 957 pp.

Rechenbach, Charles William. 1967. *Swahili-English Dictionary*. Washington. Catholic University of America Press, xi–641 pp.

Reh, Mechthild (comp.) with the assistance of Sam A. Akwey and Cham U. Uriat. 1999. *Anywa-English and English-Anywa Dictionary* (Nilo-Saharan Linguistic Analyses and Documentation; volume 14). Köln. Rüdiger Köppe Verlag, xvi–134 pp.

Richardson, Irvine. 1966. "A Vocabulary of Sukúma" [edited by Michael Mann], *African Language Studies*, v. 7, pp. 1–79.

Rood, N. 1958. *Ngombe-nederlands-frans Woordenboek. Dictionnaire ngombe-néerlandais-français* (Annales du Musée Royal du Congo Belge, Tervuren; Série in 8°; Sciences de l'Homme, Linguistique, Volume 21). Tervuren. Commission de Linguistique Africaine, l–414 pp.

Roth-Laly, Arlette. 1969–1971–1972. *Lexique des parlers arabes tchado-soudanais*. Paris. CNRS [Fascicule I (1969), 106 pp.; II (1969), pp. 107–264; III (1971), pp. 265–402; IV (1972), pp. 403–545].

Sacleux, Charles. 1939. *Dictionnaire Swahili-français*. Paris. Institut d'Ethnologie, 1114 pp.

Schrock, Terrill B. 2017. *The Ik Language: Dictionary and Grammar Sketch* (African Language Grammars and Dictionaries 1). Berlin. Language Science Press, xiv–596 pp.

Smith, Edwin W. 1907. *A Handbook of the Ila Language (commonly called the Seshukulumbwe), spoken in North-Western Rhodesia South-Central Africa, Comprising Grammar, Exercises, Specimens of Ila Tales, and Vocabularies*. London. Oxford University Press, xii–488 pp. [Republished 1964 by Gregg Press Limited, 1, Westmead, Farnborough, Hants, England].

Smith, Ian & Ama, Morris Timothy. 2005. *Juba Arabic–English Dictionary. Kamuus ta Arabi Juba wa Ingiliizi*. Kampala. Fountain Publishers, xviii–195 pp.

Snoxall, Ronald A. (ed.). 1967. *Luganda-English Dictionary*. Oxford. Clarendon Press, xxxvi–357 pp.

Stafford, Roy Lawrence. 1967. *An Elementary Luo Grammar with vocabularies*. Nairobi. Oxford University Press, xiv–199 pp.

Swartenbroeckk, Pierre. 1973. *Dictionnaire kikongo et kituba-français. Vocabulaire comparé des langues kongo traditionnels et véhiculaires* (Série III, vol. 2). Bandundu. Centre d'Études Ethnologiques Publications, xv–815 pp.

Tirronen, Toivo E. 1986. *Ndonga-English Dictionary*. Ondangwa (Oshinyanyangidho shongelaki ELCIN/Oshako 2013. Oniipa, Ondangwe 9000). Eloc Printing Press, a-h-507 pp.

Tourneux, Henry. 1987. "Les noms des équidés en Afrique Centrale," 167–205 in Christian Seignobos, Henry Tourneux, Alain Hentic et Dominique Planchenault, *Le Poney du Logone* (Études et Synthèses de l'I.É.M.V.T., 23) Maisons-Alfort. Institut d'Élevage et de Médecine vétérinaire des pays tropicaux, 213 pp.

Vettor, G. 1933. *Petit dictionnaire français-lwéna*. Udine. G. Chiesa.

Vocabolario arabo-italiano, 3 vol. 1966–1969–1973. Roma. Istituto per l'Oriente, xiii–1763 pp.

Watson, Richard L. 1989. "An Introduction to Juba Arabic," *Occasional Papers in the Study of Sudanese Languages* 6: 95–117, edited by Wise, Mary Ruth and Richard L. Watson, SIL.

Watson, Richard L. and Louis Biajo Ola. 1985. *Juba Arabic for beginners*. SIL.

Wehr, Hans. 1966. *A Dictionary of Modern Written Arabic*, edited by J. Milton Cowan. Wiesbaden-London. Otto Harrassowitz, xvii–1110 pp.

Wexler, Paul. 1980. "Problems in Monitoring the Diffusion of Arabic into West and Central African Languages," *Zeitschrift der Deutschen Morgenländischen Gesellschaft* 130: 522–556.

White Fathers. 1947. *Bemba-English Dictionary*. Chilubula (Zambia). White Fathers, 1505 pp.

Whiteley, Wilfred Howell. 1963. "Loan-Words in Kamba: A Preliminary Survey," *African Language Studies* IV, 146–165.

Worbe, André. 1962. *Étude de l'arabe parlé au Tchad*. Fort-Lamy. S.N.O., 96 pp.

Würtz, Ferdinand. 1889/90. "Kipokomo-Wörterverzeichnis," *Zeitschrift für afrikanische Sprachen*, v. 3: 81–106.

Yoneda, Nobuko. 2006. *Vocabulary of the Matengo Language* (Bantu Vocabulary Series 12). Tokyo University of Foreign Studies. Research Institute for Languages and Cultures of Asia and Africa (ILCAA), xxi–230 pp.

Zeltner, Jean-Claude and Tourneux, Henry. 1986. *L'Arabe dans le bassin du Tchad. Le parler des Ulâd Eli*. Paris. Karthala, 161 pp.

Arabic Index

'assa 1399
'e:b 1977
'ejeb 1782
'esel 1863
'ibri:g 6
'ille 79
'Ḫ̱R 25
ʿabada 1769
ʿabara 1775
ʿabd 1770
ʿadā 1818
ʿāda 1964
al-ʿāda 1965
ʿadan 1816
ʿadara 1805
ʿadas 1806
ʿādil 1813
ʿadīm 1814
ʿadn 1816
ʿadūw 1819
ʿaḏāb 1823
ʿafārīt 1891
ʿāfiya 1894
ʿafw 1893
ʿahd 1960
ʿāhira 1961
ʿaib 1977
ʿajab 1782
ʿajam 1796
al-ʿajam 1796
ʿajamī 1796
ʿajīb 1784
ʿājiz 1789
ʿajūz 1788
ʿalam 1918
ʿalāma 1920
ʿAlī 1930
al-ʿalīm 1918a
ʿālim 1923
ʿaliqa 1915
ʿalla 1911
ʿamada 1936
ʿamal 1945
ʿamalīya 1945a
ʿamara 1939
ʿamila 1944
ʿamm 1933
ʿamq 1943
ʿanbar 1952
ʿaqd 1900
ʿāqiba 1898
ʿaqīd 1901
ʿāqid 1903
ʿaqīq 1895
ʿaqīqa 1896
ʿaql 1907
ʿaqqār 1904
ʿaqrab 1905
ʿār 1979
ʿarab 1827
ʿarabīya 1828a
ʿarabūn 1830
ʿaraḍa 1835
ʿaraq 1847
ʿarḍ 1836
ʿarīf 1839
ʿaruḍa 1835
ʿarūs 1833
ʿasal 1863
ʿaskarī 1862
ʿaṣāh 1875
ʿaṣan 1875
ʿāṣin 1878
ʿaṣr 1874
ʿāša 1983
ʿašara 1866
ʿašīq 1870
ʿatb 1779
ʿaṭila 1883
ʿaṭīya 1885
ʿawāhir 1961
ʿayyār 1981
ʿayyina 1993
ʿazara 1853
ʿazīma 1857
ʿazīz 1851
ʿaẓama 1887
ʿaẓīm 1888
ʿêb 1977
ʿged 1900

ʿibāda 1771
ʿibra 1776
ʿīd 1978
ʿidād 1802
ʿidda 1800
ʿidl 1809
ʿifrīt 1891
ʿilla 1913
ʿilm 1917
ʿilm al-jabr 434
ʿimāra 1942
ʿinād 1956
ʿīša 1985
ʿišāʾ 1872
ʿišrīn 842, 1869
ʿišrūn 1869
ʿiṭr 1879
ʿizrāʾīl 1854
ʿizza 1850
ʿRB 1826
ʿūd 1962, 1963
ʿuḏr 1824
ʿulba 1914a
ʿumq 1943
ʿumr 1940
ʿunwān 1957
ʿuqūba 1897
ʿurbūn 1830
ʿurs 1832a
ʿurus 1832a
ʿurūḍ 1836
ʿušr 1865
ʿušūr 1865
ʿuzhūl 1858
ʿuzul 1855
ʿuṭūr 1879
ʿWN 1974
aʿālin 1931
aʿḏiba 1823
aʿḏār 1824
aʿlā 1931
aʿmāq 1943
aʿūḏu bi-llāh 1966
aʿyas 1982
ab 10
abad 1769
abadan 3
abadī 4
abāḥa 334
abba 10
abḥār 163
ablaq 304
abṣaʿ 246
ādá 1964
adab 35
ādam 40
adīb 37
adrâj 892
aḍraʿ 1657
aḏāh 47
aḏan 47
aḏān 44
aḏiya 46
afʿāʾ 2170
afʿan 2169
āfa 131
afaf 76
afandī 76a
afḍal 2162
afrâh 2104
afyūn 77
agil 1907
aḡlab 2038
ahl 129
ahlī 129
ahrām 2841
ahwan 2861
al-aḥad 24
aḥad ʿašar 1867
aḥmar 710a
aḥsanta 649
aiḍan 139
ajab 1782
ajal 21
ajami 1796
ajara 15
ajīr 18
ajmaʿ 512a
ajzāʾīya 471a
ajzāḫānā 471a
aḫ 32
aḫbār 762
aḫḍar 804a
āḫir 27
al-āḫira 29
aḫtar 2401a
akram 2421
alā 90

āla 133
ālāt 133
al-ʿalīm 1918a
alf 81
alif 82
allag 1915
allāh 88
Allāhu akbar 2389
alḥarram 629
a-mā 97
almās 86
amad 100
amaliyât 1945a
amaliye 1945a
amāma 95
amân 115
amān 112
amāna 115
amara 101
ambar 2691b
amīn 113
āmīn 114
amīr 107
amīrāl 119a
ammar 1939
amr 102, 102a, 104
anâgrib 2266a
anānās 121a
anasa 125
anbār 2691b
angaraʿ 2271a
angarêb 2266a
anggreb 2266a
angumâji 2341
angumâjiyât 2341
anisa 125
ânisîn 125
anusa 125
aqall 2327
aqḥāf 2242
aqrab 2265
arabât 1828a
arabiiya 1828a
arabiye 1828a
arbāʿ 1020
arbaʿa 1023
arbaʿīn 1025
al-arbāʿāʾ 1026
arbaʿūn 1025
arḍ 55
argi 1847
arz 53
arzāq 1069
asʿār 1291
aslama 1334
aṣl 71
ašir 70
atrôn 2751
attâlago 1714
aṭlas 74
aṭrūn 2751
aṯar 12
au 130
aulā 2991
aulād 2982
aurād 2914
ausāḫ 2925
autār 2882
âwan 1974
awkât 2970
awwah 135a
awwal 134
awwalī 134
axu 32
axxar 25
āya 136
ayy 138a
ayyām 3030
ayyi 138a
ayyil 135
azal 60
azmiil 1188a
azrār 1165
aẓhār 1766

baʿā 269
baʿd 266
baʿda 266
baʿdu 265
baʿḍ 268
baʿīḍ 267
baʿṯ 262
bāba 331
bābūr 147
badal 176
badan 178
badāwa 181
badīl 177

badr 171
baḏā'iʿ 248
baḏara 184
bāḏinjān 149
bafta 274
bagar 275
bağal 161
bağl 271
bahā 328
bahar 163
bahīma 324a
bahta 323
bahw 329
bāḥa 334
baḥr 163
baiʿ 348a, 349
baiʿa 351
baiḏinjān 149
bāin 356
baina 355
bait 344, 791a
bait al-māl 345
baiṭārī 347a
bajal 161
baḫs 166
baḫīl 167
baḫšīš 166a
baḫt 163a
baḫūr 165
bal 284
bāla 339
balā' 308
balad 287b
baladī 290
balağa 297
balaḥ 287a
balğam 302
balīya 304a
balla 285
ballāṣ 293
ballūr 310, 318a
balqā' 304
bāmiya 156
banā 321
banat 313
bandēra 318
bango 321b
bank 321c
bannūr 318a
banṭalūn 321a
banzīn 318b
baqar 275
baqiya 281
baqqāriy 277
bāqūl 280
baraka 211
barāqiʿ 206a
baraza 202
barī' 192
bārid 200
bariha 222
barlamān 213a
barmīl 221
barr 189
barra 187
barwa 224
bārūd 150
barzaḫ 204
bas 231
basbās 233
bāsūr 236
baṣʿā' 246
baṣal 247, 247a
baṣīr 243
baṣura 241
bašīr 239
baškir 240a
baškīr 240a
batâtîn 260a
batâtîr 249a
battâniye 260a
battariye 249a
batūl 156a
baṭana 257
baṭar 250a
baṭāṭsa 250b
baṭāyin 259
bāṭil 256
baṭn 257
baṭṭānīya 260a
baṭṭārīya 249a
baṭṭīḫ 250
bawâlîs 341a
bawāsīr 236
bawwāb 332
bawwāba 333
baxal 271
baxat 163a

bayān 357
bāyin 356
bayyin 356
bazzāz 226
benzīn 318b
berze 202
besel 247
bēṭarī 347a
bi 143
bi'r 149a
bidʿ 173
bidʿa 173a
bidaʿ 173a
bidāwa 181
bi-diqqa 918
biḍāʿa 248
bi-ḡairi 2062
biḥār 163
bi-ismllāhi 1349
bīkār 353
bikr 283
bi-lā 144
bilād 287b
billaur 310
binya 321d
bint 313
biqaddi 2242a
bîr 149a
biric 205
birmil 221
bišāra 236b
biṭāna 260
biṭṭīḫ 250
biyâr 149a
bizr 228
BḠM 272
bôlîs 341a
bōlīs 341a
BQʿ 278
brenği 218
buʿbuʿ 261
budd 168
buḡḍ 270
buhya 328
buḫār 164
bulbul 287
buldān 289
būlīs 341a
bundug 317
bundūg 317
bunduqīya 317
bunn 315
bunya 321d
bunyât 321d
būr 335
bura 190a
burā' 192
burhān 223
būrī 335a
burj 195
burma 217
burquʿ 206a
burra 190a
burš 205
burtuqāl 194
burtuxâl 194
burûc 205
burūda 197
burūği 151
burunji 151, 218
burzul 225
busta 234
bustān 235
buṣarā' 243
bušrā 236a
būza 337
būẓa 337
BWB 329a

câbah 1431
câhid 1525
caka 1504
cam'e 1517
carak 1467
carâye 1459
cawâl 1532
cawâwîl 1532
cerî'e 1459
côra 1533
cuhûd 1525
curba 1449b
curbât 1449b
curkân 1467
currâb 1449a
currâbât 1449a

daʿa 908
da'da'a 870

dā'im 963
dā'imī 963
dā'ira 955
da'ā 908
da'ib 907
da'wā 909
dab 996
dabaaba 874a
dabah 977
dabalān 882a
dabbāba 874a
dabelān 882a
dâbit 1643a
dabra 880
daff 912
dafīna 917
daftar 913
dagîg 920a
dağdağa 911
dahab 996
dahn 946
dahr 945
dāim 963
dain 972
daḫātira 926a
daḫl 882b
dalīl 928
dalla 927a
dallāl 930
dam 937
dāma 959
damara 937a
daqīq 920a
daqīqa 921
dār 951
daraga 901
darāhim 904
daraja 893
daraka 902
darb 891
dars 899
dārṣīny 871
daula 957
daur 952
daurīya 953
dawa 969
dawā' 969
dawāh 968
dawām 961
dawāyá 968
dawwama 959
dāya 872a
debaḥ 977
deheb 996
derga 901
dībāja 877
dilāla 931
dīn 973
dīnār 974
dir' 901
dirham 904
dist 905
dīwān 965
dîxât 1670
dîxe 1670
diya 2906
dîîya 2906
dolâb 958a
dōle 957
DRK 902
du'ā' 910
dubb 874
dubbât 1643a
dūd 949
duf'a 914
duf'ât 914
dugum 938
dukkān 925
duktūr 926a
duḫān 889
duḫūl 886
dūlāb: 958a
dulum: 1757
dūn 966
dunia 944
duniyā 102a, 944
dunya 944
dura 984a
durj 892
durr 1651
durra 890
duruj 892
durūs 899
dustūr 906
ḍa'īf 1658
ḍabaṭa 1643
ḍābit 1643a
ḍai' 1667

ḍāma 1642
ḍamāna 1664
ḍamīn 1663
ḍamīr 1661
ḍaraba 1654
ḍarba 1655
ḍārib 1656
ḍarr 1651
ḍarūra 1652
ḍawārib 1656
ḍiḥk 1645
ḍīq 1670
ḍuḥan 1646
ḍurr 1651
ḏabā'iḥ 979
ḏabaḥa 977
ḏabḏaba 980
ḏabīḥa 979
ḏahab 996
ḏail 1000
ḏakar 986
ḏalīl 991
ḏalla 988
ḏanb 995
ḏāqa 999
ḏāt 998
ḏikr 985
ḏirā' 984
ḏū al-qa'da 2316
ḏull 989
ḏunūb 995
ḏura 984a
ḏurrīya 983

êb 1977
ellā 79
εaragi 1847
εugda 1900

fa:r 2069
fa:s 2070
fā'ida 2216
fa'l 2072
fa's 2070
F'Y 2169
faḍaḥa 2155
faḍala 2156a
faḍḥ 2156
faḍl 2158
fagâra 2172
fagri 2172
fahm 2206
fahrasa 2203
faḥl 2094
fairūz 2217
faj'atan 2088
fajr 2090
fakka 2175a
faḫār 2095
falak 2191
falata 2180
fals 2185
fālūḏ 2183
fanâyil 2202a
fānellā 2202a
fani' 2201
fanī' 2201
faniila 2202a
fanîle 2202a
fann 2196
fānūs 2073
fāqa 2213
faqīr 2172
faqr 2171
farāġ 2125
faraḥ 2104
faraja 2100
farâmil 2132a
faransā 2136
faraqa 2129
faras 2112
faraša 2115
farḍ 2118
farha 2104
farīd 2108
farj 2101
farḫ 2106
farmala 2132a
farrag 2129
farš 2115
farwa 2137
fâs 2070
fās 2070
fasada 2141
fasaḫa 2140
fāsiq 2146
fassar 2143
fassara 2143

faṣāḥa 2150
faṣīḥ 2149
faṣṣ 2148
fatfata 2081
al-fātiḥa 2077
fatq 2082
fattac 2079
fatwā 2086
faṭar 2165a
faṭr 2164
faṭūr 2165a
fauqa 2212
fauz 2210
fāyde 2216
fazaʿ 2138a
fī 2215
fiʿl 2167
fidya 2097
fiḍḍa 2154
fikr 2177
fikra 2178
filfil 2189
firāḫ 2106
firāsa 2113
firāš 2115
firqa 2130a
firṣād 2117
fîsân 2070
fitna 2085
fiṭr 2165
FLS 2184
FNQ 2202
FTŠ 2079
fuʾād 2068
fuḍūl 2158
fuḏḏa 2154
fuḏḏā 2154
fujl 2092
fûl 2214
fūl 2214
fulān 2193
fulāna 2193
fulānī 2193
fulk 2192
fulūs 2185
fuqāraʾ 2172
fuqqāʿ 2173a
furâc 2115
furḍa 2119
al-furqān 2131
furša 2116a
furuš 2115
fuṣūṣ 2148
futaḥ 2076
futḥa 2076
fuṭa 2166a
fuṭūr 2164, 2165a

gadda 2242a
gadiiya 1459, 2306
gallābīya 493
galōn 500a
gameh 2337
gamīs 2341
gamul 2341a
gânûn 2483
gatar 2309a
gâwas 2370
gāz 429a
gazāz 2282
gazza:za(t) 2282
gazzāzá 2282
ginēh 542
giriš 2267
girš 2267
gonella 569a
gumaar 2339
gumâj 2341
gumâji 2341
gumâjiyât 2341
gumâr 2339
gumāš 2341
gumruk 503a
gunaih 542
guniila 569a
gursaé 2267
gursaya 2267
gurus 2267
gurūš 2267
ğanna 524
ğawād 557
ğellāba 492a
ğibba 432
ğinn 523
ğinzir 535
ğuzlān 472
ġabn 1996
ġaḍab 2024

ḡafal 2033
ḡafala 2032
ḡafara 2027
ḡāfil 2034
ḡafla 2033
ḡafr 2027, 2030
ḡaib 2058
ḡaiẓ 2064
ḡalaba 2037
ḡalaṭ 2042
ḡālib 2039
ḡālin 2044
ḡamā 2049
ḡamm 2047
ḡamma 2046
ḡanīma 2051
ḡaniya 2052
ḡār 2054
ḡāra 2060
ḡaraḍ 2007
ḡarāma 2012
ḡarb 2004
ḡariqa 2010
ḡarra 2000
ḡasīl 2018
ḡaṣaba 2022
ḡaṣṣa 2021
ḡašš 2019
ḡayyara 2060
ḡinā' 2053
ḡubār 1995
ḡubn 1996
ḡubūn 1996
ḡulām 2043
ḡumiya 2049
ḡurfa 2009
ḡurūr 2002

habba 2826
hadā 2837
hadāyā' 2838
hadd 603
haddây 2837
haddâyîn 2837
hadīya 2838
hadiye 2838
hady 2837
haggá 674
haiba 2867
haikal 2869
hâja 734
hajara 2830
hāǰa 734
hakam 683
hâkûma 687
hâkûmât 687
halaka 2849
halla 692
hamm 2851
haram 2841
hasad 646
hassâ 1399
hataka 2829
hawā' 2863
hawan 2862
hayyā 2865, 2866
hdiya 2838
hiba 2997
hidir 662
hilāl 2847
hille 693
hille(t) 693
himma 2852
hîcân 741a
hiss 643
hogna 680a
hudhud 2836
hurmān 2842
huss 2843
ḥabb 583
ḥabba 577
ḥabba ṣaudā' 583a
ḥabīb 579
ḥadd 603
ḥadder 611
ḥadīṯ 607
ḥaḍara 662
ḥāḍir 665
ḥaḍra 663
ḥaḏāri 611
ḥaḏira 611
ḥāǧa 734
ḥaiḍ 760
ḥāja 734
ḥajar 599
ḥajj 592
ḥājj 595
ḥakama 683, 686a

ḥakīm 686b, 1290b
ḥākim 689
ḥakūma 687
ḥāl 745
ḥalāl 694
ḥālan 746
ḥalāwā 702
ḥalla 692
ḥalwā 702
ḥamā 723
ḥamalī 718
ḥamām 706
ḥamāmá 706
ḥamd 709
al-ḥamdu lillāh 710
ḥamīla 720
ḥamiqa 716
ḥaml 717
ḥammām 707
ḥamuqa 716
ḥana 729
ḥanw 730
ḥaqīqa 677
ḥaqīr 680
ḥaqq 674
ḥaqqa 673
ḥaqn 680a
ḥāra 735
ḥarāfa 625
ḥaraka 627
ḥaram 629, 632
ḥarām 632
ḥarāmī 634
ḥarāra 619
ḥaras 621a
ḥarf 623
ḥarīm 633
ḥarīr 617
ḥarr 614
ḥasad 646
ḥasana 650
ḥāsid 646
ḥasuna 649
ḥasūd 647
ḥaṣara 657
ḥaṣira 657
ḥāšā 654
ḥāšākum 654
ḥašīš 651a
ḥašw 653
ḥattā 590
ḥauḍ 742
ḥauz 741
ḥawāla 751
ḥawwā᾽ 731
ḥayā᾽ 755
ḥayāh 756
ḥayawān 757
ḥayy 754
ḥayya 754a
ḥaẓẓ 670
ḥèt 743
ḥifẓ 671
ḥiǧǧ 592
ḥikāya 691
ḥikma 686
ḥīla 750
ḥilla 693
ḥillé 693
ḥimāya 724
ḥiml 717
ḥinnā᾽ 727
ḥirz 621
ḥisāb 645
ḥisābī 645
ḥisān 661a
ḥiss 643
ḥiṣn 661
ḥiṣṣa 656
ḥišma 652
ḥizām 639
ḥorr 615
ḥubb 578
ḥudūd 603
ḥuḍūr 664
ḥujja 594
ḥukm 684
ḥukūma 687
ḥulqūm 701
ḥumma 705
ḥuqna 680a
ḥurr 615
ḥurrīya 616
ḥurūf 623
ḥurum 633
ḥussād 646
ḥusud 647
ḥuṣr 658

ḥuzn 640
ẖarâmi 634
ẖatta 590
ḫā'in 860
ḫabal 765
ḫabar 762
ḫabīṯ 761
ḫabl 765
ḫābūr 763
ḫadaʿa 771
ḫadam 771a
ḫādim 773
ḫafīf 816
ḫaima 869
ḫair 862
ḫaiṭ 868
ḫaizurān 785
ḫalā 834
ḫalā'iq 832
ḫalafa 825
ḫalal 818
ḫalāṣ 821
ḫalfu 826
ḫalīqa 832
ḫāliṣ 823
ḫallā 834
ḫamīra 839
ḫamīs 846
ḫamsa 841, 842
ḫamsataʿašara 844
ḫamsīn 845
ḫamsūn 845
ḫandaq 852
ḫaniṯ 848
ḫanjar 851
ḫaraba 774
ḫarāj 778
ḫardal 780
ḫarib 775
ḫarṭūš 782a
ḫarṭūša 782a
al-ḫarṭūm 782b
ḫasāra 789
ḫaṣama 798
ḫaṣīm 799
ḫaṣīy 802
ḫāṣṣ 795
ḫašaba 790
ḫašm 791a
ḫātam 766
ḫātim 766
ḫātima 768
ḫaṭar 812
ḫāṭi' 808
ḫaṭīb 810
ḫaṭm 813
ḫaṭṭ 805
ḫaṭṭ al-istiwā' 806
ḫaṭwa 814
ḫauf 857
ḫaur 855
ḫawāja 854a
ḫawātim 766
ḫazan 788
ḫazīna 786
ḫaziya 787
ḫazna 785a
ḫilāf 828
ḫilya 701a
ḫinzīr 853
ḫitām 767
ḫiyāna 859
ḫiyār 866
ḫizi 788
ḫuddām 773
ḫulq 831
ḫuluq 831
ḫums 840
ḫunṯā 849
ḫurj 777
ḫuṣan 803
ḫuṣūma 800
ḫuṣūṣ 793
ḫuṣūṣan 794
ḫuṣya 803
ḫuṭba 809
ḫuyūṭ 868

iʿlān 1927
iʿrāb 1829
iʿtibār 1778
iʿtiqād 1902
iblīs 9
ibn 312
ibna 313
ibra 5
ibrīq 6
ibzīm 230

idāra 954
iḏn 43
iġtamma 2046
iḥrām 635
iḥsān 651
ijāra 19
ijtihād 546
ikrāhī 2427
iḫtilāf 829
iḫtiyār 867
ilba 1914a
illā 79
iqlīm 2336
iqtiṣād 2297
imām 96
īmān 116
imlāʾ 2662
in šāʾa allāh 1543
ingilâb 2331a
ingilâbat 2331a
injīl 124
inna 120
inqilāb 2331a
inšāʾ 2731
iris 1832a
islām 1345
ism 1348
istihwāʾ 2863b
istirāḥa 1137
istisqāʾ 1307
išāra 1534
ittafaqa 2961
ittifāq 2966
iṯnā ʿašara 424b
al-iṯnain 425
iṯnāni 424a
izmīl 1188a

jaʾš 430
jāʾiza 563
jaʿala 484
jāba 552
jabal 438
jabara 433
jabbâr 435
jabbār 435
jabr 433
jadala 451
jadd 445
jadda 446
jadwal 453
jaḏām 455
jaḏb 453a
jafāʾ 486
jāh 431
jahada 543
jahannam 551
jahāz 547
jahd 544
jāhil 548
jāhiz 547a
jāhizu 547a
jaḥama 441
jaḥīm 442
jaib 571
jaiš 572
jaḫḫa 443
jalada 495
jalāl 490
jalāla 490
jald 496
jalīd 497, 498
jallāb 492a
jalon 500a
jamʿ 506
jamʿīya 510
jamāʿa 513
jamāl 518
jami 506
jamīʿ 511
jāmiʿ 515
janāʾiz 534
janāb 527
janaba 526
janāba 528
janāza 534
jānib 529
jānn 523
janna 524
janzîr 535
jār 559
jarâdil 465a
jaraḥa 463
jardal 465a
jarīda 465
jarraba 458
jarrāfa 465b
jarrār 457

jâs 429a
jasara 479
jāsūs 478
jauharī 570
jaur 558
jauš 565
jauz 564
jawāb 552
jawa:d 557
jawād 557
jazā 476
jāza 561
jazma 475a
jiljilān 494
jināya 541
jineena 524a
jinêne 524
jinn 523
jins 536
jinsīya 536a
jinzir 535
jinzîr 535
jinzīr 535
jinzīr 1192
jirāb 459
jīrān 559
jiṣṣ 480
jizam 475a
jizdān 472
jizma 475a
jubba 432
jubn 439
jubna 439
jubūr 433
juhhal 548
juhūd 544
jūḫ 555
juljulān 494
jumʿa 507
jumhūrīya 522
jumla 517
junāḥ 531
junaina 524a
juzʾ 471
juzâlîn 472
juzdān 472
juzulân 472
ǰinzīr 535
ǰinzīr 1192
ǰuwād 557

ka-ḏā 2376
ka-ḏā wa-ka-ḏā 2376
ka-ḏālika 2377
ka-mā 2378
kaʾs 2379
kabd 2383
kabid 2383
kabsa 2392
kadâyis 2404a
kaddâb 2407
kadîs 2404a
kadīs 2404a
kaḏḏāb 2407
kafan 2455
kafana 2455
kaffāra 2452
kāfir 2453
kāhin 2489
kahraba 2488
kahrabī 2488
kahrabāʾī 2488
kaifa 2504
kaid 2501
kalab 2466
kalamānī 2474
kalb 2465
kalifa 2467
kalima 2472
kallafa 2467
kalmānī 2474
kamala 2480
kāmil 2481
kamila 2480
kamula 2480
kanīf 1182
kanīsa 2486
kānūn 2483
kanz 2485
karāha 2425
karam 2419
karâma 2419
karāma 2419, 2419a
karâmât 2419
karâsi 2415
karbōl 2414a

kariha 2424
karīm 2420
karkadê 2417a
karkadē 2417a
karra 2408
karram 2419
kartuush 782a
karṭūs 782a
karuma 2419
kās 2379
kasātibīn 2432
kāšif 2443
kātib 2398
katkat 2270
kattān 2401
kawaaja 854a
ke:f ? 2504
kibd 2383
kibēg 2394a
kibrīt 2391
killimānī 2474
kīna 2507a
kinbār 2484
kīnīn 2507a
kirā᾿ 2430
kirbāj 2414
kirbāl 2414a
kīs 2503a
kisar 2435
kisâr 2435
kisra 2435
kitāb 2396
al-kitāb 2396
kittān 2401
kôb 2490
koreek 2430a
kūb 2490
kubri 2391a
kubrī 2391a
kūfiya 2497
kufr 2451
kufrān 2451
kuḥl 2402
kuḥūl 2402
kura 2429
kūra 2495
kurbāj 2414
kurbağ 2414
kurbāč 2414
kurēk 2430a
kurrāsa 2416
kurbai 2414a
kursī 2415
kustubān 2432
kutub 2396
kūz 2496

lā 2511
lā ilāha illā llāh 2848
lā budda 169
la ḥaula 749
laʿalla 1911
laʿana 2544
laʿb 2542
laʿba 2543
laʿna 2544
labbaika 2526
labīb 2518
laḏḏa 2533
laffâfi 2548
laffay 2548
lafẓ 2552
lâga 2558
laḥama 2531
laila 2579
laimun 2581
laita 2576
lakan 2559
lākin 2515
lamba 2561a
lampa 2561a
lāqa 2578
laqiya 2558
lastik 2537a
lastīk 2537a
laṭīf 2540
lauḥ 2567
lauḥa 2567
laulā 2566
laum 2571
lauma 2571
laun 2573
lauz 2568
layyin 2582
lazima 2534
lêmûn 2581

li 2509
li-ajli 20
libās 2521
līf 2577
lifāfa 2548
lijām 2527
lisān 2538
liyaaga 3013a
llā 79
lu'lu' 2516
lubān 2524
luffa 2570a
luġa 2547
luqma 2556
lūṭī 2570
luwwa 2574

mā dāma 960
ma'akâl 78
ma'kal 78
ma'mūn 117
ma'mūr 107a
ma'rab 49
maʿādin 1817
maʿdiya 1820a
maʿīša 1987
maʿīšī 1988
maʿbad 1772
maʿbūd 1774
maʿdin 1817
maʿjūn 1798
maʿlam 1921
maʿlūm 1924
maʿnan 1959
maʿrifa 1841
maʿrūf 1844
madâyid 2601a
madelūm 1760
madîde 2601a
Madiida 2601a
madiiya 1820a
madḫūl 888
madrasa 900
maḍbūṭ 1644
maḍlūm 1760
maḍmūn 1665
maḏāhib 997
maḏhab 997
madiyy 2606
mafâtîh 2078
magaṣṣ 2291
maḡar 2639b
maḡrib 2006
mahâbîs 586
mahbûs 586
mahd 2673
mahiiya 2583b
māhīya 2583b
māhir 2675
mahr 2674
maḥabba 580
maḥall 695
maḥaṭṭ 667
maḥbūs 586
maḥḍ 2595
maḥṭūṭ 668
mait 2679
maita 2679
majlis 500
majnūn 525
majran 469
majrūḥ 464
mājūj 3018
majūs 2594
makān 2498
makanât 2645
makina 2645
mákina 2645
mākīna 2645
makka 2640
makrūh 2428
maktab 2397a
maktūb 2399
makuna 2644
makwa 2500a
makwan 2500a
maḫāfa 858
maḫālīq 833
maḫāriz 781
maḫkama 788
maḫlūq 833
maḫṣīy 804
maḫṣūṣ 796
ma:l 2684
māl 2684
mal'ak 2657
mala'a 2648
malā'ika 2657

malāʿiq 2543a
malaga 2543a
malakī 2657a
malāla 2647
malāriyā 2648a
malāryā 2648a
malāyā 2663
mâlêc 1543a
maleesh 1543a
malik 2655
malīya 2663
mamarr 2608a
mamlaka 2658
manan 2670
manār 2815
manāra 2815
mandīl 2666
manfaʿa 2775a
manīya 2670
maniyy 2670
mannān 2665
al-mannān 2665
manzila 2721
manẓar 2755
maqāla 2359
al-maqāṣṣ 2291
maqbar 2223a
maqran 2278
maraʾa 2611
marāʾin 1010
maraḍ 2620
(maraḍ al-baul) sukkari 1314a
marājil 1045
marasa 2617
mardūd 1063
marham 1128
marḥaban bika 1050
marḥūm 1055
mariʾa 2611
marjānī 2614
markab 1110
markaba 1110
markūb 1113
marmar 2624
marra 2607
marṭis 2622
maruʾa 2611
masāʾ al-ḫair 2634
masâmîr 355
mashaama 1517a
al-masīḥ 2630
al-masīḥīya 2631
masjid 1252
maskan 1319
maskin 1319
masḫara 1263
massa 2628
maṣr 2637
maṣrūf 1583
mašʾūm 1417
mašaqqa 1493
mašhūr 1529
mašriq 1465
mašūm 1417
maṭlaʿ 1712
maṭlūb 1709
maṭrān 2639a
maṯal 2590
maṯalan 2591
mauʿiẓa 2957
mauj 2680
mauja 2680
maulan 2992
maulānā 2993
maulid 2984
mausim 2934
maut 2678
mauz 2681
maxâbir 2223a
maxbara 2223a
maxârib 2006
maxrib 2006
mayyit 2679
mazzāḥ 2627
māziḥ 2627
maẓhar 1767
maẓlūm 1760
maẕlūm 1760
melaki 2657a
mesjed 1252
meszid 1252
miʾa 2584
miʾāt 2584
miʾšār 70a
miʾūn 2584
mīʿād 2955
mibrad 200a
midakk 926

miftāḥ 2078
miḥadda 769a
miḥrāba 620
mikʿab 2445
miḫraz 781
milʿaqa 2543a
milârya 2648a
milāya 2662a
mile 2649
milḥ 2649
mili/eh 2649
milk 2654
milla 2646
min 2664
min ġairi 2062
min ḫalfu 826
min ṭaraf 1698
minan 2671
minbar 2692
mindîl 2666
mindīl 2666
minfāḫ 2767a
minẓār 2756
miqaṣṣ 2291
miqṭara 2310
mirʾāh 1010
mirāya 1010
mirabba 1033
mīrāṯ 2912
mirjal 1045
misk 2632
miskīn 2633
mismār 1355
misṭara 1286
miswāk 1403
miṣhā 1262
miṣr 2637
mitr 2584a
miṭrān 2639a
miṯāl 2592
miṯl 2588
miya 2584
mīya 2584
mīzān 2924
mizzīga 2683a
ms'id 1252
muʾaḏḏin 45
muʾmin 118
muʿallim 1925
muʿāyana 1994
muʿjib 1786
muʿjiza 1790
mubaḏḏir 186
mubhij 324
mudda 2600
mudīr 956a
mudiir 956a
muεallem 1925
mufattiš 2080a
muflis 2187
mufrad 2109
muftah 2078
muġra 2639b
muhimm 2853
muhla 2677
muhr 2676
muḥāfiẓ 671a
muḥāl 752
muḥarram 637
muḥibb 581
mūjib 2887
muḫarram 783
muḫmal 847
muḫtaṣar 797
mulkī 2657a
mumariiya 2608a
munāfiq 2777
munajjim 2701
munkar 2797
muqābil 2238
murabbaʿ 1028
murabban 1033
murābiṭ 38
murād 1140
murīd 1139a
murūʾa 2612
murūwa 2612
musāʿid 1290a, 1290b
musajjil 1254a
museer 70a
mushil 1383
mūsīqā 2683a
musîxa 2683a
muslim 1346
musmâr 1355
mustaʿidd 1804
mustarah 1138
mustarâhât 1138

mustarīḥ 1138
mustaṭīl 1744
muṣība 1627
mušāhara 1528
mušamma‘ 1517a
mušṭ 2635a
muttaka’ 2978
muṭrān 2639a
muṭrib 1692
muwāfaqa 2964
muwâtin 2951a
muwātinî 2951a
muwāṭin 2951a

na‘âm 2764a
nā’ib 2810
na‘am 2763
na‘ām 2764a
na‘ma 2764
na‘na‘ 2766
na‘nā‘ 2766
nabīḍ 2691a
nabīḏ 2691a
nabiiz 2691a
nabīt 2691a
nabiha 2694
nabīy 2697
nabl 2693a
nadā 2715
nadaara 2754a
naddâra 2754a
naddârât 2754a
nadra 2712
naḏīr 2716
naḏl 2717
naf‘ 2775
nafaḍa 2774
nafaqa 2776
nafas 2772
nâfi 2775
nafīr 2769
nafs 2770
nafsân 2770
nafsânîn 2770
nafsi 2866
nafū‘ 2775
nagal 2789
naḥs 2703
naḥw 2706
najis 2699
najjām 2701
najjâr 2697a
najjār 2697a
najjârîn 2697a
najm 2700
nakīr 2797
nāḫuḏā 2708
namā 2805
namliiya 2803
nāmūs 2690
nāmūsīya 2803
nāmūsīye 2803
nanggalu 2789
naqala 2789
naqāwa 2791
naqdī 2781
naqīy 2792
naql 2790
naqṣ 2785
naqš 2783
narjis 2718
nās 126
nasab 2724
nāsūr 2727
naṣāra 2747
naṣīb 2741
naṣīḥa 2742
naṣrānī 2747
našā’ 2738
naulūn 2818
naṭrūn 2751
nawā 2821
nāwulūn 2818
naza‘a 2720
nazīr 2719
nazr 2719
naẓar 2754
naẓīf 2759
nāẓir 2757a
naẓẓāra 2754a
ni‘ma 2764
nibla 2693a
nible 2693a
nibr 2691b
nikāḥ 2793
nīl 2825
nīla 2825
nimra 2802a

nīr 2823
nirjis 2718
niṣf 2748
nišān 2736
nīšān 2736
nīya 2822
Nûba 2811
nubāï 2811
nūbī 2811
nugat 2788
nugta 2788
nuḥūs 2703
nujūm 2700
numra 2802a
nuqāwa 2791
nuqṭa 2788
nūr 2814
nusāla 2729
nuss 2748
nuṣf 2748
nuṣra 2746
nušādir 2733

onbaši 121b

panâtilîn 321a
pantalon 321a
pêrik 357a

qāʿida 2318
qabaḍa 2224
qabala 2228
qabḍ 2224
qabīla 2233
qābilīya 2236
qabla 2229
qabr 2223
qabūl 2232
qadda 2242a
qadr 2246
qāḍin 2307
qaḍīya 2306
qāfila 2323
qahwa 2350
qaḥba 2241
qālab 2331
qalam 2335
qalāš 2332
qālb 2331
qalfaṭa 2334
qālib 2331
qamḥ 2337
qamīṣ 2341
qaml 2341a
qāmūs 2340
qanṭara 2346
qānūn 2342
qaraʿa 2271a
qaraḍ 2269
qaranful 2280
qarīb 2264
qarn 2276
qarquša 2274a
qarṭas 2270
qāsa 2370
qasam 2287
qasama 2285
qasr 2284
qaṣab 2293
qaṣaba 2294
qaṣada 2295
qaṣīda 2296
qaṣṣaba 2293
qašṭa 2289
qaṯr 2309a
qaula 2358
qaum 2359a
qawāʿid 2318
qawwād 2351
qibla 2231
qiḥf 2242
qīma 2360
qimār 2339
qindīl 2345
qirš 2267
qirṭās 2270
qissīs 2283
qiṣāṣ 2292
qiṣṣa 2290
qišṭa 2289
qiṭʿa 2312
qiyāma 2361
qiyās 2371
qizāʾiz 2282
qizāz 2282
qizāza 2282
qubūl 2232
qufl 2322

al-qur'ān 2261
al-Qur'ān wa huwa'l furqān 2131
qurūš 2267
quṣairā 2303
quṣūr 2302

ra'īs 1004
ra'ra'a 1002
ra's 1003
ra'ūf 1005
ra'y 1006
raʿaba 1093
raʿd 1094
raʿīya 1095
rabb 1013
rābbanā 1013
rabṭa 1018
radd 1060
rādiyō 1001a
radiyoo 1001a
râdyo 1001a
raḍīy 1086
rafaʿa 1098
raff 1097
rafīq 1102
ragaɛ 1106
rağa 1048
rāḡa 1145
rāhiba 1127a
rahn 1129
rāḥa 1133
raḥma 1053
raḥīm 1054
raiʿ 1150
raiḥān 1134
rajā 1048
rajaʿa 1041
rajab 1038
rajama 1046
rajm 1047
rajul 1044
rakʿa 1115
rakaḍa 1114
rākib 1112
râkûba 1109a
rakuuba 1109a
raḫīṣ 1057
raḫuṣa 1057
ramaḍān 1121
raml 1122
ramya 1124
raqaʿa 1106
raqiya 1107a
rasm 1076
rasmī 1077
rasūl 1073
raṣāṣ 1083
raṣāṣa 1083
rašḥ 1079
rašš 1078
rašwa 1082
raṭl 1092
raub 1130
rawâdi 1001a
rāwaḡa 1145
rawâkîb 1109a
raxīṣ 1057
rāy 1006
rāza 1143
razaḥa 1068
razuna 1071
razza 1066
rebb 1013
riban 1031
ribḥ 1031
ridda 1061
ridf 1064
riḍā' 1089
riḍan 1085
riḍwān 1087
rîhe 1131
rīḥ 1131
rijāl 1044
riji 1048
risāla 1074
rišwa 1082
riyāl 1149
rizq 1069
rizz 1065
RTB 1034
ru'yā 1008
rubʿ 1020
rubbān 1015
ruga 1106
ruga-u 1107a
rū(h) 1132
rūḥ 1132
ruḫḫ 1056

ruḫṣ 1057
ruḫṣa 1058
ar-rūm 1146
rūmī 1147
rušd 1080
rušwa 1082
ruṭūba 1091
ruwâba 1130
ruzz 1065

al-sâʾa 1399
saʿîd 1288
sāʾil 1223
saʾira 1219
sāʾis 1397
sāʿa 1398
saʿʿara 1291
saʿd 1288
saʿāda 1290
saʿīd 1289
sabʿa 1236
sabʿīn 1238
sabʿūn 1238
saʿūṭ 1292a
sabab 1226
sab(ā)(h) 1552
sabah 1552
sabahlalan 1241a
sabar 1555
sabb 1225
sabīl 1240
sābiq 1239
as-sabt 1230
sadaga 1571
sadaka 571
sadaxa 1571
sadaxât 1571
sadda 1267
saf 1400
safala 1298
safanj 1300
safar 1294
sâfar 1294
safâya 1591a
saffar 1592
saffara 1294
safiha 1301
safîhe 1591a
safila 1298
safīna 1299
safīr 1297
sahā 1385
sahi 1562
sāhi 1562
sahm 1384
sahula 1380
saḥana 1261
sāḥil 1260
saḥna 1261
sāj 1218
sajâyir 1248a
sajda 1249
sakarāt 1311
sakina 1316
sakra 1311
sakuus 1413a
saḫā 1266
saḫiya 1266
salām 1338
salāma 1341
salāsil 1327
salaṭa 1328a
salaṭā 1328a
salīm 1342
salima 1333
salīqa: 1331
sallam 1333
sallama 1333
salsala 1327
sam 1634
samʿan wa-ṭāʿatan 1358
samāʾ 1362
samaḥa 1353
samak 1359
samakī 1359
samāwāt 1362
samāwī 1363
sambala 1241a
sameh 1352
samhîn 1352
samḥ 1352
samīr 1354
samīy 1364
samm 1350, 1361
samūm 1350
sana 1365
sanā 1378
sanā makkī 1377

sanad 1372
sandarūs 1374
sandiwic 1374a
sanna 1366
sanṭūr 1375
saqf 1304
saqīfa 1305
saqīm 1306
sâr 1409
sāra 1409
sarāb 1274
sarāya 1273a
sarīya 1283
sarj 1275
satara 1242
satâyir 1242
saṭḥ 1284
sauq 1401a
sawā 1407
sawāʾ 1407
sawād 1386
sawaga 1402
sawāḥil 1260
sawīy 1408
sawiya 1405
sawīyan 1408
sayyār 1411
sayyid 1389
sayyida 1390
seber 1555
sedd 1267
selāt 1612
serğ 1275
serj 1275
siʿr 1291
sibāb 1229
sidar 1270
sidr 1270
sifanji 1300
sigāra 1248a
sihir 1257
siḥr 1257
sijâra 1248a
sijda 1249
sijin 1254b
sijn 1254b
silāḥ 1323
silik 1332
silk 1332
silsila 1327
simsim 1356
sīn: 1413, 3011
sinn 1367
sirāj 1276
sirr 1272
sirsir 1327
sirwāl 1282
sitār 1242
sitâra 1242
sitr 1242, 1247
sitt 1246
sitta 1243
sitta ʿašrata 1244
sittīn 1245
sittūn 1245
siwāk 1403
siyāsa 1396
siyâsî 1396a
siyâsîyîn 1396a
SLṬ 1328
sorōya 1273a
sruwāl 1282
suʿâd 1288
suʿūd 1288
subūt 1230
sūdānī 1388a
suds 1271
sudus 1271
su:g 1402
sûg 1402
sūg 1402
suhail 1380a
suḥba 1255
sujūd 1250
sujûn 1254b
sūk 1403
sukkān 1317
sukkar 1314
sukkarī 1314a
sukūt 1308
sulaimān 1343
sullam 1337a
sulṭān 1329
sumsum 1356, 1357
sunna 1368
sunnī 1369
sūq 1402
sūra 1392

sūs 1394, 1395
sutur 1242
sutūr 1242
SWL 1403a
ṣāʿa 1639
ṣāba 1624
ṣabāḥ al-ḫair 864, 1553
ṣabar 1555
ṣabara 1555
ṣabir 1556
ṣabr 1555, 1556
ṣābūn 1557,
ṣadaqa 1571
ṣādiq 1573, 1575
ṣadrīya 1568
ṣafara 1592
ṣafīḥa 1591a
ṣāfīn 1598
ṣafrāʾ 1595
ṣaḡan 1588
ṣaḡār 1587
ṣaḡīr 1586
ṣaḡw 1588
ṣahi 1562
ṣaḥāba 1563
ṣaḥḥa 1560
ṣāḥib 1565
ṣaḥīfa 1566
ṣaḥīḥ 1562
ṣaḥn 1567
ṣaiḥ 1637
ṣalāh 1612
ṣalāt al-istisqāʾ 1307
ṣalāt at-tarāwīḥ 1136
ṣalīb 1601
ṣaliba 1600
ṣāliḥ 1607
ṣaluba 1600
ṣama 1634
ṣamḡ 1616
ṣanʿa 1620
ṣanam 1622
ṣanaubar 1623
ṣandal 1618
ṣandūq 1617
ṣanf 1621
ṣaqīʿ 1599
ṣāra 1638
ṣarf 1580
ṣarfīyāt 1581a
ṣarfīye 1581a
ṣarīn 1585
ṣariya 1585
ṣarrāf 1581b
ṣārūj 1576
ṣāta 1628
ṣaub 1625
aṣ-ṣaum 1635
ṣaut 1628
ṣeber 1555
ṣidq 1573
ṣidrīya 1568
ṣifa 2939
ṣifr 1596
ṣiḥḥa 1560
ṣiḥḥi 1561
ṣinf 1621
ṣīnīya 1641
ṣirāṭ 1578
ṣiyām 1636
ṣubḥ 1552
ṣūf 1632
ṣūfī 1633
ṣufr 1593
ṣufrīya 1593
ṣuḥba 1565
ṣulbān 1601
ṣulḥ 1602
ṣulub 1601
ṣumūḡ 1616
ṣunʿ 1619
ṣūra 1629
sha:ba 1431
shanta 1520
sharak 1467
shemsiiya 1514
shoGol, shuGul 1484
shurba 1449b
shuwa:l 1532
šaʾn 1418
šaʿbān 1477
šaʿīr 1480
šāʿir 1482
šāba 1431
šabāb 1422
šabah 1431, 1431a
šabaḥ 1424
šabakī 1429

šabb 1421
šābb 1423
šabḥ 1424
šabih 1431
šabīh 1432
šadda 1442
šadīd 1444
šafʿ 1486
šāfa 1537
šafāʿa 1487
šafaqa 1490
šahāda 1523
šāhèd 1525
šāhī 1420
šahīd 1522
šāhid 1525
šahwa 1530
šaḥm 1440
šaḥna 1441
šaï 1420
šaib 1544
šāib 1544
šaiḫ 1546
šaiṭān 1548
šakā 1504
šakk 1497
šakkak 1497
šakūš 1413a
šākūš 1413a
šāl 1414
aš-šām 1415
šamʿ 1517
šamʿa 1517
šamaʿ 1517
šamaʿa 1517
šamāl 1518
šamar 1512
šammās 1515
šams 1513
šamsīya 1514
šamš 1513
šanṭa 1520
šaqīy 1495
šarā 349
šarāb 1450
šarābāt 1452
šaraḥa 1453
šarak 1467
šāriʿ 1460
šarīʿa 1459
šārib 1451
šāriɛ 1460
šarīɛa 1459
šarīf 1463
šarika 1468
šarīṭ 1456a
šarmūṭa 1471
šarr 1448
šarṭ 1456
šāš 1535
šatm 1435
šaṭr 1474
šaṭranj 1475
šaṭṭa 1473
šauḡara 1483
šauk 1539a
šauq 1538a
šāwara 1533
šawārib 1451
šāwuš 1419
šawwāl 1541
šawwar 1533
šāy 1420
ŠBH 1431
aš-šiʿrā 1479
šibʿ 1427
šibaʿ 1427
šiber 1425
šibr 1425
šijāʿ 1438
šikāya 1504a
širāʿ 1458
širās 1455
širka 1468
šīša 1547
šitta 1473
šī/ēṭān(e) 1548
šiṭranj 1475
šiṭṭa: 1473
šiwāl: 1532
ŠMR 1511
šorba 1449b
šuʾm 1416
šuʿarāʾ 1482
šubbāk 1430
šuḡl 1484
šuhūd 1522
šujāʿ 1438

šukr 1500
šumūs 1513
šurba 1449b
šurrāb 1449a, 1452a
šuwāl 1532

ta'ḫīr 31
ta'ammul 110
ta'rīḫ 50
ta'ab 380
ta'allum 1922
ta'bīr 1777
ta'rīf 1842
ta'rīfa 1843
ta'ziya 1859
ta'ẓīm 1889
tâba 363a
tāba 396
tabalo 363b
tabaṣṣur 245
tabgât 1683
tabge 1683
tabliiya 363b
tabrīd 199
tadbīr 882
tadkara 986a
tadkira 986a
tafa''an 2169
tafaḍḍal 2157
tafakkur 2179
tafarruj 2103
tafāwut 2209
tafsīr 2144
taftiš 2080
tāgiya 1672
tâgiye 1672
tahlīl 2848
tâhûna 1689
tahuuna 1689
taḥarruk 628
taḥīya 758
tāj 400
tâjir 366
tājir 366
tajmīl 520
takâsi 385a
takbīr 2389
taklīf 2467
takrima 2422
takrīm 2422
taksi 385a
taḫfīf 817
talā 388
tâlab 1707a
talag 1714
talbīs 2522
talifa 386
talij 416
tallag 1714
talqīn 2557
tamaaragi 394a
tamaddun 2605
tamalluk 2659
tamarāt 394
tamma 391
tamr 394
tamarǧī 394a
tanabbuh 2696
tanaffus 2773
tanaka 397a
tannūr 397
taqabbul 2235
taqṣīr 2304
taqwīm 2364
tar'āb 1093
tarâbîz 369a
taraka 373
taraddud 1062
tarabēza 369a
tarbêza 369a
tarḍiya 1088
târi 1006
tarifa 372
tarîxa 1702
tarkīb 1111
tarqīm 1107
tartīb 1036
tarzī 371a
tasbīḥ 1235
tashīl 1382
taslīm 1344
tašdīd 1445
tašwīš 1536
taṭā 379
tauba 396
taufīq 2962
taukīl 2981a
taurāh 401

tawaḍḍu’ 2948
tawâgi 1672
tawahhum 3003
tawakkul 2981b
ṭawaali 1742
tawwal 1742
tazkara 986°
telej 416
temm 391
temma 391
terezi 371a
tîbân 1733
tībān 1733
tibḡ 363a
tijāra 365
tilifūn 387a
tin 403
tisʿa 375
tisʿīn 377
tisʿūn 377
tôb 1733
tōb 1733
trimbîl 374a
trimbîlât 374a
trombīl 374a
tuffāḥ 384
tujjâr 366
tujjār 366
tukl 385b
tukul 385b
tumbâk 363a
tumūr 394
turjumān 371
turux 1702
tusʿ 376
tûta 399
tūtiyā 399
ṭā’ifa 1738
ṭā’ira 1751
ṭāʿa 1731
ṭāʿūn 1704
ṭāba 1748
ṭabaq 1682
ṭabaqa 1683
ṭabīʿa 1679
ṭabīb 1675
ṭābūr 1671a
ṭāf 1733
ṭāfa 1733
ṭafar 1705
ṭāgīyé 1672
ṭahāra 1724
ṭāhir 1725
ṭahûna 1689
ṭāḥūn 1689
ṭāḥūna 1689
ṭaiyāra 1751
ṭalā 1717
ṭāla 1742
ṭalaba 1707a
ṭalāq 1715
ṭalaqat 1714
ṭalāsim 1711
ṭāliʿ 1713
ṭalīq 1716
ṭamiʿa 1721
ṭāq 1740
ṭāqīya 1672
ṭalīʿa 1711a
ṭaraʿa 1690
ṭarab 1691
ṭaraf 1698
ṭarbūš 1693
ṭarīq 1701
ṭarīqa 1702
ṭarrār 1689a
ṭarz 1695
ṭāsa 1728
ṭauf 1734
ṭawāla 1742
ṭawwāfa 1736
ṭayyāra 1751
ṭayyiʿ 1730
ṭayyib 1746
ṭīb 1747
ṭibb 1674
ṭilasm 1711
ṭillasm 1711
ṭimm 1718
ṭiwāla 1742
ṭūb 1726
ṭufāl 1707
ṭūfān 1737
ṭumāṭa 1720
ṭurumba 1702a
ṯābit 408
ṯafar 410
ṯalāṯā 413a

ṯalāṯā' 415
ṯalaṯīn 414
ṯalj 416
ṯallāja 416a
ṯaman 418
ṯamānīn 422
ṯamāniya 419
ṯamāniyata ʿašara 420
ṯamara 417
ṯamra 417
ṯanā' 424
ṯawāb 427
ṯubūt 407
ṯulṯ 413
ṯulūj 416
ṯum 429
ṯūm 247a
ṯumn 421
ṯurayyā 409

uʿjūba 1785
ufura 75
ugûl 1907
ujra 17
umma 94
al-untayān 122
ūqīya 132
usquf 68
uyûb 1977

wa 2870
waʿd 2954
waʿẓ 2956
waʿẓa 2956
waba' 2877
wabā' 2877
wabīl 2879
wabr 2878
wadaʿa 2902
wādin 2907
wafiqa 2961
waḥā 2898
wāḥid 2895
wail 3006
wa-illā 2872
wa-in 2873
wajāḫ 2888
wajh 2893
wājib 2886
wajuha 2891
wakala 2979
wakāla 2981
wakīl 2980
wakit 2970
wa-lā 2513
walad 2982
walad an-nās 2983
wa-lākin 2874
wa-lakinna 2874
wali 2987
wālin 2995
walīy 2987
waliya 2986a
wallâ 2872
wa-llāh 2871
wanasa 125
wannas 125
wannâs 125
wannâsîn 125
wannisîn 125
waqaʿa 2971
waqafa 2973
waqf 2974
waqt 2970
waragá 2917
waraq 2917
waraqa 2917
ward 2916
warīṯ 2911
wariṯa 2908
warša 2916a
wâsa 1405
wasaʿ 2931
wasaḫ 2925
wasax 2925
wasâya 2943
wasiye 2943
wassa 2943
wassaf 2938
waswās 2935
wasxân 2925
wasxânîn 2925
wasṭānī 2928
waṣāh 2943
waṣala 2940
waṣīy 2944
waṣīya 2945
WṢY 2943

watar 2882
watr 2881
wazaʿa 2923
wazīr 2922
weððân 44
weike 3005a
wēka 3005a
wêke 3005a
wennes 125
wiʿā 2959
wibār 2878
wijih 2893
wilāya 2990
wilyân 2987
wiqīya 2976
wird 2914
witr 2881
wuḍūʾ 2947
wujûh 2893
wuqifa 2973

xabar 762
xaber 762
xacum bêt 791a
xādum 773
xala:s 821
xalâs 821
xamsa 841
xanzīr 853
xarib 2004
xarṭūš 782a
xarṭūša 782a
xasâra 789
xasâm 798
xasîm 799
xātem 766
xâtim 766
xawâtim 766
xeir 862
xelās 821
xêr 862
xēr 862
xêt 868
xucûm buyût 791a
xusmân 799
xuyût 868

yā 3008
yā laita 2576
yāʾ 3011
yaʿabid 1769
yaʾmuru 101
yaʿanī 1958
yaʿged 1900
yabis 3015
yadʿi 908
yadbah 977
yaġfara 2027
yahdar 662
yahkim 683
yahūdī 3027
yājūj 3018
yalla! 3009
yā-llāh 3009
yamīn 3025
yangul 2789
yāqa 3013a
yaqīn 3022
yāqūt 3014
yarja 1048
yasallim 1333
yasbur 1555
yasmīn 3019
yacki 1504
yatīm 3017
yatlig 1714
yaum 3030
yaum al-baʿṯ 262
yiʿallig 1915
yiʾaxxir 25
yifarrig 2129
yifassir 2143
yigâwis 2370
yigidd 2242a
yihill 692
yilâgi 2558
yingariʿ 2271a
yisaffir 1592
yisâfir 1294
yicâbih 1431
yitâlib 1707a
yitallig 1714
yitimm 391
yittâlago 1714
yiwannis 125
yiwâsi 1405
yiwassi 2943
yiwassif 2938

yizîd 1213
yôm 3030
al-yūnān 3032

zāʾida 1214a
zaʿfarān 1171
zabad 1155a
zabād 1157
zabat 1157
zabīb 1155
zabūn 1160
zabūr 1158
zâd 1213
zād 1202
zāda 1213
zaǧala 1175
zaǧara 1174
zahari 1765
zahariyîn 1765
zāhid 1197a
zaḥala 1162
zaḥama 1164
zait 1211
zaitūn 1212
zakāh 1180
zalāqa 1182
zalāqa al-kanīf 1182
zām 1210
zamān 1189
zamr 1185
zāna 1216
zānin 1197
zarā 1170a
zaraʿa 1169
zāt 998
zaura 1205
zāwiyal 1210a
zayyana 1216
zeytûn 1212
ziʾbaq 1152
zibāna 1160a
zikka 1179
zillīya 1181
zimmīr 1186
zina 1196
zināʾ 1196
zindīq 1194
zinjafr 1191
zinjīr 535, 1192
zink 1195a
zīq 1215
zirr 1165
ziyāra 1206
zubb 1154
zuhara 1199
zuḥal 1163
zumūr 1185
zunjufr 1191
zunnār 1195
zunnāra 1195
zūr 1203
ZWD 1201a
ẓahara 1764
ẓālim 1759
ẓann 1762
ẓarīf 1755
ẓāt 998
ẓuhr 1766
ẓulm 1757

English Index

a few of 2327
a lot 517, 823, 2401a
abase 680
abasement 989
abattoir 977
abdication 1855
abet 1289
abhor 2424
abhorred 2428
abhorrence 270, 2425, 2427
abhorrent 2428
abide 961
abject 991, 2717
ablution 2947, 2948
about 1733, 2378
above 2212
abridged 797
abridgement 797
abscess 818
abscond 2180
absence 1058, 2058
absolutely 2481
absolution 2027, 2030
abstain 373, 1634
abstemious 1197a
abstract 797
absurd 752
abundance 832, 1087
abuse 1225, 1229, 1301, 1435
academy 900
accent 2552
accept 1573, 1575, 2228, 2232, 2235
acceptance 1089, 2232
accepted 1844
accessible 1786
accident 21, 812, 1418, 2741
accompany 2902
accomplishment 2419
accord with 2961
account 645, 2290
accurate 1644
accurately 918
accusation 1504, 1504a, 3003
accuse 1504
accustom 125
acknowledge 2235
acquiescence 1086
acridity 625
act 1900, 1945, 2167
action 1945, 2167, 2703
active 1805
activity 1484, 2167
acumen 2113
Adam 40, 312
add 1213
addition 139, 1213
address 809, 1957
Aden 1816
adept 2675
adequate 2991
adherent 1139a
adjective 2939
administration 1396
admirable 1784, 1786
admiral 119a
admonition 1776, 1784, 2742, 2956
ado 380
adoration 1771
adore 1250, 1769
adorn 1216
adroit 2675
adulteration 2019
adulterer 1197
adulteress 1961
adultery 1196, 1197
advance 1107a, 2269
advantage 862, 2775, 2775a
adventure 1418
adversary 798, 799
adversity 75, 1448
advice 1533, 2358, 2742, 2837, 2943, 2945, 2957
adviser 2742
advocate 2980
affable 1786
affair 104, 762, 1418, 1533, 2290, 2306
affection 578, 580, 1588, 1870, 2862
afflict 1225
affliction 2046, 2047, 2851, 3006
affluence 2764

after a bit 826
after that 826
after 266
afternoon 1874
afterwards 266, 826
age 945, 633, 1544, 1940
age-mate 914
agency 2979, 2981
agent 2980
aggrandizement 1889
aggression 46
agitation 2138a, 2156, 2680
agony 544
agree 1602, 1624, 2232, 2961
agreeing 1086
agreement 351, 1089, 1602, 1900, 1960, 2964, 2966
agriculture 1169
aid 1290, 1974, 2746
aim 49, 1424, 2007, 2295
aimlessly 1241a
air 2863
aircraft 1751
airplane 1751
alarm 2138a, 2392
album 1567
alcohol 1847
alertness 2696
algebra 434
Ali 1930
alibi 1525
align 1405
alike 1407
alive 754
all together 517
all 511, 512a, 517, 2481
Allah 88
allegation 909, 2085
allegory 2588, 2592
allot 2923
allow 334
allowance 1528
allowed 1058
allude 1835
allusion 1534
almond 2568
almost 2378, 2719
alms 650, 1571, 2165
aloe 1556, 2574
aloes 1962
alone 2108, 2895
along 1742
alongside of 1742
alphabet 82, 2788
already 821
also well 2378
also 139
alter plan 2060
alter 177, 2060
alteration 177
alternate 177
alternatively 1210
although 2873
alum 1421
always 3, 4, 945, 963
amateur 581
ambassador 1297
ambergris 1952
amen 114
amenable 2644
amidst 355
ammonia 2733
among 355
amount 2246
amulet 621, 2917
amuse 125
amusement 2103
analogy 2371
ancestor 445
and ... too 2870
and also 2870
and not 2378, 2513
and then 97
and 97, 2870
anecdote 691
angel 1854, 2657
Angels 2797
anger 657, 716, 1670, 2024, 2064
anguish 1670
animal 324a, 757, 804, 2106
ankylostomiasis 1595
anniversary 2984
announce 2715
announcement 1842
annoy 988, 2829
annoyance 47, 1536, 1670, 2467
annul 256, 2060, 2140
answer 552

ant 1357
antagonism 800, 2085
antagonist 798, 799
antecedent 1239
antimony 2402
antipathy 486, 800
anxiety 1670, 2138a, 2851
any 138a
anyhow 765
anyway 266, 1140
apart from 79
aperture 2076
apology 1086
apostasize 1061
apostasy 1061
apostatize 2451
apostle 1073
apparatus 133, 1216
apparent 356
apparition 1424
appeal 1098, 1760
appear 1835
appearance 1261, 1431, 1432, 1629, 1767, 2755, 2893
appendix 1214a
applause 2939
apple(s) 384
application 546
apply force 2370
appointment 902, 2955, 2981
appreciation 424
apprehension 857
apprising 1843
approach 2228
approval 649, 2964
approve 1624, 2235
approximately 2246
Arab 492a, 1827
Arabic 1343
Arabicize 1826
arbitration 684
archbishop 2639a
ardor 544, 2852
area 1384
argil 1707
argue 451, 798, 1403a
argument 594
arid 3015
aristocrat 2233
arithmetic 645
arithmetical 645
arm 984, 1323
armature 901
armor 901, 1323
arms 1179, 1323
army 572, 953, 1862
arrack 1847
arrange 1034, 2923
arrangement 351, 684, 902
arrive 2940
arrogance 250a, 2002
arrogant 2156a, 2158
arrows 1179, 2693a
arsenic 1576
art 1620
artful 2675
article 2359, 2501
as a rule 2038, 2039
as also 2378
as for 266
as if 2378
as long as 960
as to 2215
as 2378
ascertain 1573
ascetic 1197a
ask 451, 1223, 1533, 1707a
aslant 730
aspect 2755
aspirant 1139a
assail 1818
assault 558
assemblage 572
assembly 513
assent 2232, 2235
assign 2467
assist 1289, 1974
assistance 1290, 2746
assistant 1290a, 2980
associate 2987
association 510, 1468
astonishment 323, 1782, 1784
astrologer 1925, 2594, 2701
astrology 2191
astronomy 2191
at one! 746
at that time 1408
at the back 826

at your service! 1358, 2526
at 2215
atheist 1194
atmosphere 2863
attach 1915
attachment 580, 1588
attack 886, 2392
attain puberty 297
attain 902
attempt 458
attend 662, 2534
attendance 664
attendant in hospital 394a
attendant 773
attendants 771a
attention 2754
attestation 1562
attorney 2980, 2981
attraction 453a
attribute 2939
aubergine 149
auction 927a, 931
auctioneer 930
audacious 479
audience 202
auspice 2072
auspicious 1289
authentic 1562
authority 102, 2658
authorization 43, 102, 1058
automobile 374a
autonomy 2336
avaricious 167
avenue 189
average 2928
aversion 2425
avert 526
awakening 2696
awe 857
awl 781
awning 1109a
awoke love 577
ax 2070
axis 2567
Azrael 1854
azure 1363

back 826
bad 761, 966, 2797
badge 2736
bag humbly 1561
bag 459, 1483, 1520, 1532, 2503a
bail 2534
baking oven 397
balance 1092, 2924
bale 1018
ball 1734, 2429, 2495
ball-bearing 1083
ballet 1124
bamboo 785
banana 2663, 2681
band 1468, 1921, 2130a, 2769
bandit 634
banjo 1963
bank 321c
bankrupt 2187
bankruptcy 789
banner 318, 1918
banquet 2419
barbarians 1796
bargain 2964
barley 1480
barn 2691b
barrel 221, 397a, 2294
base 1658
bashfulness 652, 755
basil 1134
basin 280, 742, 2559
basket 1483
bastard 634
bath 707, 742, 1182
bathe 707
bathroom 707
battalion 1671a
battery 249a, 599
battlement 195
bay 855
be a duty 673
be a man of distinction 2891
be a student 388
be alarmed 1093
be alerted 2694
be alive 1983
be allowed 561, 692
be apart 267
be apparent 1764
be arrogant 1301
be ashamed 787

be astounded 2049
be at side of 526
be attached to 1683
be attached 1915
be awake to 2696
be away 1714
be bad 2141
be bankrupt or insolvent 2184
be beautiful 328
be below 1298
be bold 1805
be bustled 628
be careful 241, 611, 2271a
be cautious 611
be changed into 2981b
be changed 2789
be cheap 1057
be civilized 1826
be clear 1764
be close 2986a
be cold 197
be companionable 125
be complete 2480
be complete 2480
be completed 391
be congested 2021
be consumed 1667
be contradictory 825
be contrary 825
be converted 1345
be cool 197, 1079
be cured 2774
be damaged or spoiled 386
be deformed 1883
be dependent 1915
be despicable 787
be destitute 1883
be destroyed 386, 937a, 2849
be devoid 1883
be disgusted 2424
be distracted 1385
be distressed 1667, 2046
be docile 1730
be due 692
be dumbfounded 2049
be duty of 561
be easy 1380
be educated 1922
be empty 834
be ended 391
be enough 1903
be entitled 673
be equal 1407
be equivalent 1405
be excited 628
be favored 2961
be finished 391, 2480
be firm 1442
be fitting for 561
be fitting 673
be free 2052
be freed 2180
be friendly 125
be generous 1266, 2419
be glad 1453, 2104
be good to 2157
be good 1746
be handsome 649
be happy 1453, 2104
be hard driven 1667
be hard 1442, 1600
be harsh 1328
be healthful 2611
be healthy 1560
be heir 2908
be hidden 257
be hurt 46
be ill 1306
be imperative 2534
be imprudent 2034
be impudent 1301
be in a dilemma 657
be in a fix 657
be in a hurry 628
be in charge 2986a
be in difficulties 1068
be in front 2228
be in good condition 1405
be in time 2898
be inattentive 1385, 2034
be injured 1883
be inquisitive 2079, 2080
be insolent 1301
be jammed 2021
be jealous 646, 2060
be late 25
be learned in 1922
be left (over) 2156a

be left behind 281
be level 1405
be liberal 1266
be like 1431
be long 1742
be lost 2010, 2849
be low 988, 1298
be moist 1079
be more and more 1201a
be moved 1409
be neglectful 2034
be new 446
be noble 2419
be nubile 391
be obligatory 673
be obstinate 2501
be off 2032
be old 297
be on the alert 2696
be opened 1453
be opposite 2228, 2891
be overcrowded 2021
be packed 2021
be palatable 2611
be patient 1555
be permissible 561
be permitted 561
be pleased with 577
be pleased 2104
be present 662
be priced at 2973
be promoted 1107a
be prompt 2898
be proper 2578, 2961
be proud 2792
be pubescent 297, 391
be put off 25
be quite! 2843
be ready 547a, 2696
be released 2180
be respected 673
be rich 2052
be right for 561
be right 2961
be rigid 1600
be rotten 2141
be ruined 1667, 2184, 2849
be sad 2046
be safe and sound 1333
be same as 2961
be sarcastic 1328
be separate 267
be serious 446
be silent 1308
be silly 1301
be smooth 1380
be sociable 125
be solid 1442, 1600
be spoiled 1667, 2141
be strong 2644
be stupid 716, 1301
be suitable 561, 2961
be surplus 2156a
be surprised 2032
be suspended 1915
be taken unawares 2032, 2034
be terrified 1093
be the successor 825
be thoughtless 2034
be tired 1162, 1311
be to the point 1624
be transferred 2789
be transformed 2789
be transported 2789
be true 673
be tyrannical 1757
be uncertain 911
be unjust and tyrannical 379
be unmindful 2032
be updated 1922
be vile 787
be visible 1764
be wary 611
be weary 1162
be wet 1079, 1746
be whole 2480
be wholesome 2611
be wide 1835
be wise 1826
be worried 2046
be worthy 673
bead 1357, 2294
beam 1585
bean 2214
bear fruit 417
bear 874
beast 324a, 757
beat 1624, 1654, 2039

beating 1656
beautiful 328, 1352, 2611, 2612
beauty 518, 2867
because of 20
because 960, 2590
become a Muslim 1334
become an Arab 1826
become an unbeliever 2451
become angry or furious 716
become apparent 1764
become bad 2141
become bankrupt or insolvent 2184
become brownish red 2467
become civilized 2605
become clear 1764
become complete 2480
become covered with freckles 2467
become damaged or spoiled 386
become despicable 787
become easy 1380
become familiar with 125
become finished 391
become firm 1442
become greater 1213
become hard 1442, 1600
become known 334
become long 1742
become more 1201a, 1213
become Muhammadan 1345
become pregnant 720
become rigid 1600
become rotten 2141
become ruler 2986a
become serious 446
become solid 1442, 1600
become strong 2644
become vile 787
become visible 1764, 1835
become whole 2480
become wide 1835
become 1638, 2578
bed sheet 2662a
bed 2115, 2266a, 2673
Bedouin 181
bedsheet 882a
bedstead 2266a, 2673
beef 275
beer 337, 2173a
befall 2971
befit 2578
before 663, 2229
beg 1637
beggar 1223, 2172, 2633
begin 1939
beginning 134
beguile 1996, 2000
behavior 2158, 2422
being offended 2427
being 998
belief 116, 1902
believe 113, 1575, 1762
believer 113, 118
believing 118
bellows 2767a
belly 257
belonging to 2664
beloved 579, 581
belt 639, 1195
bench 925
bending 730, 1115
benediction 211
benefaction 650
Benefactor 2665
beneficence 651
Beneficient 2665
benefit 862, 1619, 2158, 2216, 2775a
benevolent 1005
benign 2665
benzine 318b
bequest 2997
beseech 1561, 1637
besiege 658
bet 2339
betrayal 859, 2085
betrayer 860
better 187, 2162, 2991
between 355
beverage 1450
beware of 2271a
beware! 135a
beware 611
bewitch 1145
bewitchment 1257
Bible 2396
bicarbonate 2751
bid 1160a
bier 534
bile 1595

bill 645, 751
billow 2680
bind (a book) 495
bind 497
binocular 2754a
bird 1056, 2106
birth 126
birthday 2984
birth-mark 278
bishop 68, 2639a
bit 686a , 813, 2527
blabber 2081
Black 2811
blame 1435, 1779, 2571
blanket 260a, 2115
blaspheme 2451
blasphemy 749
blemish 829, 1913, 2785
blessing 211, 1053, 1069, 1086, 2764
blindness 2002
bliss 2104
block 1707
blood money 2906
blood price 2906
blood 937
blossoms 2170
blot 1776, 1913
blow 1654, 1655
blue 1765
bluestone 2622
blurred 1424
board 1629, 2567
boast 443
boat 164, 1110, 1299, 1736, 2708
body 178, 2679, 2770
body-guard 621a
bogey 261
boil 818
boiler 742, 905, 1045
bold 479
bolt 1355
bonds 1327
bonus 1213
book 136, 471, 497, 899, 1392, 1566, 2270, 2396, 2917
booklet 913, 2416
boot 475a
booty 2051
border 603, 1000, 1215, 1695
boredom 2647
borer 1394
boss 2708
Botheration! 1966
bottle 2282
bottom 1943
boubou 2341
boulevard 189
bouleversement 2331a
boundary 603
bovine(s) 275
bow down 1249, 1250
bow 2414a
bowing 1115
bowl 280, 1567, 1682, 2394a, 2429
bows 317
bowsprit 906
box 75, 459, 785a, 1520, 1617, 1914a, 2490
boxing 321d
boy 2043, 2982
bra 1568
brag 443
brake 2132a
brandy 1847
brass 1431, 1431a, 1593, 1596
brassiere 1568
brave 408, 435, 479, 1438, 1805
bravery 1495
bravo! 649
brazier 2483
breach 2101
bread 2274a
breadth 1836
break in 1690
breaker 2680
breakfast 1420, 2165a
breath 1132, 2770, 2772, 2773
breathe 2773
breech 785a
breed 71, 2233
bribe 1082, 1420, 2556
brick 1707, 1726
bridegroom 1833
brideprice 2684
bridge 893, 2346, 2391a
bridle 686a, 813, 2527
briefcase 1617
brigand 634
bright 1598

brightness 1513, 2814
brilliance 1378
bring about 1944
brinjal 149
broadcloth 555
brocade 877, 2293
broker 930
brooch 230
brooding 2177
brother 32, 1933
brotherhood 1702
brush 2116a
brutal 486
brutality 558
brute 757
bucket 465a
buckle 230
buffalo 275
buffoon 525, 2627
bugaboo 261
bugle 151, 218, 335a
build 321, 1939
building 951, 1942
bull 2094
bullet 1083
bullock 804
bum 1981
bundle 1018, 2115
burden 717, 1617
bureau 2397a
burial place 1206
bushing 766
business deal 351
business 104, 349, 366, 734, 1418, 1468, 1484, 1533, 1945, 1988, 2290
bustle 627, 2021
but 79, 284, 2515, 2874
butcher 1267
butchery 1323
butter 1361
buttermilk 1130
button 1165, 2154
buy 349
buyer 1160
buzzer 335a
by chance 654
by God! 2871
by no means! 654, 2511
by your leave! 1349
by 143
Byzantine 1146, 1147

cabinet 958a
cable 2617
cables 1332
cadi 2307
caftan 555
Cairo 2637
calabash 2496
calamity 131, 269, 304a, 308, 640, 858, 1416, 1627, 1654, 2703
calculation 645
calculus 645
caldron 1045
calendar 2364, 2987
calico 274, 882a
calioune 1547
calk (a ship) 2334
call of the muezzin 44
call to prayer 44, 45
call together 2715
call 908, 2715
callosity 1249
calm 1071, 1138, 2644
calotte 1672
calumniate 1229
can 397a, 1591a, 2490
cancel 2140
candelabrum 1736, 2345
candid 1562
candle 1517, 1736
candlestick 2345
candy 702
cane 785, 1875, 2294
canister 2490
cannabis 321b, 651a
canoe 1110, 2342
Canopus 1380a
canteen 1617
canvas 1517a, 2341
cap 1672, 2082, 2497
capable 1804, 2113
capacity 2236, 2246
cape 1003
captain 1015, 2708
captivation 453a, 2863b
car 189, 874a, 1828a
caravan 492a, 1294, 2323

caraway 583a
carcass 2679
card game 2270
card 2917
card-board 2917
care 611, 773, 2224, 2851
careless 2034
cargo 717, 1441
caring 1345
carnation 2280
carnelian 1895
carpenter 2697a
carpet 1181, 2115
carriage 1828a
carrier 718
carrion 2679
carry 2789
cart 1828a
cartridge 782a, 1083
carving 2783
case 1617, 1914a, 2306
cash 785a, 2154, 2185, 2267, 2684, 2781
cashier 1581b
cask 221
cassette 1456a
cassock 493
castle 195, 661
castrate 802
castrated 804
cat 190a, 1416, 2404a
catalogue 913
catamite 1587
catapult 2693a
category 331, 536
caterpillar 949
cathedral 2486
cattle 275
cauldron 1593
cause courage 407
cause expense 2973
cause 20, 734, 1226, 1239, 1959, 2290, 2306
causing offence 2427
caution 611
cedar 53
cedar-tree 53
ceiling 1304
celebrate 1888
celebrated 1529
celebration 1889
celestial 1363, 2700
cement 1576
cemetery 2223, 2223a
censure 1779, 1853, 2571
center 2383
central 2928
century 2276
ceremony 1889
certain 3
certainly not! 654
certainly 120, 169, 1543, 2763
certainty 407, 677, 3022
certificate 1525, 1664
chagrin 2046
chain 535, 1066, 1192
chains 1327
chair 2415
chalk 1576
challenge 1639
champion 1438
chance 2741
chandelier 409
change (money) 176, 177
change into 1638
change the mind 1048
change 177, 1580, 2060, 2072, 2175a, 2267
changer 1581b
channel 852, 2101
chapel 1210a, 2486
chapter 471, 1392, 1413
character 623, 831, 1331, 1418, 1679, 2644, 2938, 2939
characteristic 2939
characteristics 1771
charge 559, 1504, 2224, 2467, 2571, 2818, 2943, 2945
charges 2467
charitable 1345, 1571
charity 650, 1571
charm 621, 969, 1711, 1857, 1945, 2452
charming 324, 1755
charms 3011
chastisement 2292
chat 125
chatting 125
cheap 166, 1057
cheapness 1057
cheat 771, 980, 1981, 1996, 2000
chechia 1672

check 751
checkers 1642
cheeky 1170a
cheer 125
cheers 1453
cheese 439
chef 1546
chemisette 1568
chess 1475
chest 565, 1617
chew 911
chief 689, 1003, 1004, 1329, 1389, 1546, 2757a
chiefly 2038, 2039
child 634, 2982, 3017
chill 200
chilliness 197
chimney 889
chisel 1188a
chit 224
choice 866, 867, 2754
choke 2021
cholera 2877
choose 867
Christ 2630
Christ's-thorn 1270
Christendom 2631
Christian 2631, 2747
Christianity 2631
chronology 2364
chunk 2435
chunky 2332
church 2486
cigarette 1248a, 2917
cinnabar 1191
cinnamon 871
cipher 1596
circle 952, 955
circuit 1734
circumambulate 1733
circumcise 1725
circumcision 1724
circumstances 670, 1418, 2721
cistern 6, 742
citizen 1095, 2951a
citizenship 536a
city 693
civet 1157
civil 37, 2657a
civilian 1095, 2657a
civilization 1826, 2605
claim 673, 734, 908, 1707a
clamor 1637
clan 791a, 2233
clarinet 1185
clasp 230
class 331, 536, 899, 900, 1993
clay 1707
clean 1598, 1725, 2759, 2792
cleanness 1724
clear off! 2826
clear 356, 823, 1598, 2791
clearness 356, 357
cleft 2082
clerk 2398
clever 2675
clientele 1160a
cliff 438
clinic 471a
clip 230
cloak 432
clock 1398, 2924
close a hole 653
close at hand 2264
close up 1267
close 2264
closet 1138, 1182
cloth 274, 555, 1733, 1740, 2166a, 2293, 2341, 2548, 2666, 2888
clothe 493
clothes 635, 2521
clothing 1386, 2522
cloud 1995
clove 2280
cloves 417
coachman 1397
coast 1260, 1409
coat of mail 901
coat 432, 1717, 2341
coco-nut 2289
coerce 2022
coercion 2284, 2427
coffee beans 315
coffee berry 315
coffee 315, 2350
coffer 785a
coffin 1617
coin 974, 1149, 1580, 2154, 2185, 2684
coincidence 2966

coition 886
cold 200, 705
coldness 197
collapse 1068
collar 1215, 3013a
colleague 914
collect 1612
collection 511, 832
collector 515
color 328, 1982, 2573
column 2323
comb 2635a
comb-like 2129
come back 1041
come in! 2264
come in 2158, 2264
come into power 2986a
come on! 2865, 2866
Come on! 754a
come to (sexual) maturity 297
come to meet 2558
come to 2940
come unexpectedly 1639
come 754a, 2940
comfort 222, 1133, 2100, 2103
comfortable 2861
command 101, 102a, 683
commander 107, 1901
commendable 1368, 1619
commendation 424, 2939
comment 1453, 2143
commentary 2144
commerce 349, 365
commiserate 729
commission 1965, 2467, 2945, 2979, 2981
commissioner 107a
commit injustice 1757
commit sacrilege 2451
commit sodomy 2570
common 2318
commotion 1652
community 510, 513, 2646
compactness 1942
companion 1565
companions (of the Prophet) 1160a
Companions 1563
companionship 1862
company 511, 572, 1468
compare 1431
compass 353, 955
compassion 1053, 1490
compassionate 1005, 1054
compatriot 2951a
compel 433
compendium 797
compensation 2012, 2674
competent 1903
competition 2037
compile 2203
complain 908, 1504, 1504a
complete 391, 2480, 2481
completed 821
completely 2481
complexion 1261
compliance 2371
compliant 1730
complicate 2021
compliments 1338
compose 321, 1621
composition 1111, 2731
comprehension 2206
compulsory 2427
computation 1802
computational 645
comrade 1565
conceal 2046
concealment 1247
conceive 720
concern 104, 1484
concerning 1698
conciliation 1602
conclude 2480
conclusion 767, 768
concord 2966
concrete 1576
concubine 1283
concur 1573
condemnation 684
condition 2861
condition 745, 831, 989, 1150, 1456, 1560, 1679
condolence 729, 1859
confectionery 2289
confer 1266
confidence 112, 116, 1902, 2981b
confinement 1670
confirm 407
conflict 828
confuse 2021

confusion 75, 246, 765, 1164, 1536, 2156, 2720
congratulate 1333
conscience 1661
consciousness 1661, 1907
consent 1624
consequence 1898
consider oneself pure 2792
consider 645, 798, 985, 1143, 2177, 2821
consideration 110, 245, 2178, 2754
consign 1333
consolation 1859, 2100
console 433
conspiracy 2085, 2964
constancy 407
constant 963
constantly 79, 945, 963
constipation 658
constitution 906
constraint 1652
constraint 2284
construct 321
consult 1533
consultation 1533
container 6, 397a, 742, 1591a, 2959
contaminate 2699
contemplation 110
contempt 1170a
contemptible 680, 991
content 1085, 1086, 1288
contention 2720
contentment 1085, 1086, 1089
contest 451
continually 963
continuance 1987
continue 961, 1985
continued 963
continuous 963
contract 1900
contrary 284
contrast 828, 2209
contrive 321
control 2659
controversy 829
convention 1456
conversation 125
converse 125
convert to Islam 1334
convert 2837
convict 586
conviction 3022
convoy 2323
cookies 2274a
cooking-pot 1593
cool 199, 200
coolie 718
cooling 199
coolness 200
co-operation 351
copper 1431a, 2622
copy 2789, 2790
coral 2614
cord 667, 868, 2484, 2617, 2882
coriander seed 494
corn 2337, 2776
cornstarch 2738
coronach 2848
coronet 400
corporal 121b, 1419
corpse 2679
corpulent 225
correct 1408, 1644, 2149, 2150
correction 684
correspond to 2961
correspondence 2964
corresponding 1809
corrupt 761
corrupter 2141
cosmetics 520
cost of living 2776
cost 348a
costly 1851, 2044
costs 2012
cotton 274, 882a
council of state 965
council 500
councilor 965
counsel 1533, 2957
counsellor 2742, 2837
count 645, 1802
countenance 1289, 2573
counter 369a, 2891
countries 289
country 951
coup d'etat 2331a
couple 564
courage 479, 1495
courageous 1438, 1805
course (of events) 469

course of a ship 469
court (case) 1459
court 125, 688, 1760, 2397a
courtesy 518, 2887
couscous 1356
covenant 1523, 1960
cover of a book 495
cover 1242, 1255, 1683, 2046, 2115, 2455
covering 1247
coverlet 2729
covet 1721
cow 275
coward 2138a
cowardice 2138a
crack 818, 2082, 2164
cradle 2673
craft 750
crane 1981
cranium 2242
crate 1617
crazy 525
cream 1798, 2289
create 831
created 833
creation 832, 2731
creature 832, 833
credit 427, 2269, 2940
creed 973, 997, 1523
creek 855
crescent 2847
crest 2676
crime 541, 808, 995, 1757, 2304
criminal 541
criticize 2080
cross 1601, 1775
cross-grained person 1429
crowbar 1262
crowd 75, 94, 832, 944, 1164, 2359a
crown 400
crucify 1601
cruel 761, 2453
cruelty 761, 2451
crupper (of the saddle) 410
crupper 1705
crush 75, 911
crusher 1689
cry 643
crying 1637
crystal 310, 318a
cubit 984
cuirass 901
culpability 808
cultivate 1169
culture 1826, 2605
cultured 37
culvert 893
cumin 583a
cunning 379, 750, 771, 1907
cup 1728, 2379, 2394a, 2496
cupboard 958a
curator 2987
curb 2923
curd 1130
curiosity 1418, 1851
curious 2777
curl 2293
currency 904
curry 228
curse 1046, 1897, 2451, 2544
curtain 1242, 1247, 2888
curving 730
cushion 2115, 2978
custody 621a
custom 445, 906, 1160a, 1964, 2119, 2318, 2646
customer 1160
customhouse 503a
customs 503a, 997
cut in slices 1453
cut into strips 2242a
cut lengthwise 2242a
cut 70a, 2312
cyclone 1654

dad 10
dagger 851
damage 131, 308, 775, 789, 818, 858, 1651
daman 2878
damn 1046
dampness 1091
damsel 313
dance 955
danger 21, 812, 857, 1493, 2680
dangerous 812
dare 479
date (fruit) 287a
date 50
dates (fruit) 394

daub on 1078
daub 1717
daubing 946
daughter 313
dawn 1552, 2090
day 50, 1978, 3030
daybook 913
daybreak 2090
dazed 1796
deacon 1515
deadline 21
deal 1145, 1623
dear 581, 2044
death 21, 1854, 1859, 2088, 2670, 2678
Death 2797
debased 2717
debate 451
debris 1718
debt 192, 972
decay 1394
deceased 756, 1055, 2679
deceit 750, 859, 1996, 2019, 2543
deceitful 379, 980, 1145
deceive 771, 1757, 1996, 2000, 2042
deceiver 2489
decency 652
deception 771, 859, 2002, 2501
decide 101, 2842
decision 684, 1533, 1857, 2086
deck 1284, 2391a
declare bankrupt 2184
declare lawful 692
decoction 2173a
decorate 1216
decoration 701a, 2736
decorous 37
decrease 817
decree 2246
dedication 2716
deed 650, 1731, 2167
deem desirable 577
defeat 798
defect 829, 1913, 1977, 2167, 2304, 2785
defend 723, 1098
defended 632
defenseless 1855
deficiency 1913, 2302
deficient 1658
deficit 2304, 2785
defile 2699
defilement 528
deflection 730
degradation 2156
degree 893, 2721
deity 1774
delay 25, 31, 1219, 2677
delectation 2533
delicate 1658, 2540
delight 125, 702, 1087
delightful 324
deliver 1333
deliverance 821, 1893
delivery 1344
deluge 2010
demand 1707a
demon 523, 1891, 1548
demonstrability 356
demonstration 1453, 1836
demoralize 775
denarius 974
denomination 997
departed 756
department 954
departure 628
deposit 786, 1830, 2902
depressed 668
deprived 1814
depth 1625, 1943
deputy 2810, 2980
derangement 1536
derision 70, 2627
dervish 1633, 2172, 2987
descend 1690
descendant 1463, 2982
descendants 983
descent 445, 2595, 2724
describe 2938
desert 181
deserve 577
deserving 2991
design 1036, 1076, 1111
desire 446, 1088, 1530, 1538a, 1709, 1721, 1870, 2770, 2851, 2862
desired 1140
desk 892
despicable 1658, 2717
despise 680, 798, 1657
destiny 670, 1069, 2741

destroy 386, 774, 775, 937a
destroyed 775
destruction 789
detach 692, 1714
detention 1219
determination 1857, 2064
determined 1924
detested 2428
devasted 775
device 750
devil 9, 1548, 1891
dhow 547
diabetes 1314a
diagram 1711
diamond 86
dice 1642
dictation 2662
dictionary 2340
dictum 2358
die 2010, 2849
difference 825, 828, 829, 2209
difficult 668, 752
difficulties 750
difficulty 308, 380, 1493, 2284
dignity 652, 692, 1432, 2644, 2721, 2867
diminution 817
dinar 974
direct 107, 683
direction 1625, 2557, 2893, 2945
directly 1742
director 956a, 2757a
dirge 2848
dirhem 904
dirt 1718, 2925
dirty 2925
disagreement 828
disaster 131, 269, 858, 1448, 1497, 2703
disbursements 1581a
discernment 2113
discharge 1855, 2180, 2925
disciple 1139a
discomfort 47, 1536, 2467
discord 829, 2085, 2169
discredit 798
discrepancy 2209
discretion 2754
discuss 125
discussion 125, 1533
disdain 1170a
disease 304, 1595, 2018, 2620, 2877
disgrace 531, 755, 788, 1853, 1913, 1977, 2155, 2829
disgust 2424, 2425, 2427
disgusting 2428
dish 280, 1567, 1682, 2959, 3005a
disharmony 2209
dishonest 1145
dishonor 787, 788, 1977, 1979, 2054, 2155
dislocate 2140
disloyalty 859
dismay 2156
disobedient 825, 1878
disobey 1878
disorder 765
disparage 1853
disparity 828
disperse 1639
display 369a, 1453
displeasure 76
dispose 2923
disposition 832, 1331
dispute 451, 800, 1533, 2720
disrespect 2156a
disrespectful 1170a
disseminate 184, 1639
dissension 2085
dissimilarity 829, 2209
dissolute 2146
distance 100
distinguish 2129
distinguished 1851
distress 308, 380, 1164, 1652, 1670, 2047, 3006
distresses 668
distribute 2285, 2923
district 289, 693, 735, 951, 2990
disturbance 2138a
ditch 852, 2101
divan 965
dive 2010
divergence 828
divide 329a, 2129, 2285
diviner 2489
division 136, 471, 1474, 2129, 2285
divorce 1714, 1715, 1716
do a kindness to 2157
do accurately 1643
do evil 1757

do join 2158
do quickly 627
do right 649
do superficially 1078
do work 1621
do 90, 1944
doctor 686b, 926a, 1290b, 1675
doctrine 997
document 2917
Dog Star 1479
dog 2465
doing 2167
dole 166a
dollar 1149, 2976
dollars 2267
domestic 129
domicile 1319
dominant 2039
dominate 683
domination 2659
dominion 1850, 2654, 2658
dominoes 1642
donation 2997
door 891
door-keeper 332
doorman 332
dot 78, 2788
double (a garment) 257
double 1064
doubt 169, 1493, 1497, 1536, 2935
dove 706
dower 2674
dowry 2674
drachma 904
draft 751
drag-net 465b
draper 226
drawback 1913
drawer 892
drawers 2521
drawing room 329
drawing 1076, 1622, 1629
dread 857, 858
dream 1008
dregs 1718
dress for the grave 2455
dress up 443
dress 432, 493, 555, 1423, 2341, 2729
dressing 653
drill 1836
drink 1449b, 1450, 2417a
driver 1397, 1401a
drop 2788
dropsy 1307
dross 1155a
drug 1904
drum 1689a
drunkenness 1311
dry 3015
due 656, 674
dulcimer 1375
dupe 225
duplicate 2790
durability 1983
durable 1644
duration 961, 1987
during 1742
durra 984a
dusk 2006
dust 1995
duty 674, 1865, 2118, 2886, 2887
dwelling 1319
dwelling-place 2498

eagerness 1538a
earnest 1805
earth 55, 944
ease 222, 2764
East 1465
east 1552, 1712
ease 2100
easy 1057, 2861
easy-chair 2415
eat 1311
economization 2297
economy 2297
ecstasy 453a
Eden 1816
edging 1695
education 1917, 1922
effect 484, 1898, 1944
effective 2775
effeminate 848
effigy 1629
effort 173, 543, 544, 546, 1809, 1902, 2518
effrontery 1170a
egg-plant 149
Egypt 2637

eight 419
eighteen 420
eighty 422
either ... or 97
elastic 2537a
elder 1546, 3008
election 867, 2271a
electric 2488
electrician 2488
electricity 2488
elegance 1767
elegant 324, 1755, 2149, 2150, 2611, 2612
elephantiasis 455
eleven 1867
eloquence 2150
eloquent 2149, 2474
emasculated 804
embarrassment 2171
embellishment 520, 701a
emblem 2588, 2592
embrasure 1430
embroider 2293
embroidery 2293
emigrate 2830
emir 107
emotion 628
emotional 430
empire 2658
employee 773
enable 484
enchain 1327
enchantment 2863b
encircle 657
enclose 657
enclosure 1028, 1734
encounter 2558
encourage 433
end 27, 100, 767, 768, 1898, 2295, 2303
endeavor 543, 2852
endeavor 546
endowment 2973, 2974
endure 961, 1555, 1985
enduring 963
enemy 171, 646, 1819
energetic 1805
energy 173, 2852
enforced 2427
engage in aggressive 1818
engine 2645
enjoy oneself 2104
enjoyment 125, 2103, 2533
enmity 800
ennui 2647
enough 231, 821, 2371
enrich 1201a
ensured 1665
entertain with 2542
entertain 125
entertainer 1354
entertainment 2103, 2419
enthusiasm 1809
entice 1996
enticement 453a
entire 511, 512a, 2481
entirely 794, 795, 2481
entirety 511
entitlement 674
entreat 1637
entrust with 2973
entrust 2979
entry 886
envelope 2548
envier 646
envious 646, 647, 860
envisage 2891
envoy 1073, 2415
envy 646, 647, 1530, 2085
epidemic 1704, 2877
epistle 2917
epoch 1189
equal 1407, 1809
equality 1407
equalize 1405
equator 806
equipment 547
eraser 2537a
erroneous 808
error 2042
escape 168, 2180
escort 621a
especially 794
essay 2731
essence 570, 998, 1879, 2770
establish as ruler 1328
establish 1366
establishment 707
esteem 1778
eternal 4, 60, 963

eternity 60, 945, 2648
ethnicity 2359a
eulogy 424
eunuch 802
Europe 2663, 2990
European 854a
Eve 731
even if 2873
even 284, 590
evening 1872
event 2290
ever 3, 4
every 138a, 512a
evidence 356, 1522
evident 356
evil 269, 761, 1448
exact 794, 796, 1562, 1644
exactly 794, 795, 823, 918
exalt 1888
exaltation 1887
exalted 1731
exaltedness 1887
examination 1994, 2080
examine 1143, 1223, 1713, 2079, 2080
example 2591, 2592
exasperation 2024
excellent 2162
except 79, 130, 654, 2062
exchange 177, 1580
exchequer 786
excitement 627
excrement 1138
excreta 1138
exculpate 187
excuse 1242, 1824
execration 2544
executor 2944
exercise-book 2396
exert vexations, persecutions 379
exertion 446, 544, 2064
exhibition 1836
exhortation 2945, 2956, 2957
existence 756
expect 1048, 1555
expectoration 302
expedient 1240
expedition 1294
expense 778, 1580, 2012
expenses 1583
expensive 2044
experience 458
experienced 1804, 2675
expert 1839, 1923, 2113, 2675
expiations 2452
explain 1764, 1777, 1835, 2143, 2938
explanation 357, 2143, 2144, 2706
explore 2079
expose 1835
exposure 2156
expound 1777
expression of annoyance 90
expression of impatience 90
expressly for 2295
expressly 794, 795
extend 1742
extent 2246
extort 2022
extract 2720
extradition 1344
extravagant 186
extreme 27
extremes 2928
exuberant 70
exude moisture 1079
eye 1174
eyeglasses 2754a
eyesight 243
eyewitness 1525

fabric 1106, 1372, 1733
fabricate 321
face 1629, 2893
facile 2582
facilitation 1382
facing 2238
faction 1738
factory 1468
faculty 2236
fail 90, 2184
faint 2049
fairness 674
faith 116, 997, 1523, 1702, 1778, 1902, 2631, 2646
faithful 113, 118, 1575
faithfulness 113
faithless 860
fakirism 2419
fallow 335

false 1145
falsehood 1203
fame 2939
family 129, 506, 513, 1993
famous 1529, 1844
far away 267
far 267
fare 2818
fart 1131
fascicle 2416
fascination 2863b
fashion 1695
fast 1634, 2164, 2165
fastener 230
fasting 1635, 1636
fat 225, 1440
fata morgana 1274
fate 21, 670, 1069, 2670, 2741
father 10
fatherless 3017
fatigue 380
fault 808, 995, 1757, 1913, 1977, 2042, 2304, 2785
favor 520, 563, 650, 651, 1087, 1619, 2158, 2232, 2764
fear 857, 858, 2138a, 2867, 2935
fearless 435
fearlessness 1785
feast 1832a, 1896, 1978, 2419
features 1261, 1629
fee 1965, 2430
feeble 1658, 2582
feel compassion 729
feel disgust 2424
feel pleasure 2104
feel 643, 2628
fellow 1298
felony 541, 859
fels 2185
fence 1028
fennel 233, 1512
fermata 667
ferment 839
ferry 1820a
ferryboat 1820a
fervor 614
feud 2720
fever 705
few 583
fez 1693, 2497
fibers 2577
fibre 2401, 2577
fibrils 2577
fidelity 113
field 202
fifteen 844
fifth 840
fifty 845
fig 403
fight 2720
figure 1107, 2893
figure-head 2383
file 200a, 1671a
filigree 783
fill 1427, 2648
filth 1718
finally 821
finance 2684
find fault 1170a, 1779
fine 231, 683, 1823, 2012, 2097
finery 701a
finger 2628, 2639b
finish 391, 1903, 2480
finished 821
fire 442, 2561a
firearms 317
firm 408, 1644, 1805, 2644
firmness 1600, 1942
first 134
first-born 283
fish net 465b
fish 1186, 1359
fishing net 1429
fissure 818, 2164
fistula 2727
fit 2961
fitness 2578
fitting in 1111
fitting 1607, 2201, 2578, 2991
fittings 1216
five 841, 842
fix somebody 441
fix them on a point 441
fix 1444
fixed 408, 1924
flabby 2582
flag 318, 1918
flageolet 1185

flank 526, 529
flannel 555, 2202a
flap 2538
flashlight 249a
flat 2009
flattery 2939
flavor 2533
flaw 1977
flax 2401
flexible 2582
fling 1124
flog 495
flogging 496
flood 2010
floor 2009
flour 920a
flourish 1405
fluctuate 1062
fluency 2150
foam 1155a
fog 1518
fold 1683
folder 224
foliage 2917
follow 902
folly 2002
food 78, 1033, 1069, 2556
fool 117, 246, 272, 525, 907
foolish 525
foot-ball 2495
foot-gear 1113
for example 2591
for 2509
forbid 2943
forbidden 629, 632, 633
force 433, 2022, 2284
forced 2427
forearm 984
forefather 445
forego 334
forenoon 1646
forepart of ship 95
foretell 239
forever 3
forge 1366
forgetfulness 1385
forgive 334, 1352, 2027
forgiveness 192, 2027, 2030
fork 1539a
form a conclusion 2696
form 1432, 1629, 2331, 2893
formerly 1189
fornication 1196, 1197
fort 195, 661
fortress 661
fortune 163a, 211, 1288, 1290, 1897, 2684, 2700, 2741
forty 1025
foundation 2318
four 1023
fourfold 1028
fraction 1384, 2312
fragment 2312, 2435
France 2136
frankincense 2524
fraud 1757, 1996, 2019
free 192
free-born 615
freedom 616, 1240, 2931
freeman 615
freethinker 1194
freight 1441, 2818
freightage 2818
Friday 507
friend 32, 581, 1102, 1565, 2742, 2987
friendship 577, 578, 580
fright 2138a
frighten 1639
from among 2664
from 355
front 2893
frost 498, 1599
froth 1155a
fruit 417
fuel 429a
fulfilment 2962
full moon 171
full stop 2788
full up 2805
fumigation 165
fun 70, 2627
function 1484
fundament 2318
fundamental 134
funeral 534, 1859
fur 2137
furnace 397
furniture 958a

further 139
fury 2024
future life 27
futwa 2086

gadgets 1216
gage 1830
gain 2775a
gait 1767
galabia 493
galette 2435
gall 1595
gallon 500a
gamble 2339
gambling 2270
game warden 1862
game 1734, 1748, 2542, 2543
garbage 1718
garden 235, 524, 524a
garlic 247a, 429
garment 432, 2137, 2663
garments 635
gas 429a, 1131
gasoline 318b
gate 333
gatekeeper 332
gather up 1511
gathering 506, 513
gauge 667
gears 958a
Gehenna 551
geld 802
gelding 804
gem 570, 2148
gender 536
genealogy 445, 2724
general 515
generation 2359a
generosity 1352, 1353, 2419
generous 1352, 2420
genie 523
gentle 1005, 2540, 2582, 2644
gentleman 76a
gentleness 1396, 1858, 2540, 2540
genuine 823
genus 536, 1993
get along 2961
get going 1409
get in motion 2826
get money 365
get ready 1511
get rich 365
get the better of 2039
get understanding 1826
get up 2973
get used to 125
get 177, 1328
ghee 1361
giant 435
gift 166a, 563, 1202, 1885, 2419, 2838, 2997
girdle 639
girl 313
girth 639
give almsgiving 2419
give an account 1354
give attention 2696
give credence 1575
give honor to 2863b
give information 2938
give light 1174
give more 1213
give o.s. airs 443
give offence 2424
give peace 1333
give permission 1058
give power 1328
give up 373, 1333, 1714
give 484, 2943
given 1924
glad tidings 236a, 239
gladness 236a, 2104
glance 2754
glass 310, 318a, 2282, 2490, 2756
glasses 1994, 2754a
glisten 1174
globe 2429
glorification 1889
glorify 1888
glory 431, 490, 1850, 1887, 2095
glow 2814
glue 1128, 1455
go ahead 754a
go back 1041
go fast 2898
go here and there 1062
go straightaway 2295
go to meet 2228, 2558
go! 2826, 3009

go 754a
goal 100
goat 1896, 2106
go-between 2081
goblet 310
God forbid! 654, 1966
God is great 2389
God preserve us! 1966
God willing 1543
God 88, 435, 490, 1013, 1349, 2993
godfather 2987
godmother 2987
Gog 3018
gold 996
gonorrhea 161
good evening 2634
good luck 670
good mannered 37
good manners 35, 518
good morning 864
good news 236b
good! 821
good 862, 1345, 1352, 1368, 1607, 1619, 1746, 1931
goodbye 1382
good-for-nothing 1145
good-humored 2582
good-looking 2791
goodness 1747, 2540
goods 184, 2684
gospel 124
gourd 2570a
govern 683, 2986a
government 684, 687, 957, 965
governor 671a, 689, 956a, 2995
gown 2341
grab 1643
grace 1053, 2158, 2764
graceful 1755
gracious 1005
grain 2776
grains 583
grammar 2706
gramophone 1375
grandeur 1887, 2095
grand-father 445
grant a favor 476
grant 1266, 2997
grape 1155
gratification 1088
gratitude 649, 1500
gratuity 166a
grave 1071, 2223
graveyard 2223, 2223a
gravitation 453a
grayness 1544
grease 1211, 1440
greasing 946
Greece 3032
greed 2466
greedy 2770
Greek 3032
green 804a
greet 1333
greeting 1338
grief 640, 2047
grilling 1332
grinder 1689
groom 1397
ground 55
groundnut 2214
ground-rent 1865
group 511, 914, 1400, 2359a, 2769
grow longer 1742
grow 1201a, 1213, 2805
grudge 1651, 2292
grudger 646
gruel 2183
grumbling 76
guarantee 1562, 1664, 1830
guaranteed 1665
guarantor 1663
guaranty 1664
guard 621a
guard 671, 723, 953, 1643, 1862
guardianship 724, 2224
guarding 671
guide 1015, 2837
guile 2019
guileless 192
guilt 808, 2571
gulf 855
gullet 701
gum 1367, 1374, 1616
gumbo 156, 3005a
gun 317, 1083, 2082
gunpowder 150
gypsum 480

habit 1771, 1964, 2646
habous 2974
hadith 607
hadj 592, 595
hairstyle 1672
half 2748
half-breed person 1474
half-caste 1474
half-piastre 2267
hall 329
halyard 457
hammer 1413a
hand over 1333
hand 1905, 3025
handful 2224
handicraft 1620
handing over 1344
handkerchief 2166a, 2666
handle 2628
handwriting 805
hang 1915
hanging 1242
haphazardly 1241a
happen unexpectedly 1690
happen 2971
happening 2290
happenings 1652
happiness 236a, 862, 2104, 2764
happy 1288, 1289
hard to get 2044
hard 3015
hardness 1942
harlot 2663
harm 131, 1651
harmony 2966
harrow 465b
harsh 1445
harshness 486
hart 135
hashish 321b, 651a
haste 627
hat 1672, 1682, 1693, 2497
hatchet 2070
hate 2424
hated 2428
hatred 270, 2425
hauberk 901
have courage to 407
have courage 479
have enough 1427
have in mind 2821
have under control 1643
haversack 1520
hawk about 2715
hawser 2617
head 956a, 1003, 1004, 2383
headman 2995
heal 222
healer 1925
health 745, 1150, 1341, 1560, 1746, 1894, 2861
healthy 1561
heap 1625
heart of the night 565
heart 430, 1661, 2068
heat 614, 619
heathen 2453
Hebrew 3027
heed 2271a
heir 2911
hell 442, 551
hellfire 442
helmet 1693
helmsman 1015
help 1289, 1290, 1974, 2746, 2774
helpless 2172
hem 1215
hemorrhoids 236
hemp 321b, 651a, 2401
henna 727
herbs 651a
here I am! 2526
hereafter 29
heritage 2912
hermaphrodite 849
hermit 1633
hero 1438
hesitate 1062
hesitation 1062
hidden 2058
higher 1931
highest 1931
highway 189
hill 438
hinge 333
hint 1534
hire 17, 18, 19
history 50, 691, 762, 2290

importer 492a
impose 1328
impossible 752
impost 1865
impostor 1981, 2777
imposts 2467
impotence 1587
impotent 848, 1658
imprecation 2544
impression 1076
imprisoned 586
improve 1602
impudicity 1196
impure 2699
impurity 528
in addition 139
in common 1408
in favor of 2509
in front of 95, 663
in order that 2509
in particular 794
in the presence of 95, 663
in the rear 826
in whole 2481
in 143, 2215
inadvertence 2033
inasmuch as 960
inattentive 2034
inauspicious 1417
incantation 171, 1857
incense 165
incident 691
inclination 1588, 2862
inclined 1804
income 882b, 888, 1150, 2583b, 2940
inconceivable 752
incorrect 808
increase 1201a, 1213, 2805
increment 1213
incumbent 2886
indecision 1062
indemnity 2012, 2906
independence 616
index 2203
indicate 2938
indication 928, 1534
indifferently 1241a
indigence 2213
indigenous 290
indigo 2825
indisputably 1241a
individuality 2770
indivision 1468
indulgence 1086
industry 1468
inebriety 1311
infatuation 2002
inferior 966
infidel 2453
infidelity 2451
infirm 1658
inflection 1829
inflict 1328
influence 1444
inform 1835, 1839
information 1841, 1842, 1843
informer 1272, 2777
inherit 2908
inheritance 2908, 2912
iniquity 1757
injection 5, 680a
injure 463, 775, 789
injured 464, 1760
injury 789, 818, 1651
injustice 558, 859, 1757
inkwell 968
inlet 855
innate 831
inner nature 71
innocent 192
innovation 173a
innovator 173
inquire into 1713
inquire 451, 2079
inquiry 1403a, 2080
insanity 765
insect 949
insertion 1111
inside 257
insignificant 816, 817, 1658, 2719
insinuate 1835
insinuation 2935
insolent 70
insolvent 2187
inspection 1994, 2103
inspector 2080a

inspire 2898
installation 1111
instance 914
instead of 176
instinct 1331
instruction 2557
instructions 973, 2945
instrument 133
insubordination 684
insufficiency 2302
insult 787, 788, 2424, 2427
insulting 2158
insults 1225
integrity 1080
intellect 246, 1907
intelligence 1841, 1907
intelligent 2518
intend to 2822
intend 1936, 2295, 2821, 2842
intensification 1445
intention 1140, 1661, 1665, 1857, 2007, 2169, 2295, 2822
intercession 1487
intercessor 1487
interdicted 629, 632
interdiction 2129
interest 1031, 2216
interior 257
interpret 1777, 2143
interpretation 1777
interpreter 371, 2474
interrogation 1403a
interval 204, 1398, 2209, 2600, 2677, 2772
intrigue 2085
inundation 1737
inveigle 1396
invent 321, 1621
investigation 2080
inviolable 633
invite 908, 1048
invoke 908
Iran 1796
irascible 765
iron 2500a
irresponsible 765
is? 2872
Islam 1345
it must 2534
it should 2534

jacket 1568
jam 1033
jar 293
jasmine 3019
jazz 2130a
jealousy 647, 2054, 2085
jersey 2202a
jest 1263
jester 525, 2627
Jew 3027
jewel 570, 701a, 2516
jeweler 570
Jewish 3027
jinn 523
job 1484
joint pin 1066
joke 70, 2542, 2627
joker 2627
joking 907
journey 1294, 1583, 2608a
joy 236a, 862, 1691, 2104, 2533
judge 683, 684, 689, 2307
judgement 684, 686, 1907
judgment 1459, 2754
judicial act 683
jug 6, 280, 1728, 2496
jugular 701
junk 2925
just as 2378
just so 918
just then 1408
just 1562, 1813
justice 674, 1459
justify 334

kaffiyeh 2497
kapok 1632
kasida 2296
keep 1643
keepsake 1202
keg 221
kerchief 2497, 2666
kerosene 429a
kettle 6, 905, 1045
key 2078
Khartoum 782b

kiblah 2231
kill 977
kiln 397
kin 506
kind 331, 536, 1005, 1621, 1695, 1993, 2196, 2233, 2573, 2665
kindness 650, 651, 1053, 2158
king 1329, 2655
kingdom 951, 2654, 2658
kinsfolk 2359a
kinship 2724
kinsman 2264, 2265
kiosk 363b
kitchen 385b
kite 1751
knapsack 1520
knave 1981
knickers 1282, 2521
knife 1827, 2414
knitting 1900
knock 2271a
knot 1900, 2278
know 902, 1922, 2206
knowing 1839, 1923
knowledge 686, 1841, 1917
known 1844, 1924
kofia 2497
kohl 2402
kurbash 2414

labor 2534
laborer (day) 18
laborer 1945
lack 1883, 2171, 2302
lacking 1814
ladder 1337a
lading 1441
lady 1246, 1390, 2639b
lagging behind 1219
lagoon 163
lake 163
lamp glass 310
lamp 1276, 2345, 2488, 2561a, 2814
lampstand 2815
land 55, 189
landmark 1921
landscape 2755
language 2538, 2547
lantern 2073, 2345, 2561a
lapse of memory 1385
lard 1440
larva 949
last long 1742
last stage 27
last will 2945
last 27, 902, 959, 1742, 1985
lasting 963
late 1055, 1219
lateness 1789
later 265, 826
latrine 1138
laudation 709
laugh 1645
laughingstock 1263
lavatory 1138, 1182
law of Moses 401
law 1459, 2342, 2690
lawfulness 674
lawsuit 800, 909, 1459
lawyer 2307
laxative 1377, 1383
layer 1683
lazy 1442
lead aright 2837
lead on the right way 2837
lead 1083
leader 96, 107, 1711a, 1901
leaf 1566, 2416, 2917
learn 388, 1713
learned 1923
learning 1917, 1922
lease 18
leave behind 826
leave off 834
leave 834, 1058, 1409, 2830
leaven 839
leaves 2917
lecturer 810
ledge 1097
ledger 913
leer 1174
legacy 2908, 2945, 2997
legal suit 1504a
legal 694
leisure 2125, 2772, 2931
lemon 2581
lengthen 1742
lentil 1806

leprosy 206, 455
less 2327
lessening 817
lesson 899
let be 373
let's go myself! 2866
let's go! 2865, 2866, 3009
letter 82, 224, 623, 1957, 2270, 2399, 2917
letting 19
level 1405
lexicon 2340
liar 980, 2407, 2777
libation (of milk) 1571
liberal 2420
liberality 1352, 1353, 2419a
liberate 1714
liberation 821
liberty 1058
lice 2341a
lid 1683
lie close to 1683
lie 2042
life 181, 756, 758, 1940, 1983, 1985, 1987, 1988, 2764
lifeless 2679
lift 1098, 1511
light (the fire) 441
light 816, 1276, 1380, 2814
light-hole 1430
lighthouse 2815
like this 2377
like 577, 1407, 1432, 2378
likeness 1407, 1431, 1431a, 1622, 1629, 2573, 2588, 2590, 2592
likewise 2377
lime 200a, 2581
lime-kiln 397
limit 603, 2303, 2677
limpid 1598
line 805, 1286, 1400, 1671a, 1683, 2617
lineage 445, 2724
linen 2401
linger 1742
lingerie 569a
lining (of a garment) 260
lining 1683
link together 1327
liquidation 821
liquor 337, 1847, 1904
liquorice 1395
litany 2914
litigation 1459
litter 1718
little (in quantity) 583
little 166, 816, 1586, 2719
littoral 1260
live in opulence 372
live long 1939
live luxuriously 125
live 754, 1983, 1985
livelihood 1069
liveliness 756
lively 70
living 754
load 717, 1441, 1511, 1939
loaf 2331
loafer 1981
loam 1707
loan 972, 2269
loathe 2424
locality 529
lock of hair 357a
lock 2322
locker 785a, 1617
locomotive 147
lodge 2902
loft 2009
loftiness 490
lone 2108
long ago 1189
long 1744
longing 2851, 2862
look at him with fixed eyes 441
look at 1537
look for 2079
look into 1713
look like 1431
look 241, 1261, 1629, 1707a, 2754
loom 2129
loop 230
loop-hole 1430
lord it 443
lord 1013, 1389, 2992
Lord 2992, 2993
lose consciousness 2049
lose hope 373
loss 789, 1667
lot 2271a

lottery 163a
lotus-tree 1270
louse 2341a
love 577, 578, 580, 1769, 2851, 2862
lover 581, 1870
loving 581
low 166, 668, 680, 966, 991, 2717
lowly 966
lowness 989
loyalty 115
lubricant 1211
lucid 2149, 2150
luck 131, 163a, 211, 1288, 1416, 1762, 2051, 2076, 2700, 2703, 2741
lucky 1288, 1289
luffa 2570a
luggage 734
lunacy 1386
lunch 2242a
lust 1721
lute 1963
luxurious 125
luxuriously 125
luxury 125

mace 233
machine 133, 2645, 2924
madam 1390
madman 525
madrasah 900
magazine 2396
maggot 949
Magi 2594
magic 1257
magician 1925
magistrate 2307
magnanimity 1352, 1353, 2419
magnanimous 1352
magnificent 1888
magnify 1888
Magog 3018
Mahdi 2595
maid 771a
mail 234, 2917
mailbag 234
mainly 2038, 2039
mainsail 1242, 2548
maintain 773
maintenance 1069, 1580
majesty 490, 1887
majority of 2039
majority 2038
make a Muhammadan 1334
make a present 476
make amends 902
make an effort 543
make clear 1764
make confusion 2021
make equal or similar 1431
make familiar 125
make fun 2156a
Make haste! 754a
make haste! 2865
make less noise! 2843
make longer 1742
make peace 2902
make public 665
make ready 547a
make sure 1573
make trial of 458
make up one's mind 2821
make way! 1349
make 484, 1305, 1602, 1695, 1944, 2032
make-up 1767
malady 2620
malaria 705, 2648a
male 86, 2094
malefactor 634
malevolent 2797
malice 1170a, 1448, 1907, 2167, 2451
malicious 761, 1891, 2777
man 126, 225, 312, 1044, 1422, 1544, 1788, 2043, 2236, 2983
manage 1643, 1944
manager 956a
manhood 2612
manifestation 1829
manipulation 1396
manner 1964, 1702, 2939
manners 2612
manually 1958
manufacturing 1111
many 832
marble 2624
marching 1671a
marine 2708
mark 12, 136, 1046, 1424, 1920, 1921, 2736, 2788

market 1402
marriage 1832a, 1900, 2674, 2724, 2793
martyr 1522, 1525
marvel 1782, 1785
mast 1585
master 366, 579, 1013, 1389, 2992
master 76a
mastery 2659
mat 205, 2115, 2522
match 321d, 2391, 2495
matchbox 2391
material 2537a
mathematical 645
matrix 2331
matter 104, 1263, 1418
mattress 2115
mature 1405
maturity 1080
maybe 169
Mazdaism 2594
meal 920a, 2164
mean 1658, 2717
meaning 1665, 1959
meanness 1956
means 1240, 2931
measure 1020, 2246, 2294, 2370, 2371
meat 2679
Mecca 635, 2640
medal 2736
mediation 1487
mediator 1297
medicament 969, 1904
medicine 818, 969, 1071, 1674
meditate 2177, 2179
meditation 110, 2177, 2178
medium 2928
meek 991
meet 662, 2558, 2891
meeting 513, 522, 900
melancholia 1386
melon 250
mend with someone 2902
mend 1106, 2531
mendicant 2172
menses 760
menstrual date 50
menstruation 760
merchandise 248, 349, 1836
merchant 226, 366, 492a
merciful 1005, 1054
mercury 1152
mercy 1053
merit 427, 673, 692
meritorious 1368, 1619
message 986a, 1074
messenger 1073, 1074, 2657
Messiah 2630
metal 1817
metaphor 2590
meter 2584a
method 1702, 2318
metropolitan 2639a
middle 565, 2928
middling 2928
midway 2970
midwife 872a
might 1850
mihrab 620
military 572, 1862
mill 1689
millet 2189
minaret 2815
minbar 2692
mind 246, 1661, 1907, 2694, 2770
mine 1817
minister 2283, 2922
ministry 2922
minority 1738
mint 2766
minute (time unit) 921
miracle 136, 1776, 1782, 1785, 1790, 2419
miracles 2419
mirage 1274
mirror 1010, 2754a, 2756
mischief 2085
mischievous 2703
misdeed 2167
misdemeanor 531
miser 167
miserable 2172
miseries 1493
misfortune 21, 304a, 308, 789, 1225, 1416, 1627, 1897, 2680, 2703
mishap 21, 1418
mislead 771, 2000
mist 1518
mistake 2042
mistreat 988

mistress 1390
mixture 75
mockery 1645, 2158
model 1695, 2331
moderation 2246, 2371, 2938
modesty 652, 755, 1247
modify 2060
Mohammed 1563
moisten 285
moisture 1091
mold 2331
moment 921, 1398, 2970
monarch 2655
Monday 425
monetary 2781
money order 751
money 78, 176, 177, 184, 186, 786, 904, 972, 1580, 1581b, 1593, 1830, 2154, 2185, 2224, 2267, 2269, 2674, 2684, 2781, 2818, 2906
monsoon 2934
month 637, 1038, 2316
moon 171, 2847
more frequently 2401a
more often 2038, 2039
more than 1201a, 2212
more 1213, 2212, 2401a
moreover 139
morning 1552, 1553, 1712, 2090
morsel 2556
mortgage 1129
mosque 515, 1210a, 1252
mosquito net 2803
mosquito wire 2803
most of 2039
most 2401a
motherless 3017
mothworm 1394
motion 628
motive 1226
mount 1112
mountain 438
mourn 729
mourning 1386, 1627
mouth 791a
mouthful 2556
move about 870
move away 1162
move from one place to another 526
move house 2830
move restlessly 870
move 1409, 2789
movement 627, 628
Mr. 854a
much 832
muezzin 45
mug 1728, 2394a, 2490, 2496
Muhammadan 1345
Muhammadans 635
mulberry 2117
mule 271
multiplication 1654
multiply 1201a
munch 911
munificence 2419a
music 1691, 2683a
musician 1692
musk 2632
musket 317
Muslim 1343, 1345, 1346
muslin 1535
must 957
mustache 1451
mustard 780
mutiny 1878
muzzle 813
my Lord 579
mystery 1272

nail 1355
name 82, 86, 1348, 2690
napkin 2166a
narcissus 2718
narghile 1547
narrate 1354
narrative 691, 2290
narrowness 1670
nation 94, 536, 1738, 2359a
nationality 536a
native 290
natron 2751
nature 570, 998, 1418, 1679
naught 1596
naughty 1495
nautical term 95
navigate 2192
nay 284
Nazarene 2747
near 2264

nearby 2264
nearer 2265
nearly 169, 2264, 2719
neat 2759
necessary 3, 1580, 2534
necessitating 2887
necessities 734
necessity 734, 1456, 1652, 2118, 2534
necklace 2516, 3013a
need 594, 734, 1824, 2171, 2213
neediness 2213
needle 5
needy 2172
neglect 90, 373, 2032
negligence 2033
negligent 2034
neighbor 559
net 1467
net-like 1429
netting 1430
network 1430
never mind 1543a
never 3
nevertheless 2515, 2874
new moon 2847
New Testament 124
news 236b, 762, 1841, 2290
newspaper 465, 2917
next world 29
next 139
nice 2611
night 2579
nightingale 287
nine 375
ninety 377
ninth 376
no doubt 169, 654
no more 79
no 2511
Noah's ark 1299
nobility 2419
noble 615, 1463, 2233
noise 643, 1164, 1628, 2720
nomad 181
nomadism 181
non-Arabs 1796
nonsense 1170a
nor 2513
normal 2318
nose 639, 813
not enough 583
not even 2513
not so! 2511
not so 590
not yet 821
not 2511
notable 1851
notch 2119
note 224, 986a, 2694
notebook 2396, 2416
note-case 472
nothing 79
notice 1927
notification 1842, 1843
notion 1762
notorious 1529
notwithstanding 2874
novelty 1418
novice 1139a
now then! 2865
now 1399
Nubian 2811
nuisance 1651
null 256
number 517, 1486, 1802, 2376, 2802a
numbering 1107
numeral 1107
numeration 1107
numero 2802a
nun 283, 1127a
nuptials 1833
nurse 394a
nut 2568
nutmeg 233

oak 1218
oath 1960, 2287, 2544, 3025
obedience 1731
obedient 1730
obey 1730
object 511, 629, 734, 2007, 2295
obligating 2887
obligation 192, 972, 2118, 2534, 2886, 2887
obliged! 710
oblique 730
oblong 1744
oboe 1185
obsequious 991

observation 2103
observe 241, 2694
obstinacy 1956
obstinate 2501
obvious 356
occasion 914, 2607, 2772
occident 2004
occupancy 1484
occupation 1484, 1620, 1988, 1945
occur 1690, 1835
occurrence 1417, 2033, 2607
ocean 163
odd 2881
odor 625, 1131
of course 1543
of 2664
offender 2146
offense 46, 192, 541, 995, 2424, 2427, 2304
offensive 2428
offering 1571, 2452, 2902
office 2397a
officer 107, 1643a
official 1077
officially 1077
officious 2158
oftener 2401a
Oh God! 3008
oh that 2576
Oh yes 1543
oh! 135a
oil 429a, 1211
oil-cake 1442
oiling 946
ointment 1128
okay 231
okra 156, 2639b, 3005a
Old Testament 401
olive 1211, 1212
omen 1416, 1534, 1762, 1897, 2072
omens 171
omnipotent (God) 435
Omniscient 1918a
on behalf of 1698
on the spot 1408
on 2215
one fifth 840
one ninth 376
one third 413
one 2895
one-eighth 421
one-sixth 1271
onion 247
only 79, 231, 2895
open 441, 2100
opening 2076, 2101, 2119
operation 1945a
opinion 828, 997, 1006, 1762, 2086, 2358
opium 77, 321b
opponent 798, 799, 1819
opportunity 814, 1824, 2772, 2931
opposite 2238
opposition 825, 828
oppress 658, 1757
oppression 558, 1164, 1670, 1757, 1785
oppressive 1759
oppressor 1759
option 866
or else? 2872
or 130, 2513, 2872
or? 97, 2872
orange 194, 2581
orator 810
order 101, 102, 102a, 1036, 1444, 1707a, 1850, 2943
orderliness 1396
ordinance 1036
organization 882
Orient 1465
origin 71, 445
original 71
ornament 639, 701a, 2783
orphan 3017
ostentation 2095
ostrich 2764a
other than 2062
otherwise 2872, 2873
ounce (weight) 132
ounce 2976
out of the road! 1349
outcast 181
outcome 1898
outfit 547
outlaw 634
outlay 778, 2012
outpost 953
outrage 558
outward 1432
over 821, 2212

overeat 1311
overlay 1717
overplus 2158
ownership 2658
ox 275

pace 814
package 1018, 2115
packet 1018, 2115
pack-saddle 1483
pact 1960, 2964
pad 2978
padlock 2322
page 1566, 2416
pail 465a
pain 380, 1493, 1823, 2047, 2100
pains 544
paint 328, 1078, 1717
paint-brush 2116a
painting 328, 946
pair 564, 1486
palace 951, 1273a
pall 1255
palpate 2628
paludism 2648a
palwine 1847
pamphlet 2396
pan 1593
pancake 2435
pander 2351
panic 2138a
pannier 1483
pants 321a, 1282
paper 224, 986a, 2270, 2567, 2917
parable 2588, 2592
parade 1671a, 1836
Paradise 1816
paradise 27, 204, 524
paraffin 429a
paragraph 136
paramount chief 107a
paramour 1961
parasite 2770
parasol 1514
parcel 1018
pardon 1086, 1349, 1352, 1353, 1893, 2027, 2030
parents 129, 513
parish 2990
parliament 213a
parlor 329
parrot 890
parsimonious 167
part of 2664
part 471, 656, 670, 952, 1020, 1384, 1738, 2285, 2312, 2748
particular 794, 795, 796, 1924
partition 1474
partnership 351, 1468
party 997, 1738, 1901, 2419, 2769
pass a verdict 683
pass judgment 683
pass over 1775
pass 561, 891, 986a, 1818
passage 469, 1305, 2608a
passenger 1775
passion 657, 1538a, 2024, 2862
paste 1798
pastor 2283
pastry 2435
patch 653, 1106, 2531
path 1578, 1701
patience 1555
patrol 953
patronage 724, 1160a
pattern 1036, 1111, 1143
pause 2974
pay a visit 729
pay homage 652
pay 1581a, 2583b
payment 166a, 821, 1344, 1528, 2012, 2781
payments 1581a
peace 112, 1133, 1338, 1602
peacefully 1338
pearl 2516
pederast 2570
pedestal 2318
pedigree 445, 2724
peg 763
pelt 2137
pen 2335
penalty 1897
penance 2452
pence 2267
pencil 2335
pendant 639
penetration 886
peninsula 1003

penis 1154
penis 986
pennon 318
Pentateuch 401
people 32, 94, 126, 1422, 2359a
pepper 1473, 2189
peppermint 2766
perceive 643, 1537, 2206, 2694
perception 643
perfect 2481
perfectly 823, 2481
perfidy 859
perforate 2242a
perforated 783
perform 2948
perfume 1131, 1747, 1879
perhaps 169, 654, 1911
peril 812
period 100, 469, 1189, 1398, 2600, 2677
periods 50
perish 937a, 2010, 2849
perjury 1203
permanence 1983, 1987
permanent 408, 963
permanently 963
permission 43, 1058, 1240
permit 334, 692, 1058
perpetually 959, 963
perpetuity 2648
perplexity 323, 1497, 1536, 2138a, 2156, 2935
perseverance 1809, 1902, 2518
Persia 1796
Persian 1796
person 167, 186, 225, 324, 435, 464, 478, 774, 1804, 2679, 2770, 2797
personal 86
perspicacity 245, 2113
perspiration 430, 1079
persuasion 997
perversity 1956
pest 308
pestilence 1704
petitioner 1223
petticoat 569a
phantom 1424
pharmacy 471a
phenomenon 1767
phlegm 302
phonograph 1567
photo 1629
phylacteries 621
piaster 2267
picked up 2332
picture 1629
piece 1106, 1384, 2312, 2435, 2556
pierce 2242a
pig 853
pigeon 706
piles 236
pilgrim 595, 635
pilgrimage to Mecca 592
pilgrimage 635, 1206
pillow 769a, 2115
pilot 1015
pimp 2351
pin 763, 1355
pincer 2291
pine 1623, 1667
pineapple 121a
pious 1607
pipe 1175, 1547, 2101
pipeline 2101
pirate 634
pit 397
pitch 1147
pitcher 6, 2496
pity 116, 729, 1053, 1490, 3006
place 134, 529, 633, 707, 1384, 1921, 2498
plague 308, 1704, 2877
plain 202, 356
plan 1076, 1140, 1533, 1841, 2821
planet 1411
planning 882
plans 1857
plant 1169, 2401
plaster of Paris 480
plaster 1128, 1717, 2522
plate 1567, 1591a, 1641, 1682, 1717, 2500a
play with 2542
play 1263
playful 907
playing-card 2270
plead 1098
pleasant 324, 1786, 2103, 2612
please 125, 1085, 2157
pleasing 125, 2611
pleasure 125, 351, 1085, 1087, 1691, 2104, 2533
pledge 1129, 1830

pledged 2716
pledges 1581a
Pleiades 409
plenty 1087
pliable 2582
plight 1652
plot 2964
plug up 1267
plunderer 2501
plunge 2010
plural 506
pocket 571, 2503a
poem 2296
poet 1482
poetry 965, 1482, 2109
point! 821
point 1712, 2788
pointing 1107
poison 1350
poker 2339
pole 1585, 2617
police officer 341a
police 341a, 1862, 2788
policeman 341a, 1862
policy 1396, 1396a
polite 37
politician 1396, 1396a
politics 1396
poll-tax 1865
pollute 2699
pollution 528
pomp 1453
pond 852
ponder 2177, 2179
poor 816, 817, 991, 2172, 2633
porridge 2173a, 2601a
portal 333
portent 1416
porter 718
porthole 1430
portion 268, 471, 656, 674, 1384, 2285, 2312, 2748
portmanteau 777
portrait 1629
position 652, 2721
positively 2481
possession 741, 2654, 2658, 2659, 2684
possibly 169
post office 234
post 234, 2788
pot 217, 397a, 1593, 2490
potato 250b
potency 1850
potion 1449b
pound (sterling) 542
pound 1092, 2670
pour out 1175
poverty 1068
poverty 2171, 2213
powder 228, 920a, 1982, 2018
power 223, 484, 684, 957, 1850, 2236
powerful 1444, 1888
powerless 1658
practice 1945
praise be to God! 710
praise 424, 709, 1235, 2938
pray 908, 1205
prayer for rain 1307
prayer 910, 1136, 1210a, 1612, 1766, 1872, 1874, 2006, 2090, 2947
prayers 197, 2557, 2914
preacher 810, 2697
preamble 877
precedent 445, 1239
precious 1851
précis 797
precise 1644
predisposed 1804
prefect 2995
prefer 577
pregnancy 717, 720
prelude 2077
prepare 547a, 1511
prepared 1804
presbyter 2283
prescribe 101, 1366
presence 663, 664
present 665, 1202, 1525, 1885, 2430, 2838, 2997
presentation 1344, 1836
presently 746
preservation 671
preserve 1033, 1333
preserved 1033
president 1004
press 1164, 1442, 2628
prestige 2867
pretender 2777

pretext 1242, 1824
prevent 902
price 176, 348a, 418, 1291, 2360, 2674
pride 250a, 1887, 2095
priest 10, 2283, 2489
prime 134
principle 2318
prior to 2229
prison 586, 1254b
prisoner 586
privacy 2125
privilege 2158, 2419
probably 169
problem 1403a
process 908, 909
procession 534
proclaim 2715
proclamation 1927
procurer 2351
prodigy 1790
profane 2699
profit 821, 2216, 2775, 2775a
profligate 2146
program 1857
progress 469, 814
prohibited 632
prohibition 629
promise 1960, 2716, 2954, 2955
promontory 1003
promote 1107a
pronoun 1661
pronouncement 2358
pronunciation 2552
proof 223, 928, 3022
prop 1936
proper 1924, 2578
property 186, 345, 2654, 2658, 2674, 2684, 2939
prophecy 2697
prophet 1073, 2697
Prophet 1563
propitious 484
propose 2821
prospect 2755
prosperity 211, 431, 2051, 2202, 2764, 2962
prosperous 2201
prostitute 1471, 1961, 2241, 2663
prostrate 1250
prostration 1249, 1250
protect against 1643
protect 723, 1333
protection 671, 724, 901
protector 2987
protégé 559
proud 435
prove 1573
proverb 2588, 2592
province 2336, 2990
provisions 1202, 1583, 2775a
provocation 1445, 1956, 2427
provocative 1445
provoke 2424
prow 95, 2383
proxy 2981a
prudence 243
pry into 2079, 2080
psalm 1158
psalter 1158
pudendum 2101
puff 2772
pull-over 2202a
pulpit 2692
pump 1702a, 2767a
punch 781
punish 683, 1823
punishment 603, 683, 684, 787, 788, 1060, 1823,1897, 2292
pure 823, 1598, 1725, 2149, 2150, 2792
purgative 1377, 1383
purity 1724, 2947
purity 2150, 2791
purpose 49, 1665, 1709, 1857, 1936, 2295, 2821, 2822, 2842
purse 472, 786, 2503a
purses 2125
pus 2925
push 1164
put down 2902
put in order 1034
put off 25
put on sale 927a
put together 1511
putsch 2331a
puzzle 1272
pyramid 2841

quadrangle 1028
quadruped 324a

quadruple 1028
quality 187, 615, 2939
quantity 1718, 2401a
quarrel 451, 798, 800, 2703, 2720
quarrelling 2169
quarrelsome 1429
quarter 735, 1020, 1210
question 451, 1223, 1403a
questioner 1223
quick 2675
quicklime 1576
quickly 627, 1382
quiet! 2843
quiet 2644
quilt 777, 2115
quinine 2507a
quire 2416
quite 1598
quiver 1179
quotient 656
Qur'an 136, 471, 1413, 1566, 2131, 2261, 2396, 3011, 3025
Qur'anic 136

rabies 2466
race 536, 2233, 2359a
rack 1097
radio 1001a
radish 2092
rage 657, 2024
raid 2392
railing 1435
rain 1625, 1995
raise up 262
raise 1213
raisin 1155
rake 465b
Ramadan 1121, 2316
rammer 926
ramrod 926
randomly 1241a
rank 431, 652, 893, 1378, 1400, 1901, 2246
ransom 2097
rap 125
rare 583, 1814, 1851, 2044, 2712
rareness 2712
rarity 1851, 2712
rasp 200a
rate 176, 1865, 1931
rather than 2378
rather 284, 2162
rattan 785
ravine 2907
ray of light 2814
reach puberty 297
reach 902, 1405, 2940
read 388
ready 547a, 821
real 823, 1562
reality 677
realize 241, 2696
really! 3009
really 823, 1598
rear man 1064
reason 20, 49, 1226, 1239, 1824, 1907, 1959, 2290, 2842
reasonable 2518
rebel 825, 1878, 2501
rebuke 1170a, 1779, 1853
receipt 2224, 2940
receipts 888
receive 2228
receptacle 2959
reception hall 329
reception room 500
reception 2232
receptivity 2235
recess 1097
recite 388, 2408
reckoning 645, 1802
reclusive 586
recognize 643
recognized 1924
recommendation 2943
recommendations 2945
recompense 427, 476
reconcile 2902
reconciliation 1602
record 1567
recorder cassette 1254a
recover 2774
rectangle 1028, 1744
red 710a, 2614
reddish 2639b
redemption 2097
reduction 817, 2785
reduce to straits 658
reed 785, 2294, 2335

refinement 2605
reflect 2177, 2179
reflection 245, 2178, 2179
refresh 199
refrigeration 199
refrigerator 416a
refugee 559
refuse 2129
refuse of seed 1442
refuse to obey 2501
regard as permissible or lawful 692
regarding 1698
region 951, 1384, 2336
register 913
regular 2318
rehearse 2408
reimbursement 1060
reins 813
reiterate 2408
rejection 1063
rejoice 2104
rejoicing 2104
relation 2264
relations 129
relationship 506
relative 2264
relatives 129, 513, 2265
relaxation 1137, 2103
relaxing 1138
release 692, 1714, 2180
reliable 117, 1575, 1644
relief 2100, 2746, 2772
religion 973, 1702
reluctance 1062
rely on 1721
remain in a place 1316
remain 281, 961, 1219, 1985, 2156a
remainder 281
remark 2358
remedy 969, 1904
remember 985, 2694
remembrance 2984
remissness 1789
remit 1352
remote 267
remove 2830
remunerate 15
renew 446
renounce 373
renowned 1529
rent 17, 18, 19, 1865, 2419a, 2430, 2938
repair 1106
reparation 2452
repeat 2408
repent 396
repentance 396
replacement 176
reply 552
report 762, 1354, 1842, 1843, 2290
reporter 2777
repose 1133, 1137, 1138
representation 2981
representative 2980
reprisal 2292
reproach 1435, 1779, 1979, 2571
reproaches 1504
reproof 1779, 2571
reprove 1853
republic 522
repudiate 334, 1714
repudiation 1063, 1715
reputation 2939
request 734
require 673, 908
requital 2292
rescue 1333
resemblance 1431, 1431a, 2588, 2592
resemble 1431
resembling 1432
reserve(s) 1898
reservoir 6, 742
residence 695, 1316, 1319, 2498
residue 281
resign 1333, 1555
resin 1616
resolute 1644
resolution 1661, 1857, 2064
resolve 1140, 1857
respect 629, 652, 670, 1778, 1889, 2419, 2612, 2867
respectability 1778
respectable 1463
respected 1851, 2421
respiration 2773
respite 2677
responsibility 1664, 2534
responsible 1663
rest 222, 1133, 1137, 1138, 2103

restaurant 2350
resting 1138
restore 433
restored from illness 2774
restrain 2923
restriction 1670
result 1898
resurrection 262, 2361
retard 25
retention 658
reticence 1308
reticular 1429
reticulate 1429
retirement 2125
return 1041, 1060, 1063
returns 882b, 888, 1150
reveal 2898
revealing 2443
revenge 1651, 2292
revenue 882b, 888
reverent 187
revile 1229, 2451
revolution 2331a
reward 15, 166a, 427, 476, 563
ribbon 1018
rice 1065
ride 1112
rider 1112
ridicule 70, 1263, 1645, 2627
ridiculous 1263
riding 1112
rifle 317, 2082
rift 2164
right away 746
Right Honorable 527
right 674, 1408, 1562, 1644, 1813, 2886
right angle 1028
rights 2658
ring screw 1066
ring 639, 766, 1628
ringworm 278
riot 2085
rise 1107a, 1712
rising 1713
risk 479, 812
rival 798, 799
rivalry 2037
river bed 2907
river 163
riyal 1149
road 189, 1578, 1701
robber 634
rock 438
rock-rabbit 2878
rod 790, 958a
rogue 1981
role 952
roll one's eyes 1002
roll up 1511
roll 1733
Romaeans 1147
Roman 1147
Rome 1147
roof 951, 1284, 1304, 2049
roofing 1305
room 2009, 2772, 2931
rope 457, 2401, 2484, 2617, 2882
rosary 1235
rose 2916
roseate 2916
rotl 1092
roughness 486
round 952, 953, 1734
roundabout 1641
row 1286, 1400, 1683, 1711a
royalty 957
rubber 2537a
rubbish 1145, 1576, 1718
ruby 3014
rucksack 1520
rudder 1317
ruddle 667
rudeness 46
ruffian 774
rug 2115
ruin 937a
ruined 775
rule 1093, 2318, 2342, 2658, 2659, 2690, 2986a
ruler 689, 1286, 1329, 1546, 2655
rumor 2196
run alongside 526
run at full speed 870
run away 2180
run side by side with 526
run 1114, 1818
rupture 818, 2164
ruse 2501

rush 1114, 1654
russet 2639b

Sabbath 1230
sabdariffa 2417a
sack 1532, 2503a
sacking 2401
sacred 629, 633, 1731
sacrifice 979, 1571, 2452, 2902
saddle 777, 1275, 2115
saddlebag 777
sadness 640
safari 1294
safe 785a, 1342
safety 112, 1341, 1342
saffron 1171
sagacity 243, 686
sage 686b
sail 1255, 1297, 1458, 2888
sailor 163
saint 1633, 2987
sake 1226
salad 1328a
sal-ammoniac 2733
salary 1528, 1581a, 2419a, 2583b
salat 1612
sale 348a, 349, 351
Salomon 1343
salt 2649, 2751
saltpeter 150
salts 1383
salubrious 1561
salutation 758, 1338, 1344, 1553
salute 1338, 1889
same 998, 1407
sample 1143, 1993
sanction 43, 2232
sand 1122, 1576
sandals 1113, 2445
sandalwood 1618, 2574
sandarac 1374
sand-glass 1547
sandwich 1374a
sapphire 3014
sapphism 1154
sari-like 1733
Satan 9, 1548
satchel 1520
satin 74
satisfaction 1088
satisfied 1086
Saturday 507, 1230
Saturn 1163
sauce 3005a
saucepan 1593
saucer 1567
savate 1113
save 654, 2774
savings 1898
savior 1487
saw 70a
say over and over again 2408
say 2246
saying 1911
scale 2924
scales 1092
scandal 2155
scar 278
scarce 583, 2044
scarf 2666
scene 2755
scent 625, 1747, 2879
scents 2170
schedule 453
scheme 1857
scholar 2172
school 900, 997
schoolmaster 1925
science 1917
scimitar 851
scissors 2291
scold 1170a
scorn 372, 1645, 1657
scorpion 1905
scoundrel 1145, 1495, 1981
scourge 497
scrap 224
screen 901, 1010, 1242
scribe 2398
script 805
scruple 2935
scrutiny 2080
sculptor 2697a
sculpture 2783
sea 163, 189, 1718, 2680
seal 766, 1711, 2676
seaport 2119
search 882, 1707a, 2079, 2080

seashore 1260
season 469, 2934, 2970
seat 2415
seclusion 2125
secrecy 1272
secret 1272, 2058, 2125
secretion 1079
sect 997, 1619, 1702, 1738, 2129
section 136, 471, 735, 2312
secure 1342
security 112, 115, 1129, 1338, 1341
sedition 2085
seducer 2141
seduction 2863b
see 241, 1537
seed 228, 583
seeing that 2590
seek pleasure 125
seek 1002
seize 2224
seizure 2224
select 867
selection 867
self- control 2371
self 998, 2770
self-asserting 2158
self-conceit 2002
self-control 2246
self-denial 2284
selfish 2770
self-possessed 1071
sell up 2184
sell 349, 927a
semen 1530, 2671
senna 1377
sennaleaflets 1377
sensation 643
sense 243, 643, 1907, 1959, 2754
sensibility 2235
sensible 2518
sentence 684, 2358, 2945
separate 2129, 2830
serf 1770
sergeant 1419
series 1400
serious 668, 1071
seriousness 446
sermon 809, 2956
servant 771a, 773, 1770
serve yourself 1580
serve 1769
service 773, 1771
servile 991
sesame 494, 1356
set before 1835
set free 1716
set ready 547a
set up 1328
set 433
setting up 2364
settle down 1316
settlement 2674
seven 1236
seventy 1238
sex 536
Shaban 1477
shake 870
shame 531, 652, 755, 788, 1679, 1853, 1977, 1979, 2054, 2155
shape 1366, 2573
share 656, 674, 793, 1150, 1384
Sharia 1459
sharpen 1366
shawl 783, 1414, 2666
Shawwal 1541
shears 2291
shed 1109a, 2691b
sheep 1896, 2106
sheet 224, 1591a, 2270, 2416, 2567, 2662a, 2917
sheik 1546
shelf 1097
shelter 901, 1109a, 1305
sherbet 1450, 1452
sherif 1463
shield 901
shilling 1020
shillings 1149
shine 1174
ship 95, 147, 164, 259, 547, 1110, 1299, 2192, 2708
shipment 1074
shirt 2341
shock 1655
shoe 475a, 1113, 2445
shoemaker 781
shoot 2106
shooting 317

shop 925
shopkeeper 366
short (in amount) 583
shorten 2302
shortened 797
shortly 2264
shorts 1282
shot 5, 1124, 1424
shotgun 150, 782a, 2082
shout 2715
shovel 1262, 2430a
show off 526, 927a, 2125
show 665, 927a, 1453, 1764, 2755, 2938
shroud 274, 1372, 2455
shyness 755
sick 1306
sickness 705, 2620
side 529
sidepiece 529
sideways 730
sieve 2414a, 2803
sight 1424
sign 136, 928, 1534, 1829, 1920, 1957, 2072, 2736, 2788
signal 1534
signature 1562
signet 2676
significant 2853
signification 1959
silence! 2843
silence 1308
silk 617
silver 2154
similar 1432
similarity 1431, 1431a, 2588
similarly 2377
simile 2590
similitude 2588, 2592
simpleton 117, 225, 443, 907
sin 531, 808, 995, 1679, 1878
since that 960
since 284, 960, 2590
sincere 1573, 1575
sinful 2146
sing 2052
single 2109
sink 2010
sins 2027, 2030
sir 579, 854a , 2993
Sir 76a
Sirius 1479
sister 1127a
situation 695, 1418
six 1243
sixteen 1244
sixty 1245
sketch 1036, 1111
skilled 1804
skillful 2149, 2675
skin 304, 2137
skirt 526, 569a
skull 2242
skullcap 1672
skull-cap 287, 2242
sky 27, 1362, 1363
skyblue 1363
slackness 1789
slander 270, 1229, 1853, 2085, 2443
slate 2567
slaughter 977, 979
slaughterhouse 977
slave 773, 1770
slave-boy 1827
slay 977
sleeping-sickness 2647
slice 2435
slight 372, 816, 1657
slingshot 2693a
slipperiness 1182
slit 2082
slowness 1858
sly 478, 1145
slyness 2501, 2543
small 1586, 2332
smear 1717
smell 625, 1131, 2108
smells 2170
smoke 889
smooth 2582
snare 1429
snow 416
snuff 1292a
so and so 2376
so be it 114
so that 590
so what 3009
so 266, 2376, 2377
so-and-so 2193

soap 1557, 2331
society 506, 510, 1468
sock 1449a, 1452a
sodium 2751
sodomite 848, 2570
soft 2582
soil 55
solace 2100
solder 1083, 2531
soldering-iron 1083
soldier 1862
soldiers 1160a
soldiership 572
sole 2895
solid 1644, 2644
solidity 1942
solve 692
some of 2664
some 268, 2327, 2664
someone 2895
something 734
sometimes 2607
son 312, 2982, 2983
song 1482, 2052, 2053, 2848
soothsayer 1925, 2489
sorcery 1257
sore 463
sores 2622
sorghum 984a
sorrel 2417a
sorrow 640, 2047, 2851
sorry! 112
sorry 1353, 1543a
sort 331, 536, 1621, 1695, 1993, 2233, 2573
soul 430, 1132, 2770
sound 643, 1607, 1628, 2769
soup 1450, 3005a
source 71
South 1380a
souvenir 2997
sovereign 689, 2655, 2993
sovereignty 2658, 2990
sow 184, 1169
spa 707
space 202, 2600, 2677, 2772, 2931
spade 2430a
span 479, 1425
sparrow 1656
speak scornfully, disparagingly 441
speak secretly 2081
speak 798
speaker 810, 2474
special 794, 795, 796, 1924, 2853
specialist 1839
specialness 793
species 71, 536, 1993, 2233
specific 795
specifically 794
specimen 1621, 1993, 2196
speck 1776
spectacles 1010, 1994, 2754a
speech 762, 809, 2358, 2547
speed 1382
spending 1580
spendthrift 186
sperm 2606, 2671
sphere 2191, 2429
spice 228
spindle 958a
spirit 523, 1132, 1956, 2657, 2770, 2842
spirits 1548
spite 2085
splattering 1078
spoil 775, 937a
spoiler 774
spoke 1332
sponge 1300, 2570a
spoon 2543a
spot 12, 278, 1106, 2788
spout 2106
spread 184
spring (water) 149a
sprinkling 1078
sputum 302
spy 478, 953, 1272
spyglass 2754a, 2756
squad 953
squalor 2925
squander 184
square 1028
stability 1942
stable 1805
stableman 1397
staff 277
stag 135
stage 1683
staid 1071
stain 278, 1776, 1913

stair 1337a
staircase 1337a
stake 2674
stall 363b, 369a, 925
stallion 2094
stamp 766, 1046, 2676
stand over 25
stand 2973
standing 2246
stanza 344
staple 1066
star 2700
starch 2738
start moving 2826
start 134, 1297
state 745, 831, 957, 1418, 1679, 2658
statement 684, 2290
statements 2443
station 693, 1702a, 2788
statue 1622, 1629
status 745, 1036
staunch 496, 497
stay back 1162
stay long 1742
stay 281
steadfast 496, 497
steamer 164, 1110
steel 1083
steeple 2815
step out! 2865
Step out! 754a
step 814, 1337a
steppe 335
sterling 542
steward 2980
stick to 1683
stick 1403, 1875
still 265
stipulation 1456
stock 1898
stockings 1449a, 1452a
stocks 2310
stomach 257
stone 599, 1046, 1047, 2148, 2622, 2888
stoning 1047
stop 231, 667, 693, 821, 834, 2271a, 2973, 2974
storage 199
store 925, 1898, 2009
story 1273a
stories 762
storm 1654, 1655, 1737
story 125, 607, 691, 762, 1683, 2009, 2290
stoutness 1943
stove 147, 2483
straight ahead 95
straight away 1742
straight 1408
strain 544
strap 496
stratagem 750
stratum 1683
street 189, 1460
strength 1150, 1560, 1600, 1942
strengthening 1445
stress 1652
stride 814
strike with terror 1639
strike 1654
string 1332, 2882
strip 2416
stripe 1921
strive 543
stroke 1654
strong 496, 497, 1444, 1644, 1805, 2644
strophe 344
structure 321d, 1111, 1942
struggle 2720
stubborn 2501
student 900, 1923
study 388, 899, 1713, 2754
studying 1922
stuffing 653
stupefaction 323
stupid 246
sturdy 496, 497
style 1695
subject 1095, 2290
sublime 1364
sublimity 490, 1378
submission 1344
submissive 991, 1657, 1730
submissiveness 1731
submit 1333, 1730
suborning 2557
subsistence 1069, 1987
substitute 176, 177, 2810
succeed 1405, 2210
success 862, 1288, 1290, 2202, 2210, 2962

successfulness 2962
successor 826
succumb 1068
such and such 2376
such as 2378
such 2193
Sudanese 1388a
suddenly 2033, 2088
suddenness 2033
suet 1440
suffer damage 46
suffer 988, 1068
suffering 380, 1670
suffice 391, 1903
sufficiency 2371
sufficient 1087
Sufi 1633
sugar 1314
suggestion 1006
suit 909
suitable 2886, 2991
suitcase 1520
suit-case 1617
sulfur 2391
sulphate of copper 399
sulphate 2622
sultan 1329
sum 511, 517, 645
summary 797
summit 1003
summon 1707a, 2715
sun 1513, 2004
Sunday 24, 1230
sunglass 1010
Sunna 1368
Sunnite 1369, 1619
Sunnitic 1369
sunrise 1712
sunset 2004, 2006
sunshine 1513
superior 1931, 2991
supervisor 2080a, 2757a
supervisory 671a
supple 2582
supplicate 1561, 1637
support 1289, 1290, 1936, 1974, 2419
Supreme Ruler 435
sura 1392, 2077
surely 677
surety 1664, 2534
surgery 1945a
surplice 2341
surplus 2158
surprise 1790, 2032, 2034
surrender 1333
surveillance 1994
survey 1994
susceptibility 2235
suspend 1915
suspicion 1497, 1762, 3003
Swahili 1260
swallow 2772
swearing 1203
sweat 430, 702
sweater 2202a
sweating 1079
sweetheart 579
sweetness 1314, 2183
swimming pool 707
swindler 2489
swing 980
sword dance 851
symbol 1920
syntax 2706
syphilis 161
Syria 1415
syringe 5, 680a
syrup 1452, 1863
system 2318

table 369a, 453
table-bench 369a
tail 1000
tailor 371a
take a fancy to 577
take away 2022
take by surprise 2032
take care of 1484
take care! 135a
take care 241, 2206
take more 1213
take on lease 18
take up 1936
tale 607, 691, 762, 2290
tale-bearer 2081
talent 2419
talisman 621, 969, 1711, 1857
talk 125, 1403a

talker 125
talking 125
tambourine 912, 1689a
tank for water 363b
tank 6, 742, 874a
tankard 2496
tantamount 1809
tap 285
tape recorder 1254a
tape 1456a
tar 1147
tarboosh 1693, 2497
target 1424
tartar 1394
taste 458, 999, 2533
taunt 911
tax 778, 1180, 1571, 1865
taxation 1865
taxes 2467
taxi 385a
tea 1420, 2350
teacher 1546, 1925
teachings 2957
teak-tree 1218
teapot 6
tear apart 2829
tear 2082
teasing 1445
telegraph 1332
telephone 387a
telescope 2754a, 2756
tell a story 125, 1354
tell 607, 1839
temper 716
temperance 2246, 2938
temperature 430, 619
tempest 1655
temple 1772, 2869
tempt 458
ten 1866
tenderness 1490
tenets 997
tent 869, 1458
tenure 741
term 2303, 2600
terminus 100
terrace 1284
terrify 1639
terror 2138a
test 458
testament 2945
testicle 803
testicles 2125
testimony 1522, 1525
thaler 1149, 2267
thank you 1050
thank 1500
thankfulness 1500
thanks! 112
thanksgiving 1500
thank you 649
that is 1958
that 130, 2509
then 139, 265, 284, 590, 603, 826, 1408
there, didn't I tell you so? 2865
thickness 1943
thief 634, 2501
thimble 2432
thing 734, 762, 1484
think 985, 1661, 1762, 2177, 2179
thinking 1006, 2179
thirst 2466
thirty 414
this or that 2376
thong 496, 2882
thought 110, 1661, 1762, 2177, 2178
thoughtfulness 110, 2178
thousand 81
thread 1332, 2293
three 413a
thrift 2297
throat 701
throne 2415
throughout 1742
throw 1124
thrums 2729
thunder 1094
Thursday 846
thus and thus 2376
ticket 177, 986a, 2270
tickle 911
tilde 2497
timber 790
time 469, 814, 914, 945, 1189, 1294, 1398, 1712, 2600, 2607, 2677, 2772, 2934, 2954, 2970, 2971
timetable 453
timidity 755

tin 1083, 1591a, 2490, 2496
tin-can 2490
tip 166a, 1355
tired 1442
tithe 1180, 1865
title 1957
to 355
tobacco 363a
together 506, 1408
toil 380
toilet 1138, 1182
tomato 1720
tomb 1206, 2223, 2223a
tomorrow 2006
tongue 2538
tool 133
tooth 1367
toothbrush 1403
Torah 401
torch 249a, 1276, 1736, 2561a
torment 1670, 1823
torrent 2907
torso 178
torture 1823
total 511, 517, 645
totality 517
touch 2628
tow 2484
towel 240a, 2166a
tower 195, 2815
towing launch 457
town 287b, 290, 735
trace 1076, 1921
tractor 457
trade 349, 366, 925, 1620, 1944
trademark 1046, 1765
trader 226, 366, 492a, 854a
tradition 445, 2646, 2790
traditions 1619
train 1000, 2309a
traitor 860
tranquility 2772
transaction 166a, 351
transcription 2790
transfer ownership 1266
transfer 2789
transformed into 2981b
transgression 808
transistor 1001a
transition 2608a
translate into Arabic 1826
translate 2143
translation 2143, 2144, 2790
transport 2790
trap 1332, 1467
travail 380
travel 1294, 1297, 1409
traverse 479
tray 1641
tread 868
treason 859
treasure house 345, 786
treasure 785a, 786, 917, 1851, 2485
treasury 965
treat disrespectfully 2424
treat in a scornful manner 1301
treat like a fool 1301
treat unjustly 1757
treat with contempt 372, 680, 988
treat 2419, 2451
treatise 2359
treaty 2399
tree 200, 417
trench 852
trespass 1114
trial 308, 1459
tribe 1738, 2233, 2359a
tribesmen 2359a
tribulation 308
tribunal 688
tribute 2422
trick 750, 1396, 2451, 2543
trickery 771
trip 565, 1294, 2608a
triumph 1453, 2210
troops 572
trouble 47, 308, 380, 750, 1484, 1493, 1497, 2156, 2169, 2467, 2829
troublesome rascal 1145
trough 6
trousers 321a, 1282, 2521
truck 1828a
true 823, 1562, 1573, 1575
truly 120
trumpet 151, 218, 335a, 2769
trunk 178, 1617
trust 115, 1721, 1778, 2961, 2981b
trustee 1663, 2944

trustworthy 113, 1644
truth 677, 3022
truthful 1562
try out 999
try 458, 999
tube 2101, 2561a
Tuesday 415
tugboat 457
tumbler 310
tunic 493
turban 783
Turkey 1146
turn (of fate) 880
turn around and attack 2408
turn around 1733
turn off 1145
turn over and over 1062
turn the mind to 2696
turn up 1511
turn 1210, 2607
turncock 285
turning 730
turquoise 2217
tusk 335a, 2332
twelve 424b
twenty 842, 1869
twenty-five 842
twine 868
twist tight 451
two 424a
two-color 304
tying 1900
type 1695
typesetter 515
tyrannical 1759
tyrannized 1760
tyranny 486, 558, 1757, 1785
tyrant 1759

U bolt 1066
ulcer 463
ultimate 27
umbrella 1514
unarmed 1855
unaware 2034
unawares 2088
unbelief 2451
unbeliever 1194, 2453
uncertainty 1497, 2935
uncle 1933
unclean 2699
uncleanness 2699
uncommon 2712
uncovering 2443
uncultivated 335
underlines 1286
underpants 1282
undershirt 2202a
understand 902, 2696
understanding 1907, 2518, 2842
underwear 2521
undiluted 1598
unfair 860
unfaithful 2453
unhealthy 2879
unimpaired 2481
unite 2940
universal 515
universe 944
unlawful 629, 632
unless 79, 130, 2566
unlucky 1417, 1495
unmixed 823
unobtainable 1814
unpleasant 2428
unthinkable 752
untie 692
until 590, 603, 2229
untruth 1203
untruthfulness 2543
unwholesome 2879
up to 590
up! 2865, 2866
upgrade 1915
upshot 1898
upstairs 2009
urbane 37
urgency 2852
urgent 2853
urinate 339
usage 2318, 2646
usages 997
use influence 1444
use 2094, 2775a
useful 2775
uselessness 76
usual 2318
usually 2038, 2039

usury 1031
utensil 133, 547
utility 2216, 2775a

vacate 834
vagabond 1981
vain 256
vali 2995
valley 2907
valuable 1851
value 348a, 418, 1291, 2246, 2360
vandal 774
vanity 250a, 2002
vapor 164, 889
variegated 304
variety 2196
various 2376
vase 1593
vastness 2931
vaunt oneself 526, 2125
vehicle 1828a
veil 206a, 1242, 1247, 2046
vein 701
velvet 847
vendor 718
venom 1350
venture 479
Venus 1199
veranda 202
verb 2167
verdict 684
verify 1573
verily 120
veritable 1562
vermin 949
verse 136, 344, 1286, 2053, 2109
very much 424, 1378
very well! 1358
very 823, 1598
vessel 547, 905, 1110, 1299, 2559, 2959
vest 1568, 2202a
veterinarian 347a
veterinary 347a
viaticum 1197a
vice 2167
victim 979, 1896
victory 2037, 2210
victuals 78
view 1006, 1994, 2755
vigorous 1444
vigour 1600
vile 1298, 2717
vilification 1435
village 693
vine 1155
vineyard 1155
violate 2022
violence 486, 558, 1651, 1757, 1785
violent 435
viper 2169
virgin 156a, 283
visage 1629, 2893
visible 356
vision 1008, 2754
visit 664, 1205, 1206, 2891
vitriol 2622
vituperation 1225, 1229
vizier 2922
voice 643, 1628
void 2125
vote 2271a
vow 1960, 2716
vowel 627, 2788
voyage 1294
vulva 2101

W.-C. 1138
wag 2627
wages 15, 17, 19, 888, 1528, 1581a, 2419a, 2583b
wagon 1828a
waistband 1000
wait 1048, 1555
wakefulness 2696
walking stick 277
wall 1734
wallet 459, 472
walnut 564
wand 1875
wander about 1062
wanderer 181
want 594
ward off 526
ward 2691b
warehouse 2691b
warmth 619
warn 2943
warning! 3009

warning 2945, 2956
warrant 1664
warrantor 1663
warrior 1438
washed 2018
waste away 1667
waste 184, 224, 386, 2729
wastefulness 184
waster 186
wastrel 1145
watch out 611, 2206
watch 621a, 671, 1002, 1398, 2924
watchman 1862
water closet 1182
water pipe 217
water tank 6
water 1625
water-channel 2101
watercourse 469, 2907
watermelon 250
waterspout 1737
wave 2680
waver 1062
wax cloth 1517a
wax 767, 1517
way out 168
way 1240, 1533, 1578, 1701, 1702, 2939
weak 1658, 1789
weakness of intellect 1062
weakness 76, 246, 1587, 1913
wealth 2654, 2684
weapon 1323
wear 1983
weariness 2647
wedding party 1832a
wedding witness 2979
wedding 78, 1832a, 1833
wedding-feast 2419
wedge 763
Wednesday 1026
week 507, 1230
weight 132, 1092, 1775, 2370, 2670, 2976
welcome! 1050
welcome 2158, 2558
welfare 862
well (water) 149a
well decorated 2863b
well dressed 2863b
well known 1529
well never! 749
well! 649
well 862, 1352, 1746
well-being 1341
well-dressed 324
well-informed 1844
well-known 1844
well-mannered 37
west 2004, 2006
wet nurse 872a
wet 285
what a calamity is ... ! 3009
what next ! 749
What next! 1966
wheat 2337
wheel 952, 958a
when 960, 2590
while 960, 1398, 2590, 2600
whip 495, 496, 497, 2414
whiplash 2414
whiskey 1847
whistle 1592
whistleblower 2777
white 1982
whitewash 1078
whole 511, 512a, 2481
wholesale 517
wholesome 1561
wicked 761, 2797
wickedness 1448
wide eyes 441
wife 129
wig 357a
wilderness 335
wilds 335
willfulness 1956
will 1087, 1538a, 2943, 2945
win 2210
wind 200, 1131, 1518, 1712, 2863
winding-sheet 1372
window 1430, 2754a
windward 565
wine 1450, 2691a
wineglass 310
winning post 100
wire net 2803
wire 1332

wisdom 243, 686, 1841, 1907, 1917, 2945
wise 686b
wish 1709, 1870
wishes 1338, 2945
witchcraft 1257
with 143, 2215
within a little 2719
without beginning 60
without others 1241a
without 144, 2062
witness 1522, 1525, 2557
woe 3006
woman 1422, 1460, 1788
wonder 1418, 1782, 1784, 1790
wonderful 1784
wood 790
woodworm 1394
wool 1632, 1733
word 2358, 2472
words 2945
work away! 2865
work 783, 1484, 1620, 1944, 1945, 1988
workman 18
workshop 2916a
world 102a, 944
worm 949
worn out 1311
worry about 1643
worry 1484, 2138a, 2467, 2851, 2935
worship 973, 1249, 1250, 1769, 1771, 1772, 1774, 2914
worthless 966
worthy 2201
worthless 1145
would God! 2576
wound 463
wrap 2455, 2662a
wrath 657, 2024
wretched 991
write 2398
writer 2398
writing 805, 2731
writing-case 968
writing-desk 968
written 2399
wrong 762, 808, 1757, 2428

yard 1028
yaws 206
year 1365, 2934
yearning 2851
yeast 839
yes sir / madam! 2526
yes 2763
Yes? 2526
yet 265, 2515
yield 1063, 1150, 1333
yoghurt 1155a
yoke 2278, 2823
young lady 313
young 1586, 2043
youth 261, 1422, 2043
youthful 1423

zeal 544, 546, 2054
zero 1596
zinc 399, 1195a
Zodiac sign 195

French Index

abandonner 373, 1333, 1714
abattoir public 977
abcès 818
abdication 1855
abhorrer 2424
abîmer 775
abjection 2925
ablutions 2948
abnégation 2284
abondance 832, 2764
aboutissement 1898
abrégé 797
abrègement 797
abreuvoir 6
abri 901, 1109a, 1305
absence 2058
abside d'une mosquée 620
absolument 2481
absolution 2030
abstinent 1197a
absurde 752
académie 900
accent 2552
acceptation 1089, 2232
accepter 1573, , 2228, 2232, 2235
accident(s) 21, 812, 1418, 1883, 2741
acclamation 1453
acclamer 125
accommodement 2097
accomplir avec effort 2284
accomplir son devoir 1878
accomplir 391
accomplissement 2962
accord pour arrêter une dispute 1602
accord 351, 1089, 1900, 1960, 2964, 2966
accorder 2961
accorder foi à 1575
accorder une faveur à 476
accorder 484, 1266
accouchement 1025, 2173a
accroc 2082
accrocher 1915
accueillir 2235, 2558
accusation(s) 1504, 1504a, 2571, 3003
accusé 586
accuser 1504
acheter et vendre 349
acheter 349
acheteur 1160
achever 391
acier 1083
acompte 1384, 1830
acte judiciaire 683
acte juridique 1900
acte(s) 1945
actif 1805
action 1060, 1944, 1945, 2167, 2866
activité 1484, 2167
actuellement 746
Adam 40, 312
Aden 1816
adeptes du mazdakisme 2594
adhérer 1683
adjacent 559
adjectif 2939
administration 1396
admirable 1784, 1786
admiration 1782, 1784
admonition 2956
adoration 1771
adorer 1769
adresse 1957
adroit 2675
adultère 1196, 1197
adversaire 798, 799
adversité 75
aéroplane 1751
affaire(s) 104, 349, 351, 366, 734, 762, 1418, 1468, 1484, 1533, 1945, 1988, 2290, 2306
affection 578, 580, 1588, 1870, 2862
affliction 308, 2046, 2047, 2851, 3006
âge 633, 945, 1940, 1988
agence 2979, 2981
agent 2980
agitation 2138a, 2156, 2680
agiter 870
agonie 544
agrafe 1066
agrandissement 1889
agréable (dégager une odeur -) 2108

agréable (distraction -) 2103
agréable (personne -) 1786
agréable(s) 125, 324, 1086, 1786, 2611
agression 46, 558
agriculture 1169
aide collective 2769
aide 1290, 1364, 1974, 2746
aider 1289, 1974, 2774
aïeul 445
aigle 1751
aiguille 5, 1905
aiguiser 1366
ail 247a, 429
aimable 1005, 2665
aimer beaucoup 1769
aimer passionnément 109
aimer 577
ainsi 2376, 2377
ainsi soit-il! 114
air pensif 110
air 2863
airs (se donner de grands -) 443
aise (personne à l' -) 1755
aise 222, 2100, 2764
ajouré 783
ajout 1213
ajouter 1213
ajuster 2370
alarme 2138a
album record 1567
alcool de mil 1847
alcool toxique 337
alcoolisée (boisson -) 1450
alcôve 1097
alène de cordonnier 781
alène 781
alerte au feu 2392
algèbre 434
Ali 1930
alibi 1525
aligner 1405
aliment 78
Allah 88
allez 754a, 2826, 2865, 2866
alliance 2724
allonger 1742
allons 754a, 2865, 2866
allumer (le feu) 441
allumette(s) 2391
allure 1261
allusion 1534
aloès 1556, 1962, 2574
alors 1408
altérer 2060
alun 1421
amande(s) 2568
amateur 581
ambassadeur 1297
ambre gris 1952
âme 430, 1132, 2770
améliorer 1602
amen 114
amende 683, 1823, 2012, 2097
amène 2644
ami(s) 32, 581, 1102, 1364, 1563, 1565, 2742
amidon 2183, 2738
amiral 119a
amitié 578, 580
ammoniaque 2733
amorce de fusil 2082
amour 578, 580, 2862, 2851
amoureux 579, 581, 1870
amulette(s) 621, 969, 1711, 1818, 1857, 1945, 2452, 2917, 3011
amusement 70, 2627
amuser 125
analogie 2371
ananas 121a
ancêtre 445
Ancien Testament 401
ancre 2278
âne 410, 1705
anecdote 691
ange(s) 1854, 2657, 2797
angoisse 1670
animal(-aux) 324a, 278, 2679
ankylostomiase 1595
anneau 639, 766
année(s) 1038, 1365
anniversaire 2984
annonce 1842
annuler 256, 2060, 2140
anse(s) 2496
antagonisme 800, 2085
antagoniste 798, 799
antérieur 1239
anthroponyme 86
antimoine 2402

antipathie 486, 800
anxiété 2138a, 2851
apercevoir 643
apostasie 1061
apostasier 1061, 2451
apôtre 1073
apparaître 1764, 1835
appareil 133, 1216
apparemment 169
apparence 1261, 1431, 1629, 1767, 2755, 2893
apparent 356
apparition 1424
appauvrir 2140
appel de trompette 2769
appel du muezzin 44
appel 1760
appeler à la prière 44
appeler 908, 2715
appendicite 1214a
appendice 1214a
applaudissement 2939
application 546
appréciation 424, 1088
appréhension 857
apprendre 388
apprentissage 1922
apprêter 547a
approbation 649, 2232, 2964
approcher 2228
approuver 1624, 2235
après 266, 826
après-midi 1874
arabe(s) 492a, 1343, 1827
arabiser 1826
arachide 2214
arak 1847
arbre 53, 194, 202, 384, 417
arche de Noé 1299
archevêque 2639a
arcs 317
ardeur 544, 619
area 1384
argent 184, 186, 365, 904, 1031, 1580, 1593, 1866, 2154, 2175a, 2185, 2267, 2269, 2674, 2684, 2781, 2976
argile 397
argile de potier 1707
argument 594
argumenter 451
aride 3015
aristocrate 2233
arithmétique 281, 645, 1654
arme(s) 1179, 1323
armée 572, 1862
armoire 958a
armure 901, 1323
arrangement 351, 684, 902
arranger 1034, 2923
arrêt 667
arrête 231
arrhes 1830, 2224
arrière 826
arriver 2971
arrogance 250a, 2002
arrogant 1301, 2156a, 2158
art 1620
article 2359
artifice 2501
ascendance 445, 2724
ascète 1633
ascétique 1197a
aspect(s) 1261, 1629, 1717, 2755, 2867
aspersion 1078
aspirant 1139a
assaillir 1818
assemblée 513, 572
assentiment 1086
assez 231, 821, 2371
assiette 1567
assigner 2923
assistance 1290, 2746
assistant 1290a, 1290b, 2980
assister 662, 1974
association de bienfaisance 510
association en affaires 351
association 1468
assumer la responsabilité 2986a
assuré 1665
assurer 1573
asticot 949
astrologie 2191
astrologue 1925, 2594, 2701
astronomie 2191
astucieux 2675
atelier 2916a
athée 1194
atmosphère 2863
atrocité 558

attaché (être -) 1915
attache (mettre à l' -) 1327
attaché à (être -) 1683
attache 230
attachement 580, 1588
attacher (fait d' -) 1900
attacher 1467, 1915
attaquer (faire volte-face et -) 2408
attaquer 2032
attaque-surprise 2392
attarder (s' -) 1742
atteindre l'âge de la puberté 297
atteindre la maturité (sexuelle) 297
atteindre le but 1624
atteindre qqn et lui nuire par son mauvais œil 269
atteindre 902, 2940
attendre (s' -) 1048
attendre 1048, 1555
attends! 1555
attention! 611, 3009
attention (faire -) 241, 611, 2271a, 2534
attention (fais -!) 611
attention (prêter -) 2696
attention 2206, 2754
attentive (surveillance -) 671
atténuation 817
attestation 1562
attraction 453a
attribuer 2467
attribut 2939
aube 2090
aubergine 149
audacieux (être -) 479
augmentation 1213
augmenter 1107a, 1201a, 1213, 2805
augure 269
aumône 166a, 650, 1571, 2165
aurore 1552, 2090
auspices 2072
aussi 139, 2870, 2378
authentique 1562
automobile 374a
autorisation 43, 102, 1058, 2981a
autoriser 334
autorité 102, 1850, 2658
autre monde 29
autrefois 1189
autrement 2872, 2873
auvent 1109a
avance 2269
avancer 1107a, 1409
avant 2229
avantage 862, 2202, 2216, 2775, 2775a
avare 167
avec 143, 2215
avenir 1898, 2697
aventure 1418
avenue 189
aversion 270, 2425
avertir 611, 2943
avertissement 1776, 2945, 2956
avertisseur sonore 335a
aveuglement 2002
avidité 2466
avilissement 989, 2156
avion 1751
avis 1573, 1927
avocat 1098, 2980, 2307
Azraël 1854
azur 1363

badge 2736
bagage(s) 734
bague 766, 1895
baguette 926, 1875
baie 855
baie (de café) 315
bain 707
balance 1092, 2924
balancer 980
balle(s) 1018, 1083, 1124, 2429, 2495
ballon 1734, 2495
baluchon 1018, 2115
bambou 785
banane 2681
banc 925
bande(s) 1468, 1921, 2130a, 2769
banderole 318
bandit 634
banjo 1963
bannière 318, 1918
banque 321c
banquet 2419
baquet 465a
barbare(s) 1796
barbouiller 1078
baril 221

bas 668, 680, 966, 991, 1449a, 1452a
bascule 2924
basilic 1134
bassin 742, 2559
bassine 280
bât 1483
bataillon 1671a
bâtard 634
bateau 164, 259, 457, 1110, 1299, 2278
bâtiment 329, 951, 1942
bâtir 321
bâton 277, 1875
bâtonnet 1403
batterie 249a, 599
battre 1654, 2039
béatitude 2104
beau 1352, 2611, 2612
beaucoup 823, 1087, 2271a, 2401a
beaupré 906
beauté 518, 2867
bêche 2430a
Bédouin 181
belle 1352
bénédiction(s) 211, 1069, 1086, 2764
bénéfice 862, 1619, 2158, 2202, 2216, 2764, 2775a
berceau 2673
besogneux 2172
besoin(s) 594, 734, 1824, 2171
bête(s) 324a, 757
béton 1304
beurre 702, 1361
Bible 2396
bidon 397a
bien(s) 184, 186, 862, 1031, 1266, 1352, 1746, 2674, 2684, 2973, 2974
bienfaisance 651
Bienfaisant 2665
bienfait 650
bienséance 652
bienveillant 1005, 1345, 2665
bienvenu 1050, 2158
bière 337, 534, 920a, 2173a
bijou 570, 701a, 2516
bijoutier 570
bile 1595
billet 177, 986a, 2270, 2584
blagueur 907, 2627
blâme 1435, 1779, 2571
blâmer 1779
blanc 304
blasphème 749
blasphémer 2451
blé 2337, 2776
blennorragie 161
blessé 464
blesser 463, 775, 1651
blessure 463, 1651
bleu(e) 1765
blindage 901
bœuf 804
bois de santal 1618
boisson(s) 1449b, 1450, 2417a, 2419
boîte 75, 1520, 1617, 1914a, 2490
bol 280, 2429
bon! 821
bon(s) 1345, 1352, 1368, 1607, 1619, 1813, 1931
bonbon(s) 702
bonheur 236a, 862, 1133, 1288, 1290, 2104, 2764
bonjour 864, 1553
bonnet 1672, 1693, 2497
bonsoir! 2634
bonté 650, 651, 1747, 2158, 2540
bonus 1213
bord 603, 1215
bordure 1695
bossoir 2278
boubou 2341
bouche 791a
boucher 1267
boucherie 1323
boucle 230
bouclier 901
bouffon 525, 2627
bougie 1517, 1736, 2345
bouillie 2601a
bouilloire 6, 742, 905, 2331
boulevard 189
boulon 1355
bourse(s) 472, 2125, 2503a
bousculer 1164
boussole 955
bouteille 2282
boutique 925
bouton(s) 1165, 2154
boutre 547
bouviers 277

bovin(s) 275
boxe 321d
bra 1568
bras 984
brasero 2483
brassière 1568
brave 408, 1438, 1805
bravo! 649
bravoure 1495, 2612
brebis 1896
brèche 818
breuvage 1450
bride 686a, 813, 2527
brigand 634
brillant 1598
briller 1174
brique(s) 1707, 1726
brise-fer 774
brocart 877, 2293
broche 230, 958a
brochure 2396
brosse 2116a
broyeur 1689
bruit 643, 1164, 1628, 2720, 2843
brunes 304
brutalité 486, 558
brute 757, 774
bulbe 2718
bureau de poste 234
bureau 892, 2397a
buses 2331
but 49, 100, 1665, 1857, 2007, 2295, 2822
Byzantine(s) 1146, 1147

cabane 385b
cabinet(s) 1182, 1138
câblage 1332
câble 1332, 2278, 2484, 2617
caboter 1409
cacher 2046
cachet 766, 1046, 2676
cadavre 2455, 2679
cadeau(x) 166a, 277, 1202, 1885, 2430, 2838, 2997
cadenas 2322
cadi 2307
café 315, 2350
cahier 2396, 2416
cailles 1130
caisse 785a, 1617, 1914a
caissier 1581b
calame 2335
calamité 131, 269, 304a, 308, 640, 858, 1416, 1627, 2703
calcul 645, 1802
calebasse 2496
caleçon 321a, 1282
calendrier 2364
calicot 274, 882a, 1372, 1740
calioune 1547
callosité au front 1249
calme 1138, 2644
calomnie 2085
calotte 287, 1672, 2242, 2497
camarade 1565
camaraderie 1862
camion 1828a
canal 852, 2101
candélabre 1736, 2345
cannabis 321b, 651a
canne 277, 785, 1875
canon 2294, 2342
Canope 1380a
cantine 1617
caoutchouc 2537a
cap 1003
capable 2113
capacité 1942, 2236, 2246
capitaine 1015, 2708
caporal 121b, 1419
caractère 623, 831, 1331, 1418, 1679, 2644, 2938, 2939
caravane 492a, 1980, 2323
carcasse 2679
cardamome 2173a
carène 946
cargaison 717, 1441
carnet 2416
carpette 2115
carquois 1179
carré 1028
cartable 1520
carte 2917
carton 2917
cartouche 782a, 1083
case 1459
casier 785a, 1097, 1617
casque 1693

casquette 2497
casserole 1593
cassette 1456a
castré 802, 804
catalogue 913
catapulte 2693a
catégorie 331, 536
cathédrale 2486
cause 20, 734, 1226, 1239, 1959, 2306
causer 125
causerie 125
caustique 2622
caution 1664, 2534
cavalier 1112
céder 1333
ceinture 639, 1195
célébration 1889, 2984
célèbre 1529, 1844
célébrer 1888
céleste 1363
cinquième 840
censurer 1853
cent(s) 2584
centaine 2584
centre 2383
cependant 284, 2515, 2874
cercle 952, 955
cercueil 1255, 1617
céréale(s) 2776
cérémonie 767, 1889
cerf 135
cerf-volant 1751
certain 2193
certainement 120, 677
certificat 805, 1525, 1664
certitude 407, 677, 3022
chagrin 308, 640, 2046, 2047, 2851
chaîne(s) 535, 1192
chaire 2692
chaise 2415
châle 1000, 1414, 2888
chaleur 614, 619
châlit 2266a, 2673
champ 202
champion 1438
chance(s) 163a, 211, 1288, 2072, 2700, 2741
chandail 2202a
chandelier 409, 2815
change 176, 177, 1580, 2175a
changer 177, 2060, 2175a
chanson 2052, 2053
chant(s) 1158, 1482, 2053
chanter 2052
chanteurs 1691
chanvre 651a
chapeau(x) 1672, 1682, 1693, 2497
chapelle 1210a, 2486
chapitre 899, 1392
chaque 512a
charge(s) 717, 1441, 1504, 2224, 2467
chargement 1441
charger 2467, 2943
chariot 1828a
charitable 1345
charité 650, 1571
charmant 324, 1755
charme 621
charnière 333
charogne 2679
charpente 790
charpentier 2697a
charrette 1828a
chat 190a, 2404a
château 195, 661
châtiment 2292, 2310
chaudière 2331, 1045
chaudron 1045, 1593
chauffer 1401a
chaussette(s) 1449a, 1452a
chaussure(s) 475a, 1113, 2445
chaux 946
chéchia 1672
chef 956a, 1003, 1004, 1329, 1389, 1546, 1711a, 1901, 2757a, 2922, 2995
cheik 1546
chemise 2341
chemisette 1568
chenille 949
chèque 751
cher 581, 2044
chercher 882, 1002, 1707a, 2079
cheval 271, 410, 557, 661a, 1275, 1705, 2112
chevaucher 1112
cheveux 1896
cheville 763
chien 2465
chiffre 1107, 1596
chirurgie 1827

choc 1655
choisir 867
choix 866, 867, 2754
choléra 2877
choquer 2427
chose(s) 734, 762, 1348, 1484, 1683, 2284
chrétien(s) 88, 2631, 2747
chrétienté 2631
Christ 2630
chronologie 2364
cicatrice 278
ciel 27, 1362, 1363, 1578, 2191
cigarettes 1248, 2917
cinabre 1191
cinnamon 871
cinq cents 2584
cinq 841, 842
cinquante 845
circoncision 1724, 1725, 2548
circonstance(s) 1418, 2721
cisailles 2291
ciseau(x) 1188a, 2291
citerne 6, 742
citoyen 1095, 2951a
citoyenneté 536a
citron 2581
civette 1157
civil 37, 1095, 2657a
civilisation 1826, 2605
clair 356, 823, 1598, 2149, 2150, 2791
claires 304
clairon 151, 218, 335a
clameur 1637
clan 791a, 2233
clarifier 2143
clarinette 1185
clarté 356, 357
classe 331, 536, 899, 900, 1993
classer 2203
clé 2078
clément 1005
clerc(s) 1546, 2398
client 1160
clientèle 1160a
clocher 2815
clôture 1734
cocher 1397
cochon domestique 853
cocotier 2577
coercitif 2427
coercition 2284
cœur 430, 2068
coffin 1617
coffre 785a
cohue 75
coïncidence 2966
col 432, 1215, 2137, 2496
colère 657, 1670, 2024, 2064
colis 1018
colle 1128, 1455
collecte 1612
collègue 914
collier 2516, 3013a
colline 438
colombe 706
colonne 2323
combat 1639
combattre 2720
combiner 321
commandant 107, 1901
commande 101, 102, 102a
commander 101, 107, 683, 2943
comme 2378
commencement 60, 134
commencer 1939
commentaire 2144
commenter 1453, 2143
commerçant 226, 366
commerce 277, 331, 349, 365, 366, 925, 1620
commercer 349
commissaire 107a
commissariat 2788
commission 19, 1965, 2945, 2979
commun 2318
communauté 510, 513, 2995
Comores 1978
compagnie 511
compagnon 1565
compagnons (du Prophète) 1160a, 1563
comparaison 2590
comparer 1431
compas pour dessiner 353
compassion 1053, 1490
compatissant 1005, 1054
compatriote(s) 2951a
compensation 2012
compétition 2210
complet 511, 1427, 2481

compléter 2480
compliments 1338
compliquer 2021
complot 2964
comportement 184
composer 321, 1621
composition 1111, 2731
compréhensif 2518
compréhension 1907, 2206
comprendre 643, 2206, 2696
comptage 1107
comptant 2781
compte 645, 1802, 2940
compter 645
comptoir 369a
comput 1802
concevoir 720
concerne 1698
concierge 332
concitoyen 2951a
conclusion 767, 768
concorder 2961
concubine 1283
condamnation 684
condition 745, 989, 1456, 2721
condoléances 1859
conducteur 1397
conduire 2837
conférencier 810
conférer 1266
confession 997
confiance 112, 115, 116, 1721, 1778, 1902, 2981b
confirmation 407
confirmer 407
confiserie 702, 1798, 2289
confiture 1033
conflit 828
confort 222, 1133, 2202
confortable 2861
confrérie 1702, 2914
confusion 75, 765, 1164, 1536, 2156, 2720
congé 1058
connaissance 1841, 1917, 1923
connu 1844, 1924
conscience 1661, 1907
consciencieux 1805
consécration 2716
conseil d'État 965
conseil(s) 500, 1533, 2742, 2837, 2922, 2943
conseiller 1364, 2742, 2837, 2943
consentement 1088, 2232
consentir 1624, 2961
conséquence 1898
conserve 1033
considération 110, 245, 2178, 2179, 2754
considérer 645, 1143, 2177, 2179
consigne 2943
consolation 1859, 2100
consoler 433, 2100
conspiration 2085
constamment 79, 963
constance 407
constant 963
consternation 2156
constipation 658
constitution 906
construire 321
consultation 1533
contaminer 2699
conte 607, 691, 2290
contemplation 110
contenance 2573
conteneur 742
content 1086
contentement 1085, 1086, 1089
contester 451
continuation 1987
continuer 961, 1983
contradiction 2209
contraindre 2022
contrainte 1652, 2284
contraire 825
contraste 828, 2209
contrôle 2659
contrôler 1643
controverse 828, 829
convenable 2886
convention 1456
conversation 125
converser 125
convertir à l'Islam 1334, 1345
convertir 2837
conviction 997, 3022
convoi 2323
convoquer 1707a, 2715
coolie 718
coopération 351
copain 32

copal 1374
copie(s) 2790
copier 2789
coquin fâcheux 1145
coquin 1495
corail 2614
Coran (lecture du -) 809
Coran 136, 471, 523, 710, 1392, 1566, 2077, 2131, 2144, 2261, 2396, 3011, 3025
coranique 136
cordage 2882
corde (anneau de -) 1467
corde d'instrument 2882
corde 457, 868, 2278, 2401, 2484, 2617, 2882
cordeau 667
cordon 2484
cordonnet 868
cordonnier (alène de -) 781
coriandre (graine de -) 494
cornaline 1895
corporelle (marque -) 278
corps (maillot de -) 2202a
corps céleste 2700
corps mort 2679
corps 178, 2770
corpulent 225
correct 1408, 1644, 2149, 2150
correction 684
correspondance (nécessaire de -) 968
correspondance 2964
correspondant 1809
corrompue 761
corrupteur 2141
cortège funèbre 534
cosmétique 1982
cosses 2189
côté (de l'autre – de) 2238
côté (qqn qui habite à -) 559
côte 1260
côte à côte (courir -) 526
côté de (être à -) 526
côte Swahili 1260
côté (de -) 730
côté 529
côtés (aux - de) 1742
coton (calot en – blanc) 1671a
coton 2334
cotonnade 2990
cotte de mailles 901
couard 2138a
couardise 2138a
couche 1683
coucher du soleil 1136, 2004, 2006
coude 730
couleur 304, 328, 1106, 1765, 1921, 2573
coup d'État 2331a
couper 2312
couple 564
couplet 344
coupon 2312
cour 329, 1028
courage 1495
courageux 1438, 1805
courbe 730
courir 1114, 1818
couronne 400
courrier 234, 2917
courtier 930
courtoisie 518
couscous 1356
cousin 312
coussin 2115, 2978
coût 348a
couteau(x) 1366, 1827
coûteux 1851, 2044
coutume(s) 445, 906, 997, 1160a, 1902, 1964, 2318, 2646
couturière 2291
couvercle 1682, 1683
couverture 260a, 1242, 1247, 1255, 1682, 2115, 2548
couvrir 1242, 1683, 2046, 2455
cravache 2414
crayon 2335
création 832, 2731
créature(s) 832, 833
crédit 2269
créer 831
crème 2289
crêpe(s) 2435
crépuscule 2006
cri 643
crier 2715
crime 541, 808, 995, 2304
cristal 310, 318a
critiquer 1779
croire 113, 1762
croître 1213, 2805

croix 1601
croque-mitaine 261
croyance 116, 973, 1902
croyant 113, 118
cruche 6, 2496
crucifier 1601
cuillère 2543a
cuir 1113, 2882
cuirasse 901
cuire 2559
cuisine 1109a
cuivre 1045, 1431, 1431a, 1593, 1596, 1641
culotte(s) 1282, 2521
culpabilité 808, 2571
culte 973, 1771, 1774, 2914
cultiver 1169
culture 1826, 2605
cumin 583a
curateur 1663
curcuma 228
cyclone 1654

daman 2878
dame 1246, 1390
dames (jeu de -) 1642
danger 812, 857, 1493, 1652, 2680
dans 143, 2215
date 50
datte(s) 287a, 394, 1483
davantage 2212
David 1158
dé 2432
débattre 451
débauché 2146
débours 2012
déboursements 1581a
débris 1718
début 134
décent 37
décès 1800
décharger 2180
déchet 224
décider 101, 2821
décision 1533, 1857, 2677
déclaration(s) 2358, 2443
décoration 701a
décorer 1216
décrire 2938
dédaigner 1657
défense d'ivoire 2332
défaut 829, 1913, 1977, 2042, 2167, 2302, 2304, 2785
défendre 723
déficit 2304, 2785
dégât 818
dégoûter 2424
degré 893, 1378, 2721
délai 2677
délateur 2777
délectation 2533
délit 46, 531, 1757, 2304
délivrance 821
déloyauté 859
déluge 2010
demande 734
demander 451, 1223, 1707a
démarrer 1297
déménager 834, 1409
démence 765
demeure 1319, 2498
demeurer 281, 961, 1316
demoiselle 313
démon 9, 523, 1548, 1891
dent 1367
département 954
dépensier 186
déplacer 2789
déposer 2902
depuis 2590
dérision 70, 2627
Dernier Jour 2361
dernière 2945
derviche 1633, 2987
désagrément(s)s 1670, 2467
désastre 131, 269, 858, 1497, 2703
descendant(s) 983, 2982
descendre 1690
déshonneur 1977, 1979, 2054, 2155
déshonorer 787, 788, 2155, 2829
désir(s) 594, 1530, 1538a, 1709, 1721, 1870, 2770, 2851, 2862, 2962
désirer 1088, 1721
désobéir 1878
dessin 1036, 1076, 1122, 1622
destin 21, 670, 1069, 2741
destructeur 774
destruction 789
détacher 692, 1714

détente 1137, 1138
détermination 1857, 2064
détester 2424
détourner 771, 2000
détresse 380, 668, 1164, 1652, 1670, 2047, 3006
détruire 386, 774, 775, 937a
dette(s) 192, 334, 972, 2184
deuil 1386, 1627, 1800, 2848
deux cents 2584
deux 424a
deuxième fois 1063
devant 95, 663, 2893
devenir 1638, 2578
déviation 730
devin 1633, 1925, 2489
devoir(s) 674, 1210, 2886, 2887
diabète 1314a
diable(s) 9, 523, 1548, 1891
diacre 1515
diamant 86
dictionnaire 2340
dicton 2358
Dieu 88, 211, , 435, 490, 749, 979, 985, 1013, 1543, 1772, 2030, 2665, 2716, 2871, 2992, 2993
diffamation 270, 1229, 1435
diffamer 1225
différence 281, 825, 828, 2209
difficile 668, 1068
difficulté(s) 308, 380, 750, 1484, 1493, 2284, 2467
digne 2201
dignité 652, 692, 1432, 2419, 2644, 2721, 2867
dilapider 184, 2184
dimanche 24, 1230
dîme 1180, 1865
dinar 974
dire 1839
directeur 956a, 2757a
direction de la Mecque 620, 2231
direction 1625, 2557, 2893, 2945
dirham 904
diriger 107, 683
disciple(s) 1139a
discorde 2085, 2169
discours 762, 809, 2547
discrétion 2754
disculper 187
discussion 125, 1533
discuter 125, 451
disgrâce 531, 755, 788, 1853, 1913, 1977, 2054
disposer 2923
dispute(s) 800, 828, 1533, 1602, 2720
disputer (se -) 451, 798, 2720
dissimulation 1247, 2543
distance 100
distinguer 2129
distraire 125
distribuer 2285, 2923
divan 965
divergence 828, 829
divertissement 2103
divin 1054
divination 1122
divinité 1774
diviser 329a, 2129, 2285
division 471, 921, 1474, 2285
divorce 1715, 1716, 1800
divorcer 1714
dix 1866
dix-huit 420
dixième (un -) 1865
djellaba 493
djinn(s) 523
docile 1730
docteur en médicine 926a
docteur 686b, 1290b, 1675
doctrine 998
document(s) 805, 1365, 2917
doigt(s) 480, 984, 1425
dollar(s) 1149, 2267
domestique 129, 773, 1587, 1770
domicile 1316, 1319
domination 1850, 2659
dominer 683
dominos 1642
dommage 46, 131, 789, 818, 858, 1651
don 563, 1885, 2838, 2997
donation 2997
donner 484
dossier 224
douaire 2674
douane 503a, 2119
double 2790
doubler 274, 1064, 1683
douceur 1314, 1858, 2183
douleur 640, 1823

doute(s) 1493, 1497, 1536, 2935
douze 424b
drachme 904
drapeau 318, 1918
drogue 1904
droit 674, 1408
droite 3025
dur 1445, 3015
durable 963, 1644
durer 902, 959, 961, 1742, 1985

échecs (jeu d' -) 1475
échelle 1337a
éclat 1378
école 900, 997
économie(s) 1898, 2297
écran 1242
écraser 911
écrire 2398
écrit 805, 1843, 2399, 2731
écrivain 2398
Eden 1816
éducation 1917, 1922
éduquer 2837
effet(s) 1818, 1898
effectuer 484, 1944
efforcer (s') 543
effort 173, 446, 544, 546, 1809, 1902, 2054, 2064, 2852
égal 1407, 1809
église 2486
égoïste 2770
égorger 979
Egypte 2637
élastique 2537a
élection 867, 2271a
électricité 2488
élégance 1767
éléphantiasis 455
élève(s) 900
éloge 424, 709, 2939
éloquence 2150
éloquent 2149, 2474
émancipé 615
émasculé 804
emballage 2115
embellissement 520
embêtement 1536
embêter 988
emblème 2588, 2592
émigrer 2830
émir 107
empire 2658
emplir 2648
employé(s) 771a, 773
empoignade 2224
emprunt 972, 2269
en 2215
enceinte 720
encens 165, 1879, 2524, 2574
encercler 657
enchantement 2863b
enclin 1804
enclos 1028
encore 265
encourager 433
encrier 968
endommager 789
endroit 667, 695, 1921, 2498
enduire 1717
énergie 173, 2852
enfant(s) 1071, 1896
enfer 442, 551, 1578
enfin 821
engrenages 958a
ennemi 171, 646, 799, 1819
ennui(s) 47, 308, 380, 750, 1493, 2647
ennuyer 2829
enquête 1403a, 2080
enregistrement 2307
enrichir 1201a
enseignant 1925
enseignement(s) 2957
ensemble 506, 914, 1408
ensevelir 2455
ensorceler 1145
ensorcellement 1257
ensuite 139, 265, 266, 826
entendement 2842
entendre 1358
enterrement(s) 1255, 1372, 2557, 2848, 2914
enthousiasme 1809
entier 511, 512a, 2481
entièrement 794, 795, 2481
entourer 1733
entraide 1290
entre 355, 2264
entrepôt 329, 2691a

entreprise 1468, 1944
entretenir 773
entretien 1580
entrez 2158, 2264
enveloppe 2548
envelopper 2455
envie 646, 647, 1530, 1721, 2085, 2851
envier 646
envieux 646, 647, 860
environ 2246, 2378
envisager 2821
envoi 1074
envoyé 1073
épaisseur 1943
épice 228
épidémie 1704, 2877
épingle 763
éponge 1300, 2570a
époque 1189
épouse(s) 129, 2674
épreuve 223, 308
équateur 806
équipement 547, 1216
équitation 1112
ermite 1633
erreur 2042
escalier(s) 893, 1337a
esclave 615, 773, 1770
escorte 621a
escroc 2489
espace 202, 2209, 2772, 2931
espèce 71, 331, 536, 1621, 1695, 1993, 2233
espérer 1048, 1721
espion 478, 953, 1272
espoir 1721
esprit(s) 523, 979, 1132, 1548, 1661, 1818, 1907, 2770, 2842
esquisse 1036, 1111
essai 2731
essayer 458, 999
essence 318b, 570, 998, 2488, 2770
Est 1465, 1552, 1712
estime 1778
estomac 257, 2173a
et 97, 2870
établir 1366
étage 1273a, 1683, 2009
étagère 1097
étain 1083
étal 369a
étalage 925
étalon 2094
étamer 1083
état 745, 1418, 2658, 2861
étayer 1936
étendard 318
éternel 4, 60, 963
éternité 60, 945, 2648
ethnie 2359a
étiquette 35
étoffe(s) 1372, 1733, 2341
étoile(s) 2700
étonnement 323, 1782, 1784
étouffer 2021
étude(s) 1922, 2754
étudiant 1923
étudier 1713
eunuque 802
Europe 2990
européen 854a
évacuer 2101
évangile(s) 124
évanouir (s' -) 2049
Eve 731
événement(s) 1776, 2290
évêque 68, 2639a
évidence 356
éviter 526
exact 794, 796, 1644
exactement 169, 794, 795, 823, 918
exaltation 1887
exalter 1888
examen 1994, 2080, 2210
examiner 1143, 1713, 2079, 2080
exaspération 2024
excepté 79, 654
excréments 1138
excrétions 1138
excursion 1294
excuse(s) 1086, 1242, 1824
exécration 2544
exécuteur 2944
exemple(s) 2592
exhortation 2945, 2956, 2957
exiger 673
existence 756
expectorations 302
expédient 1240

expédier 1333
expérimenter 458
expert 1633, 1804, 2113, 2675
expiation 2452
exemple 2591
explication 357, 2143, 2144, 2706
expliquer 1764, 1777, 1835, 2143, 2938
explorer 2079
exposer 1777, 1835
exposition 1453
expressément 794, 795
expression 1629
extase 453a
extorquer 2022
extradition 1344
extrême 27
extrêmement 1378
exubérant 70

fabrication 1110, 1111
fabriquer 321
face 2893
facile 1057, 1380, 2861
facilitation 1382
façon 2196, 2939
faction 1738
facture 645
faculté 2236
faible 1658, 1789, 2582
faiblesse 76, 1587, 1913
faillite 789, 2187
faire 484, 1944
fait 1945
fait 2167
fakirisme 2419
falaise 438
falsification 2019
famille 129, 506, 513, 1993, 2724
fanfaronner 443
fantôme 1424
farceur 2627
fardeau 717, 1617
farine de maïs 2183
farine 702, 839, 920a
fascicule 2416
fascination 2863b
faste 1453
fatigue 380
faute 808, 1757, 1913, 1977, 2042, 2304
fauteuil 2415
faux 808, 2428
faveur 520, 563, 650, 651, 1087, 1619, 2158, 2764
femme(s) 1267, 1568, 1588, 1800, 2173a, 2663
fênetre 1430
fenouil 233, 1512
fer 2500a
ferme 408, 496, 497, 1644, 1805, 2644
fermer 1145, 1267
ferry-boat 1820
fête de mariage 2419
fête nationale 522
fête(s) 767, 1896, 1878, 1978, 2419
feu de l'enfer 442
feu 442, 1055, 2561a
feuille(s) 1566, 2917
fez 1693, 2497
fiabilité 113
fiable 117, 1644
fibre(s) 2577
fidélité 113, 115
fièvre 614, 705
figuier 403
figure 1629, 2383, 2893
fil de moustique 2803
fil 868, 1332
file 1286
filet(s) 465b, 1430, 1467
fille 313
fils 277, 312, 1902, 2982
fin du ramadan 2165
fin 27, 100, 391, 767, 768, 1898, 2295, 2303
finir 1903
fissure 818, 2082, 2164
fistule 2727
fixer 2278
flagellation 496
flageller 495, 497
flambeau 2561a
flanc 529
flanelle 555, 2202a
flanquer 526
flasque 2582
flatterie 2939
flèches 2693a
flegme 302
flemmard 1981
fleuve(s) 163, 1775

foi 116, 997, 1575, 1702, 1778, 1902, 2646
fois 2302, 2607, 2971
fonction 1484
fond 1097, 1943
fondamental 134
fondation(s) 2318
fondement 2318
football 2495
force 1150, 1560, 1600, 1942, 2284
forcer 433, 2022
forger 1366
forme 1432, 1629, 2331, 2573
former 1366
fornication 1196, 1197
fort 195, 496, 497, 661, 1444, 1644, 2644
fortune 211, 862, 1288, 2684, 2700, 2741
fou 525, 2310
fouetter 495, 497
fouiner 2079, 2080
foulard de tête 2666
foule 75, 94, 832, 944, 2359a
four 397
fourberie 2019
fourchette 1539a
fourmi rouge 1357
fraction 413, 1384, 2312
fragment 2312, 2435
fraîcheur 197, 200
frais 200, 778, 2012, 2430
franc 1562
France 2136
franchir 1775
frapper 1624, 1654, 2271a
fraternité 510
fraude 1757, 1996, 2019
frein(s) 2132a
frère du père 1933
frère 32
fret 1441, 2818
fripon 1981
froid 197, 200
fromage 439
froment 2337
fronde 2693a
frontière 603
fruit 384, 417
fuite 168
fumée 165, 889
fumigation 165, 1962
funérailles 767
fureur 2024
fusil 317, 1083, 1424
fût 221
futilités 2002

gâcher 937a
gage(s) 1129, 1528, 1581a, 1830, 2419a
gagner 365, 2210
galette 2435
gallon 500a
garantie 1562, 1664, 1830, 2534
garçon 2043, 2982
garde 621a, 671, 1210, 1862, 2224
garder 723, 1643
gardien 332, 1862
gaspiller 184, 386
gaz 429a
gel 498, 1599
gemme 2148
gêne 1536, 2467
généalogie 445, 2724
générale 515
génération 2359a
généreux 557, 1352, 2420
générosité 1352, 1353, 2419, 2612
génie(s) 523
genre 536, 1993, 2233, 2573
gens 32, 126, 2359a
gentil 2540, 2582
gentillesse 1053, 2540
ghee 1361
gilet 1568, 1695
girofle 417, 1747, 2280
glace 416, 498, 1599
glaise 1707
globe 2429
gloire 431, 1850, 1887, 2095
Glorieux (le) 490
glorification 1889
glorifier 1888
gobelet 310, 2490, 2394a, 2496
Gog 3018
golfe 855
gombo 156, 3005a
gomme 1616
gond 333
gorge 701
gosier 701

goudron 1147
gourde 2570a
goût 2533
goûter 458, 999
gouvernail 1317
gouvernement 684, 687, 957, 965, 2995
gouverner 683
gouverneur 671a, 689, 956a, 2995
grâce! 112
grâce 1053, 2039, 2158, 2764, 2962
grains (de café) 315
graissage 946
graisse 946, 1440, 2334
grammaire 2706
gramophone 1375
grand 1751, 2101
grandeur 490, 1887, 2095
grand-père 445
gras 1440
gratification 1088
gratitude 649, 1500
gravitation 453a
Grec 3032
Grèce 3032
gredin 1495, 1981
grenier 2009
grillage 1332, 2803
gronder 1170a
gros 225
grossesse 717, 720
groupe 511, 914, 1400, 2769
guérir 222
guérisseur 1925
guerrier 1438
guide 1015
gypse 480

habit 2341
habitude(s) 1771, 1964, 2646
habituer 125
habous (loi islamique) 2974
hache 2070, 2567
hadith 607
hadj 592, 595
haï 2428
haine 270, 2425
haïr 2424
halte 667, 693
hangar 2691a
harceler 658
haricot(s) 2214
harmonie 2966
haschisch 321b, 651a
hâte 627
haubert 901
hémorroïdes 236
henné 727
herbe(s) 651a
héritage 2912, 2945, 2997
hériter 2908
héritier(s) 2908, 2911
hermaphrodite 849
héros 1438
hésitation 1062
hésiter 1062
heure(s) 424b, 1136, 1210, 1398, 1766, 2006, 2090, 2898
histoire(s) 50, 391, 607, 691, 762, 1354, 2290
hocca 1547
homme(s) 126, 223, 312, 1044, 1546
homosexuel 1587
hongre 802, 804
honnête 1562, 1598, 1644
honnêteté 113, 1813
honneur 431, 652, 1850, 1889, 2095, 2419, 2422, 2612, 2690
honorable 527
honoraires 2430
honorer 1888, 2419
honte 531, 652, 755, 788, 1679, 1977, 1979, 2155
hôpital 926a
horloge 1398, 1905, 2924
hors-la-loi 634
houe(s) 1366, 2070
huile 1211
huit 419
huitième (un -) 421
humain(s) 2679
humble 966, 991, 1657
humidité 1091
humiliation 2156
humilier 680
humilité 755, 989
huppe 2836
hydrophobie 2466
hydropisie 1307, 1595
hypocrite 2777
hypothèque 1129

idée(s) 997, 1533, 1762, 2178
idiome 2538, 2547
idiot 117, 443, 525
idole 1622, 1774
ignare 443, 1796
ignominie 788, 1979
ignorant(e) 548, 1796, 2034
illusion(s) 2002
illustration 1629
image 1622, 1629
imam 96
imbécile 117, 272, 246, 525, 907
immédiatement 746, 1399
immerger 2010
immoler 979
impie 2453
importance 2775a, 2852
important 2853
importer 492a
imposer des impôts 1865
imposer 1328
impossible! 654
impossible 752
imposteur 1981, 2777
impôt(s) 1865, 2467
imprécation 2544
impression 1076
impudent 1301
impudicité 1196
impuissant 848, 1587, 1658
impur(e) 1025, 2699
impureté 528, 2699
incantation 1857
incertitude 2935
inclination 1115, 1588, 2862
incompréhensible 223
inconvénient 1913
incorrect 808
incrédulité 2451
incroyable! 1966
incroyant 1194
indécision 1062
indemnité 2012
indéniablement 2481
indépendance 616
index 2203
indication 928, 1534
indifféremment 1241a
indigence 2213
indigène 290
indigne 1658
indigo 2825
indigotier 2825
indiquer 2938
indulgence 1086
industrie 1468
infatuation 2002
inférieur 966
infidèle(s) 860, 1522, 2453
infidélité 859, 2451
infirmière(s) 394a, 926a
infliger 1328
informateur 1272
information 1843
informer 1835, 1839
injection 5, 680a
injures 1225, 1229, 1435
injurier 1225, 2451
injuste 860
injustice 558, 859, 1757
innocent 192
innovateur 173
innovation 173a
inondation 1737, 2010
inquiétude 2138a, 2156, 2935
insalubre 2879
insectes 949
insertion 1111
insignifiant 816, 817, 1658, 2719
insinuation 2935
insinuer 1835
insistance 2852
insolent 70
inspecteur 2080a
inspection 1994, 2103
inspirer 2898
instinct 1331
instruction 1878, 2557
instrument(s) 133, 1185, 2129, 2310, 2882
insuffisant 583, 2044
insulte(s) 1225, 1229, 1435, 2427, 2465
insulter 787, 788, 1225, 1301, 1657, 2424
intellect 1907
intelligence 1841, 1907, 2206
intelligent 2518
intensification 1445
intention(s) 257, 1140, 1665, 1709, 1857, 2007, 2295, 2822, 2842

intercesseur 1487
intercession 1487
interdiction 2129
interdire 2943
interdit 629, 632
intérêt 1031, 2216, 2269
intermédiaire 2081
interprétation 1777
interprète 371, 2474
interpréter 1777, 2143
interrogation 1403a
interroger 1223
intervalle 204, 2209, 2600, 2677
intrépidité 1785
intrigue 2085
intrinsèque 570
inutilité 76
inventer 321, 1621
investigation 2080
inviter 908, 1048
invoquer 908
Iran 1796
islam 973, 1345, 1523, 1541
islamique(s) 2848
ivresse 1311

jalousie 647, 2054, 2085
jamais 3, 964
jardin d'Eden 1816
jardin 235, 524, 524a
jasmin 3019
jazz 2130a
Jérusalem 2869
jeter 1124
jeu d'échecs 1475
jeu de ballon 1734
jeu de dames 1642
jeu de dés 1642
jeu de hasard 2339
jeu 1263, 1639, 1748, 2210, 2542, 2543
jeudi 846
jeûne du ramadan 1635
jeûne 1635, 1636, 2164
jeûner 1634
jeune 1423
jeunesse 633, 1422
jeux d'argent 2270, 2339
joie 236a, 862, 1087, 1691, 2104, 2533
jouer 1692, 2542
jouissance(s) 125, 2103
Jour de la République (fête nationale) 522
jour de la résurrection 262, 2361
jour du jugement 2361
jour 507, 1025, 2984, 3030
journal 465, 2917
juge musulman 2307
juge 684, 689
jugement 684, 686, 1459, 1907, 2754
juif 3027
jujubier 1270
jumelles 2754a
jupe 569a
jupon 569a
jurer 683
jusqu'à 590, 603
jusque 590
juste 1408, 1562, 1607, 1644, 1813, 2886
justice 674, 1080, 1459
justifier 334
kasida 2296
keffieh 2497
kérosène 429a
Khartoum 782b
kiosque 363b
kofia 2497
kohl 2402

La Mecque 595, 635, 2640
lac 163, 1775
laine 783, 1632, 2729
laisser 373, 1714
lait caillé 1130
lampe 1276, 2345, 2561a, 2814
lancer 1124
langue 2538, 2547
lanterne 2073, 2345, 2561a
lapidation 1047
lapider 1046, 1047
larve 949
latrine(s) 1138
laxatif 1377, 1383
Le Caire 2637
leader 96, 107
leçon 899
lecture 809
légal 694
légalité 674
léger 816, 1380

legs 2908, 2974, 2997
léguer 2943, 2973
légume(s) 2092
lenteur 1858
lentilles 1806
lèpre 206, 455
léser 1757
lettre س 1413
lettre alif 82
lettre de l'alphabet 623, 2788
lettre 224
lever du soleil 1712
lexique 2340
libéralité 1353, 2419a
libération 821
libérer 1714
liberté 616, 1058, 1240, 2931
libre 192, 615
lieu 134, 202, 529, 695
lignage 445, 2724
ligne télégraphique 1332
ligne 805, 1286, 1400, 1671a, 2617
lime 200a, 2581
limite(s) 603
limon 2581
limpide 1598
lin 2401
linceul 274, 1372, 2455
lingerie 569a
liqueur 1847
liquide 2940
lire 388
lisse 1717
lit de fleuve 2907
lit 2115, 2266a, 2673, 2729
litanie 2914
littoral 1260
livraison 1344
livre (sterling) 542
livre(s) 136, 1392, 1566, 2270, 2396, 2917
livrer 1333
livret 913, 2416
localité 529
location 19, 1865
locomotive 147
loi 2342, 2690
loin 267
loisir(s) 2125, 2772, 2931
long 1744
lorsque 2590
lot 21, 517
loterie 163a
louable 1368, 1369
louange(s) 424, 709, 1235, 2939
louer 17, 18, 2430
loukoum(s) 702, 905
loupe 2756
loyer 17, 1865, 2419a
lubrificant 1211
lubrification 946
luffa 2570a
lumière 1276, 2814
luminosité 1513
lundi 425
lune (nouvelle) 2847
lunettes 1010, 1994, 2754a
luth 1963
lutter 2720
luxe 125

machine 133, 952, 2645
maçon 321
madame 1246, 1390, 2526
magasin 925
magazine 2009, 2396
mages 2594
magicien 1925
magie 1257
magistrat 2307
magnanimité 1352, 1353, 2419
magnétophone 1254a
magnifier 1888
Magog 3018
Mahdi 2595
main droite 3025
main gauche 1518
main(s) 206, 304, 1425
maintenant 1399
maintenir 2129
maïs 2183, 2874
mais 79, 284, 2515
maison 951, 791a, 1717, 1875
maître d'école 1925
Maître Suprême 435
maître 76a, 579, 1013, 1389, 1546, 1925, 2992
maîtresse 1390, 1961
maîtrise 2659
majesté 490, 1887

majorité 2038
mal 131, 269, 761, 1448, 1651
malade(s) 197, 1306
maladie 304, 668, 705, 969, 1595, 1883, 2620
malaria 2648a
malchance 131, 1416, 1448, 1897, 2703
malchanceux 1417
malédiction 1897, 2544
malfaiteur 634
malheur(s) 21, 304a, 308, 789, 1416, 1627, 1897, 2680, 2703, 3006
malice 1907
malle 1520, 1617
malsin 2879
maltraiter 988
malveillant 761, 1891, 2777
manches 2137
mandataire 2981
manière(s) 35, 37, 46, 257, 1702, 1964
manifestation 1453, 1829, 1836
manque 1913, 2171, 2213, 2302
manquer 1883
manteau 432, 571, 2137
manuellement 1958
marbre 2624
marchand 366, 492a, 854a
marchandise(s) 248, 329, 349, 1617, 1836, 2684
marché 1057, 1402
mardi 415
mariage 1823a, 1832a, 1833, 1900, 2516, 2793
Marie-Thérèse (dollar de -) 2267
marmite 1593
marque 12, 136, 1424, 1695, 1776, 1920, 1921, 2788
marteau(x) 1366, 1413a
martyr 1522, 1525
Mascate 1518
mât 1585
match de boxe 321d
match de football 2495
matelas 2115
matelot 163
mathématique 645
matière 104
matin 424b, 1552, 2090
matinée 1646
matrice 2331
maturité 1080
maudire 1046, 2451, 2544
mauvais 761, 966
méchanceté(s) 1170a, 1448, 2167, 2451
méchant 761
médaille 2736
médecin 926a, 1675
médecine 969, 1674
médersa 900
médiateur 1297
médiation 1487
médicament 969, 1904
méditation(s) 110, 2177, 2178
méditer 2177, 2179
méfait 2167
meilleur 2162, 2991
mélancolie 1386
mélange 75
melon 250
même 590, 918, 998, 1348, 1573
mémorandum 805
mendiant 1223, 2172, 2633
mensonge 1203, 2042
mensonger 2543
menstruation 760
mensualités 1528
menteur 980, 2407, 2777
menthe 2766
mépris 1170a, 1645
méprisable 680, 991, 1658
mépriser 372, 680, 798, 1657, 2451
mer(s) 163, 189, 1297, 1718, 1775, 2680
merci 231, 649, 1050, 1137
mercredi 1026
mercure 1152
mérite 427, 692
mériter 673
méritoire 1368, 1369, 1619
merveille 1782, 1784, 1785, 1790
mesquinerie 1956
message 762, 986a, 1074
messager 1073, 1074, 2657
Messie 2630
messieurs 76a
mesure 984, 2246
mesurer 1547, 2370
métal 996, 296, 1593, 1641, 1728, 1817, 2154
métaphore 2590
méthode 1702, 2318
métier à tisser 2129

mètre 2584a
métropolitain 2639a
mettre 433, 459
meuble(s) 958a, 968
meurtrière 1430
midi (prière du -) 1766
midi 1646
miel 337, 1863, 2183
mieux 2162
mihrâb 620
militaire(s) 218, 572, 1862
mille 81
minable! 1298
minaret 2815
mine 1817
ministère 2922
ministre 2283, 2922
minute 921
miracle 136, 1776, 1782, 1790, 2419
mirage 1274
miroir 1010, 2754a, 2756
miroiter 1174
misérable 989, 991, 2172, 2633
misère(s) 1493
miséricorde 1054
miséricordieux 1005, 1054
mode 1695
modèle 1036, 1111, 1143, 1695, 2331
modération 2246, 2371, 2938
modéré 2928
modestie 652, 755, 1247
modifier 177, 2060
moineau 1656
mois 637, 1038, 1136
Moïse 401
moiteur 1091
moitié 2748
Mombasa 718
moment 921, 1398, 1874, 2970
monarque 2655
monde 29, 55, 102a, 944
monétaire 2781
monnaie 904, 2154, 2267
monseigneur 579
monsieur 76a, 579, 854a, 2526
montagne 438
monter 1112
montre 1398, 1905, 2924
montrer 927a, 1764, 2938
monture 1113
moquer 2451
moquerie 1645, 2158
morceau 813
morgana 1274
mors 686a, 2527
morsure 2556
mort 21, 204, 826, 2088, 2670, 2678, 2679
Mort 2797
mosquée 515, 809, 1210a, 1252, 2692, 2974
mot(s) 654, 1080, 1711, 2472
moteur 2645
motif 1076, 1226
mouchoir 2166a, 2666
mouiller 285
moule 1641, 2331
moulin 1689
mourant(s) 197
mourir 2010, 2849
mousquet(s) 317
mousse 1155a
mousseline 1535
mousson 2934
moustache(s) 1451
moustiquaire 2803
moutarde 780
mouvement 627, 628
moyen(s) 750, 1069, 1240, 1533, 1658, 2928, 2931
muezzin 44, 45
Muhammad 1345, 1563, 2984
mule 271
mulet 271
multiplication 1654
munificence 2419a
mur(s) 195, 620, 1097, 1576, 1717, 1875
mûre 2117
muret 1734
mûrier 2117
mûrir 1405
musc 2632
muscade 233
musicien 1692
musique 1691, 2683a
musulman(s) 88, 118, 435, 442, 490, 524, 637, 1343, 1345, 1346, 1578, 2090, 2302, 2914
musulmane(s) 1136, 1612, 1702, 1766, 2557
mystère 1272

naissance 2983
nappe 2666
nappe de table 2166a
narcisse 2718
natif 290
nation 94, 536, 1738, 2359a
nationalité 536a
natron 2751
natte(s) 205, 480, 2115
nature 570, 998, 1418, 1679
naviguer 2192
navire indigène 1585
navire 147, 164, 259, 547, 1110, 1195, 1299, 1458, 1547, 2192, 2708
néanmoins 2515, 2874
nécessaire 2342, 2534, 2887
nécessité 734, 1456, 1652, 2118, 2213, 2534
négligence 1789, 2033
négliger 90, 373, 2032
neige 416
nettoyer 2173a
neuf 375
neuvième 376
nez 813
niche 620
nigaud 117, 225, 443, 907
noble 615, 2421
noblesse 2419
noce(s) 1832a, 1833
Noé (arche de -) 1299
nœud 2278
noir 304
noix 564, 2568
nom 417, 1348, 1770, 2708
nomade 181
nomadisme 181
nombre(s) 1107, 1802, 2802a, 2881
nombreux 832
nord 1518
nord-est 2934
note 224, 986a
noter 2694
notification 1842, 1843
notion 1762
nourrice 872a
nourriture 78, 1033, 1069, 1427, 1641, 2556
Nouveau Testament 124
nouvelle(s) 236a, 236b, 762, 809, 1841, 2290
nuage 1995
Nubien 2811
nuire 1651
nuisance 1651
nuit 809, 1056, 2579
nul 256
numéro 2802a
numérotation 1107

obéir 1358, 1730
obéissance 1731
objectif 1424
objet(s) 115, 734, 2007, 2295
obligation 192, 334, 1878, 2118, 2534, 2886
obligatoire(s) 2427, 2887
oblique 730
oblong 1744
observation 2103
observer 241, , 2694, 2696
obstination 1956
obturer 1267
occasion 814, 914, 1824, 2607, 2772, 2931
occident 2004
occupation 104, 1484, 1533, 1620, 1945
occurrence 2607
océan 163
ocre 3005a, 2639b
odeur 625, 1131
œillet 2280
offensant(s) 2158
offense 192
offenser 372
office 2397a
officiel 1077
officier 107, 1643a
offrande 979, 1818, 2452, 2902
offre 1571
oignon(s) 247, 247a
oiseau(x) 1056, 1751
olive 1212
olivier 1212
ombrelle 1514
Omniscient 1918a
once 132
oncle paternel 1933
onze 1867
opération 1945a
opinion 997, 1006, 1762, 2358
opium 77, 321b, 1798
opportunité 2772

opposant 798, 799, 1819
opposition 825, 828
oppresseur 1759
oppression 558, 1164, 1670, 1757, 1785
opprimer 658, 1757
option 866
or 974, 996, 1006
orange 194, 2581
oranger 194
orateur 810
ordinaire(s) 32, 2318
ordonnance 1036
ordonner 101, 107, 2943
ordre(s) 101, 102, 102a, 1034, 1036, 1444, 1850
ordure(s) 1145, 1718, 2925
oreiller 769a, 2115
organe(s) 2101
organisation 882
organiser 2715
orge 1480
orgueil 1887, 2095
Orient 1465
orifice 2076, 2101
origine 71, 445
orner 1216
orphelin 3017
oseille 2417a
oser 479
ostentation 2095
ou 130, 2872
oubli 1385
ouest 2004, 2006
oui 2763
ouragan 1655, 1737
ourlet 1215
ours 874
outil 133
outillage 547
ouverture 2076, 2101, 2119
ouvrier 18
ouvrir 2100

pacte 1960, 2964
Padda de Java 1656
page 1566, 2416
paiement 166a, 821, 1528, 1581a, 2012, 2781
païen 2453
paillasson 205
pain 2274a
pair (nombre -) 1486
paire 564
paisiblement 1338
paix 112, 862, 1133, 1338, 1602
palais 951, 1273a
palefrenier 1397
palper 2628
paludisme 705
pan 529
panatalon court 1282
panégyrique 424
panier 1483
panique 2138a
pantalon 321a, 1282, 2521
papier 913, 986a, 2270, 2567, 2917
papyrus 205
paquet 1018, 2115
parabole 2588, 2592
parade 1671a
paradis 204, 524, 1816
paraffine 429a
paragraphe 136
parapluie 1514
parasol 1514
paravent 901, 1242
pardon 192, 1086, 1349, 1353, 1543a, 1893, 2027, 2030
pardonner 1352, 2027
parent(s) 129, 513, 2264, 2265, 2359a, 2674
parenté 129, 513, 2264, 2724
parfait 2481
parfum 625, 1131, 1747, 1879, 2170, 2632, 2879
parjure 1203
parlement 213a
parloir 329
parmi 355
paroisse 2990
parole 2358
part(s) 656, 674, 1316, 1384, 2748
partage 674
partenariat 351, 1468
parti 997, 1738
particularité 793
particulier(s) 794, 795, 796, 1563, 1924
partie 670, 952, 1738, 2006, 2285, 2312
partir 1115, 1409, 2180
partisans 1294
partition 1474
passage 469, 893, 2608a

passager 1775
passer 561, 1818
passion 657, 2024, 2862
pasteur 2283
pâte 1798, 2435
patience 1555
patienter 1555
patron 277, 366, 2708
patronage 724, 1160a
patrouille 953
pause 2974
pauvre 991, 2172, 2633
pauvreté 1068, 2171, 2213
pays 289, 951, 2990
paysage 2755
peau 480, 2137
péché 531, 808, 995, 2027
pécher 1878
pécheur(s) 1578, 2146
pédéraste 2570
peigne 2129, 2635a
peignoir 2662a
peindre 1717
peine 380, 683, 1493, 1897, 2047
peinture 328, 946
peinturlurer 1717
pelage 2137
pèlerin(s) 595, 635
pèlerinage à La Mecque 592
pèlerinage 635, 1206
pelle 2430a
pendant 960
pendentif de nez 639
pendre 1915
pendule 1398
pénétration 886
pénis 986, 1154
pénitance 2452
pensée(s) 110, 257, 1762, 2177, 2178, 2179
penser 985, 1661, 1762, 2177, 2179, 2696
Pentateuque 401
percer 2242a
percevoir 1537, 2694
père 10, 277, 1902
perfidie 859
perforer 2242a
péril 812
période 100, 469, 1025, 1189, 2600, 2677, 2788, 2970
périr 937a, 2010, 2849
perle(s) 2516
permanence 1983, 1987
permanent 408, 963
permettre 334, 484
permis 986a, 1058
permission 43, 1058, 1240
permit 1058
perpétuité 2648
perplexité 323, 1536, 2138a, 2935
perroquet 890
perruque 357a
Perse 1796
persévérance 1809, 1902, 2518
perspective 2755
perspicacité 245, 2113
perte 789, 1667
perversité 1956
peser 1775, 2370
peste bubonique 1704
peste 308, 1704
pet 1131
petit 1586
pétitionner 1223
pétrole 429a, 2488
peu 583, 2719
peuple 94, 2359a
peur 857, 2138a, 2935
peut-être 169, 654, 1911
phare 2815
phénomènes 171
photo 1629
phylactères 621
physique 1150
pian 206
piastre 2267
pichet 2496
picture 1629
pièce de monnaie 974, 1149, 1580, 2154, 2185, 2267, 2976
pièce 653, 1106, 2684
pied(s) 206, 2310
piédestal 2318
piège 1467
pierre bleu 2622
pierre(s) 480, 599, 1047, 1304, 1895, 2888
pigeon domestique 706
pilote 1015
piment 1473, 2189

pin 1623
pince 2291
pinceau 2116a
pipe à eau 217
pipe à la persane 1547
pipeau 1185
pique-assiette 2770
pirate 634
pirogue 1110
piscine 707
pitié 116, 1053, 1490, 3006
pitre 525
placard 958a
place 202, 1384, 2498, 2772, 2931
plafond 951, 1304
plaie(s) 463, 2548
plaine 202
plaint 1504a
plaire 125, 1085, 2157
plaisanterie 70, 1263, 2542, 2627
plaisir(s) 125, 351, 1085, 1087, 1691, 2104, 2533
plan(s) 1076, 1533, 1841, 1857
plancher 1304, 1305
planète 1163, 1411
plante 2417a
planter 1169
plaque 1591a
plaquer 1717
plat 952, 1304, 1567, 1682
plateau 1641, 1682
Pléiades 409
pli 1683
pliable 2582
plonger 2010
pluie 1307, 1625, 1655, 1995
plume 2335
pluriel 506
plus 1213, 1586, 2038, 2212, 2401a
poche 571, 2503a
poêle 147, 1593, 2483
poème(s) 391, 2296, 2443
poids 1092, 2670, 2924
poignard 851
point 1802, 2788
pointage 1107
pointe 1355
poison 1350
poisson 1186, 1359
poitrine 565
poivre de Cayenne 1473
poivre 228, 2173a, 2189
poix 1147
poker 2339
police 341a, 1862
policier(s) 341a, 1862
politesse 35, 2419
politicien 1396, 1396a
politique 1396, 1396a
polluer 2699
pollution 528
pommade 969
pomme(s) 250b, 384
pompe 1702a, 2767a
pont 457, 893, 1284, 2346, 2391a
porc 853
port 1816
portail 333
porte 333, 891
portefeuille 472
portemanteau 777
porte-monnaie 459, 472
porteur 718
portier 332
portion 268, 656, 674, 1384, 2285, 2312, 2748
portrait 1629
position 652, 695, 1115, 2721
possession(s) 741, 2654, 2658, 2684
poste 234
pot 280, 952, 1728, 2490
pot-de-vin 1082, 1420, 2556
poteau 1585
poterie 6, 217
potion 1449b
pou 2341a
pouce 1425
poudre 920a, 2018, 2402
poulie 457
pourboire 166a
pousse 2106
pousser 1164
poussière 1995
pouvoir(s) 223, 684, 749, 957, 1850, 2236, 2658
pratiquer la sodomie 2570
précédent 445, 1239
préceptes de l'islam 2679
précipitation 627
précis 797, 1644

prédicateur 810, 2697
prédication 809
prédire 239
prédisposé 1804
prédominant 2039
préface 877
préférer 577
préfet 2995
préjudice 789
prélude 2077
premier repas 2164
premier(s) 134
première-née 283
préoccuper de (se -) 1643
préparé 547a, 1804
préparer 547a, 1511, 1818
présage(s) 171, 1534, 1762, 2072
prescrire 101, 1366
prescrites 2302
présence 664
présent 652, 665, 2838
présentation 1344, 1836
présentoir 369a
préservation 671
préserver 1333
président 1004
presque 2719
pressentiment 1497
presser 1442
pression 1652
prestige 2867
prêt 547a, 821, 2269
prétendre 908
prétexte 1242, 1824
prêtre 2283, 2489
preuve 223, 928, 1522, 3022
prier 908, 1612
prière au coucher du soleil 2006
prière de l'après-midi 1874
prière de la prière du soir 2006
prière de midi 1766
prière du crépuscule 2006
prière du soir 1872
prière magique 910
prière(s) 44, 45, 197, 620, 910, 1136, 1249, 1612, 2090, 2302, 2557, 2914
principe(s) 997, 2318
prison 586, 1254b
prisonnier 586, 2310
privilège 2158, 2419
prix de la fiancée 2684
prix du sang 2906
prix 176, 348a, 418, 1291, 2360, 2674
problème 1403a, 1493
procédure 909
procès 800, 909, 1459
procès juridique 1504a
proche 2264
proclamation 1927
proclamer 2715
procuration 2981
prodige 1785, 1790
production 1063, 1150
produire (se -) 1690, 1835
profane 2699
profession de foi 997, 1523, 2848
profession 1988
profit commercial 821
profit 2216, 2775, 2775a
profiter 2578
profondeur 1625, 1943
progrès 469, 814
projet 878, 1111
projeter 2821
prolonger 1742
promesse(s) 1960, 2716, 2955
promettre 1960
promontoire 1003
pronom personnel 1661
prononcer un sermon 809
prononcer un verdict 683
prononciation 2552
propager 184
Prophète Muhammad 1463
prophète(s) 607, 1073, 1790, 2697
propos 952
propre 2759
propriété 345, 1266, 2051, 2202, 2654, 2658, 2684, 2939
prospère 2201
prospérité 211, 431, 2764, 2962
prosternation(s) 1115, 1249, 1250
prostitué(e) 1471, 1961, 2241, 2663
protection 671, 724, 901
protégé 559
protéger 723, 1643, 2548
proue 95, 2278, 2383
proverbe 2588, 2592

province 2990, 2336
provision de bouche 1202
provisions 1202, 1898, 2775a
provocateur 1445
provocation 1445, 1956, 2427
provoquer 1944, 2424
prudence 243, 611
psaltérion 1375
Psaumes 1158
pudeur 652, 755, 1977
puits 149a, 1101
pull-over 2202a
punir 683, 1823
punition 684, 1060, 1823, 1897, 2292
pur 823, 1725, 1598, 2149, 2150
pure 1725, 2792
pureté 1724, 2791, 2947
purgatif 818, 1383
putsch 2331a
pyramide(s) 2841

quand 960
quarante 1025
quartier 693, 735
quatre 1023
quatre-vingt-dix 377
quatre-vingts 422
querelle 800, 2169, 2703, 2720
question 1403a
questionner 1223
queue 410, 1000, 1705
quinine 2507a
quinze 844
quitter 834, 2830

rabat(s) 2538
race 71, 536, 2233, 2359a
rachat 2097
racine 2092
raconter 607, 1354
radio 1001a
radis 2092
rage 657, 2024, 2466
raid 2392
raisin(s) 1155
raison 20, 49, 734, 1226, 1239, 1824, 1907, 1959, 2842
ramadan (fin du -) 2165
ramadan (jeûne du -) 1635
ramadan 1121, 1136, 2316
rançon 2097, 2906
rancune 1651, 2292
rang 431, 652, 893, 1286, 1400, 2246
rangée 1400, 1683
râpe 200a
rapporter 1354
rapporteur 2081, 2777
rare 583, 1814, 1851, 2044
rareté 2712
ravin 2907
rebelle 825, 1878
rechercher 2079
récipient 2559, 2959
récit 607, 691, 2290
réciter 388, 2408
réclamer 673, 908, 1707a
réclusion 1670
recommandable 1619
recommandations 2943, 2945
récompense 166a, 427, 563
récompenser 476
réconciliation 1602
réconcilier 2902
reconnaissance 1088
reconnaître 643, 2235
recouvrir 1717
rectangle 1028, 1744
redevance 1965
réduction 817, 2785
réfléchir 985, 2177, 2179
réflexion 245, 2178, 2179
réfrigérateur 416a
refroidir 199
regarder 241, 1002, 1174, 1537, 1707a
région 289, 951, 1384, 2336
registre 913
règle(s) 50, 1267, 1286, 2318, 2342
réglisse 1395
réjouissance(s) 1453, 2104
relâcher 1714, 2180
relation(s) sexuelle(s) 528, 886
reliefs 281
religion 973, 1061, 1702, 1902
remarquer 2032
remboursement 1060
remède 969, 1071, 1383, 1904
remerciement(s) 1500
remercier 211, 1500

remonter 1511
remorquage (vedette de -) 458
remorqueur 458
rempart 195
remplaçant 176, 2810
remplir 2648
remuer 870
rémunération 166a
rémunérer 15
rencontre 513, 2558
rencontrer 2558
rendement 888, 1150
renforcement 1445
renoncer 373
renouveler 446
renseignement(s) 1841, 1842, 1843
rentrer 1041
rents 888
renversement 2331a
réparation 2452
réparer 1106
repas 920a
repentance 396
répéter 2408
répondre 552, 1050
réponse 552
repos 222, 1133, 1137, 1138, 2103, 2772
repousser 1714
reprendre 2773
représailles 2292
représentant 2980
représentation 2981
réprimande 1779, 2571
réprimander 1170a
reproche(s) 1435, 1504, 1779, 1979, 2571
reprocher 1779, 1853
réprouver 1853
répudiation 1063, 1715
répudier 334, 1714
répulsion 2425, 2427
réputation 2939
requête 734
réseau 1430
réserve(s) 1898, 1977
réservoir 742
résidence 1316, 1319, 2498
résigner (se -) 1333, 1555
résigner 1500
résine 1616
résolution 1661, 1857, 2064
respect 652, 1778, 1889, 2419, 2612, 2867
respectabilité 1778
respecter 2419
respiration 1836, 2772, 2773
respirer 2772, 2773
responsabilité 808, 1664, 2534
ressemblance 1407, 1431, 1431a, 1622, 1629, 2573, 2588, 2590, 2592
ressembler 1511
restaurer 433
rester 281, 961, 1219, 1985, 2156a
résultat 1898
résumé 797
résurrection 262, 2361
retard 31, 1162, 1219, 1789
retarder 25
retenir 2923
réticence 1308
réticulaire 1429
retour 882b, 1060
retraite 2125
réunion 506, 513, 522, 662, 900
réussir 1405, 2210
revanche 2292
rêve 1008
Révélations 2443
révéler 2081, 2898
revendication 909
revendiquer 1707a
revenir 1041
revenu 882b
révérence 2867
révolution 2331a
rhume 705
richesse(s) 2654, 2684
rideau(x) 1242, 2888
ridicule 70, 1263
rire 1645
risque 812
risquer 479
rivage 1260
rival 798, 799
rivalité 2037
riyal 1149
riz 1065
robe 493, 571, 1683, 2341
rocher(s) 438
roi 965, 1329, 2655

rôle 952
Romain 1147
Rome 1147
rose 1747, 2916
rossignol 287
roue 952, 958a
rouge 710a
rougeâtre 2639b
route 189, 1578, 1701
royaume 957, 2654, 2658
rue(s) 189, 1460
rupture 818, 2164
rupture du jeûne 2165
ruse 379, 750, 771, 1907, 2501
rythme 814

sabbat 1230
sable 1122, 1576
sac 459, 1483, 1520, 1532, 2503a
sacoche de selle 777
sacrifice 979, 1571, 2452, 2902
safari 1294
sagacité 243, 686
sage 686b
sage-femme 872a
sagesse 686, 1841, 1907, 1917
saint(s) 223, 1633, 2419, 2987
saisir 1643, 2224
saison 469, 2934, 2970
salad 1328a
salaire 15, 17, 18, 19, 888, 1528, 1581a, 2419a, 2583b
sale 2699, 2925
saleté 1718, 2925
salle 329
Salomon 1343
saluer 1333
salutation(s) 758, 1050, 1338, 1344
samedi 507, 1230
sanction 43
sandale(s) 2445
sandwich 1374a
sang 937
sangle 410, 1705
sans 144
santal 1747, 2574
santé 745, 1150, 1560, 1961, 1746, 1894, 2861
saphir 3014
saphisme 1154
Satan 9, 1548
satin 74
satisfaction 1088
satisfaire 1085
Saturne 1163
sauce 3005a
sauf 130, 2062
savant 1546, 1922, 1923, 1925
savoir 686, 1841, 1917, 1922, 2206
savon 1557
sceau 766, 1711, 2676
scène 2755
scie 70a
science 1917
scorpion 1905
scribe 2398
sculpture 2783
seau 465a
secourir 1289, 1333, 1974
secours 1290, 1974, 2746
secret 1272
secte 997, 1702, 1738
section 2312
sécurité 112, 115, 1338, 1341, 1664
sédition 2085
seducement 2863b
séducteur 2141
séduction 453a
seigneur 1013, 1389
Seigneur 2992, 2993
seize 1244
sel(s) 1383, 2649
sélection 867
sélectionner 867
selle(s) 410, 459, 1275, 1705
semaine 507, 1230
semence 583
semer 184, 1169
sens 643, 1907, 1959, 2039, 2140, 2754
sensation 643
sensibilité 2235
sensible 2518
sentence 684, 2358
senteurs 2170
sentier 1578, 1701
sentir 643, 2628
séparé(s) 2129
séparer 2129, 2830
sept 1236

sépulture 2974
serf 1770
sergent 1419
série 1400
sérieux 446, 668
seringue 5, 680a
serment(s) 1960, 2287, 2544, 3025
sermon 762, 809, 2956
serrure 2322
service(s) 773, 2158
serviette 240a, 1617, 2166a
servile 991
servir 1769
serviteur(s) 771a, 1294
sésame 494, 1356
sexe 536
sexuelle(s) 297, 2533
Shaban 1477
shérif 1463
shilling(s) 1020, 1149
si 1690
siècle 2276
siège 2415, 2673
siffler 1592
sifflet 1592
signal 1534
signature 1562
signe(s) 928, 1534, 1829, 1920, 1957, 2072, 2736
significatif 2853
signification 1665, 1959
silence 1308
similaire 1431, 1431a
similitude 1431, 2588, 2592
simple 356
simulateur 2777
singulier 2109
Sirius 1479
sirop 1452, 1863
sisal 2401
situation 695, 1068, 1418
six 1210, 1243
sixième 1271
société 506, 1468
sodium 2751
sodomie 2570
sodomite 848
sœur 1127a
soie 617, 1695, 2888
soierie 617
soin 611, 2224, 2851
soir (prière du -) 1872
soir 424b, 1872, 2006, 2164
soixante 1245
soixante-dix 1238
sol 55, 1304, 1305
soldat(s) 1160a, 1671a, 1862, 1901
soldatesque 1862
soleil 1513, 1646, 2006
solide 1644, 1805, 2644
solitude 2125
solliciter 1637
sombrer 2010
sommaire 797
somme 511, 517, 645, 2097
sommet 1003
son 643, 1628, 2769
sonner 1628
sorcellerie 1257
sorgho 984a
sort 21, 670, 1069, 2233, 2741
sorte 331, 433, 480, 536, 1621, 1695, 1993, 2196, 2573
sottises 1170a, 2002
souci 104, 1484, 2156, 2467, 2851
soudain(s) 2088
soudanais 1388a
souder 2531
soudure 1083
souffle 2770, 2772, 2773
souffrance 380
souffrir 1068
soufi 1633
soufre 2391
souhait(s) 1870
soulager 2100
soulever 1098, 1511
soumission 1344
soupçon 1497, 1762, 3003
soupe 1449b
source 71, 149a
sournoiserie 2501
soustraction 281
sous-vêtements 2521
soutane 493
souteneur 2351
soutenir 1568, 1936, 1974
souvenir 2997
souverain 689, 1329, 2655

souveraineté 2658, 2990
sparadrap 1128
spécial 794, 795, 796, 1924, 2853
spécimen 1621, 1993, 2196
sperme 1530, 2671, 2606
sphère 2429
statue 1622, 1629
statut 745, 1036
steppe 335
sterling 542
stock 1898
stop 821
store 925
stratagème 750
strophe 344
structure 321d, 1111, 1942
stupide 716
style 1695, 2150
stylo 2335
suaire 1372
sublime 1364
sublimité 490, 1378
subsistance 1069, 1987
substantiel 570
substitut 176, 177
subtil 2675
subvention 2997
succéder 825
succès 862, 1288, 1290, 2202, 2962
successeur 826
succession 2912
sucre 702, 1314, 1798
sud 1380a
sueur 430, 1079
suffire 391, 1903
suffisance 2002, 2371
suiveur 1139a
sujet(s) 1095, 1418, 2342
sulfate 2622
sultan 1329
Sunna 1368
sunnite 1369, 1619
supercherie 771
supérieur 1931, 2009, 2162, 2991
superviseur 671a, 2080a, 2757a
suppléance 177
supplice 1823
supplier 1637
supporter 1555, 1985
suppuration 2925
sûr 1342
sûreté 112, 115, 1341
surplus 2158
surprendre 2032
surprise 1790
surtout 2038, 2039
surveillance 1994
susceptibilité 2235
suspendre 1915
Swahili 1260
symbole 136, 1920
syntaxe 2706
syphilis 161
Syrie 1415

tabac à priser 1292a
tabac 363a
table 369a
tableau 453, 1629
tabou 629
tache(s) 829, 1106, 1484, 1776, 1913, 1977
tacher 278
taille 1000, 2888
tailleur 371a
talisman 621, 969, 1711, 1857
tambour 1689a
tambourin 912
tamis 2414a, 2803
tampon 2676
tank 874a
tape 1456a
tapis 1181
tarbouche 1693, 2497
tarder 25
tarif 2818
tartre 1394
tasse 1728, 2379, 2394a
taureau 2094
taux 176, 1865
taxation 1865
taxe(s) 1865, 2467
taxi 385a
teigne 278
teint 1261
téléphone 387a
télescope 2754a, 2756
témoignage 1522, 1523, 1525
témoin 1522, 1525

tempérance 2246, 2938
température (élévation de -) 705
température élevée 430
température 619
tempête de vent et de pluie 1655
tempête 1655, 1737
temple 1772, 2869
temps 413a, 424a, 424b, 469, 814, 914, 921, 945, 1189, 1398, 1547, 2209, 2600, 2677, 2772, 2788, 2970, 2971
tenir 2224
tente 869, 1458
tenter 458
tenture 1242
terme 95, 100, 2303
terminer 391, 2480
terrain 55, 202, 2974
terrasse 1284
terre 55, 189, 944, 951, 2496
terreur 857, 858, 2138a
Testament 124, 401
testament 2945
tester 458
testicule(s) 803, 2125
tête 1003, 1004
texte(s) 805
thaler 1149, 2267, 2976
thé 1420, 2350, 2417a
théière 6
tiers (un -) 413
tige 958a
timbre 2676
timidité 755, 1977
tissu 260, 432, 790, 1000, 1106, 1267, 1733, 1740, 1921, 2729, 2888, 2990
titre 791a, 1957
toile 1517a
toilette(s) 1138, 1182, 1467
toiure(s) 1273a, 1305, 1875
tomate 1720
tombe 1206, 2223, 2223a
tombeau 2223
tonneau 221
tonnerre 1094
Torah 401
torche 249a, 1276, 1736
torrent 2907
torse 178
tort 46, 1757
torture 1823
total 511, 517, 645
toucher 2628
toujours 3, 4, 265, 945, 963, 964
tour (du destin) 880
tour 195, 1210, 1734, 2543, 2607, 2815
tourment 1670
tournant 730
tourteau 1442
tous 138a, 517
tout 138a, 280, 511, 512a, 2481
toute(s) 952, 1683
trace 1076, 1921
trader 492a
tradition(s) 445,1902, 2646, 2790
traduction 2143, 2144, 2790
traduire 2143
trahison 859, 2085
train 2309a
trait(s) 1261, 1698
traitement 969, 2342
traité 2359
traiter 1301
traître 478, 860
tranquillité 1137, 1138, 2772
transaction(s) 166a, 351, 2964
transcription 2790
transférer 1266, 2789
transgression 808
transition 2608a
transpiration 430, 1079
transport 1617, 2790, 2818
transporter 1641, 2789
travail 166a, 380, 1210, 1484, 1945, 1988
travailler 1944
traverse 2278
traverser 479, 1775
trente 414
Trésor 345, 785a
trésor 786, 917, 1851, 2485
tribu(s) 1738, 2233, 2359a
tribunal 688, 1760, 2397a
tribut 2422
tricher 771, 1996, 2000
tricheur 980
trick 1396
tricot 1900
triomphe 1453, 2210
tristesse 640

trois 413a
tromper 771, 1145, 1757, 1996, 2000, 2042, 2543
tromperie 750, 771, 859, 1996, 2002, 2019, 2543
trompette 151, 218, 335a, 2769
trompeur 860, 2489
trône 2415
trou 1467
trouble(s) 1497
troupe 572, 2769
trusquin 667
tube 2101
tuer 977
tuile 1707
tunique 493, 2538
turban 783, 1695
Turquie 1146
turquoise 2217
tuyau 782a, 1175, 2101
type(s) 1695
tyrannie 486, 558, 1757, 1785

ulcère 463
un (numéral) 2895
un huitième 421
un tiers 413
unique 2108
uriner 339
usage(s) 997, 2094, 2216, 2318, 2646,
usine 1468
ustensile 547
usure 1031
utile 2775
utilisation 2775a
utilité 2216, 2775a

vache 275
vaciller 1062
vagabond 181, 1981
vague(s) 2680
vaisseau 547, 1110, 1299
valeur 348a, 418, 816, 1291, 2246, 2360
valise 1520, 1617
value 418
vandale 774
vanité 250a, 2002
vapeur 164, 165, 457, 889
variété 1270, 2196
vase 2959
vaurien 1981
vautour 1751
végétation 202
véhicule 1775, 1828a
veilleur 621a
veine jugulaire 701
velours 847
vendre 349, 2715
vendredi 507, 809
vengeance 1651, 2292
venin 1350
venir 2940
vent 200, 1131, 1655, 1712
vente 348a, 349, 351, 931, 1160, 2715, 2863
Vénus 1199
ver(s) 949
véranda 202
verbe 2167
verdict 684
vergue 457
vérité 677, 3022
vermine 949
verre 310, 318a, 2282
verset 2109
verset coranique 136
vert 804a
vésicule biliaire 1595
veste 1568, 2202a
vêtement(s) 178, 217, 260, 274, 493, 629, 635, 1165, 1568, 1740, 2137, 2521, 2522, 2729
vétérinaire 347a
veuvage 1800
viatique 1197a
vice 2167
victime 977
victoire 2037, 2210
vie 21, , 756, 1132, 1983, 1985, 1987
vieille 1788
vierge 156a, 283
vieux 1788
vigilance 2696
vigne 1155
vigoureux 1444
vigueur 1600
village 693, 951
ville 287b, 693
vin 310, 1450, 2691a/a
vingt 842, 1869

vingt-cinq 842
violence 46, 486, 558, 1093, 1651, 1757, 1785
vipère 2169
visage 480, 1629, 2893
vision 1008
visite 664, 1205, 1206
visiter 1205
vitre 2754a
vitriol 2622
vitupérations 1225, 1229
vivacité 756
vivre 754, 1983, 1985
vizir 2922
vœu(x) 1960, 2716
voie 1240, 1578, 1701, 1702
voile 206a, 259, 457, 1242, 1247, 1255, 1458, 2888
voiler 1242, 2046
voir 241, 1537
voisin 559
voiture 189, 1828a
voix 643, 1628
voleur 634, 2501
volonté 1538a, 2945
voter 2271a
voyage 1202, 1294, 1297, 2818, 2608a
voyager 1294, 1297, 1409, 1775
voyelle 627
vue 1006, 1802, 1994, 2754, 2755
vulve 2101

W.-C. 1138
wagon 329, 1828a
wakf 2973, 2974
wakia 1092
wali 2995
whisky 1847

yaourt 1155a

Zanzibar 718
zèle 544, 546, 2054
zéro 1596
zinc 399, 1195a
zodiaque (signe du -) 195

Index of Scientific Names

Abelmoschus esculentus 3005a
Agave sisalana 2401
Arachis hypogaea 2214

Callitris quadrivalvis 1374
Cannabis sativa indica 321b
Cannabis sativa 651a
Cassia acutifolia 1377
Cassia lanceolata 1377
Cinnamomum zeylanicum 871
Citrus aurantifolia 2581
Citrus sp. 194
Coriandrum sativum 494

Eugenia jambosa 384

Ficus carica 403

Glycyrrhiza glabra 1395
Grevillea robusta 200

Hibiscus esculentus 156
Hyrax syriaca 2878

Jasminum Sambae 3019

Luffa cylindrica Roem 2570a

Morus alba 2117

Nigella sativa 583a

Ocimum basilicum 1134
Oriza sativa 1065
Oryza barthii 1065

Padda oryzivora 1656
Pinus pinea 1623
Psittacus alexandri 890
Pygeum africanum 53

Raphanus sativus 2092

Senna alexandrina 1377
Sorghum durra 984a
Spirostachys africana 2574
Struthio camelus 2764a

Tectona grandis 1218
Triticum sp. 2337

Ziziphus jujuba 2018
Ziziphus spina Christi 1270

Printed in the United States
By Bookmasters